Victor Serge

I0109967

"Mitchell Abidor's superb and assertive writing reveals the many faces of Victor Serge, a 'troublesome witness' to some of the most decisive moments of his era. This is a vivid and deeply researched account of one of the most compelling lives in modern revolutionary history."

—Maurice Casey, author of *Hotel Lux:
An Intimate History of Communism's Forgotten Radicals*

"From anarchism to Bolshevism to anti-totalitarian socialism, Victor Serge never abandoned his passionate struggle for human freedom and a just society. Mitchell Abidor captures this rebel for all seasons in all his fascinating and tortured complexity."

—Bruce Baugh, Professor Emeritus of Philosophy,
Thompson Rivers University

"A fascinating and provocative biography of a fascinating and provocative man. Tracing Serge's tumultuous pilgrimage from individualist anarchism to revolutionary socialism to ethical personalism, Abidor testifies to his life-long courage in 'rethinking left-wing politics'."

—Geoffrey Kurtz, Associate Professor of Political Science,
Borough of Manhattan Community College

"Mitchell Abidor's new biography of the early-twentieth-century radical, memoirist, and novelist best known as Victor Serge is the tale of a left-wing 'Zelig.' In Abidor's tale we meet the leading figures of European anarchism, socialism, and communism, intellectuals as well as activist revolutionaries. Through his life of Serge, Abidor distills the history of Western revolutionary radicalism in the first half of the twentieth century."

—Melvyn Dubofsky, Professor Emeritus of History
and Sociology, Binghamton University.
Author of *We Shall Be All: A History of the IWW*

Revolutionary Lives

Series Editors:
Dr Sarah Irving, University of Staffordshire
Professor Paul Le Blanc, La Roche University, Pittsburgh

Also available

Salvador Allende
Revolutionary Democrat
Victor Figueroa Clark

James Baldwin
Living in Fire
Bill V. Mullen

Hugo Chávez
Socialist for the Twenty-first Century
Mike Gonzalez

W.E.B. Du Bois
Revolutionary Across the Color Line
Bill V. Mullen

Frantz Fanon
Philosopher of the Barricades
Peter Hudis

Mohandas Gandhi
Experiments in Civil Disobedience
Talat Ahmed

William Godwin
A Political Life
Richard Gough Thomas

Leila Khaled
Icon of Palestinian Liberation
Sarah Irving

Jean Paul Marat
Tribune of the French Revolution
Clifford D. Conner

John Maclean
Hero of Red Clydeside
Henry Bell

Martin Monath
A Jewish Resistance Fighter Amongst Nazi Soldiers
Nathaniel Flakin

Sylvia Pankhurst
Suffragette, Socialist and Scourge of Empire
Katherine Connelly

Paul Robeson
A Revolutionary Life
Gerald Horne

Percy Bysshe Shelley
Poet and Revolutionary
Jacqueline Mulhallen

Toussaint Louverture
A Black Jacobin in the Age of Revolutions
Charles Forsdick and Christian Høgsbjerg

Victor Grayson
In Search of Britain's Lost Revolutionary
Harry Taylor
Foreword by Jeremy Corbyn

Ellen Wilkinson
From Red Suffragist to Government Minister
Paula Bartley

Gerrard Winstanley
The Digger's Life and Legacy
John Gurney

Victor Serge
Unruly Revolutionary

Mitchell Abidor

PLUTO PRESS

First published 2025 by Pluto Press
New Wing, Somerset House, Strand, London WC2R 1LA
and Pluto Press, Inc.
1930 Village Center Circle, 3-834, Las Vegas, NV 89134

www.plutobooks.com

Copyright © Mitchell Abidor 2025

The right of Mitchell Abidor to be identified as the author of this work has
been asserted in accordance with the Copyright, Designs and Patents Act
1988.

British Library Cataloguing in Publication Data
A catalogue record for this book is available from the British Library

ISBN   978 0 7453 4885 8   Paperback
ISBN   978 0 7453 4888 9   PDF
ISBN   978 0 7453 4886 5   EPUB

This book is printed on paper suitable for recycling and made from fully
managed and sustained forest sources. Logging, pulping and manufacturing
processes are expected to conform to the environmental standards of the
country of origin.

Typeset by Stanford DTP Services, Northampton, England

Simultaneously printed in the United Kingdom and United States of America

EU GPSR Authorised Representative
LOGOS EUROPE, 9 rue Nicolas Poussin, 17000, LA ROCHELLE, France
Email: Contact@logoseurope.eu

Contents

Preface   vi

1   Growing Up Kibalchich   1
2   From Socialism to Anarchism   13
3   Paris   31
4   The Tragic Bandits   61
5   Man in Prison   89
6   Barcelona: Becoming Victor Serge   96
7   Serge and the Russian Anarchists   115
8   Kronstadt   126
9   The Anarchists Against Victor Serge   137
10 Victor Serge Against Kibalchich   146
11 Why?   154
12 Comintern Agent in Central Europe   162
13 Opposition   173
14 Arrest   198
15 Orenburg and L'Affaire Serge   215
16 Return to the West   238
17 Flight from Europe   275
18 Liuba   287
19 Finally Mexico   294
20 Revising the Revolution   314
21 Anti-communist?   336
22 Fisticuffs   354
23 The Final Interview   369
Epilogue   373
Conclusion   381

Acknowledgments   387
Notes   389
Works by Victor Serge in English   407
Index   411

Preface

When people learn of my involvement with the life and writings of Victor Serge, they often tell me how much they love Serge. I commend them on their good taste, but at the same time I have to hold myself back from asking them a question. I would like to ask them which Serge they admire, because there were many. Do they support the anarchist individualist of his youth, who considered the working-class to be a mass of weak-willed, spineless cowards? Or is it the syndicalist he claimed to be at one point, believing that the workers could seize power directly? Or maybe it's the Bolshevik who worked at the Communist International and propagandized for the new regime. Maybe they identify with the man who opposed Stalin and sided with Trotsky in the battle for power after Lenin's death. And then again, maybe it's the man who realized Trotsky was dogmatic and closed to the ideas of others, and who then revised all of revolutionary socialism, seeing that much of Marxism no longer applied to the world of his day.

Admirers usually developed their affection for Serge from reading his classic account of his life, the posthumously published *Memoirs of a Revolutionary*. In this book, written in his final years, Serge explains the various twists and turns of his political life, smoothing out the rough edges and minimizing his contradictions. It is the purpose of *Victor Serge: Unruly Revolutionary* to roughen the edges that need to be roughened and to examine the contradictions in the contradictory being that was Victor Serge.

It was when I first started working on this biography more than a decade ago with Richard Greeman—the greatest of English-language Serge scholars, the man who single-handedly saved Serge's writings from oblivion—that I saw that Serge's story was more complex than his memoirs would lead the reader to believe. He was a man of enormous courage, who, when interrogated by the secret police in 1933, showed no signs of fear and defended himself as few did in those circumstances. He also, in his final years while in exile in Mexico, had the insight and fortitude to insist to his fellow leftist exiles that the world had changed, and the schemas that had ruled the radical left no longer obtained. But in reading letters, manuscripts, and published articles I saw that he also minimized in his memoirs the extent and radicality of the ideas he advocated for in his anarchist youth, and elided the ways the opinions he expressed in the early 1920s contradicted what he actually felt and thought. Serge was an admirable man, but he was a flawed man, pretty much like all of us, only more so.

Unlike most of the other members of the small circle that writes about and translates Serge, I came to him fairly late in life, and not through his memoirs. I also didn't come to him through Marxism. There's no denying that when writing a biography, or indeed almost any interpretive work, our worldview guides our researches. The French psychoanalyst and literary critic Pierre Bayard has written about what he calls a reader or writer's "inner paradigm." He defines this as the worldview that "determines the types of questions asked of a work."[1] Or in our case, a life. Bayard explains that writers "project their own inner world" when examining their subject.[2] My examination of Serge is unabashedly informed by my inner paradigm. This means that in many places it doesn't chime with the image many readers have of Serge, though in many places it does. I have enormous respect for Serge, but as a phrenologist might say, I don't have the bump of veneration. That is my inner paradigm.

Reading the 1989 collection of Serge's anarchist writings edited by Yves Pagès was a revelation to me. Here was a writer, a revolutionary who believed revolutionism was an illusion; a man who believed in absolute freedom, who hated capitalism and wanted it destroyed by giving primacy to individual will and liberty. He was a man who wrote with the fire of youth (his anarchist articles were mainly written between the ages of seventeen and twenty-two) and with brutal honesty. When I translated—

in collaboration with Richard Greeman—Serge's *Notebooks (1936-1947)* I had some of the same thrill of encountering a man willing to think independently and face the contumely that came with this intellectual bravery. This biography was written in the spirit of its subject.

* * *

Note on sources: It is impossible to write about Serge without quoting extensively from his memoirs, and I have done so in the following pages. The memoirs, though, are a starting point, not an end point. My goal has been, through use of primary sources and other reports of events, to examine the veracity of Serge's account of his life and to fill in the blanks he left in his telling of it. There's more to a man's life than his version of it, and this is definitely the case with Serge. His political evolution was not as smooth as he depicted it, and it moved in directions that can most clearly be found in his private correspondence and in long-out-of-print pamphlets, but not in *Memoirs of a Revolutionary*. It is necessary to quote the latter volume as well as his *Notebooks (1936–1947)*, both widely available, in order to begin the task of establishing who Victor Serge was and what he believed. The necessary documents are in various archives around the world, many of them gathered by Richard Greeman, who granted me access and use of them. *Victor Serge: Unruly Revolutionary* is the fruit of my research in these sources.

1

Growing Up Kibalchich

We know him as Victor Serge, a pen name he adopted during the brief period he lived in Spain after his release from a French prison in 1917. He was born Victor-Napoléon Kibalchich. The future Victor Serge—he never explained the origin of the pseudonym – was also known in his youth by the pen names Le Rétif, Yor, and Ralph. His Soviet documents, including the records of his interrogations by the secret police, referred to him as Victor Lvovich Kibalchich, inserting his patronymic, as is always the case in Russia. While living in Mexico at the end of his life, mail he received was addressed to Victor Poderewski, adopting his mother's maiden name perhaps in an attempt to hide his location from possible Stalinist assassins.

Along with his many names, Serge lived many political lives. Underlying them all was the inspiration Serge drew from his Russian roots, from the role his family had supposedly played in the revolutionary struggles of nineteenth-century Russia. This inspiration appears in the very first paragraph of his *Memoirs of a Revolutionary*. Serge described his parents, Léon, originally Leonid, Kibalchich[1] and Vera Poderevskaya, as "revolutionary exiles, tossed into the great cities of the West by the first political hurricanes blowing over Russia."[2] Their story is a good deal less straightforward than the one he presented. Léon had been a student at the military academy in St. Petersburg and served as a non-commissioned officer in the tsar's Imperial Guard. Despite these impeccable tsarist credentials, he was opposed to tsarism. Serge took pride in his father's stance, but he was even prouder of what he called his "distant" and unspecified family ties to the revolutionary martyr Nikolai Ivanovich

Kibalchich, a chemist and member of the secret revolutionary group Narodnaya Volna (The People's Will). From the 1860s on, Nikolai was active in one of the many groups of young revolutionaries in Russia. Having served time in prison for possession of radical propaganda, he formally joined Narodnaya Volna in August 1879, the same month that the revolutionary organization's Executive Committee met and passed a death sentence on Tsar Alexander II.

A police report on Nikolai Kibalchich can be applied in many ways to the young Victor Kibalchich. He "can be characterized as a typical anarchist, following an evil obsession, unique from the viewpoint of applying technology to infernal machines, a monstrous criminal fanatic, a new personality type, but clearly demonstrated by the evidence of the investigation."[3]

Nikolai's chemical know-how was an important element in his being assigned to carry out the death sentence on the tsar, but it wasn't limited to that. Kibalchich worked closely with the famous revolutionary Vera Figner for almost a year and a half preparing the assassination. Nikolai had been part of a failed plot to kill the tsar in September 1880, and other plots had also been set in train between the death sentence and the final successful attack in March 1881.

Nikolai constructed the devices to be used in the attack, consisting of four grenades weighing five pounds each. On March 1, 1881, he was one of the group of five Narodniki who were present when the bomb was thrown at Alexander II. The attack did not go off as planned, as the first bomb thrown did not hit its target. The tsar insisted on examining the scene of the crime, and while he was doing so a second terrorist threw another bomb that killed the sovereign.

Serge's son Vladimir (Vlady) Kibalchich told Serge scholar Richard Greeman during one of their many conversations that his father had told him two different stories, claiming Serge's father was a part of the plot as well. The first version asserted that Léon was the second backup, assigned to kill the tsar in the event the first two assassins failed. An alternative version recounted by Vlady claimed that Léon was assigned to shoot the tsar if he returned alive to his palace. Serge never put any of this to paper, having no proof of his father's involvement, nor is there any evidence of this anywhere else.[4]

Whatever one might think of their methods, the Narodniki were courageous individuals. They didn't attempt to evade responsibility for their acts; in fact, they took great pride in them. The terrorists were almost immediately arrested, and Nikolai Kibalchich took full responsibility for the attack. The government was not having any of that and held the entire group to account. The six terrorists were tried and sentenced to death, though one, Gesia Gelfman, was pregnant and her sentence was commuted after international outcry against the execution of a pregnant woman (her baby died soon after its birth and Gesia shortly thereafter). The most thorough contemporary historian of the Russian revolutionary movement of the period wrote movingly of Nikolai Kibalchich's end: "Kibalchich revealed his true worth, and showed himself a man of genius, always concerned with the technical problems of the relations between ends and means. In his prison cell he went on designing a plan for a flying machine, which he regretted not being able to finish before he was hanged."[5]

Only one of the terrorists, Rysakov, expressed any remorse for the killing, which didn't save him from sharing the fate of his unrepentant comrades. "At 9:50 in the morning of 3rd April 1881, Rysakov, Zhelyabov, Mikhailov, Kibalchich, and Sofia Perovskaya climbed the scaffold. With the exception of Rysakov they all embraced for the last time. Then they were hanged."[6]

The self-abnegation of the Narodniki was a touchstone for Serge throughout his life. Their purity, uprightness, and courage served as an example for him in all circumstances. His pride in his Russian roots, which included his affectation of a Russian peasant blouse when a young man in Belgium and France, is largely owed to his admiration for his supposed relative and his comrades.

Despite Serge's admiration for his distant relative, genealogical attempts to find the connection between Serge's family and Nikolai Kibalchich have failed. There are several lines of the Kibalchich family, all beginning in Montenegro, but where if anywhere Serge's and Nikolai's lines intersect is unknown. Priests abound in the Kibalchich family tree, among Serge's antecedents and Nikolai's, but a direct tie can't be determined. It was at best very distant. Serge's connection was, instead, an emotional one, a political and moral one, and so became a real one psychologically. That, however, is the most that can be said of it. A mythological past is something individuals and nations not infrequently construct, taking them to be factual. This connection was a real presence in Serge's life, one he passed on to his son, who defended it when he spoke about it with admirers of his father like Richard Greeman and Suzi Weissman. As Greeman explained it:

> The Kibalchich legend presents us with the additional problem of a story already mythologized at its apparent source, the mythomania of Victor's father, the confabulator Léonid Ivanovich, who apparently traded on his famous name by elaborating a plausible self-legend around it. Yet this myth remained so vital to family identity that Victor began his autobiography with the historic date March 1, 1881, in the logical place of his birth date, and even a century later, his son Vladimir persisted in denial in the face of contradictory evidence.[7]

The fame of Nikolai Kibalchich was not an ephemeral thing. The Soviet children's author Arkadi Gaidar's most famous book, *A Tale About a War Secret About the Boy Nipper-Pipper and his Word of Honor*, published in 1933, features the character Nipper-Pipper, whose name in the Russian original is Malchish-Kibalchich. A poem about little Kibalchich is familiar to every child who grew up in the Soviet Union. Gaidar chose the name in honor of his friend Victor Serge.[8]

* * *

There are also many questions about the life of Serge's father. Serge's claim in his memoirs that his father was a political exile is, to an extent, solid, though there is some dissent on the matter and there are many unclear aspects of the tale. Léon, born in 1861 and "the son of a priest," as documents in Belgian archives describe him, was expelled from his military school in St. Petersburg in 1882 for distributing revolutionary propaganda to his fellow students, though in another version he was guilty only of possession of the propaganda. Whatever the case, he was busted down to the ranks and served as a trooper in Kiev. He likely participated in a revolutionary circle in Kiev, where his name is mentioned in a police document, but it's not certain he played any significant political role.

Léon deserted that same year and fled to Switzerland. There is some possibility he was politically active under the assumed name Ivanov while in Switzerland, but Léon's life between 1882 and 1887 is a mystery. He is supposed to have attended medical school in Geneva and seems not to have engaged in political activity there. It was in Davos, Switzerland, that Léon met the woman who would be Serge's mother, Vera Frolova, née Poderevskaya, in 1861, in Nizhni-Novgorod, Russia. Vera was a descendant of the Polish aristocratic Poderevsky family, was married to Vladimir Frolov, a wealthy Russian at the time of her meeting Léon, and had two daughters. Vera was in Davos recovering from tuberculosis when she met Léon. The young wife and mother abandoned her comfortable life for a risky one with Léon, and her travels with him would not involve stays in resorts like the one where she met Léon, but rather the slums of Brussels, Canterbury, Geneva, and London. She would experience the death of a child, the end of a stormy relationship with her husband, her return to Russia, and her own early death in 1907, worn down by the strains of her impoverished existence.

In 1889 the Belgian police requested information on Léon's political activities from the police of St. Petersburg and Geneva, and in response the Geneva police spoke of Léon's activities in Russia. In a Belgian police report from 1889 (the date is partially obscured) an agent who had been following Léon wrote that he

> [L]ed quite a mysterious life. He took long walks alone. No one visited him and no one knew of any relatives. He said he was affiliated with a foreign revolutionary group, but surveillance carried out at his home in concert with its tenants produced no results. He receives money from Russia on a monthly basis, moneys allocated by his family, his wife [*sic*] it is said. He had no other resources and sometimes found himself in a precarious position.

Another police surveillance report, from 1890, the year of Serge's birth, reports that Léon received money from Russia from his wife's family and, concerning surveillance, that "up until now no unfavorable report has reached us on the foreigner." If Léon was a revolutionary at the time of his son's birth, something the police seem to have suspected, since they were investigating him to discover if he "joined in revolutionary propaganda or if he has relations with notorious anarchists or those engaged in anarchist propaganda," no evidence for it was found.

This, though, is only part of the story. A cousin of Serge's, Irina Gogua, in a conversation with Serge's son Vlady Kibalchich recorded in 1989 by Suzi Weissman, spoke disparagingly of Léon, whom she knew personally. Léon, she said, was falsely portrayed as a member of Narodnaya Volna. "All he was," she told Vlady and Weissman, "was a real gambler." Another relative, the geologist Oleg Kibalchich, also contested the thesis that Léon was political, writing, "He was a very frenetic man, loved to gamble with cards. Gambling debts may have been the reason he fled to Belgium [*sic*]." Vlady, in response to these denials of his grandfather's revolutionary credentials, but also in defense of his father's vision of his own father as a rebel, split the difference.

Léon was both. He was a revolutionary turned ne'er-do-well. Léon, Vlady claimed to Gogua and Weissman, is mentioned in one of the definitive histories of Narodnaya Volna as a participant in the 1881 assassination plot. It is fairly certain (nothing more can ever be said about anything claimed by him or on his behalf) that Léon was expelled from the military academy for possession of illegal publications. More than that is just guesswork.

That Léon should have become a ne'er-do-well after a spell of radical activity – or might always have been both a rebel and a ne'er-do-well—can't be excluded. Given the wandering life of misery and poverty he lived as a parent and that he imposed on his wife and children, this hypothesis is more than plausible.

A 1908 Belgian police report said of Léon, who by this time had lived a decade with a Belgian woman, Marie Mouillard, whom he married—he claimed—in 1897 and with whom he had three living children, born between 1897 and 1906,

> The foreigner in question claims to be a medical doctor but does not practice. We don't know his resources, but in any case, they are not living a life of ease. He is said to be violent and crude. The residency office has not been told that Kibalchich has been married several times, and at said address no one knows of a son of the abovementioned named Victor-Napoléon.

From the last part of this report, it would seem that the true target of the police investigation was no longer the impoverished Léon but his teenage revolutionary son, Victor.

Léon eventually left Belgium for Brazil. His fate there isn't known, but we do have a clue to it. A self-proclaimed anarchist individualist and illegalist, Jorge Semnone, in an article in *La Revue anarchiste* attacking Serge for his abandonment of anarchism, wrote that it was "we and we alone, anarchist individualists, who, in 1922 in Brazil, on [Serge's] insistent request, saw to the investigation into his father, who died as the result of a fire in the state of either Santa Catarina or Rio-Grande do Sul, if I remember correctly."[9]

* * *

Victor-Napoléon Kibalchich was born in Ixelles, a municipality of Brussels, on December 30, 1890. Victor's birth records also raise questions. According to official documents, living in the house at the time of his birth were his parents and a half-sister, Helène Kibalchich, born in 1880 in Marseille. This birthplace would change according to the document, but not her birth year of 1880. Though Helène [Elena] was listed as Helène Kibalchich, she was, in fact, born to Vera Poderevskaya and her first husband, Vladimir Frolov in 1878, and was actually named Helène Frolova. But there's more. There was a child born in 1880 in the household, but it was not Helène, but Vera Frolova. Serge had *two* half-sisters in his childhood home, the error in the official records apparently caused by the family's choice to mislead the authorities for some unknown reason.

Léon's status as a doctor, which he claimed on many official documents—though those officials completing the documents accepted self-declarations—contain improbabilities, like a training period of two years that did not meet the Belgian norm of three. An undated police report states definitively that during the period he was under surveillance "he was in no way employed as an intern at Hôpital Saint-Jean," which other documents stated was the site of his internship. The files of the Okhrana, the tsarist secret police, state that Léon attended medical school in Geneva for at least the summer semester of 1888, but by 1889 he was in Brussels.[10] In any event, Léon's profession was a mutable thing on official documents. He was sometimes a "physician," sometimes had lesser medical titles, sometimes "rentier," and sometimes a combination of several professions. Because Léon and Serge's mother Vera were foreigners, they had to register whenever they moved, a regulation they were less than assiduous in complying with, which was occasionally commented on by police authorities. The five-year period 1889 to 1894 gives an idea of the family's wandering existence. In November 1889 they reported their address as "chez Monsieur Nan" at 2, Petite rue des Longs Chariots, which was a boarding house. Serge was born a year later at 16, rue Saint-Jean, in Ixelles, though the family doesn't appear on the building's official registry. On July 4, 1891, they were living in Ixelles at 199, rue du Trone, and in May 1892, the year Léon supposedly finished his medical studies, they moved in Ixelles to 247, rue du Trône. In February 1893 they moved yet again in Ixelles to 42, rue Caroly, where Serge's brother Raoul-Albert, who would die at in 1902, was born on April 11, 1893. In 1894 the family moved twice, this time in Etterbeeck, the first time on June 4 to 26, rue Antoine-Gauthier, and then in August to 4, rue de Mot. This wandering around Brussels and its bourgs later carried them further afield in Belgium, to Verviers and Liège, as well as overseas to Canterbury and London. Vera, the second daughter from Vera's first marriage to Vladimir Frolov, lived with them at all these early addresses. She thus knew Léon and his failings very well. She, like so many who had a connection to Serge, would be sent to the Gulag, where she spent the years 1936 to 1942.

Léon's marital history is also an unsettled matter. No marriage licenses have been found for his two marriages, the first to Serge's mother, the second to the Belgian, Marie Mouillard which, according to one police document, took place in Canterbury in 1897. Léon informed the Belgian police in Forest, Belgium, in 1908 that he'd never been married to Vera, that she'd left him to return to Russia in 1903, where she had died three years earlier in either Stavropol or Tiflis. Whether he married Marie in 1897, as he also claimed, is equally uncertain. Richard Greeman has determined that Léon was bigamous, marrying Marie without divorcing Vera. As we will see, the apple never falls far from the tree.

In his memoirs, Serge speaks of childhood memories of Canterbury Cathedral.[11] Town Hall records in Canterbury show that the Kibalchich family lived in Canterbury in 1897 (the year Léon is supposed to have married his second wife) in a part of the town that was highly undesirable due to the odors from a nearby soap and candle works. Léon's occupation was listed with the municipality as "physician," though he doesn't appear in any professional directories as a doctor or in any related field. Serge also speaks of memories of Whitechapel, London; the time he spent as a child there would also have been a period of poverty, as Whitechapel was a heavily Jewish slum quarter of London. It was there that Serge wrote in his memoirs that he first came to know the meaning of hunger, when he was eleven and living in England.[12] Though his memoirs give the impression that his younger brother Raoul died of starvation (Serge writing that he "wasted away"[13]), the cemetery records in Uccle, Belgium, show he died on June 1, 1902, of acute enteritis. A sign of Léon's poverty is that his son received a "fifth-class burial," the lowest possible, that of the poor. Léon is listed in the death record as "préparateur d'anatomie" at the Brussels Museum.

Serge's father had no faith in education as it was carried out in schools. As a result, Serge was an autodidact all through his youth, except for the disorganized private lessons he received from his father. Serge's half-sister from his mother's first marriage, Vera, said of Victor's childhood that "M. Kibalchich totally neglected the upbringings and education of his son, never sending him to school, giving him very occasional lessons, lacking totally in system and method. The family was not a united one, and the discord between the parents visibly weighed on the tender soul of the child."[14] Serge's self-education perhaps began in England where, when he was six or seven, "I learned to read through cheap editions of Shakespeare and Chekhov."[15] It should be noted that school attendance for children was already mandatory in England at this time, so little Victor's home education was illegal, if it truly occurred as he claimed. No records of his attendance at schools in England have been found, though many records in the neighborhoods in which he lived were destroyed during the Blitz. In Belgium, on the other hand, school attendance was not yet mandatory, and auto-didacticism was a well-established method, especially in Brussels, with its museums, public lectures, and a Royal Library open seven days a week from 9.00 a.m. until 10.00 p.m.

His half-sister Vera's description of Serge's upbringing seems an accurate one, to which must be added Serge's mother's departure when he was still a child and her replacement by his stepmother. Serge gives the age he declared independence as fifteen, but he had already been living apart from his family for a couple of years by that time. A police report from 1908 states that Victor-Napoléon had been living on his own at 56, rue du Conseil in Ixelles since March 17, 1903, when he was not even twelve and a half! According to the text of a talk given by Michel Hinaut, a local historian in Ixelles, there is no further record of Victor-Napoléon living with his family after 1903. He was barely an adolescent when he broke with his family, from that point on earning his own living however he could. He wrote in his memoirs that he was inspired by a pamphlet by the anarchist Prince Peter Kropotkin "which spoke to [him] in a language of unprecedented clarity."[16] He told his father he had no intention of being a student and set off to make a living and a life on his own.[17] Politics would soon enter his life, and he would develop his own family, an elective one drawn from among his comrades.

Serge's difficult childhood and his early escape from parental control can explain much about his family relations throughout his life. He would attach himself ferociously to his first and third wives, and, in the case of his second wife, Serge became attached to her and her family during the time of a ship's voyage between France and Russia. He needed to find the connections he'd been denied as a child and adolescent. Politics, to which he gave his all, filled much of the void he felt during his childhood, adolescence, and as an adult during his troubled marriages. He had two children, Vlady and Jeannine. Serge would be the devoted father to Vlady that he had never experienced during his own childhood. Vlady would join his father in all his struggles and exiles, would be his companion, his supporter, and his most important personal connection. They differed on many political matters in Serge's final years, but Vlady was a dogged defender of his father's memory, attacking all those who questioned his father's genius or ideas.

There is a touching coda to the story of Serge's Frolov family. In 1945 Serge contacted a family member in Louvain, which touched off a final round of correspondence with his remaining Belgian family, which lasted until just before Serge's death. He received regular mail in Mexico City from his Belgian cousins, nephews, and nieces, many of them relatives of his half-sister Helène, who after a time in Russia had settled in Belgium with her Belgian husband. The letters were often simple and chatty affairs, but the sufferings of the family under Stalin were ever present. His niece Cecile asks him, "if you haven't had any news of Aunt Vera and [her daughter] Mado, for it's already been seven years that we have completely lost sight of them." A later letter from Serge's nephew Henri explains, "We've never managed to have any news of Vera. Before the war we wrote several times to Mado, but never had any results. I'm absolutely certain that steps taken at the Soviet embassy would be completely useless."

This correspondence continued till shortly before Serge's death. He sent them his books, and his niece Cecile wrote, upon receiving his novel *Les Derniers temps*: "I admire you; how beautiful it is to be able to write something." Cecile's vision of her uncle was a touching one, speaking of the "enchanted isle" on which he must live. She worried about Vlady, wondering if he'd left for New York for an operation. Serge's interest in his family is obvious. Cecile sent him, on September 2, 1947, a "long-promised photo of Maman Frolov."

2

From Socialism to Anarchism

Serge explained the fact that he lived alone from age thirteen—actually twelve and a half—as "owing to the journeys and estrangements of my parents."[1] Whatever the journeys and estrangements, it could only have been unimaginably horrible for a child to be sent out on his own. In place of a family, he did develop close friendships with other like-minded young men, the closest of them with Raymond Callemin, son of an impoverished, alcoholic, socialist cobbler. There were other friends, friends he described as being "closer than brothers," a choice of noun that is not accidental, for they replaced the family he'd left. Callemin was the first among them, and he also developed close friendships with Edouard Carouy, a metal worker; with the printer Jean De Boë; with René Valet; and later with Octave Garnier. All of these men would, like Serge, eventually move to Paris and be friends and comrades of Serge's. Ultimately, their fates would diverge from his. It was with Callemin that he would begin reading political works like Louis Blanc's *History of the French Revolution*, and Émile Zola's novel *Paris*, set during the age of attentats and featuring a variety of anarchists, like the bomb-thrower Émile Henry, whose example Victor and Raymond would later praise. Victor read Kropotkin, whose anarchism moved him. Young as this group was, they were politically aware and they joined the youth branch of the Parti ouvrier belge (POB; Belgian Workers Party), the Jeune Garde.

At age fifteen Serge began a life of odd jobs, all poorly paid. He recalled that his best paying job brought a mere 40 francs a week. In that same year, 1905, Victor gave his first public political talk, at a gathering of the Jeune Garde at the Maison du Peuple in Ixelles, speaking about the October 1905 general strike in Russia. Serge and his friends, fervently revolutionary, formed a study group that they called Ad Lumen. The POB, though, was a solidly reformist social-democratic party, one not interested in fomenting revolution. Later in his life Serge would find kind words to say about its leadership as decent men who did not fail in their revolutionary duty because they were never revolutionaries. But as a teenager Victor and his friends found the party conservative and constricting. As Jean De Boë later recalled "I met [Raymond Callemin, Kibalchich] and other youths who, like me, became anarchists. We became extremely close since already at that time we had many affinities which placed us in opposition to the mass of Young Guards."[2] While still in the POB they regularly visited an anarchist commune in suburban Boitsfort, part of a paradoxical movement in France and Belgium of individualists living on communes. In June 1907 the friends established their own newspaper, *Le Communiste*, where Serge learned the basics of the printing trade and in which they expounded their dissident left-wing ideas.

Things came to a head for the young rebels on June 30, 1907, when, at a special congress of the POB, one of the party's leaders, Emil Vandervelde, called for the annexation of the Congo. Serge and his friends stormed out of the congress. They not only left the congress and the POB but also turned away as a group from parliamentary, reformist socialism to anarchism. The "brothers" were not seeking small, ameliorative changes: They were in quest of something greater. As Serge wrote in his memoirs:

> Socialism meant reformism, parliamentarism, and repellent doctrinal rigidity. Its intransigence was incarnated in Jules Guesde, who made one think of a city of the future in which all the houses would be alike, with an all-powerful State, harsh towards heretics. Our way of correcting this doctrinal rigidity was to refuse to believe in it. We had to have an absolute, only one of liberty (without unnecessary metaphysics); a principle

of life, only unselfish and ardent; a principle of action, only not to win a place in this stifling world (which is still a fashionable game), but to try, however desperately, to escape from it since it was impossible to destroy it.[3]

Despite their walkout, despite having their own newspaper, the young men remained members of the POB, but the situation could not last forever. Though now considering themselves anarchists, they also felt alienated from the veteran anarchists of the existing anarchist groups in Belgium, specifically the Groupe communiste libertaire, which called for anarchists to work within the POB and lead the workers to see the justice of the anarchist cause. The young rebels against the POB could not but find that tactic reprehensible, and formed their own, more radical organization, the Groupe révolutionnaire belge. Jean De Boë later told Émile Michon, a psychiatrist who examined the members of the anarchist bandits of the Bonnot Gang and who published his results as a book, *Un peu de l'âme des bandits* (A Bit of the Soul of the Bandits), that "We were young, enthusiastic; we were bound to drag the elders behind us."[4]

Le Communiste was renamed *Le Révolté*, the original name of a newspaper published by the great Kropotkin. There, Serge would write most of his articles under the name Le Rétif, an adjective with many meanings: restive, recalcitrant, refractory, rebel, stubborn, unruly.

As Jan Moulaert, a historian of the Belgian anarchist movement, explained:

> *Le Communiste* already stood out among the other papers for its youthful, aggressive style. It was felt to be less tied to the workers' movement and its attitude toward the POB was much more critical. The artisan of *Le Révolté* was the young—seventeen-year-old—Victor Kibalchich [...] His articles quickly revealed a man highly critical of "the people" [...] A virile, vitalist revolt dominated *Le Révolté*. The paper preached

permanent rebellion, at once personal and collective [...] Anarchists are in the habit of using muscular language, but the new anarchist paper beat all the records. Despite all its criticisms [of the workers], *Le Révolté* continued to care about the oppressed masses and their emancipation, but this emancipation would be mainly instinctive. This individual revolt, still peaceful but energetic, was not yet dissociated from the hope for a collective liberation. Nonetheless [when the occasion arose] *Le Révolté* and Victor Serge would line up, de facto, on the side of the illegalists and defend, in a rather radical way, forms of illegal action which would be difficult to distinguish from terrorism.[5]

Two issues exemplified the distance that separated Serge and his friends from their elders in the Belgian anarchist world, not to mention the reformist POB. Those issues were illegalism, that is, crime as a legitimate weapon of anarchist struggle, and propaganda of the deed: the indiscriminate violence, the "terrorism" referred to by historian Moulaert.

Émile Henry was the son of an exiled Communard who became the emblematic figure of the age of attentats of the early 1890s. He placed a bomb at the Paris offices of the Carmaux Mining Company (Société des Mines de Carmaux) to avenge the savage repression of the Carmaux miners following a failed strike in 1892. Henry's bomb killed five policemen. Two years later, in 1894, Henry was arrested after throwing a bomb into the Café Terminus at the Gare Saint-Lazare, killing two and wounding twenty. Henry's café bombing was intended to avenge the execution of anarchist bomb-thrower Auguste Vaillant, guillotined after he threw a bomb into the Chamber of Deputies that failed to kill any of its intended victims. For Henry, anyone who acquiesced to the existing system was guilty: There were no innocent victims.

Serge's commemorative article on the fourteenth anniversary of Henry's execution, published in *Le Communiste* on May 23,

1908, provides us with a portrait of the teenage Kibalchich, a young man boiling with hatred, rage, and a very personal idea of moral purity.[6]

Serge, writing as Le Rétif, set the tone from the start, praising "acts of brutal revolt" because "they awaken the masses, shake them up with the lashing of a whip, and show the real face of the bourgeoisie, still trembling at the moment the rebel climbs the gallows." He rejected Henry as a kind of sacralized figure for "We want neither tribunes, nor martyrs, nor prophets." But a figure like Henry could be a source of inspiration and pride. Henry handled himself with "calm and tranquility" at his trial, having "the satisfied awareness of someone certain of having lived a useful and beautiful life" that he was sacrificing at age twenty-one.

Victor's rage was directed not only at "arrivistes, crushers, [and] deceivers of all kinds," but also at "the mass of imbecilic followers and serfs." What distinguished the anarchism of Serge and his comrades was pushing contempt for the compliant masses to its furthest extreme. As Serge wrote in ending his piece, "We are merciless towards everything that blocks the road of humanity on its march towards the light!"

The other issue splitting the anarchist movement was that of illegalism. Contrary to what Serge would write in his memoirs, and despite his later reservations about illegalism as a revolutionary tactic, from age seventeen he was a supporter of crime as an inherently anarchist act. In an article published on June 20, 1908, in *Le Communiste*, he didn't mince words.[7] Defining illegalists as "people living off illicit labor" he compared them to anti-militarists, for whom anarchist support was never put in question. The anti-militarist "pits himself in open struggle against society, whose law he violates." He then asked, "After this, how can we disavow that other comrade, whose temperament bows as little before the regime of the workshop as the anti-militarist bows before that of the barracks, and who, by some *illegal* method, revolts against the law of the slavery of work?"

Le Rétif excluded from his praise those for whom crime is "nothing but an act of cowardice and weakness, for he who commits it has no other goal than that of escaping work, while at the same time escaping the difficulties of social struggle." He calls illegalism an "admissible" tactic, one whose risks often outweigh its benefits. But even so, illegalists are part of the movement. "All rebels, through their acts, are our people. Anarchism is a principle of struggle: It needs fighters and not servants, the way statist socialism does."

In these articles approving terror and crime, the battle lines are clearly drawn between Serge and his "brothers" and the anarchists of the main anarchist organization. Their elders on the left accepted the role of serfs. Not the Groupe révolutionnaire belge.

Serge and his comrades were increasingly isolated within the larger Belgian left. He was being harassed by the police—who on December 22, 1908, carried out a fruitless search of his apartment looking for the manuscript of an anarchist pamphlet and the type used in printing it, at the same time that the anarchist communes in which the libertarian left had placed its hopes were failing and incapable of serving as a lever for changing society. Serge approached his eighteenth birthday in a state of political despair, a despair—and frustration—that is apparent in the two articles he wrote to see off 1908 and greet 1909.

Serge ended 1908 with an article entitled "Christmas."[8] He derided the holiday as celebrating

the birth of the savior who saved no one, and the new year for the poor, for the workers; winter is the cruel season which torments us, which we fear, which we hate. Christmas, when the words of Jesus, "stolen by the same double-dealers and scoundrels he condemned and who crucified him" are used to preach resignation and hope for a Kingdom of Heaven [that] renders the hell of this world more acceptable.

As was often the case in the articles signed Le Rétif, the resigned are contrasted to those for whom poverty "will have removed the blindfold from their eyes." For people of this stripe, Christmas will have been "a resurrection, the resurrection of their souls, finally freed from odious Christian morality, castrator of energies." Serge thus ended the year on a note of (limited) hope. For those who have freed themselves—like Serge and his brothers—the seed of a new life will grow, "the will to live real life without restrictions or hindrances; without oppression or injustice."

This hopeful note, however vague, however disabused and limited, would not last a week, as his next article, "1909," derides New Year's wishes and resolutions, which people "know to be vain."[9] His disdain for the traditions of the holiday season spares no one: "Negro fetishists or Christians, the religious and atheists," are all mocked for expressing "the same desires and the same hopes."

The profound pessimism that lies at the heart of individualism is expressed by the eighteen-year-old rebel, since whatever people might hope for, "the hope is always disappointed. Years and centuries pass and pile up; grandiose civilizations are constructed, flourish and crumble; regimes change and races disappear without humanity's lot seeming to improve." For Serge there is really no hope: "Life will be equally cruel for all and filled with suffering"; all this because "we live in a dying society [...] a society where no one is happy." It is only through engaging in struggle that happiness is possible, not by getting drunk to welcome a New Year that will be like the old one. "But you, men of all categories, are too weak, too cowardly, too lacking in consciousness to commit to it."

Which is not to say that the teenage anarchist had no wishes for the New Year. He hoped for famine for people "too spineless to conquer their bread [...] War, causing patriots to mutually slaughter each other ... Gangrene to rage among the idiotic crowd of the lower depths." And he concludes his wishes by hoping that 1909 will "be a year of calamities and atrocious suffering that will abridge the agony of the inane world in which we vegetate."

Whatever the contempt for the spineless masses felt by Serge and many of those around him, those who were ready to risk all in confronting the state and the bourgeoisie, those willing to be what he called in his writings "men," were supported unhesitatingly. A month after Le Rétif expressed his wishes for a calamitous new year, the Hartenstein Affair, Victor's final major campaign in Belgium, was to explode.

It began on February 4, 1909, with the discovery of an unexploded device in Saint-Josse-ten-Node, a Brussels municipality, as well as an accusation of the extortion of 3000 francs from a Brussels businessman. Shortly afterwards, a manifesto issued by the Groupe anarchiste internationale (GAI) took credit for the device, saying it was intended for Jules Renkin, Belgium's former minister of justice, who was responsible for the expulsion of many foreign revolutionaries. The group also took credit for the extortion, which was an element of their campaign of "immediate expropriation of bourgeois personal property."[10] The team at *Le Révolté* responded to the manifesto in its February 16 issue, saying that though the members of the GAI "have our complete confidence," we "disapprove of their recent actions." Serge, who had recently written in support of anarchist banditry, could not have been in total agreement with the reasons for his comrades' disapproval: "We don't consider individual re-appropriation a means of social transformation [...] Violence in itself has nothing anarchist about it, and though we will resort to it when necessary, under no pretext do we want to erect it into a principle." In Paris the syndicalist *Temps nouveaux* of February 27, 1909, was especially indignant about the GAI manifesto, which had been sent to comrades in London with the *Temps Nouveaux* offices as the return address. The tone of *Le Révolté* would quickly change.

A police investigation determined that a Russian-Jewish émigré living in Ghent, Abraham Hartenstein, who possessed an array of pseudonyms (Seliger, Sokolov, Soukarov ...), was responsible for making the bomb. A warrant was issued, and on February 15, 1909, the police went to Hartenstein's residence. The story was recounted in the socialist paper *Le Peuple*:

> When the police arrived at his home Monday evening at 7:00, Sokoloff was seated at a small table on which was a gas lamp. The anarchist was reading. A revolver was within his reach. The police, having found the key in the door, entered quickly without knocking. Sukaroff [*sic*] immediately understood their intentions. With an infernal presence of mind, he knocked over the lamp that illuminated the scene with the back of his hand. It immediately became dark and before the police [...] could recover from their surprise five explosions rang out, followed by cries of pain.

Two policemen were mortally wounded, dying shortly thereafter. The Hartenstein Affair was launched.

If the Brussels anarchists of the Groupe révolutionnaire belge had expressed reservations at the time of the GAI manifesto, all hesitations fell to the wayside once an anarchist brother was in real danger. Hartenstein was one of theirs, and he would be defended to the bitter end. And not just against the state, but against the anarchists' enemies within the POB.

Le Peuple's February 20 article on the case was headlined "Where Did the Money Come From? Are Sokoloff's Relatives Named Okhrana?" The accusation was a grave one, as the Okhrana was the tsarist secret police. The article questioned the delay between Sokoloff being considered a suspect and the police's attempted search of his apartment. More importantly, *Le Peuple* spoke of the large sums of money in his possession, as well as new clothing, and men's and women's linen, "the clothing beautiful, the linens very fine." For the socialist paper, "If the generous benefactor ... is not the prisoner of Ghent, who is it? We know from many examples that the Russian secret police, the

Okhrana, is very generous with its agents, especially the provocateurs. Is Okhrana the real name of Sokoloff's relatives?" The money found in Hartenstein's possession had an "innocent" explanation. It would later develop that it was part of the 3000 francs extorted two weeks earlier, an extortion that would later figure in the indictment against Hartenstein. The newspaper *Le Petit Bleu* would make a similar claim concerning Victor, alleging he had attempted to extort 3000 francs from a certain Semen Henault. An investigator spoke to the alleged victim and determined that the charge was "fanciful."[11]

The situation for the Groupe révolutionnaire belge had become extremely ugly. The anarchist Émile Chapelier wrote a letter on February 20 to *Le Peuple*, which published it on February 23. In it, though he expressed doubts that Hartenstein was an agent provocateur, he nevertheless insisted that "It is no less true that his acts have nothing in common with anarchism." Further, Chapelier went on to attack the Groupe révolutionnaire belge for its support for Hartenstein, openly breaking ranks with his fellow anarchists in the pages of a reformist paper. But Chapelier also condemned what would soon develop into the illegalist trend: "Striking representatives of authority is not in itself an anarchist act. Otherwise, we would have to admit that the Pollet gang and, in Paris the [royalist] Camelots du Roy [*sic*] are also anarchists."

The Groupe révolutionnaire belge could not but react to this, and strongly, doing so in a manifesto published in *Le Révolté* of February 27. Far from an agent provocateur, Sokoloff was a man who, when confronted with the "watchdogs of the bourgeois safes," acted like a rebel: "An anarchist doesn't surrender." Sokoloff was an exemplary figure, one who was not one of the "spineless and moronic crowd who don't know how to rebel."

There is every reason to believe that Serge was the author of the manifesto. He would later use almost the same words in defending Liabeuf—a pimp arrested and executed after killing a policeman, a figure we will return to later—as he now did defending Hartenstein:

> Every man has the right to defend himself. Every man whose freedom another man—in the name of anything at all—wants to steal from him, has not only the right, but the obligation to defend himself. This is what Sokoloff did; attacked, his freedom and perhaps his life threatened, he defended himself.

And the line "an anarchist doesn't surrender" was a variant of the Russian cry that "An anarchist never surrenders" that Victor had already used in his article "Anarchists-Bandits" on February 6.

The Groupe révolutionnaire belge was able to defend Hartenstein's honor and probity with confidence, since they knew him well. Serge, who had originally met the "redoubtable chemist from Odessa via Buenos Aires" while putting out *Le Communiste*, wrote in his memoirs that "Sokolov was a man of icy will, formed in Russia by the inhuman struggles outside of which he could no longer live. He came out of the storm and the storm was within him." The novelist in Serge speculated that when Sokoloff fired on the police who broke into his apartment he saw before him the authorities he'd fled in Russia. "The peaceful policemen of Ghent paid for the Cossacks who'd carried out the pogroms."[12] It was only natural that Serge and his comrades took up Hartenstein's defense, both in the court of public opinion and that of justice.

The aggressiveness of the Groupe révolutionnaire belge's campaign made Serge's life difficult with the police, the latter writing no less than four reports on him in February 1909, particularly singling out his authorship of the article "Anarchists-Bandits."

The writers at *Le Révolté* seemed to have realized that their language had perhaps been excessive, and the March 13 issue led with an article entitled "Amicably," by Jean Vaillant. Vaillant bemoaned the split the case had caused among Belgian anarchists, in which one group considers Hartenstein "a hero and the others finding him clumsy, if not an imbecile. The former consider him a rebel who acted in full awareness; the latter think him an agent provocateur or an instrument of the Russian police." Vaillant, noting the small number of anarchists in Belgium, cautioned them against tearing at each other the way they were, and asking a question that is ever pertinent in internecine squabbles of this kind, in which name calling and accusations are de rigueur: "Is this really being an anarchist and working for the Idea?"

Le Rétif didn't accept this. In the same issue he let loose with a virulent defense of Hartenstein and an attack on those who failed to defend him as he deserved to be, an article whose title defined Victor's attitude: "A Man."

This piece opens with an attack on the common run of mortals, "ugly, petty, evil, hypocritical towards others, vain and conceited towards themselves," who live in "a pestilential marsh." In contrast to these people there arises a Man—Hartenstein, though unnamed—who "dared to rise up, to think freely, to speak his mind and act as he thought! ... Everyone is leagued against this madman." For the ferocious individualist Victor had become, repression not only came from the state but rose up from everyone in society, for "fear gripped the guts of the bourgeois and the workers. The crowd was anxious upon seeing their calm abjection disturbed." In the face of this ambient baseness the Man is not alone; others like him also enter the fray, and "perhaps they will fall as well, and quickly [...] But what difference does it make? They will have fought and they will have lived."

The animosity that had been percolating within the Belgian movement was reaching a boiling point. The Hartenstein Affair was a war on many fronts: of the state against the anarchists, between anarchists and socialists, and between anarchists and anarchists, and even between writers on the same anarchist paper. It was a paper that, precisely at this time, was beginning to suffer financial difficulties. These financial woes were compounded by the growing disarray of the movement. A clear sign of this was the departure of staff and supporters, departures that would soon include Victor and his original brothers, Jean De Boë, Raymond Callemin, and Edouard Carouy.

The police remained on Victor's tail in the run-up to the Hartenstein trial. On May 18, 1909, it was reported that Serge, "who calls himself an illustrator," was living with a certain Anna Estorges, better known to posterity as Rirette Maîtrejean, later Serge's companion in his Paris days and eventually his first wife. In fact, this woman in all probability was not really Rirette, but rather a friend to whom she had loaned her papers. The Serge of the report is clearly a man at sixes and sevens. "Kibalchich hasn't worked during his stay in the division's territory. He goes shopping during the day, while the mistress remains in the room. The latter only goes out in the evening and returns at around 2.00 or 3.00 a.m. Kibalchich and Estorges are reported as frequenting anarchist meetings."[13]

Hartenstein's trial began on June 16 in Ghent, and Serge and his comrades showed their support, not just in their writings but by their presence and participation. The indictment included seven charges: the defendant's having fabricated a bomb in Brussels and having transported it in order to commit a crime; extortion of 3000 francs from M. Mayer; of having fabricated a bomb in Ghent; of homicide in the death of Inspector de Smet; of committing it with premeditation; of homicide in the death of officer Ghyssels; of committing it with premeditation.

Hartenstein, as the true Russian revolutionary he was, admitted to all the facts: the extortion from Mayer in Brussels, having received a check from the victim which he immediately cashed; the fabrication of the bomb used as a threat in the extortion and which was later found planted for the planned attentat; the plans for the second device in Ghent; and even the killing of the two policemen, though the defendant denied any premeditation.

The honesty and frankness of all involved in the case is almost surreal. Mayer testified that he told his two night visitors, Hartenstein and an unidentified comrade, that he didn't have 3000 francs on him but gave his word of honor that if they came to his office the next day he'd give them the money asked for. He did and later received a receipt signed "The Anarchist Committee."[14]

The facts seemed clear, and on the second day of the trial Hartenstein's comrades testified on his behalf, having been followed by the Bureau des Étrangers from Brussels' Gare du Nord to Ghent.[15] The defense witnesses, many of them, like Hartenstein, Russian Jews, spoke highly of the defendant, of his gentleness, of his charitableness, of how he helped those less fortunate than him.

Serge, incorrectly described in newspaper reports of the trial as a student, stood by his principles from the first, refusing to swear an oath until told that he wouldn't be allowed to testify unless he did. He praised Hartenstein's studiousness and said that his comrade had often spoken to him of the persecutions to which revolutionaries were subjected in Russia.[16]

The testimony ended with the defendant's supporters, who were followed by Hartenstein's lead attorney Jofé, who spoke in his closing argument of how his client "preached love and fraternity, for he knew the Russian terror." He dismissed the seriousness of the visits to Mayer for purposes of extortion, saying "they didn't want to do him harm; they only wanted to expropriate him." As for the charge of homicide, "the honest man that is Hartenstein did not want to kill. From the first interrogation he declared he wanted to frighten the policemen in order to flee." The aim of Jofé's plea was to place Hartenstein within the context of hunted Russian revolutionaries, insisting that "all the accused's acts were inspired by the noblest sentiments towards his unfortunate brothers."[17]

The next morning the prosecuting attorney, Van Elewijck, admitted that Hartenstein had no premeditated plan to kill the policemen, "but the murder exists," and a guilty verdict was called for. M. Hirsch, another attorney for Hartenstein, closed the case by taking up the question of whether or not Hartenstein was an agent provocateur, "expressing his disgust for those abject beings" and praising the defendant's nobility.[18]

It took the jury just two hours to reach a verdict, finding Hartenstein guilty of constructing the Brussels bomb, of extortion, and of voluntary homicide of the two policemen, but not guilty of premeditated murder and the making of a bomb in Ghent. He was sentenced to hard labor for life. There were later reports of his going on a hunger strike, a method of protest familiar to Russian revolutionaries. He died in prison, though the date is unknown.

The police reported on June 21 that "anarchist pamphlets relating to Hartenstein have been found on the Grand Place [of Brussels]." The fight for their brother had not ended, but things had hit rock bottom. The time for a change of scene had come. Serge was stateless, and for a young man of his ideals there was only one possibility.

Paris called us, the Paris of Salvat, of the Commune, of the CGT [Confédération générale du travail], of little journals printed with burning zeal; the Paris of our favorite authors, Anatole France and Jehan Rictus; the Paris where Lenin from time to time edited *Iskra* and spoke at émigré meetings in little cooperative houses, where Burtsev lived, who had just unmasked, in the terrorist organization of this party, Evno Azev, engineer, executioner of Minister von Plehve and of Grand Duke Sergei, and police spy.[19]

The Paris described in this passage of Serge's *Memoirs of a Revolutionary* was most decidedly not the Paris that called Le Rétif and his comrades, though it was the one that would have called the Victor Serge who wrote his *Memoirs of a Revolutionary*, who was quite a different man. The uncompromising individualist of the articles of *Le Révolté*, whom we will soon see writing for and editing *l'anarchie*, the most important organ of individualist anarchism, would not have seen Paris as the city of the

Commune, which he mocked in several articles, or the syndicalist CGT, which he would also condemn, and certainly not Lenin, whom he would have been less familiar with than the Bolshevik's Narodnik brother, the martyred Alexander. This passage is an object lesson in how to read the *Memoirs*, for it clearly demonstrates that Serge was not immune to retrospective modifications of his point of view. This is a professional deformation of all memoirists, and Serge was no more immune to it than anyone else.

Whatever the attraction of Paris might have been, Serge did leave Belgium, not to return until 1936 after his expulsion from the Soviet Union. There is, however, some controversy as to how and why he left.

Serge recounts that he left one day "on a whim, taking ten francs, an extra shirt, a few notebooks, a few photos." At the station he by chance ran into his father, "and we spoke of the recent discoveries on the structure of matter popularized by Gustave Le Bon,"[20] who had, in fact, published a number of articles on this subject in French scientific reviews.

That it was Le Bon that the teenage individualist and his father discussed at the train station contains a certain irony. Le Bon, far more than a popularizer of science, was best known for his book *The Psychology of Crowds*, which demonstrated the suggestibility of crowds, who were easily led by strong leaders, and that, once part of a crowd, man "is no longer himself, he becomes an automaton who is no longer guided by his will." Le Bon was thus a writer who provided a scientific basis for Le Rétif's contempt for the herd.

After saying farewell to his father for what would be the last time, he left Belgium with ease, for "Europe knew nothing of passports; the border hardly existed."[21] But another version of his departure from Belgium also exists. Richard Parry, in his brilliant study of the Bonnot Gang, writes that "according to the Brussels Gendarmerie Rirette and Victor were expelled together from Belgium in August 1909." Parry speculates that "his status as a refugee put him at the mercy of the Belgian authorities and after the Sokolov Affair they had obviously had enough of him."[22] The biographical notes compiled by Serge specialist Jean Rière in the Bouquins edition of Serge's *Memoirs* say that "He leaves Belgium (or is expelled from it) shortly after [the Hartenstein trial]."[23]

Parry's version revolves around the above-mentioned fellow anarchist to whom Rirette Maîtrejean had loaned her papers and who was perhaps the (fake) Anna Estorges Victor was living with in the May police report, and who was expelled from Belgium at that time. This hypothesis is partly backed by the fact that in her own memoirs, published in 1913, Rirette says that she met Victor along with the other Rirette, and that "that young woman had just been expelled from Brussels for propaganda activity." The meeting took place in Lille while she was on a speaking tour with her lover, the individualist Maurice Vandamme, known as Mauricius. Victor "sovereignly displeased me," she told her lover at the time.[24]

There are several problems with the expulsion story, the principal one being that, in his extensive researches in the archives of Belgium and France, Richard Greeman has never been able to uncover any such order. The second is Serge's account of his departure from Belgium. No stranger to expulsions by the time he wrote his *Memoirs*, having already been expelled from several countries, he certainly would not have been ashamed to have been expelled from Belgium, especially if it occurred because of his support for a comrade. He would have had no reason to hide the story in writing his autobiography. And Rirette's account specifies that the young woman, the false Rirette, had been expelled, making no mention of Victor having met the same fate. Finally, Victor had every reason to leave Brussels and Belgium. He was just eighteen with only a loose attachment to his family, with whom he hadn't lived since he was twelve-and-a-half, and his political group had fallen on catastrophically hard times. Even if it was not the Paris of Lenin that called, the Paris of anarchy, literature, and revolution did. It is all but certain that he left Belgium—like the good individualist he was—of his own free will.

Before reaching Paris, Serge stayed in the north of France, in the mining village of Five-Lille, where he wanted nothing more than to work in the mines, though he was dissuaded by two old miners who told him "He'd die in two hours." Unable to find work, running out of money, he roamed the streets thinking of killing himself, when he ran into a comrade who found him a job, and then found another job in Armentières working in a photo lab. Though not a miner, he remained in the mining village, walking to his job alongside the leather-hatted miners. He read Jean Jaurès's French socialist paper *L'Humanité* in the evening. He listened to the sounds of the couple in the next room, the man beating the woman before making love to her, the woman telling him to beat her again. He realized he had a lot to learn about working-class women.[25]

Paris was calling.

3

Paris

Serge, feeling ever the exiled Russian, was introduced into Russian émigré—primarily Socialist Revolutionary (SR)—circles in Paris. The party was going through a period of crisis, with infiltrators and agents provocateurs being unmasked with alarming frequency. When the files of the Okhrana, the tsar's secret police, were opened after the victory of the Bolshevik Revolution, Serge reported in the slim book he assembled from what he learned studying the files, *What Every Radical Should Know to Know About State Repression*, that there were 35,000 informers in the pay of the Russian government. Serge would later learn that his contact with the SRs, with whom he discussed the Belgian writer Maruice Maeterlinck and who remained calm in the face of the surrounding collapse, was an informer as well.[1]

Serge also maintained his Russianness by working as a translator.[2] He translated three works of the now-forgotten novelist Mikhail Artzybachev: two novels, *Sanine* (1911) and *À l'extrème limite* (1913), and the short story "Le Vieux Procureur Raconte" (1913). These translations were signed not by Serge but by "an amiable Russian journalist," Jacques Povolozky. Artzybachev's articles frequently appeared in the pages of the newspaper Serge was to edit, *l'anarchie*, and we can safely assume that it was Victor who translated them as well. He also anonymously translated works by K.D. Balmont and D.S. Merezhkovski, but these works haven't been identified.

There were multiple milieux in the popular Paris in which Serge lived. Alongside his Russian activities Serge also moved among the *apaches*, the lower-class hoodlums of Montmartre, who he viewed as primitive rebels. But whatever the role played by the *apaches* or the Russians in the life of the new arrival, the one milieu that truly mattered, the one that absorbed his life from mid-1909 until his arrest on January 31, 1912, was that of anarchism, and more particularly that of the individualist anarchism centered around the newspaper *l'anarchie*, founded in 1905 by Albert Libertad.

French anarchism at the time of Victor's arrival was recovering from the crisis that had afflicted it in the 1890s, when the acts of the propagandists of the deed—the bomb throwers Émile Henry and Auguste Vaillant, the terrorist/murderer/grave-robber Ravachol, and the assassin of President Sadi Carnot, Sante Caserio—colored the entire movement and led to a wave of repression that struck all of French anarchism. The attacks led to the *lois scélérates*—the scoundrel laws—of 1894 which all but made anarchist activity and propaganda illegal.

That same year the government put on trial thirty key figures of the anarchist movement, a trial known as the Trial of the Thirty. This was intended as a show trial, and in order to put the anarchists in the worst possible light, mixed in with figures like Jean Grave, Sébastien Faure and the art critic Félix Fénéon was a large group of illegalists. The prosecution strived to demonstrate that there were large areas of agreement between the theoreticians of anarchy and the illegalists who carried out theft in the name of the anarchist ideal. The trial badly misfired, with only three of the thirty accused found guilty, all of them illegalists. The anarchist movement now entered a period of growth, but the movement Victor found on his arrival was a fissiparous one.

The French anarchism of the time can be defined as rotating around two axes. There were those who thought the revolution was imminent or, if not imminent, at least possible through mass action. These anarchists gravitated towards anarcho-syndicalism and anarchist communism. On the other hand, there were the anarchists who believed the revolution was at best a remote possibility, or who believed it wasn't possible at all. These were the individualists who drew the lesson from the Paris Commune of

1871 that the masses were not capable of carrying out a successful revolution because of their own inadequacies and the preponderant force of the enemy. Continuing the work he had begun in Belgium, Serge joined the latter group, which had two focal points, the popular educational talks known as the Causeries populaires and the newspaper *l'anarchie*—all the letters of its name in lower case, signifying their absolute equality—both founded by the fiery militant Albert Libertad.

Born Albert Joseph on November 24, 1885, he was abandoned by his parents and brought up in an orphanage in Bordeaux. He fled the home while a teenager and had a reputation as a rebel, being tracked by the police as a known anarchist from the age of nineteen. In 1897 (on August 27, according to a police report) he made the inevitable move to Paris, where he went to the offices of Sébastien Faure's newspaper *Le Libertaire*.

Libertad was disabled and required crutches to get around. Jean Maitron, the greatest historian of the French working-class movement, wrote of him that "He was feared and no one heard the sound of his canes without fear, for it was the prelude to an awful din and brawls." His militancy led him to be condemned six times during his ten Paris years, though despite his reputation the sentences were quite moderate, none exceeding three months in jail, and one a fine of but one franc.[3]

Mauricius, an individualist and later director of *l'anarchie*, said of the paper, in a volume he wrote in homage to another leader of the movement, Émile Armand, that it aimed at being the contact point for those around the world who live as anarchists, under the control of only experience and free examination. Armand, who would later edit *l'anarchie*, described its early days and its raison d'être to a journalist for *Le Temps* in its May 1, 1912, issue. "*l'anarchie* [...] was founded in 1905, its first issue dated April 13. It provoked a reaction against the traditional anarchism of men like Kropotkin and Jean Grave, against sentimental anarchism."

Armand, whom we will meet again later, described the ideas that animated the paper:

We didn't bother ourselves with a future society that was promised but never came. Economic and social points of view were left to the side. Individualism is a permanent struggle between the individual and the environment, it's the negation of authority, the law and exploitation, a corollary of authority. But all this is theoretical. How do we cast authority and exploitation out of practical life? Simply by living without authority and exploitation.

These few sentences sum up the entire program of individualist anarchism. It was at *l'anarchie* that Serge would literally and figuratively find a home.

Shortly after Serge's arrival in Paris a major change in his personal life occurred. While still in the north of France Serge met Rirette Maîtrejean, whose papers, as we have seen, an anarchist friend in Belgium was using. Rirette at the time of their meeting was on a speaking tour with her then lover, Mauricius. She was born Anna Estorges in Corrèze in 1887, and while still an adolescent began preparations to study at university. Her mother attempted to impose a husband on her, so, to avoid this fate, at sixteen she fled to Paris. She would later say that her initial attraction to anarchism, "like many anarchists," was to escape "constraints imposed by my family." Once in Paris she began attending classes at the Sorbonne, and the young anarchist would ask professors "questions official doctrines were unable to answer."

She soon joined anarchist circles, becoming part of the group around Albert Libertad. The instinctive revolt of her childhood and adolescence had changed. "I needed the suffering of thousands of workers, bloodshed, and the anger of the people to give a meaning to my anger." She claimed it was a result of her innocence that she met the man who would be her first husband. Approached in a café by a pimp who asked her to come work for him she broke down in tears. It was then that Louis Maîtrejean, an anarchist leather worker she'd met at anarchist meetings, came to her defense, and they soon became a couple.[4]

They lived together for eighteen months and had two children; they split up due to mutual incompatibility. Maîtrejean soon joined the world of the illegalists, was arrested, and sentenced to five years for counterfeiting on June 9, 1910.[5] Rirette continued to be active in anarchist circles, including participating in speaking tours with Mauricius. It was on one of these tours that she first met Victor.

Though Rirette had taken an immediate dislike to Victor, once he arrived in Paris their relationship changed. Though her friends at *l'anarchie* disliked Victor, feeling him to be nothing but an "intellectual," he regularly attended the Monday evening Causeries populaires. When he would comment on the speakers she would sharply respond to his comments. "I would have liked to slap him."

A mutual friend told Rirette that if she and Serge were to spend an hour together they would find themselves in agreement on everything, and she formally introduced them to each other. They were soon lovers and comrades and, with her husband imprisoned, Serge would become a surrogate father to her two daughters. They would also share each other's fate over the coming years.[6] They always addressed each other using the formal "vous," and not the familiar "tu" form, commonly used in their milieu, precisely to differentiate their relationship.

*　*　*

We know that Serge was in Paris by mid-September 1909 and, thanks to contacts he had already made in Brussels, particularly with Mauricius, was in immediate contact with individualist circles.[7] A month after his arrival in Paris he was witness to what he described as one of the two major events that marked him personally and Paris in general, the massive demonstration of October 13, 1909, protesting the execution in Barcelona of the libertarian educator Francisco Ferrer.[8] This demonstration was the largest working-class action since the Commune. Serge was on the scene but didn't write about it.

Ferrer—wealthy, educated, and cultivated—founded the Modern School movement upon returning to Spain in 1901 after spending sixteen years in exile for his republican beliefs. Once back in Barcelona, he remained a target of the authorities and was arrested in 1906 on suspicion of participating in a failed plot to assassinate King Alfonso XIII. He was released after a year in jail and focused on his educational activities, publishing a history of the Modern School movement in 1908.

Ferrer's execution was a result of the Bloody Week of July 25–August 2, 1909. That week the workers of Barcelona and of Catalonia in general rose up against the government of Prime Minister Antonio Maura (who was the maternal grandfather of the future member of the French Resistance, Communist leader, and prize-winning novelist Jorge Semprun), who had called up reservists to serve in Spain's colonial war in Morocco.

What began as an anti-militarist revolt quickly developed into a general strike and violent uprising. The organization at the heart of the revolt was the broad-based Solidaridad Obrera, a group whose educational activities Ferrer helped fund. Though much of the revolutionary activity that week had its source in Solidaridad Obrera, Ferrer himself did not participate in the events, and in fact wasn't in Barcelona.

Once the revolt was put down the repression that followed was fierce, with five supposed leaders sentenced to death, including Ferrer, the sentencing decree stating that he was "the author and chief of the rebellion," the proof of his leadership role being that "the names and the chiefs and principal instigators correspond with the names of those who appear as teachers placed by Ferrer in certain schools."[9]

The worldwide outrage at the execution on October 13, 1909, was immense, with demonstrations in Rome (where the Vatican supported the death sentence), Berlin, Brussels, Trieste, London, and Buenos Aires. Paris, though, was the heart of the protest movement outside Spain, and Socialist Party leader Jean Jaurès gave a succinct explanation for the results of Ferrer's trial: "The trial and sentencing can only be explained by Spanish clericalism's hatred for rationalist education."[10]

There had been hopes that Ferrer's sentence would be commuted, but when the word spread around Paris that Ferrer had been executed, demonstrators headed for the Spanish embassy. "Blood called for blood, and more than one heart was pierced with the secret hope of revenge."[11]

As they left their factories and workshops at 6.00 p.m., workers gathered and chanted, "Down with the assassin! Down with the priests! Down with Alfonso XIII!" A small number of policemen tried to block the demonstrators from reaching the Spanish embassy, but they had to retreat quickly, though not before carrying out the first arrests of the evening.

Police from the eighth, tenth, and seventeenth arrondissements arrived and attempted to block the boulevard de Courcelles, lining up in three ranks. The demonstration continued to grow around the Spanish embassy, and at 8.25 p.m. the police charged the crowd. This first charge was followed by others, with police on horseback driving into the working-class crowd. A shot was fired and the rumor spread that police prefect Lepine had been fired at and then that Lepine and the head of the municipal police force had been struck with pieces of thrown brick. Word spread that a policeman on a bicycle had been killed, which was in fact the case.

It was now 10.00 p.m. and the crowd had neither left nor its rage diminished. They managed to get control of a hose and fired water at the police until the hose was beaten out of the hand of the demonstrator holding it. The crowd was then attacked by the assembled forces of order, the prefect ordering them to have their sabers at the ready. The confusion was immense, with trams and buses blocked in the middle of the fray, more demonstrators arriving, and, in order to further confound the police, demonstrators smashing the streetlights.

Finally, at around 11.00 p.m., the police succeeded in breaking up the demonstration.

The scope and importance of the demonstration, and the anger and militancy of the crowd, which fearlessly stoned, fired on, and faced down the forces of order and attacked passing vehicles, was not missed by the reactionary press. *Le Figaro* wrote:

> [T]he aspect of the Ferrer Affair, barely a few hours old, has already changed, or rather it is no longer a question of this affair. It's a matter of preserving order here at home; it's a matter of defending our society. The threat is no longer in Spain, it is on our streets. And Ferrer is the pretext of today while we await that of tomorrow.[12]

In his memoirs, Serge recounts that the spontaneous demonstration of October 13 was followed two days later by one of 500,000, the authorities "measuring this growth of a new power."[13] The demonstration actually occurred three days later, on October 16, organized by the revolutionaries of the newspaper *La Guerre sociale* and the socialists. The 100,000 marchers maintained their discipline in the face of police provocation.[14] The Spanish ambassador on that same day attended the memorial service for the policeman killed the night of the execution, a service attended by 2000 people.

Only a couple of months later Serge witnessed and participated in the second great mass movement of his early days in Paris. On January 8, 1910, Jean-Jacques Liabeuf was arrested after having killed a policeman who was attempting to arrest him. Though Serge hadn't written any articles about Ferrer or the movement to save him, this was not the case with the Liabeuf Affair. This reversal is quite significant. The Ferrer case was clearly political, and was also part of the war on clericalism, Ferrer being a hero of the secular education movement and of all those fighting against the power of the priests. The cause of Ferrer was a cause that anyone with progressive or merely republican sentiments could support. That of Liabeuf was much less straightforward, with no overt political content. Even so, it mobilized most of the same forces, and this time Serge openly expressed his sentiments.

Liabeuf was a shoemaker from Saint-Etienne (Victor incorrectly has Liabeuf growing up in the working-class quarters of Paris).[15] He soon became a petty criminal and suffered the fate most feared and hated by members of the French lumpen, doing his military service in the disciplinary Bataillons d'Afrique.

Upon completing his military service, rather than return to his hometown he remained in Paris, where he fell in love with a prostitute (though he firmly denied that that was her profession), Alexandrine Pigeon, whose pimp was a police informer. The two lovers were arrested by officers Maugras and Mors, members of the vice squad, on July 31, 1909, and Liabeuf was accused and condemned as Pigeon's pimp. He was sentenced to three months in prison, given a fine of 100 francs, and prohibited to reside in Paris for a period of five years. Despite his sentence, at the end of his prison term he returned to Paris, explaining at his later trial that he did so because he thought the sentence was unjust. He was then arrested again and sentenced to one month in prison for violating the terms of his sentence.

Once released from this second sentence, which he considered doubly unjust, since he continued to maintain that he was not a pimp, he decided to seek vengeance on the two officers who had arrested him. His homemade weaponry was impressive, including spiked brassards wrapped around his biceps and forearms and knife blades made out of shoemakers' tools. On the night of January 8, 1910, he roamed the neighborhood of Les Halles hoping to encounter the officers responsible for his arrest. He went into a bar called the Caves Modernes, where he "[spat] out the worst imprecations, the worst threats against the police, declaring 'The cops ... I'll knock off a few of them.'"[16]

A patron went to the local police station and told them of Liabeuf's threats, and when they went to the bar he said to them, "Oh, here they are; now we're gonna have some fun."[17] Police attempted to take him into custody, but rather than surrender he lashed out at them, killing one, seriously wounding another, and slightly wounding three more. In his memoirs, Serge speaks of Liabeuf wounding four officers, omitting any mention of the officer he killed.[18]

The story of Liabeuf's rampage was covered in the mainstream press, but the Socialist Party's *L'Humanité*, which would later take up his defense, dismissed the case in a brief notice, saying simply that "it is supposed the individual is an extremely dangerous fugitive from justice."[19] The next day, accepting the police version, Jean Jaurès's newspaper dismissed Liabeuf, saying that "he worked at the profession of shoemaker but quickly left it for the more lucrative one of pimp."[20] When he was finally booked, Liabeuf's rage had not been calmed: "I'll get you when I get out of prison. I'll kill all of you."[21]

Liabeuf persisted in denying the charge that he was a pimp, and after a brief trial he was sentenced to death on May 4, 1910. After saying at the end of his testimony that "I regret that it was Officer Deray, who I had nothing against, who was killed. I only hate Maugras and Mors," the vice squad cops responsible for his original arrest.[22]

By this point, Liabeuf had already been turned into a cause célèbre, thanks to the efforts of Gustave Hervé of *La Guerre sociale* and his deputy, Miguel Almereyda, the father of the filmmaker Jean Vigo. In the January 12, 1910, edition of *La Guerre sociale* Hervé wrote an article about Liabeuf entitled "The Apache's Example," in which he said

that *apache* who just killed Officer Deray wasn't lacking in a certain beauty, a certain grandeur ... He gave us revolutionaries a good example [...] Every day there are honest workers who are victims of police brutality, horrible beatings, undeserved sentences, flagrant judicial error. Have you ever heard of one of them taking vengeance? [...] Oh, honest people, give that *apache* half of your virtue and in exchange ask him for a quarter of his energy and courage.

This article earned Hervé a prison sentence of four years and a fine of 1000 francs, but it also launched the Liabeuf Affair.

Serge, too, wrote in defense of Liabeuf, for Liabeuf was almost the model rebel in the eyes of Victor and his comrades at *l'anarchie*. His article "A Good Example," in the January 27, 1910, issue of *l'anarchie*, was a major programmatic statement. It begins with a backhanded swipe at the pro-Ferrer demonstrators. He praises Liabeuf for "wip[ing] the floor with four [cops]" while "it took a few hundred avengers on October 13 of blessed memory to take down just one." For Serge, mass action like the pro-Ferrer demonstration of October 13 accomplished nothing. That the thousands who demonstrated in support of Ferrer killed only one cop and didn't save Ferrer was further proof of the ineffectiveness of the demonstrations.

Serge's defense of Liabeuf is divorced from the motives for his acts, which are a matter of total indifference to the young anarchist. The attack occurred during an arrest "for some misdeed I don't know a thing about." He earned Serge's support strictly because he fought back, Serge finding him in doing so "quite simpatico, much more so than certain fearsome revolutionaries who, after having suffered the third degree, vehemently protest journalistically."

Liabeuf is admirable because "he acted like a man where almost everyone else—including revolutionaries and anarchists—ordinarily act like cowards." And this, for Serge and his comrades at l'*anarchie*, was all that mattered.

If Liabeuf did indeed commit a crime that set the police on his trail, it was of no consequence: "Is it not the height of illogic to accuse an individual of not recognizing the rules he is perhaps ignorant of, to which no one ever asked him to subscribe, and which others unknown to him decreed?" In cases like Liabeuf's, when the police threaten arrest, the suspect has one ultimate recourse: "The right to live implies the right to kill whoever prevents me from living. The will to live imposes on me the duty (the necessity) of killing whoever wants to rob me of freedom, without which there is no life." The crowd is weak and cowardly, and "it's necessary that there arise more often the figure of the *apache* in order to teach poltroons and tormentors respect for the individual [...] This *apache* provided a good lesson."

Articles like these would not stand Victor in good stead three years later during the Bonnot trial, when he would be viewed as the theoretician of illegalism. At this particular moment what is important is that the issue for him was not one of specific injustice. What mattered was the more general issue: Laws are always unjust and bind no one; anyone who commits an act of violence against those in authority who threaten him is justified in anything and everything he does in response, up to and including killing. Liabeuf the man mattered only up to a point; Liabeuf the symbol of the rebel was what counted.

Gustave Hervé took a similar tack, and in fact used many of the same words that Serge would a couple of weeks later. It is indicative of the relative threat posed by Hervé and Serge that, though they wrote the same things, Hervé went to jail for his opinions while Serge went undisturbed by the police. There are no police records indicating why they left Serge in peace, but the fact remains that despite his praise of the killing of police he escaped unscathed from the writing of this inflammatory article. And as we will see, he returned to this exact theme at the time of Liabeuf's execution and was again left alone.

If in the immediate aftermath of Liabeuf's attacks his case was taken up only by the fringe of the political spectrum, as the months passed Liabeuf gained support, and the vice squad, which had trumped up the case against Liabeuf as a pimp, was increasingly seen as the true villain in the piece. So broad was the support of Liabeuf that even Maurice Ravel, France's most highly esteemed composer of the period, was a supporter.[23]

Calls for clemency were issued by the left and the republican press, and their tenor was always the same: His crime was not premeditated, and it was "the abominable institution of the vice squad that drove the exasperated man to vengeance."[24]

On May 12, 1910, Serge again wrote about Liabeuf in an article for *l'anarchie* entitled "A Head Will Fall." It added little to the previous article, again saying that "there's nothing about Liabeuf that interests us." Serge concentrated instead on the fact that objectively Liabeuf's battle with the police, "viewed on its own [was] an anarchist act. In fact, he even implicitly questions the logic of the clemency appeals, saying that "there is no worse wrong that can be committed against an individual than that of depriving him of his freedom. Even death is less serious, for it is not painful, while imprisonment constitutes a continuous, abominable torture."

As he waited for the sentence to be carried out, Liabeuf handled himself with calm and dignity. He refused to pray with the prison chaplain and was haunted by one thought alone, the false accusation of his being a pimp, and he even asked his lawyer to request that he be given three minutes before the blade fell on him to repeat his assertion that he had been unjustly accused of that offense.[25]

Visits were paid to the president of the republic, Armand Fallières, asking for clemency, and *La Guerre sociale*, in its final appeal on June 28, told the president, "you know that Liabeuf doesn't deserve death and that the social order of which you are the highest representative bears a heavy responsibility for the act for which he was condemned."[26]

Fallières ignored all pleas, claiming the existence of a secret file proving Liabeuf was a pimp. In a last-ditch effort, a petition campaign was mounted that brought together the most disparate characters in French political and cultural life, including the socialist Jaurès, the anarchist Séverine, the tireless troublemaker Henri Rochefort, the great novelist Anatole France, and even France's leading antisemite, Edouard Drumont. But the president ignored all of these pleas and *L'Humanité*'s headline on July 1 expressed a widely-shared opinion: "Liabeuf Assassinated."[27]

The government had kept its plans to go ahead with the execution secret for as long as it could, in an effort to keep crowds away, even limiting the number of press members invited. A crowd gathered nonetheless outside La Santé prison at midnight of the scheduled date of execution, waiting for the arrival of Deibler, the public executioner. When the paddy wagons with the executioner and his victim left the prison they were greeted with cries of "Down with Deibler! Long live Liabeuf!" A cortege of protestors followed the vehicles to the place of execution. When the wagon with Liabeuf arrived, he got out, shouting, "Before my execution I declare that I'm not a pimp. No, I'm not a pimp!" He was placed in the guillotine and "justice was done, as the newspapers of the bourgeois Pharisees would say."[28]

Shortly before the execution was carried out, though, at 3.00 a.m., crowds arrived on the boulevard Arago, where the execution was to occur. When the wagon with Liabeuf's corpse left the guillotine for the cemetery the police guard was greeted with shouts of "Assassins!" The police attacked the demonstrators and, with the streets in the process of being repaved, the demonstrators had spare stones with which to respond to their attackers. The scene quickly resembled a battle, and the police required reinforcements from mounted cuirassiers. The police and military struck out at everyone on the street, and saber blows and kicks rained down on the protestors; they began to round up people on the scene, including journalists.[29]

The demonstration was over. At 10.00 the same morning, just hours after Liabeuf's execution, the editors of *La Guerre sociale* went to the cemetery of Ivry, where the victim had been buried. Despite resistance from the cemetery staff, they were able to leave wreaths and flowers, with ribbons saying, "*La Guerre sociale* to Liabeuf, victim of the *apaches* of the vice squad" and "To Liabeuf, odiously assassinated." The affair was over. It had allowed Serge, now in Paris just a few months, to stake out his ground, to express his ideas, his hatreds.

* * *

Rirette wrote a few years after Serge's arrival in Paris that he had been the Brussels correspondent for *l'anarchie*, though no articles appeared by him with a Brussels dateline. The two of them became a number, spending time together strolling through Paris's most romantic spots. Serge's first article for *l'anarchie*, "On Anarchist Life," appeared in the September 23, 1909, issue. It was similar to many he'd written during his Belgian years and to what he would write in the coming years, an article condemning the idea of putting off happiness until tomorrow, calling on readers to "fight to immediately wrest some of the satisfaction, some of the reality, some of the scraps of the great life that is glimpsed." The method for doing so was to "destroy dogmas, beliefs, prejudices, institutions. To strive to be, to—despite it all—realize your own personality, your own personal ideal, and our common ideal." He began his Parisian life by summing up the ideas that would animate it: "Anarchist life today can only be a unrelenting reaction against the environment."

Serge's articles appeared in almost every issue of the paper from the time of his arrival until his arrest in January 1912, under one of his three pseudonyms: Le Rétif, Ralph, and Yor. Only occasionally were his writings commentary on news of the day, events like the Liabeuf Affair and the early career of the Bonnot Gang. His writing revolved around more general themes, themes common to individualist anarchism since the first appearance of the movement in France around 1890.

Serge's key themes were anti-revolutionism, contempt for the masses, the obligation and possibility for individuals to make their own revolution immediately, and illegalism. All of these themes are intertwined. The masses being worthy only of contempt leads to the certainty that revolution is not possible, making it necessary for the individualist to make the revolution now in whatever way he or she can, the most brutal and direct form of that being illegalism.

Contempt for the masses, for the "herd," drips from the writings of Serge's *l'anarchie* period, and if there are any Rétifian adjectives they are spineless (*veule*) and cowardly (*lâche*), which recur frequently in his articles. But already in Belgium, at the time of the Hartenstein Affair, he complained of the common run of men, "how ugly they are, how petty, wicked and hypocritical they are toward each other ... can this be called living? Can these pitiful beings be called men?"

Everything the masses enjoy is subject to his scorn. From the time of Libertad individualists had ridiculed festivals and anniversaries, and following in Libertad's footsteps Serge would write that "joy on command is unhealthy, grotesque and stupid, like those who savor it," and the festivities the people engage in are "the apotheosis of the stupidity, the illogic, and the cowardice of vast human herds." Mere contact with this gutless mass is repellent to Kibalchich: "The men I rub shoulders with wrong me at every moment. Their limpness, their rapacity, their foolishness prevent me from living."[30]

When France was in an uproar over the first crime of the Bonnot Gang, the robbery and shooting on the rue Ordener of a messenger for the Société Générale bank, Victor felt no sympathy, rather contempt and satisfaction at his fate: "This poor wretch, through his submissive weakness and his stupid honesty was the accomplice of criminals of a far higher caliber than the ones they are hunting down."[31]

Despite countless comments similar to these, Serge claimed not to hate the people: "We love you, for we love men." What he hated was not "men" but what they did with their potentially exalted human status: "We deeply detest your vegetative and bestial existence, your pitiful lack of intelligence."[32]

The source of this misanthropy was the background of Serge and his fellows. None of Victor's comrades were of the leisure class; none had received a university education; and Victor had received virtually no formal education at all. To a large extent they were all autodidacts, and their feeling that if they were able to rise above their natal muck then others could do so as well is clear in their writings of the time. Since all the individual needs to do is will it for things to change, the men of the herd were complicit in the continuation of an absurd society and were worthy of scorn, if not worse.

The next logical step in this idea chain is the denial of the possibility of a successful revolution. This idea is entirely consistent with the preceding one and is far more logical than the revolutionary hopes invested in the masses by class struggle anarchists, syndicalists and socialists. All of these schools acknowledged the degraded state of the worker under the current social system. Only the individualists, and Serge foremost among them, asked the obvious question: How can we expect people who accept such a fate to be capable of making a revolution, of building a radiant tomorrow?

For Serge this was not a subjective viewpoint, but rather an objective fact settled by science: "In all areas impartial science demonstrates to us the inferiority of the working-class." What did Victor see before him but "the degenerates, the hereditary slaves, the pitiful mass of working stiffs that we know *de visu* are physiologically incapable of living in harmony." For the *ouvriéristes* the answer to the question of whether or not the workers can change society was "'Yes' (without ever explaining why)"; for Victor, given the degenerate state of the men who make up the working-class, "organizing the working-class in order to carry out social transformation means wasting time and energy."[33]

Le Rétif proved his case by attacking the most sacred of working-class cows, the Paris Commune of 1871, and in fact did so in two articles entirely dedicated to scathing attacks on its folly. The uprising that began on March 18, 1871, was pointless, for "crowds are fickle, puerile, credulous [...] They are capable of heroism, but they can also commit monstrosities. And in all cases they need masters."[34] No, there was no point in ever seizing power, for "to think that impulsive, defective, ignorant crowds will have done with the morbid illogic of capitalist society is a vulgar illusion."[35] Indeed, even though the defeat of the Commune erased all the positive changes it had made, "their victory would have annihilated them, since they'd preserved the essence of the system of social oppression through private property and the law."[36]

Not only did the Commune fail but all revolutions have failed: "They have neither destroyed what they wanted to destroy, nor constructed anything better." Serge once again turns to the root cause of this inevitable failure: "Lacking in education, not used to thinking, not knowing how to count on themselves [...] could the workers of 1912 do any better?"[37]

None of this implies that a rebel should sit idly by while the vulgar herd does nothing or foolishly attempts to rise up. There must be a change to the rotten world that created the degenerate humanity that surrounds and inhibits Serge. In answer to the question of who should be counted on—mass action being worthless—"the anarchists will answer with individual revolt."[38]

This will be done in several ways, for "anarchists liberate minds." Even the lone anarchist living his free life has great revolutionary ramifications, for "all men profit from the act of revolt of one." Unlike those who think the masses will lead the way, like the socialist Jean Jaurès and his anarchist rival Jean Grave, Victor tells us that "there is no more consistent element of progress than individual initiative"[39] and "in every social grouping the individualist will remain a rebel."[40]

The anarchist, in young Victor's eyes, echoing the Nietzschean notion of the blond beast, "is above all a person who challenges [...] In decadent civilization he is the salutary barbarian, the only one still capable of creating, of erecting his individuality above the pestilence."[41]

In his memoirs, Serge would later write that "Anarchism swept us away completely because it both demanded everything of us and offered us everything,"[42] and during his youth he had written that "we consider anarchism to be, above all, a way of life." Anarchists are creatures of pure will, in this sense again disciples of Nietzsche: "anarchists formulate neither wishes nor vows: They want and immediately act according to their will."[43]

Freedom, individual freedom, is the be-all and end-all of indidualist anarchist, and even in the unlikely event that a mass revolution were to succeed, that success would do nothing for the free individual since "the hypothesis of a collectivist tomorrow presages a ferocious struggle between the state and the few individuals desirous of preserving their autonomy."[44] Note the use of the word "few" and the implicit elitism in the phrase, since the rest will be quite content to accept the new yoke of the new order.

Serge's individualist anarchist is not only one who challenges but also and primarily one who fights, for "not to resist means not to exist."[45] Not just the conquering but the preservation of the little freedom allowed the individual today is a duty, and any challenge to it must be reacted to forcefully.

In Belgium, Serge had been extremely vocal in support of the accused anarchist bomb-maker Hartenstein—giving him the highest praise, that of calling him "a man" for having shot down the policemen who'd come to arrest him—and had not only written about him in Le Révolté but also served as a character witness at his trial. He had also defended the Russian anarchists who died fighting the police in the 1909 gun battle known as the Tottenham Outrage. "The mere act of a policeman putting his hand on your shoulder, because it signifies an attack on the human personality, is sufficient reason to justify any form of revolt," he wrote in defense of Liabeuf.[46]

For Serge and for individualists in general it is not only political rebels who are worthy of support, but rebels of almost any kind. This leads us to the vexed subject of illegalism, which had been a part of anarchist individualism for years before Victor's arrival on the scene. The belief that anarchists, recognizing no laws, were self-evidently bound by no laws found its justification in the movement's foundational text, Max Stirner's The Ego and His Own, where he writes that "since the state is the 'lordship of law,' its hierarchy, it follows that the egoist, in all cases where *his* advantage runs against the State's, can satisfy himself only by Crime."[47] Illegalists had been particularly fond of counterfeiting, but a new breed of illegalists was appearing on the scene, a breed far more violent than ever previously seen, their avatar being what came to be known as the Bonnot Gang.

At the gang's trial in 1913 Victor denied ever having advocated illegalism; he even claimed to have opposed it. There can be no question that he came to oppose it, and that at the time of his trial his condemnation of the "waste" of men and energies it entailed was sincere. What is difficult to pin down is when he became an opponent of illegalism, for no serious reader of his articles on the subject written during the years 1908–12 could find any opposition to this natural outgrowth of the insistence on the primacy of the individual and his or her will.

Particularly telling is another of his favorite epithets, "honnête," meaning "honest," "decent," or "upright," which he used as a pejorative against those anarchists opposed to illegalism, dismissed as "honest men," and the general use of the adjective against anyone who condemns rebels.[48] Paradoxically, even criminals can be smeared with that brush: "The *apaches* in general don't interest me. They differ too little from decent people."[49]

In some cases, he exercised feats of intellectual legerdemain to disguise his support for illegalism. While still in Belgium he claimed that "every revolt is in essence anarchist. And we should stand alongside the economic rebel just as we stand beside the political, anti-militarist and propagandist rebel."[50] All rebels, thus are equal. He did, however, recognize that illegalists "remain far from us, far from our dreams and wishes. But what difference does that make?" If existing means resisting, and crime is a form of revolt, then the illegalists exist "and they aren't part of the herd." The logic of their acts is patent. "An intellectual and moral rebel, it is in fact only logical that the anarchist doesn't fear becoming, whenever the circumstances seem favorable, an economic rebel.[51]

In the immediate aftermath of the first acts of the Bonnot crime wave he praised the bandits for their "daring," which was one of Serge's favored positive characteristics. And if he didn't everywhere and always advocate crime as an anarchist act, he nevertheless said, "I am with the bandits. I find their role to be noble. Sometimes I see in them men," the last word here, too, being a term of praise in the Rétifian lexicon.[52]

He perhaps came closest to open advocacy of crime in his article "Against Hunger," an article considered important enough to be issued as a pamphlet almost immediately after appearing in *l'anarchie*. In it he declares that "individual re-appropriation—theft—is the logical opposite of the monopolizing of wealth, just as individual revolt is naturally opposed to the arbitrariness of the law and its agents."[53]

Nor should we think that it was only in his writings that Serge defended illegalism and illegalists. In the notes for what must have been his final talk at the Causeries populaires, given on January 28, 1912, he says of crime that "we think this is logical/ ineluctable/necessary," and he ended his talk by saying of the illegalist anarchists, "Along with us, they are the only men who dare demand life."[54]

These themes were not the only ones current in Victor's individualist milieu, but it is significant that they were the ones that he viewed as essential. The fact that he ignored other issues like neo-Malthusianism, diet and general health-faddism, free and plural love, and the extreme biological determinism that played so important a part in the movement is significant. So strong was this current that he would later speak about a split between "scientifics" and "sentimentals," the latter allowing sentiment a part in human activity and development, the former believing that virtually everything was biologically determined. Victor was a "sentimental," while the members of the Bonnot Gang, the core of which was made up of Serge's Belgian friends Raymond

Callemin, Jean De Boë, and Edouard Carouy, were all "scientifics." Herein lies much of the tension between Serge and his erstwhile comrades. None of these forms of lifestyle anarchism held any particular attraction for Victor, and he didn't expend much energy on any of them.

When reading his anarchist writings, what is striking is something that is very much a part of the individualist tradition: the lack of references to authorities. If Marxists and, later, Leninists involved themselves in Talmudic disputes over passages in the works of the masters, individualists almost completely eschewed this practice. All of anarchist individualism grew out of Max Stirner's *The Ego and His Own*, which was originally published in Germany in 1844, and only appeared in French in 1890.But Stirner's name is never used to back up any of Victor's arguments. To do so not only would have meant abdicating his individuality, but also would have constituted erecting Stirner into a hero, an idea that was anathema in his circles. While still in Belgium, in an article written on the anniversary of the death of Émile Henry, a man he clearly admired, Serge issued this caveat: "Let them not reproach me for glorifying a man, making him into a banner. We want neither tribunes nor martyrs nor prophets."[55] Instead of relying on specific passages in Stirner's writings, it is his *weltanschauung* that serves as the foundation for almost all of Victor's positions.

A thinker who was clearly of great importance to young Kibalchich was the aforementioned Gustave Le Bon, whose 1895 work *The Psychology of Crowds* demonstrated that crowds subsume the individual and obliterate the identity of the individuals within it, ideas which Victor sometimes credited to Le Bon in his articles and other times simply paraphrased. Just as Stirner was necessary for Victor in establishing the primacy of the One, Le Bon was needed to demonstrate the dangers of the Many.

In this regard, another writer, one far less known, influenced Victor: The uncompromisingly pessimistic individualist Georges Palante. Palante not only posited the need for the Self to affirm itself, but also established that there was a clear antinomy between the individual and society, that they were eternal enemies. "Individualism," he wrote, "is the sentiment of a profound, irreducible antinomy between the individual and society. The individualist is he who, by virtue of his temperament, is predisposed to feel in a particularly acute fashion the ineluctable disharmonies between his intimate being and his social milieu."[56] If most anarchists, indeed most revolutionaries, contented themselves with viewing the state as the enemy, one that could be defeated because it was a specific entity, for Palante society itself, a far larger and more nebulous foe, was the true adversary, one whose aim was the grinding down of the individual. The same pessimism that Victor often expressed concerning the possibilities and even desirability of social change also appeared in the pages of Palante:

> In the name of his own experience and his personal sensation of life the individualist feels he has the right to relegate to the rank of utopia any ideal of a future society where the hoped-for harmony between the individual and society will be established. Far from the development of society diminishing evil, it does nothing but intensify it by rendering the life of the individual more complicated, more laborious and more difficult in the middle of the thousand gears of an increasingly tyrannical social mechanism.[57]

These excerpts from Palante's *La Sensbilité individualiste* (The Individualist Sensibility) were published in 1909, the year Victor Kibalchich arrived in Paris, and appeared in the chapter of the book titled *Anarchisme et Individualisme* (Anarchism and Individualism). Serge was certainly aware of these writings and quoted or cited Palante on several occasions, including in one of his final articles before leaving for Red Russia in 1919. Palante's influence can be seen up to the end of Victor's spell as editor of *l'anarchie*. A talk he gave on January 28, 1912, in the Causeries populaires lecture series, was titled "The Individual Against

Society," and his notes for the talk show that his opening remarks on the subject were, "It's rather the contrary that should be said: 'society is the enemy of any individuality.'"[58]

All of these influences, cited or not, fed into his thematic.

And so we can see that within Victor Serge's anarchist writings there is a natural and consistent flow. Richard Parry, in his book on the Bonnot Gang, makes the claim that Victor so loudly praised illegalism because "he simply wanted to make a name for himself as the most 'combative' writer in the milieu." As we can see, far from this being the case, Serge was being utterly consistent when he defended illegalism in the abstract and the Bonnot Gang in particular. His subsequent condemnation of it was the first step along the road to the epistemological break that would lead him to abandon anarchism completely.

* * *

While the actions around Liabeuf were going on, *l'anarchie* moved in late June 1910 from Paris to the suburb of Romainville. Such a move would have made an appreciable financial difference to a paper of reduced means like *l'anarchie*. Newspapers based in Paris had to pay a security deposit of 300 francs to the city. In his memoirs of anarchist life Jean Grave, of the far more successful *Les Temps nouveaux*, wrote that "there was a way of paying less, and that was giving the paper an address in a locale in one of the suburban departments."[59]

Rirette and Serge moved from Paris with the paper and lived in their new building with the paper's editor André Lorulot, a trio of Serge's Belgian brothers—Raymond Callemin, Octave Garnier, and Edouard Carouy—and Marius Metge. All of the Belgians would go on to be members of the Bonnot Gang and would develop sharp differences with Serge, differences that were already visible.

Serge's comrades and housemates were strict believers in the value and power of science, and had no use for irrational sentiment, rejecting any idealistic notions. Serge credited his ability to stand up against this anti-humanist trend to his background: "I was quite distant from these elementary views; other things influenced me, there were other values which I couldn't and didn't want to renounce, and that was essentially the revolutionary idealism of the Russians."[60]

Part of their scientific beliefs revolved around diet, an issue they took quite seriously, as an account of a meal at the mini-commune at the Romainville office attests. Rirette had made a plate of string beans to which she had added vinegar, which the "Scientifics" condemned as an "anti-scientific aliment." She was issued strict orders concerning what was allowed and not allowed:

"No salt," Lorulot concluded.
"Or pepper," Callemin insisted, "it's a stimulant."
"Or chervil," said Garnier, "it's an aphrodisiac."

The arrival of Maîtrejean and Serge and their less stringent eating habits broke up the communal table that had existed since the paper's move. One evening, when the couple was seated separately from the rest of the staff, they overheard their comrades saying, "They'd better straighten up or we'll drive them the fuck out of here with our revolvers."[61]

However frivolous this all might sound it in fact got to the heart of anarchist individualist practice. It has often been written, including by Serge, that anarchism was not just a politics but a life. Diet, science, illegalism, and sexual relations were parts of a whole for most individualists. Serge's insistence on drinking coffee and using vinegar placed his whole commitment in question. These simmering differences would soon explode.

Dissension didn't only exist within the group behind *l'anarchie*. On April 11, 1911, the police reported that a group of anarchists, including Serge and André Lorulot, representing *l'anarchie*, met with a certain Juin, almost certainly Émile Armand, whose real name was Ernest Juin, who had announced he would soon begin publishing in Reims a new anarchist newspaper, to be called *La Vie Anarchiste*. Lorulot and Serge were enraged by this proposal, since *l'anarchie* was struggling to survive. The publication of a new paper would disperse the available forces and deprive *l'anarchie* of funds and readers it so desperately needed. Juin insisted the paper had become a necessity since in refusing articles he had written, as well as others written by some of his comrades, the paper was no longer the organ of free discussion that Libertad had founded.[62] Juin was not convinced by Lorulot and Serge and the newspaper was indeed founded, lasting a total of twenty issues.[63] An ancillary question is raised by the source of this information. Only three people were aware of this meeting. Unless they spoke to others afterwards, one of them reported the discussion to the police. Serge could not have known of this police report, but he later considered Lorulot to be a police informer.

Despite Serge and Lorulot's united front in April against Armand's encroachments, Lorulot left *l'anarchie* due to disagreements with the paper's direction, in particular its support for illegalism, which Lorulot had written in support of in 1906 but had come to oppose. Serge and Rirette agreed to assume control of the paper on July 11, 1911, on the condition that they be able to completely change the staff of the paper. In his *Memoirs of a Revolutionary*, Serge claimed he tried to give the paper a more social outlook, in opposition to the individualism of the previous team. This social outlook, if it existed at all, never extended very far, and he admits to having continued to attack syndicalism, the wing of the anarchist movement that truly was social, which he found to be guilty of "a future statism as formidable as the previous one.[64] Despite the apparent split in the leadership, on the evening of July 11 Serge and Lorulot gave a joint talk to a large audience of some 250 people with the title "Against All Bastilles."

This talk provides us with a revealing glimpse of the ideas expressed among themselves by the anarchist individualists, and how well aligned their articles and talks were. It also demonstrates how thorough police informants were, since the transcript of this talk comes from one of their reports. Serge began the evening by pointing out that though they were just a few days away from the national holiday on July 14, "a day of national orgies, face-stuffing, and drunkenness," which celebrated the taking of the Bastille, there were still many Bastilles left, in the form of the many prisons in France.

The terms "Liberty, Equality, and Fraternity" are only vain words. Liberty collides with prison walls; equality doesn't exist because there are individuals sated with wellbeing and others who don't have anything to eat. And as for fraternity, it, too, does not exist. Men are still disposed to tear each other apart.

After saying that all Bastilles must disappear, he was succeeded by Lorulot, and it can be seen that in their main points there was little to distinguish the two men. "The main idea of the men [who compose the great mass] is to eat well, drink well, to celebrate, and to taste love. They are concerned with nothing; outside of these joys they could give a good god damn." He placed the audience on guard against any illusions concerning a possible socialist government, which "would be as authoritarian as any other. Haven't we heard [Socialist leader Jules] Guesde say that the first thing the socialist collectivists would do upon arriving at power would be to execute or imprison the anarchists, who constitute for them a real danger." He ended by saying that he hoped that all conscious anarchists would educate themselves and that those present would demonstrate their disapproval of the popular festivities of the national holiday."

Further proof of Serge's later obscuring of the facts in denying ever having preached illegalism can be found in a talk given at the Study Group of the Twelfth [Arrondissement] on August 26, 1911. The talk, on the topic of "Individualist Doctrine," ended with him mocking the CGT and the revolutionary communist anarchists, advocates of direct action by the working-class, who "instead of cutting electrical and telephone wires would better spend their time robbing banks. There are better tasks to be accomplished [...] and the individualists have understood it by carrying out 're-appropriation,' thus striking directly the safes of the bourgeoisie."[65]

Around this time, first Carouy, then Callemin and Garnier, left *l'anarchie*. Given the tenor of Serge's public talks it is unlikely it had anything to do with any disagreement over illegalism. The other issues that separated them, over lifestyle issues and science, were in all likelihood the driving force.[66]

Now at the head of *l'anarchie*, Serge spoke openly of the paper's woes at a *causerie* in late September 1911. He bemoaned the lack of interest in the paper demonstrated by the *compagnons* and complained that most of the articles submitted to the paper were full of mutual criticism, rancor, and jealousy. He addressed the issue of Armand's criticisms of the paper for refusing to accept articles by himself and his comrades, saying their work wasn't "conscientious enough." The picture he painted of the paper's state was dire on all fronts: The typesetters were no better than the intellectuals, and if for any reason he was no longer able to oversee the paper it would disappear. Not only were the human resources faulty but the printing press was in a dilapidated state and there wasn't a penny on hand to repair it. This being the case, they would now have the paper printed by an outside firm. He also announced another momentous decision: The paper would be returning to Paris, and on October 19 it—and Serge and Rirette—took up residence on the rue Fessart.

Things did not improve for the paper after its return to Paris; in fact, the situation could hardly have been more desperate. Those in the movement were surprised that the paper was able to survive at all. It was distributed by *Le Petit Parisien*, for which they had to pay between thirty and eighty francs weekly. Serge was in such an impoverished state that he was only able to eat regularly from the time he took over the paper, which also fed others involved in its production. The cash box was empty. The question that agitated both the police and the paper's rivals was just how the paper was able to survive on nothing.

La Guerre sociale, the newspaper of Gustave Hervé and Miguel Almereyda, which had supported Liabeuf as stridently as did Serge, carried out an investigation, at Almereyda's behest, of *l'anarchie*'s source of income. The rival paper questioned former writers for *l'anarchie*, like founding editor Albert Libertad's mistresses the Mahé sisters, along with the anarchist and former collaborator Leon Israel, but no one knew where the money was coming from.[67] There are two things that can be inferred, or that the investigators inferred. First, *l'anarchie* was a nest of police informants and the police were propping the paper up; second, illegalist activities were behind the paper's continued survival. This suspicion would soon motivate the police to take an even closer look at Serge and his comrades.

The hatred between *l'anarchie* and *La Guerre sociale* was mutual, though the individualists' expression of it at first was slightly veiled. At a public meeting on November 27, reported on in a police informant's report dated November 28, Serge attacked what he called "*révolutionarisme*," which makes much noise, distributes piles of newspapers and pamphlets, and holds countless meetings from which absolutely nothing comes. Anarchists, on the other hand, want to act. The acts he looked forward to would soon occur. "He said that he would with pleasure see a cop taken down for having delivered a kick on the streets. He would see with no less pleasure desertions and draft evasion increase at a time when war threatens."

Lorulot, with whom Serge supposedly had so many differences, appeared on the same program, and his statements were even more violent. He felt the acts Serge mentioned were too gentle and that "violence must be answered with violence, but with reflection and method," warning against the mistakes of the bombers Vaillant and Henry and the presidential assassin Sante Caserio, who thought that the "future society would rise from their acts." Lorulot warned that only coordinated acts would bring good results.[68]

That Serge was aware of *La Guerre sociale*'s suspicions about his paper was made clear just three days later at a talk on the subject of "Squealers." Mauricius was the first speaker, and he openly accused *La Guerre sociale* of having turned anarchists in to the authorities, followed by Serge, who revealed to the forty people in attendance that the rival paper had "cast suspicion on several comrades, notably himself and Reichmann, who has since disappeared and whose fate is unknown."

In the middle of this dissension on the revolutionary left, a hold-up occurred on the rue Ordener in Paris. The career of the Bonnot Gang had begun.

4

The Tragic Bandits

On December 21, 1911, a group of armed men attacked two bank employees in front of the rue Ordener branch of the Société Generale in Paris, seriously wounding one, Caby, who was carrying a sack of cash and bonds. The thieves then escaped in a car with their takings. The incident was marked by the boldness of the bandits and the coldness with which they shot down their victim and then fired on the crowd that pursued them. This was the opening salvo in the story of the "*Bandits en auto*," soon to become famous as the Bonnot Gang or the Tragic Bandits.

On the surface this was simply a bank robbery, albeit a particularly brutal one, made unique by the use of a speeding car as a getaway vehicle. But for Victor Kibalchich, who, not yet twenty-one, was editing *l'anarchie*, there was no mystery to the affair, nor was there any doubt in his companion and co-director Rirette Maîtrejean's mind: "It was an anarchist crime or, more precisely, the crime of illegalist extremists."[1] Serge immediately recognized the bandits' descriptions in the newspapers, particularly that of Raymond Callemin, Raymond la Science, his childhood friend and a recent collaborator on *l'anarchie*. Victor was not alone in suspecting there was more to the crime than met the eye. "Immediately the same word was on everyone's lips: 'Anarchists ... anarchist crime ....' People evoked the days of mad terror of 1894 ... the bombs ... Ravachol, Vaillant, Émile Henry. For the public there was no doubt. It was a declaration of war of the anarchists on society."[2]

The nucleus of the gang included several of those with whom Serge and Maîtrejean had had dietary disagreements at the offices of their newspaper: Raymond Callemin, Octave Garnier, and Edouard Carouy, "the very gentle, very timid, very quiet" René Valet, and Jules Bonnot, all of them anarchists, all of them illegalists, supporters of "individual re-appropriation."[3] Though most of the group was well known to Victor, Jules Bonnot, whose name was to be attached to the gang, was less familiar to him, being neither Bruxellois nor a Parisian, coming from the region of the Jura Mountains and having spent much of his life in the south of France.

The police, too, immediately suspected that "fishy individuals in Montmartre, anarchists, and car and tire thieves" were behind the theft.[4] Within a week of the attack the police were given the name of a possible accomplice, Georges Dettweiler, by one of the latter's neighbors.[5] Within days, the first of the thieves, Edouard Carouy, was positively identified by a witness.

The robbery on the rue Ordener was just the beginning. It was followed by automobile thefts and the robbery of a gun shop, the stolen weapons from which were to seal Serge's fate when they would later be found in the offices of *l'anarchie*. The first of the criminals' killings occurred on January 3, 1912, with the murder and robbery of a nonagenarian and his servant in Thiais in Paris's southern suburbs. Police suspicions at first were directed at a neighbor, but sources led the police to the identification of the actual perpetrators, Edouard Carouy again and Carouy's friend Marius Metge, like Carouy a draft dodger who had fled to London and recently returned to France.

Eyewitness descriptions of the men who carried out the attack on the rue Ordener left the anarchists in no doubt that Octave Garnier was one of the men involved, and the police were not far behind them in reaching the same conclusion. By trailing his mistress, they were able to arrest Garnier, who was positively identified by Caby, who, against all odds, had survived the shooting on the rue Ordener.

The anarchist connection was now so clear that on January 31, 1912, the police raided the offices of *l'anarchie*, where they "fell upon a few 'comrades' who were peacefully enjoying their chocolate."[6] They arrested all those they found on the premises, but the next day they released everyone except the paper's two directors, Serge and Maîtrejean, after two revolvers were found on the premises, as well as false papers. These weapons, Rirette would maintain at her trial and in her later memoirs, were not stolen by the anarchists, but by common criminals, from whom she and Victor purchased them "at a high price."[7]

The deputy chief of the Sûreté, Louis Jouin, who led the raid, spoke kindly to Serge: "I know you pretty well and I would be saddened to cause you any problems," Jouin told Serge. "You know this milieu, these men who are far from you, who shoot you in the back, in fact ... Stay here with me for an hour; no one will ever know about it and I guarantee you you'll have no problems."

Serge rejected the proposal with disgust. Although he was horrified by these crimes, if the anarchists had any law it was that of solidarity, which made it impossible for him to cooperate with the police, to turn informer. He would pay dearly for this. He and Rirette were taken to prison, and it was there they'd remain throughout the remainder of the gang's crime wave.

A report written a week after his arrest provided the leadership of the police hierarchy with a rapid, tendentious, but thorough overview of Serge's life and beliefs. The final portion of it spoke of his ideas concerning illegalism, that he "is a supporter of 'individual reappropriation,' which penal law more simply calls theft." As a result, the report summarized, "Kibalchich must be considered a dangerous anarchist." This opinion would be repeated over the following months and years and would weigh heavily in determining Serge's fate. The government had a "dangerous anarchist" in its hands, one who thought that "the man who doesn't want to produce must even so live and take what is necessary for his subsistence wherever it is, without any concern for prejudices or legality." He would suffer for this opinion of him.[8]

On February 2, 1912, a policeman attempting to check the papers of an automobile that was being driven wildly was shot down in front of the Gare Saint-Lazare. So bold were the shooters that the very night of the killing they went to Pontoise and attempted to steal a safe from the office of a notary, though their attempt was foiled. The car was found abandoned the next day and discovered to have been stolen and repaired before being used in the commission of the crimes. Witnesses described the men who'd taken the car to the mechanic for repairs, and their descriptions matched those of the thieves of the rue Ordener: Bonnot, Garnier, and Callemin.

The police were bombarded with letters reporting the bandits' presence all over France, and any violent crime within French borders and even in neighboring countries was attributed to them.

The police had several of the gang members under surveillance and, having already made a sweep at the offices of *l'anarchie*, were also keeping an especially close eye on André Lorulot's rival anarchist paper, *L'Idée Libre*. This led them to twenty-seven-year-old Eugène Dieudonné, who had been an anarchist militant since the age of fifteen, and another of Serge's Brussels brothers, Jean De Boë. Caby, the victim on the rue Ordener, who had already recognized Cardouy as the man who'd shot him, now instead recognized Dieudonné as the shooter. Deputy Chief Jouin, who had had the pleasant chat with Serge, was confident that, if they were patient, the trailing of these two bandits would lead to the rest of the gang and to its true leaders. But the killing of the policeman at the Gare Saint-Lazare had put pressure on Jouin's superiors to do something, and quickly. Jouin was ordered to arrest the criminals he could immediately get his hands on, and, at the end of February 1912, Dieudonné and De Boë were in police custody.

Serge was in jail as well, out of the limelight and out of harm's way in La Santé prison, but the police continued to keep an eye on his activities, which appear to have continued while he was behind bars. An anarchist comrade, Renaud, was reported to be seeking to visit Victor in prison in order "to take certain dispositions in the interest of his cause." Renaud "tall, blond, with long and large teeth," intended to claim he was a tailor making a suit for the prisoner, and in this guise would discuss political matters.[9] The police were able to forestall this visit by claiming that only the investigating magistrate could authorize such a visit.[10]

Not only were the main criminals still on the loose, but their boldness had increased. Octave Garnier, one of the most daring members of the band, sent a letter addressed to the Parisian police to the Parisian daily *Le Matin*, which ran it on March 19: "Ever since, to the great joy of the concierges of the capital, through your intervention the press has given my modest person a starring role, you announce my capture as imminent, but believe you me, all this noise doesn't prevent me from tasting the joys of existence in peace." Garnier went on to proclaim the innocence of Dieudonné and to denounce the "squealer" whose perfidy, rather than any particular skill on the part of the police, was responsible for the identification of the bandits. Nothing was less certain than that a squealer was directly responsible for the arrests and identifications. Illegalist circles had been followed closely by the police for some time, with *l'anarchie* and the Causeries populaires frequently visited by police or attended by informants. Garnier continued in his letter in *Le Matin*:

I know that the fight between me and the formidable arsenal which society disposes of will come to an end. I know that I WILL BE DEFEATED, THAT I WILL BE THE WEAKER, but I hope to make you pay dearly for your victory. Waiting for the pleasure of meeting you, Garnier.

On March 25 three men flagged down a car driving south from Paris to Nice. They shot the two men in the car, killing one and wounding the other. Three more men then joined them and they drove to Chantilly and the branch of the Société Générale bank there. They opened fire almost immediately, killing two employees. Public opinion was in an uproar, people shocked by the outlaws' coldness and sangfroid, and the newspapers prominently featured these sensational crimes. The matter was so serious that the minister of the interior was questioned in the Chamber of Deputies. However, "The population instinctively felt that these fearsome corsairs who had risen up against all of society, casting defiance at the police and the magistracy, were not in the classic category of ordinary bandits simply out for gain."[11]

Through all of these events, separate investigations were being carried out by the different elements of the judicial system. Finally, at a meeting held to bring together agents and investigators from the courts and the police, it was determined that one vast conspiracy was in play, and the principal culprits were named Rirette Maîtrejean, Victor Kibalchich, Bonnot, Carouy, Valet, Dieudonné, De Boë and a handful of other, lesser players.

At the heart of the conspiracy, according to the authorities, was the newspaper *l'anarchie*, where, it was alleged, the bandits gathered to plan their actions, to bring their loot, and to distribute it. It was thus no accident that Maîtrejean and Serge, nominally in charge of the paper, figured so prominently. Given the public mood, the police had to act. "The imagination had to be struck; the public had to be allowed to believe they were on the road to the truth. This singular method was to cause much suffering to most of the accused, the majority of whom, however, remained foreign to the activities of the real 'tragic bandits.'"[12]

The arrests continued, the gang members being plucked one by one. Former grocer's clerk André Soudy, whose nickname among his comrades was "No Luck," and who was known in the press as the "Man with the Rifle," the gang member who held the hostages in Chantilly under control with his rifle, was arrested on March 30, followed by Carouy. While in the offices of the Sûreté, Carouy swallowed pills, thinking they were cyanide, that he hoped would kill him, but he had the wrong potion. A week later, Serge's friend Raymond la Science was captured at the home of a friend, having in his possession three revolvers, each holding eight cartridges, and 5000 francs, most of it in large bills.

On April 14, Louis Jouin and a group of inspectors tracked down Bonnot and found him hiding at the home of a friend. In the shootout that ensued Jouin was killed, while Bonnot was able to effect an escape. The grief of the Sûreté over Jouin's killing was doubled by their anger at Bonnot's escape. Four days later another of Bonnot's hideouts was discovered at Choisy-le-Roi, and this time the police took no chances. Jouin's superior, Guichard, who had ordered the arrests of De Boë and Dieudonné, led the forces of order as they laid siege to the suburban cottage. Eventually, with the aid of three Republican Guard companies, some infantry divisions, neighborhood rifle clubs, and a good deal of dynamite, they succeeded in capturing the lone bandit. The siege had lasted several hours. When Bonnot was found, dying of self-inflicted wounds, it was discovered that he had spent his time during the siege writing a defiant declaration of principles, in which he, too, proclaimed Dieudonné's innocence, as well as that of several other accomplices. The news of Bonnot's exploits eclipsed the sinking of the Titanic on the front pages of Paris's newspapers.

Garnier and Valet were still on the run, but the police continued to follow Garnier's mistress, who led them to a building in Nogent-sur-Marne, which they were certain was the hideout of the final two gang members. On May 14, 1912, the police went to the suspected hideout and were fired on from within. Reinforcements were called for and the house was surrounded, and a scene similar to that at Choisy-le-Roi and the killing of Bonnot occurred. Zouaves dropped heavy stones on the roof of the building and punched holes in it through which dynamite was tossed. The fight continued, with the anarchists calling their attackers "murderers." Dogs were called in, machine guns were employed, and carts loaded with explosives were rolled into the improvised fortress. Legend has it that Parisians came out to the suburbs to watch the battle. When at three in the morning the bandits' bodies were removed from the bullet-riddled and dynamite-torn house, it was discovered that, like Bonnot, the criminals had died by their own hands, but not before burning any compromising documents. The drama of the Tragic Bandits was at an end. The epilogue, in which Victor Kibalchich was to be given a starring role, would take place in the Assize Court of Paris in February 1913.

While waiting for his trial, Serge remained informed on the activities of his circle, as he continued to read *l'anarchie* during his imprisonment, the paper being smuggled to him by his lawyers.[13] He remained a force on the paper. Police informants reported that there was discontent in individualist circles concerning the paper's line under the leadership of Émile Armand, its new director, and a group was agitating to have Armand removed so the paper could follow a more "vigorous" line. All that was holding them up was the expectation that Serge and Maîtrejean would be released after the Bonnot trial, but "if that hope is dashed, they will act differently."[14] At precisely the same moment, an informant was reporting that Rirette was being accused by comrades of having squandered 700 francs that were intended for the arrested anarchists.[15]

* * *

The trial of the Tragic Bandits (or the Auto Bandits, depending on the newspapers) began on February 3, 1913, in the Assize Court of Paris, in a courtroom guarded by the military, where all those entering were checked for weapons, the number of seats available was reduced to a third the usual number, and the spectators—all of whom had a long wait before entering the courtroom—were restricted to witnesses, the press, and lawyers.

The tone was immediately set for those who entered the courtroom. On display were the most fearsome pieces of evidence—Browning revolvers, rifles, burglary tools, and even some of the gym equipment that the bandits used to build themselves up (in fact, the bandits were so intent on building themselves up, on hygiene—a hobby horse of the individual- ists—that they continued to work out in their cells).[16]

The opening argument of the prosecution, along with enu- merating the bandits' many criminal acts, did not fail to stress the anarchist angle of the case. The bandits were all said to be individualist anarchists motivated by their belief in illegalism, whose hideout was alleged to be the offices of *l'anarchie*, which was also where their takings were stored. Even more, a portion of the gains from their thefts was turned over to the paper to keep it functioning. As for the directors of the paper, Serge and his lover Rirette Maîtrejean, they were charged with possessing two (sometimes reported as three) revolvers stolen from a sporting goods store that were found in their lodgings within the offices of the paper. Because the office was central to the gang's doings, and because stolen identity papers were found in their home, Serge and Maîtrejean were described as being the center of the criminal gang. Anarchy and *l'anarchie* would clearly be at issue in the trial. Rirette later wrote, "Hearing [the prosecutor] I understood the society that crushes everything that doesn't want to accept its laws. I was aware of having before me an unheard of, a prodigious force against which the pitiful theories of illegalism couldn't prevail."[17]

And yet, after stressing the role of anarchism in the indictment, the jury was informed that the trial they would be participating in was not a political one, though the accused called themselves anarchists and claimed to have simply applied their doctrine.

Anarchy as applied to daily life immediately entered the trial with the questioning of Rirette, the first of the accused to take the stand. Officially she and Serge were the directors of the paper, but to the surprise of the tribunal she denied that this was the case, informing the judges that "there is no director among us, and if her name appeared in the paper with that title it was from pure legalistic obligation; that she was simply responsible for commercial correspondence and proofreading."

The prosecution attempted to place Rirette at the center of the crime wave, saying that while she was in charge of *l'anarchie* the offices had become a center for the discussion of individual re-appropriation and that "under her leadership a great number of thefts were committed." When shown stolen objects, Rirette responded that the individuals alleged to have stolen them— Garnier, Valet, Callemin, and Carouy—never stayed at the offices of the paper and that they were given to her by comrades. She also declared that the revolvers found on the premises, which were the basis for her imprisonment, had been purchased by her from another comrade. The innocence of their presence was patent: "I attached no importance to them, since they were found carelessly sitting on the table."

It was at this point that there occurred the first hint of the breach that had developed among the defendants, most particularly between Serge and Maîtrejean and those seated alongside them. She had written a letter that had been seized by the authorities in which she harshly criticized her fellow defendants for their lack of revolutionary backbone:

> I was just seized with the greatest moral sorrow. Once they're before the judges and in prison, all these anarchists lose their assurance. For the least thing, if they were asked if they were Christians or patriots they would answer "yes." They speak of honor and honesty and all that beautiful foolishness that they deny at the drop of a hat when they're with us. It's intolerable to think that we were able to propagandize alongside such cowards. They understood nothing of what we told them.

Confronted with the evidence of revolutionary intransigence, she said that this expressed not her own opinion but rather that of those around her, that she was simply making an observation. Even the most cursory reading of the letter shows that she clearly was expressing concern about the moral backbone of those with her in court. As the trial wore on the irony of this letter became increasingly clear, as she and Serge were themselves to be scorned by their comrades for their apparent pusillanimity.

Rirette's testimony was received sympathetically, and she was described by the socialist *L'Humanité* as a defendant with a special cachet, with her "long, black blouse, her short hair, her large, turned down collar [...] She laughs all the time and is not particularly disturbed to find herself in this tragic adventure."[18] Virtually every reporter on the scene likened her appearance to that of the Claudine of Colette's novels.

Serge, too, stood out, and not only for the Russian peasant blouse he affected and which appears in all the photos and artists' renderings of the trial. "With his high forehead and his tousled hair he looks like a Russian student escaped from the nest of the 'Birds of Passage.'" He followed his lover to the stand. He had worked out his strategy prior to entering the courtroom, and laid it out in a letter to Émile Armand:

> The courtroom will not be the time or the place to speak of illegalism [...] but if the accusation makes me out to be in solidarity with acts I find repugnant (and this is the mot juste) then I'm going to have to explain myself. In that case, rest assured that I will do it in terms so clear that they won't be able to use them against my fellow defendants [...] It's that I am— we are—sickened, saddened to see that comrades for whom I had great affection at the time of their initial and beautiful enthusiasm were able to commit things as shameful as the butchery of Thiais. I am saddened to see that the others, all the others, madly threw away and wasted their lives in a sad, dead-end fight that beneath an appearance of courage they are unable to defend with pride.

Like Maîtrejean, Serge denied any leadership role in the paper, saying he was only a typesetter and that all the work at the paper was carried out "among comrades." "I was only concerned with the copy." Also like Rirette, he attempted to draw a line between himself and his fellow accused. As the anarchist writer Victor Méric, Serge's sometime comrade, sometime rival, said, "with a skillful word he separated himself from the anarchist terrorists."[19] When it was stated that upon his arrival at the paper's offices in Romainville Serge found Garnier and Carouy, "who became his collaborators," he immediately demurred: "There's no doubt they are anarchists, but there are tendencies within anarchism. They took biology to be the foundation of morality and denied the influence of affective sentiments. This separated us, so they left with Lorulot." This strict demarcation between himself and André Lorulot, between their different camps, would have long-term ramifications, and was soon brought to light during the trial.

Serge also denied the charge that the newspaper's offices were the base of a criminal association. They lived in the open, knowing that there was a special police brigade that dealt specifically with the anarchists, one that could have searched their offices at any time, since he and Rirette lived there. "But even more, if we had encouraged thefts we would have profited from them, but only forty francs were found in our cash box."

The first day's proceedings ended with a key piece of testimony, reported with slight variations in the daily papers the next day, which covered the trial extensively. In the most thorough account, in *L'Humanité*, it was reported that "with a weak voice, without raising his tone," Victor denied any support for illegalism. "As for the expression 'individual reappropriation,' which the indictment speaks of and which it claims was our customary language, it was old jargon, dating from twenty-five years ago. I defy you to find it in one of my articles. This proves how the indictment was drawn up." Serge and Rirette had made a fairly good impression, though the royalists at *L'Action française* dismissed Serge, describing him as "a phrase-mongering anarchist; fussy, monotonous and boring." Most importantly, on this first day, Serge and Maîtrejean had openly distanced themselves from their erstwhile comrades, and doing it, at least in Victor's case, with a certain disingenuousness.

As was recounted earlier, despite Serge's denial, the specific words "individual re-appropriation" *do* appear in his articles in *l'anarchie*, most importantly in one of his most famous articles, "Against Hunger," which not only appeared in *l'anarchie* in September 1911 but was also issued as a pamphlet. In it he says, "Individual re-appropriation—theft—is the logical opposite of the monopolizing of wealth, just as individual revolt is naturally opposed to the arbitrariness of the law and its servants." And the specific words were used in a talk Victor gave at an anarchist discussion group, the Study Group of the Twelfth [Arrondissement] mentioned earlier where, according to a police report, Le Rétif said that the syndicalists "instead of cutting electric and telephone cables would put their time to better use by robbing banks. There's better work to be done, Le Rétif added, and the individualists have understood it by exercising 're-appropriation,' in this way striking directly at the safes of the bourgeoisie."[20] More damning is a talk he gave just before his arrest at the Causeries populaires on January 28, 1912, after the beginning of the crime wave, in which he calls criminality "logical/ineluctable/necessary. Social organization produces crime." Moreover, as we have shown, both in Belgium and in France, he had been an outspoken defender of illegalism; indeed, he had justified many of the crimes that led him and the other defendants to the courtroom. In his January 4 article "The Bandits," he called those who shot the messenger Gaby "the champions of the human will to live," continuing that, "I'm with the bandits. I find their role to be a noble one." And in his article "Expedients," he wrote that he was "with the outsiders and bandits precisely because I love mutual aid," considering banditry, like wage labor, "a deplorable expedient." And in response to a letter in *l'anarchie* attacking his position on illegalism that appeared February 1, 1912, he said that "the anarchist must not waste the pleasure he feels in seeing such rebels." A selection from his writings on illegalism could go on for pages, but in "Anarchists and Criminals" he made a distinction between "criminals and criminals," condemning those who steal simply to fill their pockets as nothing but "honest men" *manqués*, while supporting the others, those who are "outlaws because honesty is a framework too narrow for their lives, because their desire for happiness can't be satisfied while in a state of submission." All of these articles were written while Bonnot and company were carrying out their attacks.

Technically, none of this strictly constitutes *advocacy* of illegalism, but Serge's understanding for, not to say support of, the act is clear. Even if in his view crime is an expedient, one people are forced to by an unjust society, Serge considered it to be at the same level as work. By speaking of the way that society forced people to crime Serge had annoyed his illegalist comrades, since he stripped the act of the pure freedom, the gratuitousness they granted it; but for the authorities his writings were nothing but an apology and a justification for theft. Serge's claim that this was "old jargon, dating from twenty-five years ago" was patently false, since his articles had been written over the course of the past few years. Illegalism was, indeed, an idea with a twenty-five-year history; Serge at *l'anarchie* had brought it up to date.

All this said, Serge was not on trial for his writings, but for possession of stolen goods; it had been clearly stated at the outset that this was not a political trial. Except it was. And Serge would try to recall the true charges the next day during the testimony of Dieudonné, who firmly denied any part in the bandits' acts. He claimed to know only two of the defendants well, along with "Kibalchich, because he's a propagandist." Serge called out from his seat, "I'm a propagandist. Since when is that a crime?"

Whatever the virtues of Serge's defense strategy, it was completely undermined by that adopted by his old friend, Raymond Callemin. Callemin simply denied everything, and did so in a way certain to alienate those who held his fate in their hands. He testified on February 4, and snapped at the presiding judge that he should stop interrupting him when the judge asked him a question in mid-answer. "He continued his dialogue with the presiding judge, arguing and splitting hairs over every question that is asked," even telling the judge that he was acting in "bad faith."[21] He ostentatiously read and wrote while his alleged crimes were being listed, and later in the trial he was noted to be drawing caricatures and sharing them with Carouy, "which seemed to interest them both a great deal."[22] Though he had made several self-incriminating remarks after his arrest, when confronted with them at the trial he described these statements as "*plaisanteries*." Another "*plaisanterie*," and one that was raised on a couple of occasions, was his statement to the police that "his head is worth 100,000 francs, while that of a policeman is worth seven-and-a-half centimes," the price of a bullet. He produced no evidence to back his case, simply saying that all of the eyewitnesses were mistaken. He impressed no one, and his actions not only did nothing to help his case and that of his fellow defendants but also clearly contributed to what was perhaps a foregone conclusion in any event.

Dieudonné himself ridiculed the notion that praise (*apologie*) for the crimes of Bonnot and his gang could have appeared in *l'anarchie*: "Such praise is absurd; it's idiotic. There is no praising Bonnot's crimes." But the question of illegalism wouldn't go away, and Dieudonné quoted the aphorism of a "legalist": "Illegalism doesn't free the individual, but rather leads him to the assize court," concluding by saying that there aren't many partisans of illegalism, and "my entire life proves that I am not a partisan of this."

If Serge was the alleged ideologue of the gang and propaganda his main role in its activities, for the newspaper of the French courts, the *Gazette des Tribunaux*, Soudy was the "intellectual of the gang." Soudy immediately adopted the tactic that would be called during the Algerian War the *défense de rupture*, the refusal to grant the court any right to judge the defendant at all. "I don't recognize your right to judge me. You are neither supernatural beings nor gods. You don't have the right to force an innocent man like me to sit on the bench of pain." But he would accept the debate, since even if the court had no moral rights over him, he was nevertheless forced to defend himself.

Soudy went straight to the point, adopting as his own the intellectual underpinnings of illegalism as Serge had expressed them. "It's possible that I was reduced to practicing illegalism, that is, to theft. If, like you, *messieurs*, I'd had enough to live on I never would have been driven to these methods." Soudy then fell back on what would be the predominant tactic of the defendants: Denying everything, stating that the witnesses were all in error. But he also returned to the philosophical question, drawing a distinction between thoughts and deeds: "If morally I am able to accept attacks on property, I morally condemn attacks on human life. Thus, neither morally nor materially could I have been at Chantilly."

The same day, one of Serge's Brussels "brothers," Edouard Carouy, was called to the stand. His Belgian past was recalled, as well as his relations there with Raymond Callemin and De Boë, though not with Serge. His testimony revealed splits in the anarchist ranks. He explained the numerous weapons in his possession by saying he needed them because he "was sentenced to death by the anarchists, who thought I'd betrayed them. Garnier was sure I'd denounced him." He also provided an indirect defense of Victor and Rirette, saying it was impossible to prepare burglary tools at the offices of the paper, and took personal responsibility for their manufacture.

Marie Schoots, Garnier's lover, who Carouy believed had wanted to kill him, and who was herself accused of the possession of stolen goods, said she knew nothing of her lover's activities, saying she "sometimes thought he was guilty, and sometimes not." Her testimony was interrupted by Maîtrejean, who asked Marie if she had ever come to the offices on the rue Fessart or knew of Garnier going there while Rirette was in charge of the paper. Marie answered that she hadn't.

Another of Serge's Brussels brothers, De Boë, accused of possessing the stock certificates stolen from Caby on the rue Ordener, said he'd received them from his fellow Belge Callemin. But he, too, denied participating in a criminal association: "It's not because there are anarchists who are criminals that I can be accused of being a criminal."

Indeed, the denial of the existence of a criminal association, a linchpin in the charge against Rirette and Serge, was a constant refrain in the testimony of the defendants. Léon Rodriguez, who had been expelled from Belgium for, among other things, signing a pamphlet calling for the assassination of the empress of Austria, and had deserted from the French army and engaged in counterfeiting ("my past life is pitiful," he admitted from the stand), affirmed that "this association exists only in the minds of the accusation [...] In any case, anarchy is not a criminal association; there might be criminals among the anarchists, but they're a minority."

The testimony continued, and on the third day Serge, feeling ill from the heat in the courtroom, asked if the windows could be opened. They were, and the journalists were granted permission to wear their hats.

It was on the ninth day, on February 12, that an important confrontation took place, one that was to mark a turning point in Serge's life. André Lorulot, one of the leading lights of individualist anarchism, who Maîtrejean and Serge had succeeded at the head of *l'anarchie* and who now edited *L'Idée Libre*, was called to the stand. He testified that he'd seen Soudy at the offices of *l'anarchie* and that Kibalchich "had fought against the propagandists of the deed." Serge then spoke up, "with moderation and not without eloquence," as the *Gazette des Tribunaux* put it. As Lorulot was about to leave the stand Serge stopped him and then set out, as *Le Matin* reported the next day, "to establish that *l'anarchie*—that of the rue Fessart—his—which in no way resembles that of Romainville—Lorulot's—was being slandered." He questioned his predecessor, asking if he hadn't posed certain conditions before agreeing to take over the paper. When Lorulot claimed no memory of such a conversation, Serge refreshed his memory:

> I told Lorulot that I'd only go to *l'anarchie* if those who were with him left. Lorulot: It's possible, but that had nothing to do with me. Serge: Did Lorulot receive Garnier, Callemin and De Boë in Romainville? Lorulot: Yes, for three months. It's not a crime. Serge: Well, gentlemen of the jury, I was in Romainville for three weeks and Garnier and his friends never came when I was there. They didn't go to the rue Fessart, yet I'm in prison while Lorulot is free—and I'm happy for him. The accusation thus lacks justice and logic.

His voice cracking with emotion, Victor went on:

> I am being prosecuted for being part of a criminal association. I am placed alongside the people—and I hope they prove they aren't guilty—who are accused of theft and murder. And what is horrible is that precisely these people, upon whom these accusations weigh, were our worst adversaries. The truth is that I am being prosecuted for my ideas [...] To be logical [the prosecution] should have gone further and implicated Lorulot. I am indignant at the thought that this evening I will return to prison while Lorulot (whose imprisonment I don't wish for) will leave the session a free man.

Lorulot had had enough, exclaiming: "If the fact of having received Garnier and Carouy at my home is a crime, I demand that I be arrested." The attorney general said he would answer Lorulot when the time came, at which point one of the defense lawyers, Moro-Gaffieri, leapt up and protested "against the vile articles that have appeared in *l'anarchie* over the past few days," articles written by Lorulot attacking the jury in this case. The royalists at *L'Action française* were clearly enjoying this anarcho-anarchist civil war: "All of this alludes to certain imputations in the anarchist milieu—where unlimited confidence among 'comrades' doesn't reign—against M. Roulot, alias Lorulot."[23] The imputations being that Lorulot was a police informant and was also behind a provocative attack on the jury members entitled "Twelve Puppets" that was being investigated by the authorities.

This exchange would mark a key step in Victor's march away from anarchism, and he would later make serious accusations concerning Lorulot's conduct in his correspondence with the individualist icon Émile Armand, refusing to have anything to do with any enterprise in which Lorulot was also involved. The suspicion long lingered among anarchists that Lorulot was an informer, but police records show that he was followed by informants and had in fact been involved in illegalist activity himself, implicated in the counterfeiting of post office stamps.[24] Though at the time of the Bonnot crime wave Armand would say he would "henceforth no longer propagandize for illegalism," Lorulot, according to police reports, continued to speak in their defense.[25]

Lorulot, for his part, was clearly and justifiably shocked at having a comrade say he belonged among the defendants. In an undated letter to Armand, Lorulot expanded on the events at the trial. He said that given that Serge was in the process of being judged he didn't respond, not wanting to add fuel to the fire; all the reports, however they might vary in details, agree on this. But he had much he wanted to say. He contested Serge's claim that he had always been an enemy of illegalism, citing the latter's statements in his article "The Bandits" that "the bandits are grand, the bandits are beautiful." Defending himself against the idea that he should have been among the accused, he quoted an article he wrote, published in August 1911, establishing the bankruptcy of illegalism, for which Serge mocked him in a response. Lorulot also pointed out that Victor's testimony actually exculpated Lorulot, since he left his post at the head of *l'anarchie* in July 1911, well before the beginning of the Tragic

Bandit's crime wave, which began in December 1911. Finally, he pointed out that Kibalchich was being prosecuted not because he knew the bandits, but because he had stolen goods and papers in his possession, "establishing a connection between Kibalchich and his fellow defendants." On the other hand, there was not a single material fact against Lorulot. "This is what Kibalchich didn't say when he posed as an honest journalist and when he broke ranks with those seated alongside him by charging them. This is what I didn't want to respond with! This is why I said nothing … and yet this was the only way to answer the Mr. Bad-Faith who attacked me."

Serge's rancor would fester for years, and the wound would never heal. For the moment, though, as a result of this exchange, another breach in anarchist ranks had been pierced.

At the twelfth session of the trial on February 15, Maîtrejean explained the stolen identity documents in their possession as having come from a person she didn't know, invoking her right—nay, her duty—as a journalist to protect her sources, since "it was as a journalist that I received them and as a journalist I am bound to secrecy."

Another witness, Camboulin, a gang member already serving time for a theft the gang had carried out in Alfortville (which was accompanied by the criminals "making ordure in the kitchen"), gave up Carouy as an illegalist who deposited his takings at *l'anarchie*, which he recognized by their shape and wrapping. Maîtrejean asked Camboulin if he knew what time she got up in the morning. The witness knew she got up around noon, so Rirette pointed out she couldn't know anything about any stolen goods brought there in the early morning. Serge then joined in, asking Camboulin about the shape of the packages brought to *l'anarchie*, the witness saying they could easily be distinguished from stacks of wrapped newspapers, ending on a note of levity: "You'd think *l'anarchie* had a press run as big as that of *Le Matin*."

The proceedings were suspended for the day, but when they returned the next day Serge continued his questioning of

Camboulin, asking if the packages he had spoken of were in any way suspicious. The witness could only say he knew they were stolen goods because they were all addressed to the same person, Carouy. Having finished his questions, Serge added yet another witness to the list of those who should be sharing his lot, asking why Camboulin wasn't being prosecuted, though adding that nothing indicates he knew what was going on around him.

On February 18 the final summations began. Attorney General Fabre, in this supposedly non-political trial, described anarchism as

nothing but a label serving to cover a long series of crimes. To hear them these men are partisans of a certain doctrine that commands them to fight against a social order that doesn't correspond to their desires [...] Among them, anarchy took the form of a refined and perfected banditry [...] Such an attitude should not fool us: you are standing before vulgar criminals, though of an unprecedented skill and daring, of an unmatched criminal organization.

The summation was lengthy; each crime was laid out, the lives and personalities of the defendants picked apart. Raymond Callemin was described as a Belgian "who only came to France to commit crimes [...] He loves philosophy and has a real intellectual culture: it isn't surprising he was nicknamed 'La Science.' But the philosopher was only the stand-in for the bandit."

As the summation was going on, the individualist anarchists' foe Gustave Hervé, editor of the syndicalist *La Guerre sociale*, expressed his opinion of the trial. Hervé, based on his experience as a revolutionary journalist, knew there was little doubt as to the innocence of Maîtrejean and Kibalchich. Their crime was that

they'd harbored stolen goods, notably weapons, in the office of the paper, and known the principal members of the tragic gang. The attorney general doesn't seem to know that a revolutionary journal is a veritable mill, where people enter as they will and where people leave more or less whatever they want [...] That with a little bad luck any revolutionary journalist could be sent to prison.[26]

Considering the fact that not that long before the outbreak of the Bonnot Crime wave Hervé's paper had been carrying out its own investigation of *l'anarchie*, such a defense was all the more impressive.

So lengthy were the summations that it was only two days later, on February 20, that the assistant attorney general got to Serge and Rirette, addressing them directly and telling them,

[Y]ou were the center of the association, the pivot around which everything gravitated. It was under your benevolent aegis that the products of the thefts were brought to *l'anarchie*. It is there that the items needed to forge official documents were found; it is there that contacts were maintained among various members of the gang.

Adad, Maîtrejean's's lawyer, defended her by saying she was simply interested in the propagation of the idea of anarchy, and could in no way be accused of being part of a criminal gang, since she didn't even know many of the defendants. Adad then went further, either consciously or not playing on the ambient misogyny and flying in the face of facts: "At the newspaper she had one of the least important occupations, peeling vegetables and keeping house."

Serge's defense lawyer, Le Breton, said his client had been charged with "a thought crime." Accused of the possession of the stolen weapons, both Serge and Rirette assumed full responsibility, each exculpating the other: "They are proud people, young people who didn't want to betray each other. One of them paid with eleven, the other with thirteen months for this imprudence [before going on trial]. Isn't that enough?" He then returned to the sectarian rivalry within *l'anarchie*, describing the "profound hostility that reigned between 'scientifics and sentimentals,' the former group represented by Lorulot and his friends, Kibalchich and his girlfriend in the latter." He then addressed their human side, speaking of Serge's love for Rirette, of his life split between strolling in the Luxembourg Gardens, frequenting libraries, and participating in the Causeries populaires. After citing intellectual character witnesses, including the anarchists Sébastien Faure and Han Ryner, Le Breton ended the day by saying that "Whenever France puts thought on trial, it loses." He returned the next day, February 26, to put the final touches to his plea, again stressing Victor's love for Rirette, ending by saying that the police have never been able to find anything against Victor, that he's led "an exemplary life."

February 26, 1913, was the final day of the trial, and, as some of the defendants made direct statements, Rirette cried. Serge ("as was expected," according to *Le Matin*) took the floor. For *Le Matin* "his preoccupation hasn't varied: Prove that an anarchist of doctrine has nothing to do with an anarchist of crime." The socialists at *L'Humanité* phrased it slightly differently:

He is far from the trial. He is far from his fellow defendants. He's the dreamer who, without worrying about the consequences of his words, without knowing if, despite himself, he is charging his fellow defendants, wants to defend the doctrine that is dear to him. And so, he gives a long speech.

He once again drew a sharp line between himself and the members of the gang, between himself and those who had been his comrades, his "brothers." *L'Humanité* ran a large portion of his plea, saying that "His voice became bitter. It's as if it expresses regret, suffering":

You must be saying to yourselves that they are propagandists, but it is the ideas they propagated that made those seated alongside them thieves and murderers. But I don't want to accept that moral complicity. There's a difference between the ideas we pursue and those who kill in order to steal [...] The imprisonment I had to bear up under, the suffering I put up with, the conviction of my innocence, all of this pains me less than the thought of the energy of the young men that revealed itself in the tragedies of Choisy and Nogent, that all these energies that could have served to pursue propaganda for our ideas and realize our magnificent dream were wasted in that evil cause.

The socialist paper's report concluded, "And tenaciously, almost violently, he cried out to the entire room, which listened to him: 'No! Anarchists are not those who kill in order to take money. It is vile to claim this.'"[27]

For the other defendants, Serge's distancing of himself from them, from their acts, from their fate, from his former writings, had gone far enough. Callemin, who had known Serge since they were both adolescents in Brussels, stood up: "You don't know anything. Enough of your generalities and syntheses." Serge attempted to continue, but Callemin cut him off again: "You bore me, Kibalchich. We're not murderers, we're accused of murder. You're mixing things up." As the reporter for *L'Humanité* wrote, "Realizing that he risks becoming an accuser, Kibalchich ends with an appeal to the jury: "I accuse no one. I simply ask that I be judged not based on what others did, but on what I did."

The final pleas concluded at 3.00 p.m. The presiding judge read the 540 questions to the members of the jury. They left to deliberate. The deliberations continued overnight, the security in the courtroom so tight it was reminiscent of the era of Ravachol and the bomb throwers. The charge against Serge and Maîtrejean of running a criminal association had been dropped; they were now only charged with the possession of the stolen guns.

Finally, after thirteen hours of deliberations, the jury reached its verdicts. Dieudonné, Callemin, Soudy, and Monier were sentenced to death; Carouy and Metge were sentenced to life; the various other defendants to shorter terms. Rirette was found not guilty and asked a guard what Kibalchich's verdict was. He answered indirectly. "Don't cry, madame, Kibalchich's sentence will be short, six months, a year, very little ...." Given the lightness of the charge it was hoped he'd get off with time served even if found guilty.[28] But not only was he found guilty but he was sentenced to five years, counting from the date of his pre-trial arrest.

Why Serge was found guilty and Rirette not, based on similar charges and the same evidence, is an unanswerable question, laying as it does in the peculiarities of jury mentality. Perhaps it was because Rirette was a woman, perhaps it was because of Victor's outbursts, perhaps they simply didn't like him. Or perhaps it was because of his life as an anarchist and his long-standing defense of illegalism, combined with what looked to be an eleventh-hour conversion at the trial. We are on surer ground when it comes to his harsh sentence. It should be remembered that immediately after his arrest he was described in a police report as "a dangerous anarchist." Now that he was in the clutches of the state it was unlikely they'd let him go. And as we will see, that characterization of him as "dangerous" was to hang over him until the day he left France for good.

But for the other defendants the drama hadn't ended, not at all. As the verdicts were being announced, Raymond Callemin stopped the proceedings:

I have nothing to say about myself, but as for Dieudonné, I declare he didn't assault Caby. It was Garnier and I who did. I was the one who took the sack from him, but he never described me. I'll write the attorney general with the proof of what I say.

Nor was this the end of the drama.

Carouy, who had told his fellows that he preferred death to prison, a notion that Serge had praised in his writings about Liabeuf, and who had made two suicide attempts over the course of the trial, had succeeded in obtaining cyanide—probably hidden in a piece of paper tossed to him, according to the prison warden. He had ingested it and was found dying in his cell.

When the prisoners given the harshest sentences—Callemin, Dieudonné, Monier, and Metge—were led from the courthouse to La Santé prison they were put in straitjackets to prevent them from following Carouy's example. Dieudonné's sentence was reduced to forced labor for life, and he would be pardoned after a press campaign led by the famous journalist Albert Londres. He wrote a book on the life of prisoners and died in 1944.

The death sentences were carried out on April 26, 1913. Raymond la Science remained true to his beliefs, boasting in a posthumously published account in *Le Journal*, "We were more brutal and less hypocritical, that's all." Monier expressed his hope for a better tomorrow and left his revolver to a Paris museum "In memory of an innocent victim of an affair that threw the country into a state of terror." Soudy, condemned to death, he said, "by the representatives of social vengeance, otherwise known as justice," bequeathed his burglary tools to the minister of war "to help him open the way to social militarism," his brain to the dean of the medical school, his skull to the anthropological museum, his hair to the barbers' union and to the workers, "conscious or inebriated," so it could be put up for sale to support his cause, and his autograph to *l'anarchie* "so that the priests and apostles of the philosophy may make use of it to the profit of their cynical individuality."

The men were executed, and a school of anarchism that had spilled much blood and caused even more bad blood among comrades during its twenty-five-year life span was dead as well.

At the time of Bonnot's death the revolutionaries at *La Guerre sociale* had already written the obituary of illegalism, "an imbecilic doctrine":

No, individualism colored with anarchism or illegalism leads neither to social revolution nor individual happiness [...] For pariahs there is today no means of individually escaping from the hell of wage labor; there is no individual salvation. They will only escape all together through a collective, methodical, disciplined effort, after a patient labor of organization.[29]

Jean Jaurès, the most important figure of the working-class movement, leader of the Socialist Party, and founder and editor of *L'Humanité*, wrote in a similar vein: "The spectacle of cowardice, of stammered disavowals with which the murderers ended, serves to warn any rebels who would allow themselves to be seduced by a monstrous vertigo. The only real courage lies in labor and the collective effort of emancipation."[30]

The anarchist writer Victor Méric, whom Kibalchich had singled out for attack in one of his articles for his belief in revolution, but who had also defended the illegalist impulse, wrote in his book-long account of the Tragic Bandits that they were motivated by

an instinct of revolt and much lassitude, contempt for prophets and revolutionary theoreticians, and the ardent need to live, to enjoy life at any cost. And once the finger was caught in the gears the entire soul passed, the wild beast awakening in man, in the dreamer of yesterday. He who could have been an apostle was transformed into a bandit. The ravages certain theories caused among thousands of enthusiastic young people are incalculable. For having sacrificed to the illegalist idol the anarchists populated the prison colonies and prisons.[31]

Émile Armand had been visited at his office at *l'anarchie* by a journalist for the Parisian daily *Le Temps* for an article that appeared on May 1, 1912. In it the question of the Bonnot Gang, whose trial was still months away, came up. Armand, who certainly knew better, understandably equivocated.

Bonnot? ... It's quite possible that the Bonnots are the product of individualist anarchism. They weren't satisfied with the social pact and they rebelled against its arbitrary power. They are outsiders, illegals [...] I didn't know Bonnot. I don't know Garnier. I knew Carouy, who frequented *l'anarchie*. We don't ask those who come here if they live inside or outside of society's borders. We are only concerned with knowing if they're good or bad comrades.

The historian Jean Maitron viewed the bandits as "simply victims, while they believed themselves to be victors. Victims of society, victims of their nature, victims of their youth, victims— above all—of the 'anarchy within anarchy' that was illegalism. They deserved better than their fate."[32]

Serge, who at the trial had analyzed the illegalist illusion with clarity and brutality, wrote three decades later in his memoirs that the end of illegalism was the sign of something much larger. "It also testified to the bankruptcy of a doctrine. Between the vast syntheses of Piotr Kropotkin and Elisée Reclus and the exasperation of Albert Libertad, the decline of anarchism in the capitalist jungle became obvious." And he ended echoing the words he had spoken at the trial: "I only regret the forces wasted in struggles that could not but be sterile."[33]

That night he sent a pneumatique to Rirette:

My friend, I am happy you are free and that I alone suffer. Everything will come to an end. I will return. Be happy, try to be so while you wait for me. Make sure Chinette [Rirette's daughter] keeps her affection for me. Take advantage of the sun, the flowers, good books, of everything we loved together. But I beg you, never ever return to that milieu.[34]

The four remaining years of his five-year prison sentence, his "inner nightmare," began.[35]

5

Man in Prison

Now that he'd been found guilty of a crime Serge was transferred from La Santé prison in Paris to the penitentiary in Melun on the River Marne. The conditions at Melun were harsh, with the prisoners held in isolation overnight and performing forced labor for ten hours during the day. Serge was assigned to the print shop, where he worked as a compositor, and then as a proofreader. The printshop was an island of the familiar in what he called "the city of the damned."[1]

Serge's experiences of prison were the material he used for his first novel, *Men in Prison*, published in 1930. Like all of his novels, it is autobiographical and can be mined for traces of his life.

Serge speaks in it of how easy it was to predict who would collapse under the weight of imprisonment, and how such predictions were almost always correct. "But they had been wrong about me; I had appeared fated to die before long."[2] But as he would demonstrate in all his later travails, Serge's inner strength was greater than the difficult circumstances that he was forced to face.

Though Serge remained a revolutionary and condemned the Great War as an imperialist one, he doesn't hide the fact that when the war began and the battlelines advanced towards Paris—the Battle of the Marne fought not far from the prison at Melun—he asserts about the prisoners,

If we had been outside jail I think that we would have followed the stream and felt immediately that, despite all theoretical considerations, a country under attack, unless it is at the height of a social crisis, must defend itself; primitive reflexes, infinitely stronger than principles, are at play; the sensation of "the Fatherland in danger" prevails.[3]

This passing observation is a striking one, foretelling the many ways that Serge would revise radical doctrine in the light of real—not theoretical—experience.

While in Melun, the process of reconsideration of his political course that had been long in progress deepened. As he wrote in his memoirs, "I understood pretty clearly the individualists' aberrations—but I could see no way out."[4] The appearance he likes to give that he had seen the dead end that individualism was needs to be taken with a grain of salt. Contrary to his many statements to the contrary, he remained closely tied to his individualist comrades, and this for quite some time, as we shall see in his correspondence with Émile Armand just before Serge left for Barcelona and in his early days there.

Serge maintained the elitism of the individualist stance behind the prison walls. Describing the mass of prisoners as a "mob," Serge wrote in a vein already familiar to us that in opposition to this mob "stand the men. The real men."[5] As in his days of freedom, he praises the outlaw, who "has no illusions about society's values and knows neither faith nor law."[6] As it was in his days at *l'anarchie*, the type of man he admires in prison "has self-respect, the knowledge of his own strength, and the respect of other 'men'—the strong."[7] "'I'm a man.' All his pride is summed up in these words."[8] A "man" in prison is someone who "never sells out [...] knows how to take it—and dish it out—in a knife fight."[9] As he wrote, "the greatest praise you can give [a prisoner] is to say that 'He's a man.'"[10] All his pride is summed up in this word, more than that of any idealism borrowed from the Narodniki.

Anarchists are not, as a rule, knife fighters, yet they, too, are counted among the "men" in prison. He cites the case of Julien Laherse, an anarchist who has remained faithful to his ideals, "patient, unchanging, exemplary, living on a diet of oil, studying German and English, greeting his comrades with a glance of solidarity."[11] It is from Laherse that we learn what is, according to Serge, the correct attitude to sex behind prison walls. Love has nothing to do with it; it's an outmoded notion, "a momentary conjunction of personalities and sex needs, that's all, nothing more. The rest is nothing but ignorance, outdated beliefs, prejudices, the effects of pure reproductive instincts."[12]

But even so, love existed, love for those left behind. Serge wrote movingly of the effect reading a letter from a lover outside the prison walls had on the incarcerated. Just reading the words "My darling, I love you," makes the prisoner feel "invulnerable, like someone wearing a talisman."[13] Recipients of love letters feel a "rapture" that raises them above their environing misery.[14]

Serge was not speculating on this. It was something he felt and experienced intensely. During his five years in prison—one in La Santé and four in Melun—thoughts of his lover and companion Rirette Maîtrejean kept him constant company and provided infinite torture.

While they were imprisoned, the members of the Bonnot Gang (and Serge) received visits from the psychiatrist Émile Michon, who, as we previously mentioned, published a book of his observations, *Un peu de l'âme des bandits*. Serge's letters to Rirette are singled out by Michon for their sincerity and profundity, and Michon treats the letters' author with enormous respect. Before quoting from some of them—in the end Serge wrote Rirette 500 letters—Michon says of their author that "I will never agree to see in him a criminal."[15] Michon says of the first of the letters he quotes, written before the end of the Bonnot Gang trial, when they were held in separate prisons—he at the Conciergerie, she at Saint-Lazare—that it is "a bit precious, but delicate and of a pure sentiment. He speaks to his girlfriend of the shared sufferings endured and evokes the future."[16]

Even this early in their separation, Serge's heart was overflowing with love and sorrow. "Nothing of the evil we've suffered will be wasted, nothing will have been useless. Tell yourself, my beloved friend, that every day that has passed, colored with our sorrow, will leave something within us."[17] Serge expresses regret for their political follies, saying that they "will remake [their] lives with the materials gathered now [...]; there will be no more thoughtless blunders, no more mad imprudence or costly carelessness."[18] Prison means nothing to him. "I won't allow myself to be tormented by prison itself; I will suffer only for you, through you. This is good, right? For it will be up to you to erase this evil."[19]

Once Serge was sentenced and sent to Melun, in a letter bearing the number 249, Serge speaks of feeling "a stab of jealousy, a perfectly human sentiment at such a time in life, [that] hides beneath the caress of words."[20] He's jealous that she will see the flowers blooming and the trees turning green again at the Luxembourg Gardens, but there is clearly more here than a jealousy inspired by Rirette's ability to see nature.

"If only you knew the dreams I had Tuesday night and all those that haunted me here since I saw you! If only you knew all you said to me, promised or confessed, and what absurd, what violent jealousy is at times set alight in me, momentary lightning flashes. And how much vague anxiousness. None of this has been extinguished; it all burns and lives in me, torturing me, but giving meaning to these dark days."[21] Serge wrote another letter that same night, saying, "I understand you better than ever," imploring her to "be happy and free [...] What will be left to me if I have to think that our love, instead of helping you fight, to come closer to me, instead of encouraging you, saddens and torments you." His parting wish was an ardent one: "Close your eyes, my adorable *moute* [Serge's affectionate nickname for his companion] and try to dream that I've returned for an hour in order to persuade you. I hold your hands; I speak to you softly before departing. I'll have slowly caressed your hair and will give you a gentle, a very gentle kiss."[22]

That Serge loved Rirette is not in question. But in order for her to be allowed to visit him and correspond regularly they needed to be married. In a letter to his father—whom he hadn't seen in five years—dated April 5, 1914, one read by the authorities, Serge wrote, "I only want to give legal sanction to an already old and quite stable union for entirely practical reasons having to do with my current situation: in order to be able to correspond with my partner and to see her, which would lighten my cares and would be a great comfort for me." In August 1914 Serge requested of the prison authorities that he be allowed to marry her. The matter was kicked around the prison bureaucracy, and in December Rirette asked for authorization to begin the formalities for their marriage. The lengthy delay that followed was unavoidable, as she was still married to her first husband, the father of her two daughters. Louis Maîtrejean, an anarchist illegalist, had also been imprisoned at Melun, in his case for counterfeiting. Rirette wrote to inform him that "I'm going to start divorce proceedings against you, but don't feel sad about it. I'm doing this to help a suffering comrade." She addressed her husband in the informal "tu" form, while, as we've mentioned, she and Serge continued to use the formal "vous" form. There's no doubt that Rirette was sincere in the reasons she gave for marrying Serge. Added to his imprisonment, none of this was the basis for a stable marriage.

The prison authorities refused the request to marry, the warden writing dismissively, "As far as I am concerned, I think that Kibalchich can wait till he's released (January 31, 1917) to contract marriage with Maîtrejean." The warden also cites a fear that "this person [Rirette], who shares her lover's anarchist ideas, will take advantage of the celebration of the marriage, or visits she'll be authorized to make to her husband, to attempt an escape." On April 8, 1915, the warden issued a formal refusal of Serge's request. Serge and Rirette persisted, and in May the prison director relented, laying out the conditions for the ceremony. Kibalchich "will be taken from the establishment by guards in civilian attire and brought before the officiant of the civil registry. At the end of the ceremony, and if they have a religious ceremony, after the church ceremony, he must be immediately returned to the prison." On August 3, 1915, the marriage was celebrated.

Serge was disappointed in the relative infrequence of his wife's visits. There's every reason to believe that Rirette, an anarchist through and through, just as she'd moved on to Serge after Louis Maîtrejean was arrested, moved on after she was found not guilty and Serge held in the penitentiary.

On January 31, 1917, Serge was released from prison, having served the full five years of his sentence in the Bonnot trial. He would leave for Barcelona two weeks later.

Important insights into Serge's state of mind upon his release can be obtained from an article headlined "From Criminal Court to the Trenches" that appeared in October 1917 in the daily newspaper *L'Excelsior*. It reported that "the war has permitted some men to rehabilitate themselves, weapon in hand."[23] Presenting the story as a sequel to that of the Tragic Bandits, the paper reported that Louis Maîtrejean had been cited in the army's order of the day and received the Croix de Guerre. But that wasn't all. In order "to serve France at the same time as his country of origin," Rirette's second husband, Victor Kibalchich, "after having played the role of anarchist intellectual in the Bonnot Affair, now wants to enlist."

Rirette proudly showed the journalist from *L'Excelsior* a postcard she'd received from Louis informing her of the reason for his decoration. He had served as a liaison agent who, under bombardment and bullets, unstintingly transmitted orders during the August 16, 1917, offensive." Rirette was proud to point out that she was the first person her ex-husband had informed of his bravery and commendation.

"Smiling and shaking her curly hair," she told the reporter of how Maîtrejean, because of his arrest record, had at first been prevented from serving, but was finally able to enlist and was wounded three times. His conduct so impressed his superiors that he was given his position as courier. For Rirette, "his merits were born of his sentence."

As for Serge, released from prison and living in exile, and still Rirette's husband, he had lived a miserable life in Barcelona, "in a city full of spies and deserters," till the Russian Revolution gave him a new concept of duty.

6
Barcelona:
Becoming Victor Serge

Serge, in his memoirs, as well as in *The Birth of Our Power*, the novel he wrote about his time in Barcelona , focuses on his exposure to revolutionary syndicalism and his participation in the struggles of the anarcho-syndicalists there. He reported that he more or less experienced a kind of conversion experience in Spain, one that he had been mulling over during his prison years, if not the time before that, as his relationship with the Bonnot Gang deteriorated. He now saw individualist anarchism as a dead end; in his subsequent telling, in Spain he learned of the need for mass action. The process was in reality a far from immediate one.

In his memoirs he wrote angrily that, because of his support for the Russian Revolution of February 1917, "Certain French Individualists mocked me with their store of cynical stock phrases: 'Revolutions are useless. They will not change human nature. Afterwards reaction sets in and everything starts all over again.'"[1] And yet, his one article written in Spain about events in Russia was not the full-throated endorsement of the February Revolution that he claimed. Serge's account of his relations with the French individualists requires some modifying.

Serge was engaging in revisionism when he wrote in his memoirs what he then thought of his erstwhile comrades:

You people are no longer good for anything. You're at the end of your tether: you won't march for anything anymore— because you yourselves are not worth marching for [...] Your kind are the products of the degeneration of everything: of the bourgeoisie, of bourgeois ideas, of the working-class movement, of anarchism. My break with these "comrades," who were no more than the shadows of comrades, became complete: it was useless to argue, and difficult to endure one another.[2]

In a letter written to Émile Armand on February 12, 1917, during the brief time he spent in Paris before departing for Spain, Serge reminded Armand of what he insisted were the true reasons for his imprisonment. "I had to answer for the triple crime of being a foreigner, of being an anarchist, and refusing to be a rat." As we saw at the trial, his relations with his comrades were already souring. At the Bonnot trial he had more than implied that André Lorulot was a police informer, and his anger had not calmed in the years since. Speaking of an unnamed individual, he told Armand that

> as soon as I will find it possible to elucidate this affair, I will. In the meanwhile, I cannot agree to collaborate in any way with a man upon whom weigh such grave suspicions and who, in any case, had been in regard to me and my partner a backstabber in the saddest sense of the word.

He told Armand he wouldn't name the person in question, but it is certain that it was Lorulot.

Serge certainly had disputes with his former comrades, and disagreements over Russia would become increasingly prominent in the deteriorating relations between Serge and the French individualists. But when he arrived in Spain, as his correspondence with Armand shows, these men and women he wrote of so disdainfully in his *Memoirs* decades later helped him out financially. On March 19, 1917, about a month after his arrival in Barcelona, he continued to say that he was at one with the individualist movement Armand was at the heart of. His departure from the movement was not as overnight as he wanted us to believe. Émile

Armand opened a subscription in support of Serge in the individualist review *Par delà de la melée*, explaining that "For many years he played too important a role in our intellectual activity for us to not think about his material situation, which is necessarily precarious."[3]

Far from having jettisoned anarchist individualism, upon arriving in Barcelona Serge continued to place himself among the individualists, describing Armand's paper, *Au-dela de la melée* (not to be confused with *Par delà de la melée*, though very similar and both edited by Armand), "the only paper that today represents *our* tendency" (emphasis added). A lengthy letter of March 3 to Armand demonstrates that his disagreement with the individualists was not political but rather personal, revolving principally around his detestation of Lorulot.

Serge lists his points in the lawyerly fashion he would adopt over the course of his remaining decades when involved in politico-personal disputes. A comrade had questioned whether the time was right to air the movement's dirty laundry in public through "reciprocal accusations." Serge was angered by the use of this phrase: There were no "reciprocal accusations," since Lorulot has nothing to reproach him for. Serge was furious with Armand and said he—Serge—needed a "strong dose of courage" in order to continue the discussion with him. He was angry that he was being asked to provide proof of his accusations against Lorulot when his circumstances—his exile to Spain—didn't allow any such thing. "I have other things to do at present," he wrote, and, what's more, Lorulot had had five years to prepare his defense against any charges made by Serge. Serge's rage is unlimited, explaining his refusal of collaboration with the individualists as a group by likening it to collaborating with Azev, the Russian secret police agent who infiltrated revolutionary groups in that country.

The French comrades, for their part, were angered by Rirette's ghostwritten memoirs of her time at *l'anarchie* with Serge, which had been published in *Le Matin* in 1913. Serge was being told to disavow his partner's articles. He, with great justice, asked if it was right that he be asked to "disavow writing I never avowed? That isn't mine in any way?" He correctly points out that "Rirette alone is responsible" for the articles and "I don't think I have the right to demand an accounting for her acts." He then goes on to defend the work. "She doesn't hide her disgust and absolute discouragement in the face of the men and the acts which, in her eyes, wasted, profaned and degrades the ideas. She has her bitter experience against which I can do nothing." But he issues a warning to Armand: "I have not (not yet?) reached the same point as her."

In closing, he returns to his refusal to have anything to do with any undertaking that includes Lorulot. "If in one way or another it would later be possible to collaborate with you without agreeing to this neighborly relation, it would be with real joy." He requested that his letter be made known to their comrades, and then gave precise instructions for how they should send him money.

The only sociopolitical issue that is brought up in this series of letters to Armand is Serge's dismissal of Armand's "sexological" writings, "which have nothing to do with the development of our ideas," and which Serge said were nothing but "vulgarity" and "purely ridiculous."

Serge did not stop writing while he was in Spain, his articles appearing in both the Spanish and French anarchist press. It was at this point that he adopted the name Victor Serge, sometimes Victor-Serge, a choice he never explained, and which would henceforth be the principal name by which he wrote and was known. His Spanish articles, written in French and translated by one of his comrades, the individualist anarchist Manuel Costa Iscar, appeared in the newspaper *Tierra y Libertad*. Serge published five articles in that paper, the most important of them a study of Friedrich Nietzsche, which extended over four issues that appeared between August and December. They display a push/pull relationship with his past ideas but are clear proof of the persistence of some of his prior notions and the arrival in force of others that were previously subterranean.

Tierra y Libertad was a forthrightly anarchist communist newspaper, fiercely internationalist and insurrectionist, perhaps the most radical of the newspapers in Spain. Its anarchism, though, was open to all schools. His closest friend when he arrived in Spain, as well as his host, Costa Iscar was a postman by vocation and an active individualist by avocation. He was a close friend of Émile Armand and shared with Armand two of the trends of anarchism that held little appeal for Serge: free love and nudism.

The April 4, 1917, issue of *Tierra y Libertad* included Serge's first article on the revolution in Russia, still in its pre-Bolshevik phase, entitled "A Tsar Falls." This article, his first signed Victor Serge, shows that Serge was a hopeful but not unbridled enthusiast for the new post-tsarist Russia. He feared that "the liberal bourgeois will end up taking power in Russia and will do the same as their predecessors: they'll exploit, execute, and send male youth to war. There are not two ways of governing." A nagging pessimism persisted in Serge: "This is why there is no reason to expect great results from political revolutions, even victorious ones." The overthrow of the tsar and the recent events in Russia "constitute nothing but an episode" in a great struggle that began in 1860. The bourgeois revolution, "imbued with modern ideas against the representatives of the ancien régime, can reach an end. The social struggle, no." The social transformation that is a real revolution cannot be changed by an insurrection, due to "the slow evolution of the collective souls." The weight of the bourgeois presence will impede this process. "There will not be one less miserable, exploited individual, soldier, degraded man or parasite in Russia."

But Serge insisted there was reason to hope, that the change in consciousness would eventually come, for much is owed to Russia. "We owe a part of our valor to Russia. It has given new forces to the world that have borne fruit everywhere." The struggle of the Russians is not only theirs, but that of all revolutionaries: "Russians, in the course of their painful ascents to betterment have worked for all men, because their sufferings and hopes enrich the common patrimony." The messianic hopes placed in Russia by the young man who was Victor Kibalchich are here given body. "They have succeeded in dethroning a tsar. And they continue their work, helping us through their example, when it's not their efforts, to live our life, fighting for LIFE."

In a subsequent article, "Extreme Moments," Serge explained his vision of how a revolution occurs, one that shows him to be miles from the Bolsheviks who were now achieving growing influence in Russia. Ever the anarchist, Serge rejected the idea of a guiding minority. "All I know is that revolutionaries do not prepare the revolution; I know that revolutions are detonated in people who lose hope in the reform of those who govern; I know that revolutions are not forestalled through repression, that at most, it manages to postpone them." The man who wrote "The Revolutionary Illusion" is beginning to fade into the distance.

His lengthy analysis of Nietzsche was the most important of his Spanish writings. As Annick Stevens, who assembled and prefaced the first French edition of the essay, which only appeared in 2018, wrote: "[T]his text is an occasion to clarify the extent to which [Serge's] individualism is compatible with his profound desire to participate in the decisive historic movements that were underway."

The frenetic individualism of Nietzsche, particularly that of *Thus Spake Zarathustra* and its proclamation of the Superman (more accurately Overman), appealed to individualist anarchists, who, as we've discussed, often felt an elitism that was an outgrowth of their ideology. In this lengthy essay, his longest to date, he describes Nietzsche as "a philosopher of violence." As such, "he was and, since his thought continues to live, is our sole and unique enemy."[4]

However "vigorous" Nietzsche's "ideal of life, one not without a certain beauty," might have been, it was, according to

Serge, nevertheless "profoundly barbarous and an enemy of the progress for which we are fighting." The force Nietzsche grants the individual is no longer enough for Serge. Nietzsche's vision of the individual and the society in which he moves is inimical to progress, something whose attainment through struggle he'd doubted prior to his imprisonment.

The Bakuninist ideal of destruction as a positive good is present in Nietzsche, but "he destroys in order to make room for an ideal probably quite distinct from ours." The differences between Nietzsche and the anarchists are clear:

If [Nietzsche] seeks to smash the tablets of current values, it's not in order to substitute for them a new order founded on the free development of every human personality, where the only law will be consciousness's inner law finally sublimated and made glorious by a free life, but rather to rejuvenate the old order, which he believes in and wants to be eternal.

Both Nietzsche and the anarchists feel the "grandeur and value of strength." But for Nietzsche force is a positive good, a way for the strongest and most able to impose their way and will. Anarchists view the matter differently:

Our "noble ideal par excellence" is the humble and purified man who overcomes the ancestral instincts of the bestial struggle because he desires another struggle, one that demands no less courage or strength, but which is more worthy of him. One needs more courage to smash a sword than to use it, to be free and libertarian than to be an oppressor.

In defending anarchist individualism from any Nietzschean connections, Serge modifies his ideology. The harsh, cynical elitism of his youth is softened, and he now resembles a gentler school of individualist anarchism, one represented by Han Ryner. He casts aside the "authoritarian individualism" of Nietzsche:

The individualist asserts himself through his own internal worth; through the domination of the self; through the cult of impartial reasoning; through generosity, disinterest, and the idealism that are the characteristics of higher egoism; and through the intense effort of fervent and judicious will, all of which is much closer to true nobility.

Serge's ideal is someone who "will be the guide, the example, the wise man, the hero, never the man with the whip."

Far from being the exemplar of the new man of the anarchists, Nietzsche is a "German imperialist," someone "manifestly of the race of Bismarck and Hindenburg, of the race of predators."

Between his vision of the future and ours there is an abyss impossible to fill. Two ideals remain present in our poor destroyed humanity: imperialism and libertarianism. One asserts itself through fratricide, through victory by the knife and fire, oppression, the perpetual crucifixion of another species; the other points out a new path, the only one that can lead humanity toward a healthy perfection without bestiality; toward victories that aren't tarnished by descent into the dregs, blood, falsehood, mad hatred, and blindness.

It's unlikely that the Le Rétif of the years 1908–12 would have subscribed to the ideas of the Victor Serge who writes now: "He who wants to go freely toward the future with his brothers must rebel in the name of the shared suffering of which his is but an infinitesimal part." The path to mass action Victor Serge will soon take is being constructed before the reader's eyes.

Nietzsche is described by Serge as "our enemy," though still someone who brings with him something essential: "His truth, a precious truth." Among anarchists this truth has only been felt by the individualists, but only the intellectuals among them, for workers "don't have sufficient education to confront the energetic seduction of the passionate imperialist with a critical spirit." The exercise of this critical spirit reveals Nietzsche to be nothing but a "Social Darwinist." Now sounding like Kropotkin, Serge says that no conclusions about humanity can be drawn from the mutual slaughter occurring across Europe, for "[t]he immense crime that is currently being committed will not testify against the law of mutual aid."

And then Serge again pivots, asserting that Nietzsche

> was the philosopher of violence and authority, but like us he felt an immense love for life and knowledge, the invincible desire to fight for his cause, disgust for the current social order and the rule of the mediocre to which we are descending. He felt the need to destroy old ideas and things, to assist in destroying what is collapsing so that we can then be reborn.

He was an anarchist despite himself.

Serge ends with a striking and perspicacious conclusion. He states that he loves Nietzsche, "And I listen to and am largely inspired by his oeuvre. But I don't follow him. Imitating his example as a critic and free-thinker I only ask him for assistance in finding *my truth*." And that is what is essential to the anarchist Victor Serge, as it was to the anarchist Le Rétif. There is no authority to which the anarchist owes obeisance. The important thinkers—the Max Stirners, the Bakunins, the Kropotkins— open a road that those who think like them can take. And as the cult of Nietzsche took hold in France, and not only there, he offered the highest praise possible from a man who rejected any form of discipleship:

> I have no illusions concerning the value of his prejudices and I don't close my eyes to his errors. He looked men and things in the eye with a rebel's insolence and lack of respect. How he would have despised the blindness of those who today want to set up a vain cult to him, because this master wanted no disciples.

* * *

Serge wrote of his Barcelona experiences in his novel *Naissance de notre force* (*The Birth of Our Power*), published in French in 1931 and in English for the first time in 1967. In a 1929 letter to his friend, the Romanian-born French-language novelist Panait Istrati, he spoke of it under two alternative titles, *Les Hommes en marche* (Men on the March) and *Nous voici sortis des ténèbres* (Here We Are, Out of the Darkness).

Written after his first Soviet imprisonment of 1928, this, Serge's second novel, reflects the thoughts and feelings of a Serge long out of his individualist anarchist phase. His friend Costa Iscar, who had housed him and translated his articles into Spanish for *Tierra y Libertad*, appears briefly as Tibio, called "The Postman," who "studied the art of living and wrote commentary on Nietzsche."[5] The appearances of the individualists in the book are almost always taken as occasions for denigrating them. A revolution is in preparation in Barcelona, but the individualists, most of them exiles from other lands, stand apart from events. One, Zilz, informs a group of revolutionaries that "You can count me out. My skin is worth more than any republic."[6] A Russian individualist, named Lejeune, intends to participate in the planned uprising in his own way, reverting to the methods of the Bonnot Gang: "There are bound to be a few days of disorder, you see. So I'll hit the banks. My revolution will be over quickly. I don't believe in *theirs*. Monarchies, republics, unions, I don't give a damn, you understand?"[7] It's a Spanish anarchist who passes judgment on Serge's former comrades: "The ego-anarchist poison. People like that, you see, don't risk their necks any more except for money."[8]

Serge gives further and more direct vent to his disgust with his former comrades, who are infected with "the old poison of Paris." Speaking in the first person he recalls the follies of the illegalists, those "happy counterfeiters, carrying [their] bundles of 'merchandise' stuffed in [their] left pants' pockets, [their] right hand resting on [their] Brownings!"[9] He knows these men and women well, "More than anyone else—since I had seen them kill off the strongest—I was conscious of certain imponderable poisons, synthetic products which combine bourgeois temptations with a natural love of life, intelligence, and energy with rebellion and poverty."[10]

He bids a final farewell to the Bonnot Gang, who were the purest representatives of all Serge had grown to hate: "[B]orn to adventure, the gray autos carried you off to the guillotine—five thousand francs sewn into your pants' lining, three clips of ammunition (twenty-one bullets, nicely pointed and explicit) and: 'We're nobody's fool anymore.'—'We no longer believe anything.'—'We will carve out a new life for ourselves.'"[11] Is Serge referring yet again to Lorulot when he adds: "But one of the boys, who didn't believe in anything either, found it even more convenient to make blood money on you and sold you out to fat policemen—cash on the line."[12]

Placed against these "conscious egotists" are the members of the Comité Obrero, the revolutionary syndicalists preparing an uprising in alliance with the liberal bourgeois parties. Serge continues that "I much preferred the very different truths held by [the syndicalists] El Chorro, Eusebio, and a few thousand other comrades who, at every hour, were crossing and recrossing the teeming city, running secret errands."[13]

Serge's novel is set against the background of the preparations for an uprising in Barcelona in 1917. The uprising was planned by what the anarchist historian and theorist Murray Bookchin called a "curious bloc."[14] Aiming at the establishment of a Constituent Assembly that would produce a more progressive constitution, the anarchists found themselves allied with Catalan industrialists and nationalists, military men, conservatives, republicans, and socialists, all of whom had a shared desire to rid Spain of the landowning oligarchy that had ruled it for centuries.

The anarchist labor union, the Confederación Nacional del Trabajo (CNT), was led in Catalonia by Salvador Seguí, the model for Dario in Serge's novel, and by Angel Pestaña, editor of the anarchist newspaper *Solidaridad Obrera*. Though their overarching views differed, as Bookchin explained, both men were sincere anarchists, and "their practical views were shaped by day-to-day issues and organizational exigencies. They placed a strong emphasis on the need for immediate gains, often at the expense of their libertarian principles."[15] According to Bookchin, Seguí, for whom Serge had great admiration, felt far more comfortable with socialists like Largo Caballero than with the more militant anarchists of *Tierra y Libertad*, who had published Serge's writings. Serge, in his memoirs, expresses the same opinion of Seguí, who had no use for the matter of a future world, more concerned with "immediate problems of wages, organization, rents and revolutionary power."[16]

The CNT entered into an alliance with the Union General de Trabajadores (UGT), a non-anarchist union, and in December 1916 the two unions called for a twenty-four-hour general strike protesting the high cost of living, a call that was largely honored.

The CNT–UGT alliance grew stronger, and in the early summer of 1917 it was time for the "curious bloc" to move into action. The prime minister, Dato, dissolved the legislature—the Cortes—and suspended constitutional liberties, and then set out to provoke a confrontation, one he hoped would frighten the bourgeois opposition into returning to the fold and abandon its left-wing allies. Serge called the alliance of the revolutionaries with the bourgeoise "dubious," and quoted Seguí as being aware of the instability of the union: "They would like to use us and then do us down. For the moment they are useful in their game of political blackmail. Without us they can do nothing: we have the streets, the shock troops, the brave hearts among the people. We know this, but we need them."[17] A first rebellion occurred on July 19, which was quickly crushed. Though preparations were begun for a larger uprising, some workers in other parts of Spain went on strike as a first step, and the Socialists, realizing the cause was lost in advance, told the CNT to call off any strikes in Barcelona. Despite this, a general strike was called for August

13, and was quickly smashed, where barricades went up and the workers were fired on by the military. Bookchin sums the episode up by saying, "The strike proved to be entirely political, its demands influenced not by Anarchist demands but by those of the Socialists."[18] But he also points out that the battlelines were henceforth drawn, with the workers lined up against the bourgeoise. Serge, in his *Memoirs*, sees matters differently. For him the demands drawn up in June 1917 "were borrowed from the accumulated experience of the Russian Soviets."[19]

In any event, by this time Serge was out of Spain.

* * *

Though we are jumping ahead a bit, an interesting critique of the picture Serge painted of Spain and himself in 1917 appeared in 1931, the year of the publication of *The Birth of Our Power*. A critique of the novel in the *La Revue anarchiste* described it as "perfectly constructed, written in a beautiful descriptive language, clear and precise."[20] The critic continued that such words did not suffice "when it's a matter of a revolutionary work." Treating the novel as an autobiography, the critic pointed out that "it contains no small number of inexact ideas and, as concerns the life of the author, [possesses] a dryness of heart, an astounding power of forgetfulness." The critic was well placed to know. It was, Rirette Maîtrejean.

Maîtrejean questions the veracity of almost everything in the novel. In her eyes, it could just as well have been called "The Art of Evolving." The evolution she refers to is not so much the political one, from individualism to Bolshevism, since she claims—oddly—that Serge's evolution towards Bolshevism was clear since 1911, "though Bolshevism did not yet exist." Her former lover's change of line was one due not just to his evolving ideas but also to his national background, for "Russians rarely have an individualist consciousness, and it is within communism that they find their true element."

Rirette's primary concern is for what she describes as Serge's "moral evolution." With more than a little justice, she reproaches Serge for his "disdain," his "scorn for individualists, which is for the most part laughable, and in others painful." Maîtrejean doubts Serge's sincerity, asking, "Was he sincere when he professed individualism or is he only so now? Or in both cases?" Maîtrejean cited in support of her case the atmosphere in which they lived between 1907 and 1912, when in their circles "there was no lack of sincere and disinterested individuals, who fought with fervor (for a cause either good or bad is of no matter here)." The prisons were full of these sincere rebels, but "Serge doesn't remember them; he's erased them from his memory. No one could ever guess, on reading him, that he lived among them, with them, shared their very existence."

Maîtrejean also questioned Serge's claims in the novel (and later in his *Memoirs of a Revolutionary*) that he returned to France in order to go to Russia, pointing out that this road is "bizarre," and his claim that he did so "an infringement on the truth." Let us recall that Rirette herself had told a journalist in October 1917 that Serge had indeed followed this route she now calls into question. "'Don't lie to others, don't lie to yourself' Victor Serge says on page 247 of his book. But Victor Serge's book is from one end to the other a lie to himself, a lie against friendship, a lie against honesty. Victor Serge's book is a wicked act against himself."

On November 8, 1931, Serge responded to Maîtrejean's article in a letter to the editor, datelined Leningrad. Serge denies speaking ill of individualists in *Birth of Our Power*, saying that it is only "incidentally a question" of these circles. The focus is on the "anarchist and syndicalist circles in Spain in 1917–18, [in which] I praise their solidarity and their spirit of revolt." He claims that "In doing so I render justice to my former comrades and I believe I am alone in having done so, at least in a literary work." Serge here evades Maîtrejean's question: The mentions of the individualists can, if push comes to shove, be considered "incidental," but they are almost uniformly negative. The "former comrades" he praises are the anarcho-syndicalists, not the individualists of whom Rirette spoke. He also points out that there is a positive portrait of an individualist, that of Broux. For the rest he dismisses everything his former companion has to say as the fruit of "an arbitrary carving out of texts."[21]

* * *

It was some time after the defeat of the first uprising on July 19 that Serge, admitting he thought the situation was hopeless in Barcelona, began his convoluted voyage to Russia. He went to see the Russian Consul General in Barcelona, who had been converted to support for the Provisional Government, and told him he wanted to go to Russia to fight for the new Russia. He was referred to the Russian headquarters in Paris—where he was still banned—and was told his request would not be easily filled. He was advised to enlist in the Russian troops fighting for France, but the list for volunteers was closed. He continued to search for other means to get to Russia.

In her interview given in October 1917 to *L'Excelsior*, Maîtrejean said that Serge, in order "to serve France at the same time as his country of origin, after having played the role of anarchist intellectual in the Bonnot Affair, now wants to enlist."

> Since his brothers no longer fight for tsarism, but for freedom, he wants to be among them and help them realize an ideal. He came back to Paris, but he learned that all enlistments to go to Russia or for Russian contingents are suspended. All that's left is the Foreign Legion. He is currently in a concentration camp near Paris awaiting the results of the steps I'm taking on his behalf. I'll be very happy if I succeed.

Helping Serge get to Russia was her main task of the moment and tells us just how important getting to his ancestral homeland was to him. The reporter asked Rirette what she was busy with.

"Not much, alas. For the moment I'm busy with Kibalchich's enlistment. I think you'll agree with me that this is not a waste of my time."[22]

While seeking a route to Russia, Serge worked at a printshop, though the ban on his residing in France was still in place. In October 1917 Serge was arrested on the streets for his violation of the ban and was first sent to the prison in Fleury-en-Bière, outside Paris, and then to the camp at Précigné.

He wrote in his memoirs of finding there a group of revolutionaries of various stripes who were labeled Bolsheviks, "without being anything of the kind." They constituted themselves as a group within the camp, and if there was, in fact, only one Bolshevik among them (who later refused to leave for Russia when the opportunity arose), the rest "desired a libertarian, democratic revolution," one that would be "egalitarian and tolerant towards ideas and people, which would employ terror if it was necessary, but would abolish the death penalty."[23] Their Bolshevik-leaning anarchism—or anarchist-leaning Bolshevism—he would later write, was his guiding light, which manifested itself during the nearly sixteen months he spent in Précigné.

Serge didn't find the conditions there too terrible, though hunger dogged the prisoners. While he was held there he was able to write for the anarchist review *La Melée*, edited by Pierre Chardon. Chardon was an individualist anarchist who had assumed the editorship of this publication after the arrest of its founder, Émile Armand. Here again we see that Serge had maintained his contact and involvement in the individualist circles he later claimed to have left behind.

These articles are tremendously important if we are to understand Serge's state of mind during the period immediately preceding his departure for Soviet Russia. Writing again as Le Rétif, the name he used as an individualist, and not Victor Serge, the supposed syndicalist who wrote from Barcelona, he strives to open his individualism to mass struggle in a way he'd almost never done previously. In his November 15, 1918, "Lettre d'un emmuré," he still said of crowds that "they are always inferior to the lone man." But he shifts gears further on and says of the Russian Revolution, as he did in Spain, that "They are attempting to construct something else. Will they succeed? I hope so, and nothing more." As a result, "We can't retreat from social life. Whether we like it or not, we are social animals, and we can't, when we want to improve our personal lot, do anything but work to improve the common lot." Here we have, just months before Serge's departure for Russia, the ideological basis for his adoption of Bolshevism. Concern for "the common lot" was once a foreign notion to Serge; it was now central.

In his final articles for *La Melée*, published in February 1919 after he was already in Soviet Russia, though written in December 1918, he spoke of how he and his individualist comrades lacked "an elevated idealism," and how "everything that was grand was done by great idealists."

As for Russia, Serge asked "What is the scope of the social transformations accomplished in Russia? No one can predict it [...] Revolutions take decades to be completed," the French Revolution, he asserted, only reached its end in 1850. Individualists must take part in the events that are unfolding; "Whatever the errors of the moment, we can't be indifferent to historic events upon which the future will be founded and which permit the greatest hope." Serge wants this participation to grow from his anarchist beliefs. "[E]ach must occupy himself with himself [...] to be a new man. To cultivate his intelligence, his will, his originality, his independence his sentiment life, his physical life." But at the same time that the individual must be cultivated, he must "league together in labor, consuming, study, pleasure, the education of children and solidarity."

In concluding this last communication written from France to his French comrades, Serge tells of his "inexpressible joy at going to play my part in the sufferings and labors of all those in Russia who continue the immense undertaking of social transformation."

Serge left his comrades with a final word: "For my part, I head off into the uncertain and the unknown with absolute confidence. The harshest trials only confirmed and ensured my ideas, my concept of living. I remain faithful to my clear ideas, happy to soon be able to serve and realize them through my activities."

The longed-for moment finally arrived. Included in a prisoner exchange for French officers held in Russia, Serge set out for Russia on what he described in his memoirs as a "fine voyage in a first-class berth."[24] It was on this voyage of departure from the West that Serge met "an amazing girl-child of twenty," whom he called "The Bluebird." He spoke of how she invited him and his comrades for tea in a cabin occupied by an old anarchist "who was more enthusiastic than even we were" about Soviet Russia. The Bluebird is unromantically described as the person who brought him news of the murder of Karl Liebknecht and Rosa Luxemburg.[25] The Bluebird was the woman who would be his second wife, Liuba Russakov, who was traveling from France with her entire family, headed by her anarchist father, Alexander. Serge found in the Russakovs the family he was constantly in search of. Just as Rirette and her two daughters served as a ready-made family, the Russakovs gave him a set of like-minded relatives. Victor and Liuba married soon after arriving in Russia, and would eventually have two children, Vlady, born in 1920, and Jeannine, born in 1935. History would put paid to the family idyll. Unhappiness, persecution, madness, and separation would be their fate.

There is a legal twist to Serge's marriage with Liuba. French newspapers reported on February 15, 1927, that the previous day Mme Rirette Maîtrejean had appeared in civil court to obtain a divorce from her husband, Victor Kibalchich. The latter had sent a letter to his estranged spouse, telling her that "I can confirm what you know. I have established myself in the Union of Soviet Socialist Republics, where I have made a new life. It's for you to deduce from these facts all the legal and moral consequences."[26]

The court found for Mme Maîtrejean, granting the divorce for reasons of abandonment. Serge had been bigamous at this point for eight years, having married his second wife Liuba on August 18, 1919.

7

Serge and the Russian Anarchists

Serge arrived in Soviet Russia in January 1919, and in March began working in Petrograd as a deputy to the leader of the Comintern, Grigory Zinoviev. Because of what he considered the weakness of his Russian, he at first turned down the proposed position, but acquiesced when Zinoviev assigned a native Russian speaker to work along with him. The new immigrant was now a senior official and thus enjoyed the perks of members of the *nomenklatura*, like living at the Hotel Astoria, "the foremost 'House of the Soviets,' where the most responsible of the Party's militants resided under the protection of machine guns posted on the ground floor." He and his family were better fed than the common run of the population. Though he was occupied with administrative tasks big and small, propaganda was a key part of his role.[1]

He arrived during a dark period of hunger, of rationing of many goods, but also of enthusiasm, as the Reds and their newly organized Red Army fought off the Western-backed White armies. In the first year of his Soviet life Serge witnessed the victorious resistance of the Red Army:

Yudenich is crushed under the very walls of Petrograd, where Trotsky has set up barricades; a defeat north of Orel disposes of Denikin; his army, harassed in the rear by Makhno and his black [i.e., anarchist] troops, disintegrates and finally, in total disarray, boards ship at Novorossisk; a Red Army, led by Ivan Smirnov, hurls the Whites back in the Urals, while the Red guerillas begin their pitiless campaigns in Siberia. A few months later Admiral Kolchak is handed over to the Reds by Allied officers afraid for their own skins, and shot one moonlit night near Irkutsk with one of his weeping ministers. Their bodies are thrown into the Angara through a hole dug in the ice. In 1920 the English set sail from Archangel, as the French set sail from Odessa the year before; a Revolutionary Committee, presided over by Ivan Smirnov, organizes Soviet Siberia.[2]

These are times of enormous optimism, despite the problems of building a new type of society from scratch. It's little wonder that Lenin celebrated the day in 1918 that the new Soviet state outlived the Paris Commune. And Serge was at the heart of it all, working at the general staff of world revolution, the Third International.

Despite his rapid rise in the Communist hierarchy, Serge always said that he went to Soviet Russia in 1919 as an anarchist and that it was as an anarchist that he joined the Bolsheviks.[3] It was in order to attempt to synthesize these two traditionally opposing schools of revolutionaries that he wrote some of his most important theoretical pieces for *Bulletin Communiste* in the first years of the 1920s. These articles constitute a critique of anarchist activity, but implicitly of Bolshevik activity as well. He attempted to draw out the best of both tendencies, and to have the best of each nullify their worst. They are also revelatory of Serge's state of mind in his first years in Russia. The tragic misfortune of these articles, though, is that they were written at the height of Bolshevik repression of anarchism, and published after the brutal suppression of Kronstadt, of the anarchist forces of Nestor Makhno in the Ukraine, and of anarchist groups in general. His ideas, which might have been fruitful had they been applied, were moot almost before they were published.

The articles examine an essential group of subjects: What is the current state of anarchism, what are the differences between the anarchists and the Bolsheviks, and can they work together?

The pre-Revolutionary anarchist movement had two important things working against it: its own internal divisions and the
harsh repression the tsarist government exercised against it. The
outbreak of the war in 1914 caused even greater disarray in anarchist ranks when the central figure of Russian, indeed, of world,
anarchism, Peter Kropotkin, came out in support of the Russian
war effort, taking a certain number of militants with him. The
result of all this was that "almost all the Russian militants could
be found either overseas [...] in prison, or deported to Siberia."[4]

The February Revolution gave the movement new life, and
from a pre-war total of about 220 members in six groups, their
numbers grew to 40,000 adepts in twenty-three cities in 1917.
Though still not a large movement, it was nevertheless a vibrant
one, containing all the many trends common to anarchism at the
time, and some of its own. Expropriation, for example, was not
an act specific to the better-known Bolshevik groups, of which
Stalin had been a member, and the anarchists had had a strong
and influential wing involved in that activity. Among its most
prominent figures was the later leader of the Ukrainian anarchist
army, Nestor Makhno, who even received a death sentence for his
activities at age nineteen. There were also anarcho-communists,
anarcho-syndicalists, individualists ... Within each wing there
were splits, splits that would grow more important when they
had to decide whether or not to support the Bolsheviks. These
many trends did not constitute an advantage for the movement,
as Serge clearly saw: "The anarchists constituted a scattered,
varied movement divided into poorly delineated and short-lived
movements."[5]

At the sight of this movement rife with internecine disputes,
Serge made an immediate choice:

It was during the first winter that, seeing that in all of the
immense Russia there was only one force—one heroic and
unshakeable—alive and capable of defending the revolution at
a time when no one saw clearly, and even many old militants

despaired, I thought it was my duty to rally to it. I joined the Russian Communist Party as an anarchist, without in any way abdicating my ideas, except for what was utopian about them in contact with reality.[6]

But for Serge, his adherence to communism also represented continuity with his past activity, for he refused the equation that communism equaled dictatorship.

I am only a communist—of libertarian philosophy and ethics—because I see no possibility for the future liberation of the individual outside of a communism called on to evolve a great deal (once it has emerged victorious). To claim that communist ideology leaves no room for the individual thus seems to me to be inexact, though there are unquestionably communists who understand it in this way.

We can read between these lines the fear that the first years of Serge's Soviet life had instilled in him, and the hope it would change. But the change could only occur "once it has emerged victorious." Until then, the choice of communism was clear.[7]

The heart of Serge's criticism of the anarchists was their lack of contact with the real world, their inability to bring their anarchism up to date, to confront the new realities created by a successful revolution. In order to demonstrate the anarchists' isolation from reality he derisively reviewed various of their tendencies, their absurd neologisms (the new group of "interindividualists"), and the bizarre notion of inventing a language constituted of words of one syllable (AO).[8] Remaining in the realm of the vague in which they had long lived, "the lack of a practical program for action— their utopianism—and their lack of organization have killed the anarchist movement in Russia which has expended a prodigious amount of energy in service to the revolution."[9]

But he would always feel that the anarchists had something specific to contribute to the Revolution, that their presence would negate the worst tendencies of Bolshevism. Two decades later he would still write, "If the libertarians were to join in with this movement wouldn't they be enormously useful tomorrow, when it will be a matter of protecting society from bureaucratic sclerosis?"[10]

Writing for a French audience, he pointed out that the Russian anarchists were not alone in this. Serge's anarchist comrades in France had remained stuck in their old ways, and as he piquantly put it, while perusing *Le Libertaire* he felt the pages "could have been published in 1912." The changed circumstances of a world war and a socialist revolution appeared to have been passed over by the anarchists.[11] Twenty years later he would accuse Marxists of the same error.

What then were the issues dividing the Bolsheviks and the anarchists? The principal one was that of dictatorship. Also important was the question of what was to be done during the transitional period after the revolution. For the anarchists, any dictatorship at any point was anathema, a violation of their core principles. Serge quotes the anarcho-syndicalists as saying that "The dictatorship of the proletariat, as the expression of the domination of the organized class, leading to the dictatorship of one party and transforming the Soviet system itself into a bureaucratic, police, and primitive machine, is inadmissible to the anarchist syndicalists." Serge concedes that this is an issue of great consequence, for "in all of history there is no example of a dictatorship that died on its own." But the anarchists (including the just-quoted anarcho-syndicalists) were far from united on this issue, and Serge responded to the syndicalists with the words of the Russian anarchists who had been expelled from the US and settled in Russia, among them Emma Goldman and Alexander Berkman: "The principle of dictatorship must be accepted because organized violence is much more rational than chaotic and arbitrary violence"; because in social revolutions, which are above all the work of "united, convinced, conscious, energetic, and advanced revolutionary minorities," there is no other final recourse than violence. "Precursors of a superior society, the anarchists, in the period of humanity's great revolutionary struggles, must adopt a realistic and positive attitude."[12]

Many anarchists did take such a "realistic and positive attitude." Some of them were close friends of Serge's. The American anarchist Bill Shatov was a particular favorite of Serge. Despite his anarchism, Shatov was a member of the Revolutionary Military Committee that led the October Revolution and a Red Army Commander during the Civil War. (It almost goes without saying that he was shot during the Stalinist purges.) Shatov was not the sole anarchist in the insurrectionary leadership in October 1917. He was joined there by at least three others from various tendencies in the movement, the anarchist-communist Bleikhman, the independent anarchist Bogatsky, and the anarcho-syndicalist Yarchuk.[13]

For many anarchists the threat of a White victory was more dangerous than the Bolshevik dictatorship, which at least had expropriated the capitalists. Anarchists were divided into three groups, those who actively supported the Bolsheviks (and even joined the party, like Shatov), those who were neutral, and those who actively opposed them, opposition that included acts of terror, like the bombing on September 25, 1918, of the Moscow headquarters of the Communist Party, which caused twelve deaths. Anarcho-syndicalists, though, for the most part, supported the Bolsheviks, either actively or passively.[14]

During the Civil War there was no better example of the initial support given the Bolsheviks by anarchists than that of Emma Goldman and Alexander Berkman; their explanation of their reasons holds good for their comrades. Goldman wrote of the moment of her arrival, when her "heart trembled with anticipation and fervent hope"; of "Soviet Russia! Sacred ground, magic people! You have come to symbolize humanity's hope, you alone are destined to redeem mankind. I have come to serve you."[15]

The relations between the two movements constituted a kind of hesitation waltz, with the Bolsheviks alternately welcoming alliance with the anarchists, and even adopting elements of their program. Lenin's *The State and Revolution*, for example, with its promise of an ultimately withered-away state, can be seen as an attempt to use the anarchist program to woo the anarchists. At other times the Bolsheviks actively combatted them. The anarchists acted in a similar fashion, at times working with the Bolsheviks, at others totally rejecting them, although it would probably be more accurate to say that at least until 1921 it was more the case that certain anarchists consistently tried to find a modus vivendi with the Bolsheviks, while others rejected them as enemies of all the anarchists stood for.

In 1919, Lenin praised the anarchists, saying that "many anarchists were becoming the most dedicated supporters of Soviet power."[16] And there were a number of significant figures among the Russian anarchists who supported the Bolsheviks. One, Iuda Roshchin, making the case clearly in 1920: "It is the duty of every anarchist to work whole-heartedly with the Communists, who are the advance guard of the Revolution. Leave your theories alone, and do practical work for the reconstruction of Russia. The need is great, and the Bolsheviks welcome you." Another group, the Universalists, maintained that a temporary dictatorship was a necessary step on the road to anarchism.[17] Other anarchists condemned these supporters of the Bolsheviks, of the "social vampires," as traitors to the cause, sell-outs. "Anarchists," they proclaimed, "must be purged of this watery mixture of Bolshevism in which it is being dissolved by the Anarcho-Bolsheviks and the Anarcho-Syndicalists."[18] Kropotkin himself, the doyen of anarchists, maintained a position of nuanced support for the Bolsheviks:

Not only the workers, but all the progressive forces in the civilized world should put an end to the support given until now to the enemies of the revolution. Not that there is nothing to oppose in the methods of the Bolshevik government. Far from it. But all foreign armed intervention necessarily strengthens the dictatorial tendencies of the government.[19]

The vacillations of Bolshevik policy towards the anarchists are nowhere clearer than in their relations with Nestor Makhno, the Ukrainian anarchist leader. Before the October Revolution Makhno, after being amnestied for his activities as an expropriator, was the head of the Soviet of Guliai-Polei and assembled a peasant army that expropriated large estates. These activities came to an end with the Brest-Litovsk treaty between the Germans and the new Soviet state, which Makhno, like most anarchists, opposed as a surrender to imperialism.

Makhno went to Moscow in the spring of 1918 and met there with Kropotkin and Lenin, who told the anarchist leader that "if only one-third of the Anarchist-Communists were like you, we Communists would be ready, under certain well-known conditions, to join with them in working towards a free organization of producers."[20] Serge reports that he was later told by Trotsky that the Bolshevik leaders had considered granting autonomy to the anarchist peasant region, continuing that "that arrangement would have been just and diplomatic, and perhaps an outlook as generous as this would have spared the Revolution from the tragedy towards which we were drifting."[21] Just two months before Lenin's meeting with Makhno, before the treaty of Brest-Litovsk was even signed, the first serious outbreak of violence between the anarchists and communists had already occurred, when on April 11 the Cheka, the Bolshevik force charged with crushing counter-revolutionary activity, attacked twenty-six buildings occupied by anarchists. The latter, believing their attackers to be Whites, fought back against the Bolsheviks with machine guns. In the aftermath of that fight anarchist organizations were dissolved and the anarchist press banned, though the ban would soon be lifted and then re-imposed and then lifted and then re-imposed.[22]

Upon his return to his native Guliai-Pole, Makhno found the region occupied by Austrian troops and their Ukrainian collaborators. He went to war with them, which ended with the signing of the armistice on November 11, 1918. Makhno and his group seized power, and by early 1919 had begun the establishment of a mini-anarchist state, one which the Bolsheviks left in peace. In March 1919 the Communists even signed a pact for joint action with the anarchists to fight against the White forces under General Denikin. But the friendliness of the Bolsheviks was one of appearance and convenience, and when Makhno called a congress in April the Bolsheviks decreed it to be "counter-revolutionary" and Makhno to be a kulak. The Cheka sent assassins to Guliai-Polei to finish off Makhno, a plot that failed. When in June Makhno called for yet another anarchist conference, the Bolsheviks outlawed Makhno and attacked the region with the Red Army.

But in a clear demonstration of the opportunism of Bolshevik policy, when White General Denikin again became a serious threat in the summer of 1919, the Bolsheviks no longer found Makhno a counter-revolutionary and on September 26, 1919, the Makhnovtsi dealt Denikin his first defeat, at Peregonovka, and Makhno then occupied and communized Ekaterinoslav and Alexandrovsk. Makhno, with the support of anarchist intellectuals like Voline, turned Guliai-Polei into a liberated zone, with a free press and free association, and the dissolution of the Bolshevik-run Revolutionary Committee.

In late 1919 Trotsky ordered Makhno's army to the Polish frontier, but his motives were all too obvious: remove the Makhnovtsi from their base and destroy their anarchist society; the *batko*—the father, as Makhno was called—refused. War broke out between the two revolutionary forces, a war that lasted eight months, until the Whites made their reappearance, when Wrangel launched an offensive, and Makhno and the Bolsheviks became allies yet again. Until, of course, Wrangel was defeated, and in November 1920, the Bolsheviks again turned on Makhno, seizing his commanders and killing or imprisoning them, attacking Guliai-Pole, and ultimately crushing the Makhnovtsi. Makhno had managed to escape the Red clutches, and after a year of wandering, fled Russia and ultimately went to France, where he ended his days as a factory worker.

We can see, then, that the Bolsheviks made use of the anarchists when they needed them, and attempted to destroy them when they didn't. Serge's later analysis of this conduct was justifiably harsh:

> This fantastic attitude of the Bolshevik authorities, who tore up the pledges they themselves had given to this endlessly daring revolutionary minority, had a terribly demoralizing effect; in it I see one of the basic causes of the Kronstadt rising. The Civil War was winding to its close, and the peasantry, incensed by the constant requisitioning, was drawing the conclusion that it was impossible to come to any understanding with "the commissars."[23]

The Bolsheviks' opportunism and wavering didn't only apply to Makhno. In April 1918, months after banning all anarchist activity, the ban would be lifted, and anarchist activity, which was largely based on factory and union organization, began anew. The anarchists' situation would become exceedingly difficult, with Bolshevik–anarchist relations reaching their nadir with the bombing of the Moscow offices of the Communist Party. By 1920 many of the important voices of anarchism, like Voline and Aron Baron, were behind bars. Despite the harsh repression, anarchist ideas were still able to make headway, and Lenin found himself obliged to ban the writings of the French syndicalist Fernand Pelloutier, along with some of the writings of Bakunin and Kropotkin.[24]

Kropotkin, thanks to the aura that surrounded him, was untouchable, though he had been forced to leave Moscow for rural Dimitrovo. There he received a steady stream of visitors, including Berkman and Goldman, who wanted to know why he remained silent as the Bolsheviks warred on his comrades. "Peter smiled sadly. I would know better, he said, after I had been awhile longer in the country. The gag was the most complete in the world." But Kropotkin continued, and explained in a lapidary fashion the core of the anarchist dilemma. "The anarchists in particular are between two fires. They could not make peace with the formidable power of the Kremlin, nor could they join hands with the enemies of Russia. Their only alternative at present, it seemed to Peter, was to find some work of direct benefit to the masses."[25]

Kropotkin died in February 1921. The divided anarchists united for a massive funeral, organized by many of those who had been imprisoned in November of the previous year and who were freed in order to attend.

Serge had never visited Kropotkin, "fearing that any conversation between [them] would be painful," but he was admitted among the anarchist mourners, the only Communist Party member granted this status. The Communists harassed the anarchist attendees, and after lengthy negotiations the Communists allowed black flags to be borne by those marching to the cemetery. The procession headed to the cemetery at Novodevichy, "carrying black flags and banners denouncing tyranny." At the graveside, Aron Baron condemned "the new despotism[,] the butchers at work in their cellars, the dishonor spread upon socialism. The official violence that was trampling the Revolution underfoot."[26] Many of those attending would later be arrested and either imprisoned or expelled from Russia. Serge remained torn.

And then, eighteen days after what would turn out to be the final officially sanctioned anarchist demonstration, Serge received a call during the night of February 18–19, 1921. "Kronstadt is in the hands of the Whites."[27]

8
Kronstadt

By late 1920 the situation in Soviet Russia was critical, and discontent with the Bolsheviks had reached its height. Famine was widespread, and so were revolts: In February 1921 the Cheka reported there were 118 separate peasant uprisings across Russia.[1] Serge, in his novel of an exhausted Petrograd, *Conquered City*, depicts the popular disgust with their plight and the privileges granted those in power:

> The half-empty slums were hungry. The factory chimneys no longer smoked, and when by chance one started smoking, the women, huddling in their rags at the door of a communal store, watched that bizarre smoke climb with bleak curiosity. They're repairing cannons. They get extra rations...—How much? How much?—four hundred grams of bread a day; yeah; but it's not for us, it's only for *them*.[2]

This feeling of "them" versus "us" would culminate in the most wrenching threat to the Bolshevik regime, the Kronstadt uprising. If the Civil War was, in its pitting of Red against White, a black and white affair, Kronstadt, in which the revolutionary sailors of the naval base of Kronstadt, located on an island off Petrograd in the Gulf of Finland, rose against the state they had helped found, posed a threat both existential and moral to the Revolution. For Serge, as with many others, the state's reaction to it would have grave consequences. Serge, based in Petrograd, whose hierarchical superior, Zinoviev, played an important role in the events, was confronted with the most serious of dilemmas: How does a self-proclaimed anarchist-Bolshevik react when those same Bolsheviks attack the people who are defending ideals shared by anarchists?

The sailors revolted as the country descended into the famine that the Civil War and the government policy of War Communism had given rise to, and as the Bolsheviks grew ever closer to the one-party state they would soon officially become. At around this same time a series of strikes were called in Petrograd. The sailors rose in the name of free soviets and a free press, and "the revolt of 1921 was at bottom an effort by the Kronstadters to recapture [the] golden age of spontaneity, and 'All Power to the Soviets' was their slogan."[3] Though motivated by legitimate grievances, there was also an undeniable anti-communist and antisemitic element within the revolt.

There is little doubt that the uprising of March 1921 was spontaneous. Various elements opposed to Bolshevism joined in, not least among them the anarchists, who distributed leaflets among the sailors saying that "Where there is authority, there is no liberty," and condemning the militarization of labor imposed by the Bolsheviks.[4] But Kronstadt was not the work of the enemies of the Revolution; it was the act of a population that felt its revolution had been betrayed.

The Bolsheviks didn't see it this way, and when the revolt broke out on the night of February 28 to March 1, Serge received a call informing him of the uprising and ordering him to his post. Zinoviev quickly had posters put up around Petrograd claiming that the revolt was the work of the counter-revolutionary general Kozlovsky, but those around Serge knew this wasn't the case.

I met comrades, rushing out with their revolvers, who told me that it was an atrocious lie: the sailors had mutinied, it was a naval revolt led by the Soviet [...] The worst of it all was that we were paralyzed by the official falsehoods. It had never happened before that our Party should lie to us like that. "It's necessary for the benefit of the public," said some, who were nonetheless horror-stricken at it all.[5]

Serge's French comrade and future brother-in-law Pierre Pascal, also resident in Russia, confirms that Serge knew the truth of the matter. He later wrote of how the French communists in Russia knew that the news being spread about the revolt was false. And "in order to confirm our judgments we had an antenna in Petrograd in the person of Victor Serge. His presence alongside Zinoviev and his relations in all the circles of the former capital made him the best informed of men."[6]

The government stood firm against the Kronstadt demands which, based on the thesis that "the present Soviets do not represent the will of the workers and peasants," called for the establishing of free speech, press, and assembly, though only for "workers, peasants, anarchists, and left socialist parties," peasant control of the land, and the end to privileges for Communists.[7] The Kronstadt program, as Serge would later say, was a program for "the renewal of the Revolution."[8]

The Communists carried out clumsy attempts at negotiation with the rebels, which were firmly rebuffed, and the situation became increasingly threatening. The revolt couldn't be allowed to continue until the spring thaw, since at that time the rebels' defenses would be impregnable.

In an effort to prevent a catastrophe, Emma Goldman and Alexander Berkman, the two deported American anarchists who had gone to Russia supporting the Revolution but had developed second thoughts while there, attempted to mediate between the two parties, mediation which Serge (whom Goldman refers to in her memoirs as "Kibalchich") was aware of and encouraged. In fact, the group of anarchists met at the home of Serge's in-laws, the Russakovs, though Serge did not attend the sessions, "since it had been decided that only the anarchists would undertake this initiative (in view of the influence they exerted within the Kronstadt Soviet) and that, as far as the Soviet Government was concerned, the American anarchists would take full responsibility for the attempt."[9]

The plea to the Bolsheviks, signed by Goldman, Berkman, and their Russian anarchist comrades Perkus and Petrovsky, said that they would

> fight with arms against any counter-revolutionary attempt, in co-operation with all the friends of the Social Revolution and hand in hand with the Bolsheviki [...] Resort to bloodshed on the part of the Soviet Government will not—in the given situation—intimidate or quiet the workers. On the contrary, it will only serve to aggravate matters, and will strengthen the hands of the Entente and of internal counter-revolution.[10]

At the same time that this plea was being composed, though, Leon Trotsky, a particular bête noire of the rebels for his role in promulgating War Communism and his implementation of the militarization of labor, as well as a lightning rod for the antisemitism that simmered below the surface of the revolt and of all the opposition to the Bolsheviks, went to Petrograd on March 5 and called for immediate surrender by the rebels. "'Only those who do so,' he stated, 'can count on the mercy of the Soviet Republic. Simultaneously with this warning I am issuing instructions that everything be prepared for the suppression of the mutiny by armed force ... This is the last warning.'"[11]

Serge, for his part, later admitted that "After many hesitations, and with unutterable anguish, my Communist friends and I finally declared ourselves on the side of the Party," a decision he reflected on many times in the future, as we will soon see.[12]

On March 16 the Bolsheviks began their attack on the rebels. By March 18, the anniversary of the founding of the Paris Commune, the revolt was over. The fight was brutal, and though estimates of casualties vary wildly, the figures are probably about 10,000 killed and wounded on the Bolshevik side, and 600 dead, 1000 wounded, and 2500 taken prisoner on the rebel side. Of those captured, hundreds were executed.[13]

At the same time that the Kronstadt uprising was occurring, the Communist Party was holding its Tenth Congress, and the

Bolsheviks applied the lesson they'd just learned. Lenin said that Kronstadt proved that "the White Guards strive, and are able, to disguise themselves as Communists, and even as the most left-wing Communists, solely for the weakening and destroying of the bulwark of the proletarian revolution in Russia." The time had come for "the complete elimination of all factionalism," and the Congress "hereby declares dissolved and orders the complete dissolution of all groups without exception on the basis of one platform or another."[14]

Serge summed the situation up in his *Memoirs*:

Emergent totalitarianism had already gone half-way to crushing us [...] What with the political monopoly, the Cheka and the Red Army, all that now existed of the "Commune-State" of our dreams was a theoretical myth. The war, the internal measures against counter-revolution, and the famine (which had created a bureaucratic rationing apparatus) had killed off Soviet democracy.[15]

The crushing of Kronstadt was a climacteric in relations between the Bolsheviks and the anarchists, but even more, in the relations between the Bolsheviks and the masses and any elements of society, within the party or without, with any velleities of opposition. For someone of Serge's libertarian background, for someone who had joined the Bolshevik Party as an anarchist, the experience of the brutal crushing of a working-class revolt can only have been a wrenching event. His contemporary reaction existed on two opposing levels, the public and the private; it is a sign of how painful this event was for Serge that even decades after the fact he was still attempting to come to a final judgment.

The contemporary article in which he wrote most directly about Kronstadt, "The Tragedy of a Revolution," appeared in *La Vie Ouvrière* a year after the event, an article for which French anarchists would never forgive him.[16]

Serge, in this lengthy overview of the difficulties that confronted and continued to confront the Revolution, espoused the point of view of Lenin and Bolshevik theoretician Nikolai Bukharin, that the revolt was one of

"The peasant, petit-bourgeois mentality," which doesn't aspire to socialism and whose sole ideal is the peaceful enjoyment of a plot of land cultivated for the profit of the individual, the lucrative commerce of regional fairs, and the free speech of a rural democracy that, if it were realized would, through its obscurantism and conservatism, be a powerful force for reaction.

Serge also adopted in a mildly modified form the opinions of his boss Zinoviev, and saw the rebels' demands for free soviets as being "exploited by the Social-Revolutionaries, the Mensheviks, the anarchists, even by Communists carried away by the storm who lacked clear-sightedness or were embittered by even more suspect elements, foreign espionage agents and former officers." But these reactionary forces didn't just "exploit" the revolt: They were behind it: White general "Charnov rushed to Reval, [and] Wrangel telegraphed from Constantinople. The Cadets [the Constitutional Democrats, a moderate political party] in Berlin rejoiced. 'Slaughter the Jews' was chalked on the walls of Petrograd." These slogans, Serge omitted to mention, predated the revolt and were the fruit, not of Kronstadt, but of hatred of the Bolsheviks, viewed by the populace as a band of Jews.

He then took his negative view of the rebels to a higher level, and gave voice to the Bolshevik Party's substitution of itself for the masses: Kronstadt "expressed the revolt of backward elements, of an exhausted population, against the stoic and inflexible party that was holding on when everyone else was too tired to, when people would have gladly capitulated in order to have white bread."

A year after Kronstadt, after the crushing of the revolt and the repression of anarchists and the banning of factions at the Tenth Party Congress, Serge had gone public defending the harshest anti-Kronstadt line.

But who was speaking here? Did he truly mean what he was saying, or was he acting as an agent of the government he supported despite it all and which fed him and his family? As we will see, there is much evidence to suggest that Serge, far from believing what he wrote, had great reservations about the event, reservations that appeared in various forms and forums, some authorized by Serge, some not.

A year after this article, another article appeared in the British *Communist Review* in which Serge repeated some of what he said in *La Vie Ouvrière*, but now with more than a hint of sympathy for the rebels and the discontented people.[17] He now admitted that the revolt was set off by legitimate complaints:

> The long winter of famine after the war. Nerves at last stretch. The guns of Kronstadt. Sailors and peasants risen against the Communist Revolution because after such suffering they can do nothing, can understand nothing, and wish for nothing but one thing; cultivate their land and sell what they want to appease their hunger [...] This peasant people need repose. It has bled too much.

A year after "The Tragedy of a Revolution" the desire to cultivate land and to be able to eat are no longer condemned. And though he continues by saying that "too much [is expected] from a wavering mass," he accepts that "a halt is necessary." This understanding of the causes of the revolt brings us closer to what appear to have been Serge's true feelings at the time, feelings reported by anarchist comrades.

The French anarcho-syndicalist Gaston Leval, whom Serge had first met in Barcelona, where Leval had fled after deserting the French army, met with Serge around the time of the revolt. He twice reported Serge's private sentiments, sentiments he would only express to those sharing his (former?) anarchist beliefs. In his first report of their private conversations, Leval reports Serge as having said that "The Kronstadt Affair was a revolt of the masses against the dictatorship of the leaders," and that the party's actions "were the last straw."[18] In his second report he reminds Serge that "during the events at Kronstadt you were in Petrograd with Emma Goldman and Alexander Berkman. 'Something has to be done; we can't allow those people to be massacred like that; we can't just stand by and do nothing.'" Serge then revealed to Leval his dilemma, one that serves as a key to so many of the apparent contradictions between Serge's avowed anarchism, his lifelong belief in liberty, and his propaganda in support of virtually every Bolshevik measure. When Goldman and Berkman asked him to speak out, he said, "I can't do it. I'm known in the party as an anarchist. If I did anything I'd be arrested." Leval also makes the claim that so strong was Serge's disgust that "you, Novomirsky, and two other Communists decided to resign from the party. Only Novomirsky did so."[19] Serge was a prisoner of his past and of his post. His anarchist comrades would show him little forgiveness and understanding, and he remains a pariah to anarchists. In 2011 a book-length attack on Serge was published by an anarchist press entitled *Victor Serge: L'Homme Double* (Victor Serge: The Double Man).

In 1938–39, when he was free to discuss Kronstadt, he wrote several articles on the subject. In these articles, responding to Trotsky's defense of the brutal suppression of the uprising, Serge took the position held by the anarchists at the time, the one he privately expressed in the 1920s.

The event, he said, was not subject to just one interpretation:

Bourgeois liberals, Mensheviks, anarchists, and revolutionary Marxists consider the drama of Kronstadt from different standpoints and for different reasons, which it is well and necessary to bear in mind, instead of lumping all the critical minds under a single heading and imputing to all of them the same hostility towards Bolshevism.

The country was at an impasse, and questions needed to be posed then that have to be posed now. "Who then was right? The Central Committee which clung to a road without issue or the masses driven to extremities by famine? It seems to me undeniable that Lenin at that time committed the greatest mistake of his life."[20]

Despite his outrage, he had remained silent, and in 1942 he wrote in his notebooks that he had had "sympathy for the Workers' Opposition, but feared[ed] that its faculty for falling apart was greater than its capacity for organization and rebuilding."[21]

Shortly after publishing his reevaluation of Kronstadt in *New International*, he returned to the subject for the French syndicalist magazine *La Révolution prolétarienne*, discussing the matter of the severity of the repression, and again echoed the theses of the anarchists in 1921:

Living in Petrograd I lived among the leaders of the city. I know through eyewitnesses what the repression was. I visited anarchist comrades at the Chpalernaya Prison, imprisoned, by the way, against all good sense [...] I repeat, the repression was atrocious. According to Soviet historians, insurgent Kronstadt had at its disposal around 16,000 combatants. A few thousand succeeded in reaching Finland over the ice. The others were massacred in the hundreds, and more likely in the thousands, at the end of the combat or later.[22]

Facts that drove anarchists away from the revolution in its early days and that Serge had denied at the time were now openly discussed and accepted.

But Serge was far from through with his reflections on Kronstadt, and in an unpublished document, dating probably from 1943, he once again spoke critically of the rebels, saying that "the sailors' demands were just, but their rebellion placed the revolution a hairsbreadth from its destruction," and then goes further, alleging that "while the attack on Kronstadt was being prepared [...] the party committee learned that an infantry regiment, arrived from Lithuania, was going to go over to the insurrection under the command of officers who were nothing but counter-revolutionaries." And so, once again, the rebels were opening the door to counter-revolution.[23]

His final public word on the subject appeared in his memoirs. There Serge makes his sympathies abundantly clear. "Kronstadt had right on its side. Kronstadt was the beginning of a fresh, liberating revolution for popular democracy: 'The Third Revolution!' it was called by certain anarchists whose heads were stuffed with infantile illusions." But Serge, recognizing the justness of the Kronstadt cause almost a quarter century after the event, remained steadfast that opposing it was the only way to ward off the worst:

> However, the country was absolutely exhausted and production practically at a standstill [...] The Party, swollen by the influx of power-seekers inspired little confidence [...] If the Bolshevik dictatorship fell, it was only a short step to chaos, and through chaos to a peasant rising, the massacre of Communists, the return of the émigrés, and in the end, through the sheer force of events, another dictatorship, this time anti-proletarian.

The sailors were right, as the anarchist Kibalchich knew, but their timing was wrong, the Communist Serge wrote.[24]

In his autobiographical account Serge confirms Gaston Leval's claim that he had intended to leave the Communist Party at this time and provides an explanation for failing to do so. When told by a group of comrades that he couldn't involve himself in mediation efforts between the government and the rebels because he was bound by party discipline, he responded, "One can leave a party. They replied, cold and serious that a Bolshevik does not leave his Party. And anyway, where would you go? You have to face it, there is no one but us."[25]

Finally, the sailors he had once called "a powerful force for reaction" he now, and no doubt then, judged differently. "Those defeated sailors belonged body and soul to the Revolution; they had voiced the suffering and the will of the people; the NEP [New Economic Policy] had proved that they were right."[26]

The massacre of the sailors and Serge's silence in defense of them would serve to irreparably envenom his relations with the anarchists in France.

9

The Anarchists Against
Victor Serge

The French anarchist reaction to the Bolshevik Revolution was filled with the same enthusiasm, fears, and confusion as among anarchists all over the world. Here, at last, in the home of the *knout*, Siberian exile, and fierce repression was a successful revolution, and for many anarchists it deserved at least reserved support.

The French anarchist Rhillon, who also contributed to the Belgian anarchist press, wrote in 1919 that it was "thanks to the libertarian economic program that the revolution won." Rhillon harbored no illusions concerning the Bolsheviks, who won "because they were better organized and, even more, because they were devoid of any scruples." The anarchists were, of course, angered at the government's repression of anarchist activities, but

> despite espionage, despite denunciations, despite repression, the libertarian idea continues to progress and be put into practice. A clear evolution towards federalism is making itself manifest. From the force of events, Bolshevism itself is evolving, and in evolving it is disappearing. It is making way for a more flexible, a more fertile organization.

All was far from lost, and the Revolution was on its way to fulfilling the anarchist dream.[1]

Even in 1921, after Kronstadt and the Bolshevik ordered dissolution of anarchist groups, as important a figure as Sébastien

Faure could recall the anarchists' support for the Bolsheviks, who founded their state on a "federalist" basis, a foundation dear to the anarchists. Faure, like Serge, viewed the early days of the Revolution as days of promise, despite their evident flaws: "It must be said that this wasn't the immediate and complete realization of the anarchist ideal, but was it possible with one leap to jump over the abyss separating bourgeois society from libertarian communist society? But it opened the door to all the possibilities for the future." Whatever negative stories were spread concerning the Soviet state about "workers' riots in the cities and peasant uprisings in the countryside" were subject to caution, being "visibly tendentious and even made unlikely by their obvious exaggeration or their manifest falsehood."

Eventually, though, it became clear to Faure that many of the falsehoods were truths, and that the comrades who reported the facts "attempted to justify as imperious necessity all the acts, measures, and attitudes that alone could excuse and explain the problems of life or death."

He ultimately found himself forced out of his silence, as the uncontested pro-Bolshevik campaign took on such a scope that the communists were able to win over large masses of French workers and confuse anarchists, who were left with no weapons to win back the workers. The silence of the most outspoken anarchists left the impression on some that "there were no more anarchists in Paris, and on others that we'd entered the Communist Party en bloc. Finally, others interpreted our reserve [...] as tacit adherence to the thesis of dictatorship during a revolutionary period."[2]

In this post-Kronstadt period the anti-Bolshevik heat—and with it anti-Serge sentiments and resentments—could only mount. Gaston Leval wrote of a visit with Alexandra Kollontai, one of the leaders of the left-wing Workers' Opposition within the Bolshevik Party, a faction that had been attacked and banned at the party congress in March 1921, at the exact moment of the defeat of the Kronstadt rebels. Kollontai spoke of the impossible position of the Oppositionists, saying how "we can't do anything, not publish a newspaper or organize a single meeting to speak of our theses on the role of unions."

Serge was attacked for his silence concerning all these events, Leval throwing back at him words spoken in private conversation. In the wake of Kronstadt and the banning of all anarchist groups, thirteen Russian anarchists had gone on a hunger strike, and Leval claimed that Serge said at the time that "their opposition was always perfectly legal and that they are individuals above any suspicion [...] Aside from Voline [the publicist of the Makhno movement], none of them have gone beyond the framework of Bolshevik legality." Leval reminded Serge of the latter's private defense of the sailors and told Serge that "I reproduced in *Le Libertaire* what you told me about Kronstadt, which is the exact opposite of what you wrote in *La Vie Ouvrière*."[3]

As the Russian Revolution strayed further and further from those of its ideals that were consonant with those of the anarchists, and as Serge became more deeply involved in Bolshevism and increasingly visible as a propagandist for the ruling party, anarchist hatred, particularly the hatred of his former French comrades, grew increasingly fierce. The campaign against Serge in France became especially virulent in 1921, after the publication of his previously mentioned articles on anarchism, which attempted to draw more anarchists over to Bolshevism, while condemning anarchists for their refusal to accept that times had changed. But these articles, and the attacks, also coincided with the crushing of Kronstadt, which definitively alienated many anarchists from the Revolution. When anarchists were being executed by the government Serge so adamantly defended, no other reaction could be expected. Any anarchist who would have followed Serge's advice to come and support the new state now risked imprisonment or Siberia or worse.

The anti-Serge chorus was loud and large, some of its soloists having a long and unpleasant history of relations with Serge.

Rhillon had locked horns with Le Rétif in 1908 over the question of violence and re-appropriation, which Rhillon strongly supported. At that time, Serge criticized his older comrade for his apparent acceptance of the notion that the end justifies the means and for his advocacy of hatred as a positive factor in the revolutionary struggle. Serge had written, "An end always implies a morality from which the means to attain it automatically follow."[4] Rhillon's response was derisive, referring to Serge as "juvenile" (Serge, it should be noted, was seventeen when the article appeared) and claiming that his ideas were full of "Tolstoyan resignation and Buddhist passivity."

Rhillon's scorn for Serge had only grown over the years, and he wrote a scathing attack in *Le Libertaire* entitled "A 'Virtuous Revolutionary': Victor Serge."[5] The direct pretext for this article was not Kronstadt or the Bolsheviks, but rather Serge's article in the January 5, 1922, issue of the Comintern publication *Bulletin Communiste* on "Bakunin's Confession," which had raised the hackles of many anarchists for its depiction of Bakunin as an erring mortal who, in a moment of weakness, had written a confession of his activities to the tsar. For Rhillon, Serge was nothing more than "a paid liar and slanderer."

Rhillon presented the French readers of 1921 with a review of Serge's Belgian life, one they might not have been familiar with. Along the way he also revised his own version, portraying the young Serge as an individualist extremist, attributing to Serge the positions Serge had criticized him for a decade earlier. Rhillon recounts how Serge and a "half-dozen of his 'buddies'" founded a group, took control of the newspaper *Le Révolté* and turned it towards support of illegalism. Serge and his Belgian brothers did, indeed, convert the newspaper *Le Communiste* to *Le Révolté*, and though Serge had written in support of illegalism while in Belgium, Rhillon had done so in far stronger and more uncompromising terms.

Rhillon attempted to establish continuity between the "indignity" of Kibalchich and that of Serge by describing how

Victor left Brussels after the Hartenstein Affair of 1909, "but not until having extorted 50 francs from me on the pretext of providing urgently needed assistance to Hartenstein." Rhillon, who in 1908 condemned Serge's "Tolstoyism" now implied that his opponent was an active illegalist, "never working, but living on who knows what and practicing counterfeiting." He claims that these practices continued in Paris, where counterfeiting was carried out at *l'anarchie* "in broad daylight, on a large scale, and openly bragged about."

Serge was, according to Rhillon, nothing but a swindler and a fraud, cheating a Bulgarian comrade of money and then having his friends pull guns on the latter when he asked for it back. Rhillon rehearsed the history of the Bonnot Gang, but in his version it is Serge who was the one who led his comrades down the garden path. None of them had "ever strayed from anarchist principles as we see them in our classics. But from the day these young men left their country to place themselves under the moral rule of the Smerdiakov of anarchy nothing could save them."

In summary, for Rhillon Le Rétif should have on his conscience the deaths and imprisonments of the members of the Bonnot Gang, "but the Dostoevsky character that is Le Rétif—today Victor Serge—has this particular trait: he has no conscience. What difference are corpses to him?"

In this perfect exemplar of anarchist attacks on Serge, his anarchism and his Bolshevism are consistent:

It is every bit as natural that a Kibalchich be elevated to honors by a regime that owes everything to force and ruse, to violence and lies, as it is understandable that the real anarchists—I mean those of inflexible morals—suffer in the prisons or are murdered by that same regime.

The task assigned by the Soviets to Serge, "that of preparing in France a working-class mentality suitable for the exercising of a dictatorship [...] at least called for it to have been taken up by serious and disinterested spirits; that Moscow's theses be spread by men who are clean." For Rhillon, in setting Serge to this task the Bolsheviks found "the most cynical and most rotten of the rejects of anarchy." A Kibalchich who remembers having been "consciously unscrupulous" was what the Bolsheviks needed to unfailingly exercise a profession that was, after all, nothing but the continuation of his former life."

Rhillon's vision of Serge is a looking glass version of Serge's own. For Serge, his Bolshevik life was, indeed, "a continuation of his former life," but in a radically different way. It meant the injection of anarchism into Bolshevik statism; it was an attempt to ensure the growth of freedom under the new state. For Rhillon, Serge had never been sincere in anything he'd done, and now his insincerity had found a boss willing to pay him for it. There was really no way for these two viewpoints to meet.

Rhillon was far from alone in his visceral and unmeasured criticism of Serge. For the French anarchists there is no baseness Serge isn't capable of now, or wasn't capable of in the past, however absurd.

Maurice Wullens, an anarchist whose review *Les Humbles* Serge would later write for, recounted his meeting with a former fellow prisoner of Serge's at Melun, a man who "neither theorizes nor pontificates," as Wullens phrases it. Having taken up his old life of crime and feeling the need to get out of France, Wullens suggested to his anonymous source that he go to Russia to meet up with his former fellow prisoner, Serge. Wullens's informant was horrified by the suggestion.

You see all of this from a distance, with the halo of legend. Kibalchich a theoretician of anarchism? He's nothing but one more idol to be torn down. He explained to me how in prison Victor Serge would show off to the prisoners, talking to them about his relations in the imperial Russian court and how, less brilliantly, he abandoned all dignity in the face of the guards

[…] Doesn't this unpretentious little tale fill out the portrait of this sad little man?

That Serge had no such relations at the court, that he had never in his life demonstrated a tendency to invent such relations, and had always proposed not the court but those most violently opposed to it as exemplary figures, none of this mattered to the editors of *Le Libertaire*. Serge had betrayed them and there was nothing he wasn't capable of.[6]

Gaston Leval drew the widow of Peter Kropotkin into the ad hominem war. Leval proposed to the anarchist prince's widow that he publish a rectification to an account Serge wrote of Kropotkin's funeral, which was the last hurrah of the anarchist movement Kropotkin had so nobly represented. She rejected this idea. "No, I beg you, don't respond. Kropotkin's name is too great to be placed alongside that of Kibalchich."[7] And in a footnote to an article Leval wrote on repression in Russia, he tells his readers that "in a future issue I will say what we should think of the wretch named Kibalchich."[8]

In the introduction to an article by Alexander Berkman on Kronstadt, Louis Lecoin, a militant anarcho-syndicalist, pacifist, and anti-militarist, disposed of Serge with disgust:

> As for Kibalchich, well-known to his old comrades for his backtracking and thousand acts of cowardice, we'll talk about him later. We'll pass the pen to friends who saw him in Russia and who will prove that the protagonist of illegalism, the pre-war anti-communist and anti-revolutionary, is even more abject today.[9]

No response is possible to such vicious and unprovable attacks, which could do nothing but drive Serge, a man always certain of his own rectitude, further into the adverse camp.

Serge did, however, reply to his detractors in an open letter published in the March 11, 1921, issue of *Le Libertaire*, though the letter was written on February 21, just before the sailors' uprising.[10] Serge defends himself against the personal attacks of which he was victim, in which he had even been mocked for his past affectation of a Russian blouse and for living in Russia in a relatively luxurious hotel. The predominant tone of his response, though, is one of hurt and genuine puzzlement. Never having insulted anyone in any of his articles, he asks, "In what way have I deserved to be insulted by you, comrades of *Le Libertaire?*" He wonders if it was because he said that the recently deceased Kropotkin had died "surrounded by the best of care and the greatest respect?" But most importantly, he condemns the campaign against him for being "unworthy of anarchists [...] Your entire campaign against the dictatorship is carried out in a tone that is far from being that of a discussion of ideas and facts." He condemns the French anarchists for their "false allegations and their many tendentious interpretations," but renounces correcting them, certain as he is that his responses "would not be published." The timing of his response could not have been worse, for he also wrote that "a great number of Russian anarchists would not understand your way of posing the question, and many of them accept the principle of proletarian dictatorship." Though the last clause was certainly true, by late March, 1921, many anarchists had been executed or imprisoned and could neither accept nor deny Serge's claims. Serge was not naïve enough to think this response would put matters to rest or calm anarchist rage, and ended it hoping he would not be insulted. That hope would be denied.

Le Libertaire's response appeared directly beneath his letter, and he was immediately accused of "playing fast and loose with the truth." He was accused of backtracking on statements he had previously made about anarchist opposition to the Bolshevik dictatorship, about anarchists being counter-revolutionaries. The paper's final word on Serge was that he was an acknowledged agent of a government that imprisons and executes our brothers in anarchy [...] And Victor Serge, who still proclaims himself an anarchist, should blush in shame for enjoying certain favors, for certain tasks and for his ability to flood the Bolshevist press of this country while the anarchists over there are doomed to the cruelest silence.

Serge could not win, and it was partially because of things he had said in private conversations, conversations that had been leaked to the wider anarchist world.

10
Victor Serge Against Kibalchich

Whatever the veracity and sincerity of what Serge was writing or not writing for public consumption, we have several accounts by ex-comrades that his private sentiments were not the same as his public ones. His libertarian sentiments had not been completely expunged, nor were his eyes closed to the disaster that surrounded him.

Angel Pestaña was an anarcho-syndicalist from Barcelona who attended the second congress of the Communist International, a congress at which he made three speeches "on the alleged necessity for the existence of the Communist Party."[1] Unlike so many of the attendees, Pestaña was unafraid to play the part of the "heretic," and "laid out the point of view of the syndicalists of the CNT ... [which] had nothing in common with the state system established in Russia by Lenin, or the organizational principles adopted by the Congress for the parties that intended to join the Communist International."[2] Serge met often with the anarchist attendees, who included the Italian Armando Borghi and the Frenchmen Augustin Souchy (representing the Swedes and Germans) and Jules Lepetit, a group Serge found "admirable" but who were "ignorant of political economy and had never posed the problem of power," and so were stuck in their "romantic position of the 'universal revolution' as it was represented by the libertarian artisans between 1848 and 1860, before the formation of large-scale modern industry and the proletariat."[3] His discussions with these anarchist attendees were to play a vital role in his analysis of the role of anarchists in his article "The Experience of the Russian Revolution."[4]

Installed like most of the delegates at Petrograd's Hotel International, "Pestaña received an unexpected visit from an old fellow-warrior and friend, Victor Serge [...]. In private conversations the latter told him about the negative aspects of the revolution, showing him, so to speak, the dark side of the moon."[5]

Armando Borghi left a longer account of his conversations with Serge. Borghi was a *rara avis* in Petrograd, an Italian anarchist, and he was invited to meet with countless individuals, always accompanied, or rather, as he termed it, "guarded," by his interpreter.[6] Borghi and Serge had known each other in Paris, so it was natural that the two would meet privately in Petrograd.

Serge and Borghi made an appointment to meet, and Borghi went to see Serge, accompanied by a Spanish comrade. When Serge opened the door and saw Borghi and the Spaniard he asked what he could do for them. Borghi reminded him of their appointment and Serge explained that "he had misunderstood and that, in any case, he had to leave on important matters."

Borghi returned to his room, and when his phone rang it was Serge, who repentantly invited Borghi back to see him immediately. Serge explained that he had told Borghi to come alone, but that he'd been accompanied by the Spaniard. "'But the Spaniard is a comrade,' [Borghi] said." "'I understand. You come from Europe.'"

Serge then unburdened himself: "The soviets were swallowed up by the Communist Party. The leaders all spy on each other. Any dissent is treason and any act of treason results in elimination. The factory system is ruthless. Trotsky is a perfect tyrant. What we have is neither communism, nor socialism, nor anti-communism, but Prussianism."

Borghi wanted to know why Serge continued to support the Bolshevik state. Serge explained that "He was and remained an anarchist, but what was the sense of having himself killed for an opposition that was worth less than zero? No one would understand; no one would follow. No one would know. He'd be taken for a spy and nothing else. This was the horrible logic of totalitarianism." It's a demonstration of the strength of the revolutionary dream that despite what Serge had told Borghi, the latter did not reject the revolution, but rather exercised "prudence" in his observations.[7]

Marcel Body was a French socialist who, after participating in the French military mission in Russia stayed on and was a founder of the French Communist Group, of which Serge was a member. Body, who would become disenchanted with Soviet Russia and leave both it and communism behind, was a co-worker of Serge's, writing and translating for the Comintern.

He later wrote of what he called Serge's "split personality." Body recalls that "whenever Victor Serge thought he could express himself freely, he delivered a withering attack on the party and the state system established by Lenin and Trotsky [...], [w]hich didn't prevent him from glorifying the party and its actions in his writings." Body observed that Serge, as we have seen in these examples, carefully chose who to unburden himself to, and he only did so "if he had before him an interlocutor who contested the party and the Soviet bureaucracy." Body in his memoirs expanded on this, finding this split characteristic of Serge until his death. "On one hand, there was in him the eternal Le Rétif, and on the other, the writer with a fertile imagination." Body even credits the bursting forth of Serge's talents as a writer to his woes under Stalin.

> As long as Victor Serge applied himself to sticking to the party line in his writings, he produced nothing interesting. His Bolshevik conformism sterilized him. He only began to find his true literary stature from the moment Stalin's henchmen deported him. He then found himself, discovered his own literary vein, and allowed it to flow.[8]

There is much to be said for Body's point of view.

Maurice Vilkens was another French anarchist to whom Serge opened himself, and who revealed what was said. Vilkens, who spent six months in Russia and sent regular articles to *Le Libertaire*, wrote in February 1921 that Serge attacked the Bolshevik government's policy on foreign concessions. He had told Vilkens that, in this system of coming to terms with foreign capital, "it's entirely likely that we'll lose and we'll expose ourselves, even if the communists remain in power, to re-establishing in Russia a more or less disguised form of capitalism." There was a way out though, and that was

allowing the working people to take the initiative, to have the freedom to take production into their own hands and allow them to live under their own responsibility with the cooperation of all revolutionary elements. End the terror and work with the masses to realize their aspirations and initiatives. In truth, in doing so we will expose ourselves to being crushed by the people, who will take revenge for the failings and errors from which they have suffered.[9]

The best known of the anarchists to report on Serge's real feelings was Maurice Vandamme, better known as Mauricius, Serge's wife Rirette's former lover, and one of the leading figures of individualist anarchism. During his difficult visit to Russia in 1920, during which he was arrested for his alleged activities as a police informant in France, he visited with Serge in Petrograd. Mauricius tells us that, when discussing the state of the Revolution, "the words that fall from his lips are implacable and ferocious verdicts." Mauricius asked about the Bolshevik policy regarding the elderly, and received "a surprised look," and then Serge responded, "The elderly?" he said. "There are no more elderly, they're all dead."

Mauricius also reported on a conversation between the French Communist journalist Raymond Lefebvre and Serge. Lefebvre told Serge that whatever else was the case,

There's at least one indisputable fact, and that's that the peasants own the land and are free.

Kibalchich looked at him with an ironic smile on his face and said, in his gentle voice: "It's true that the peasants are free, but it's because there aren't enough militia to oppress them. They own the land, of course, but that's because a way of taking it from them hasn't yet been found."

I heard this with my own ears. You can draw your own conclusions.[10]

The most significant first-person account of Serge's feelings appeared in *Le Libertaire* in March 1922.[11] It was the result of a conversation he'd had with Gaston Leval. A member of the Spanish CNT, he was sent by that organization to Soviet Russia in 1921, where he met with Serge on June 1. Twenty years later Serge would write in his notebooks that Leval's publication of their discussions was an act of "perfidy," and it is easy to see why.[12] Leval clearly knew that publication of their talks would be controversial, and that there was every chance Serge would deny that any such conversations took place, as he begins the article by saying, "let him dare to deny me." The title of the article sums up Victor's situation in Russia: "Victor Serge against Kibalchich. Kibalchich against Victor Serge."

Leval brought out the schism within Serge, as over the course of their lengthy conversation, "Kibalchich often again becomes Victor Serge or, more precisely, he was at one and the same time both men. At 2.00 p.m. the implacable demolisher of the Bolshevik state and government, and at 2.15 the ardent defender of the Bolshevik state and government." Serge's conflicted state in the early 1920s can't be better or more simply expressed.

Leval asked Serge what he thought of the general situation. "I am very pessimistic. We've survived four winters but we won't survive a fifth. The people are exhausted and the counter-revolutionaries are gaining ground every day. We're in retreat.

"And how are things going in the Communist Party?"

"The latent argument between the masses and the leaders is only growing worse. The former complain of too much centralization and dictatorship. They demand the right to more initiative, more freedom of thought and action. But since the vote on Lenin's motion at the Tenth Congress of the Party, the repression against the left has only increased. Lenin is a veritable dictator. He doesn't discuss, he punches. He gags the opposition by using all possible means: imprisonment, deportations, mobilization ... That's why I intend to leave here. Maybe I'll go to Spain."

"But you know the repression we're suffering under."

"It's better to have to fight against the bourgeoisie than against revolutionaries."

"So centralization hasn't been a success?"

"Centralization has ruined industry and disorganized production."

"And the unions?"

"There are no unions. On paper there are eleven million mandatory union members, threatened with sanctions in the event of refusal .... The unions play no role ...."

Of course, the two key questions of the moment were Kronstadt and the Cheka, and Serge was equally categorical on both subjects:

"What was the Kronstadt Affair?"

"The Kronstadt Affair was a revolt of the masses against the dictatorship of the leaders."

"And the Cheka?"

"The Cheka has become a counter-revolutionary institution that no one knows how to rid us of ...."

Leval could hardly allow these obvious contradictions between Serge's writings and his thoughts to pass unchecked, and pointed this out. Serge answered: "Everything I wrote was written before the Kronstadt insurrection. I've written nothing since, for that was the last straw." And in a moment of bravado and shame, Serge told Leval, "We're reaching a moment when it will be shameful to remain at liberty. I've reached a point where I want to be arrested."

The overall tone of Leval's article is an angry one, typical of the articles written by French anarchists about Serge, arraigning him for "his lies and sophisms," for his "conscious falsehoods," and finally, condemning him as "the most contemptible scoundrel I met in Moscow." That wasn't all. He said of Serge that he was still "the same amoral or immoral man he once was, not caring a whit for those who read him, wanting only to attain renown as a writer and to live well."

But Leval, though he had no sympathy for Serge's plight, reported him as saying that "if it was known that I told you all this I'd be executed." And yet, we know of no ill consequences suffered by Serge when what he said was published. We can easily understand why Serge would consider the publication of these conversations an act of "perfidy." Gaston Leval, in order to attack the Bolsheviks, placed Serge's life and freedom at risk. But Serge couldn't deny what was reported, and Vilkens for his part had named several witnesses to his conversation with Serge who could verify that his reporting was exact.[13] Serge, the Comintern functionary, considered Lenin a dictator, the Cheka counter-revolutionary, the unions a sham, and Kronstadt legitimate.

There was, however, one anarchist visitor to whom one would have expected Serge to have made similar comments but who, at least in her memoirs, gives no hint of this. Shortly after Emma Goldman's arrival in Russia she visited "the young anarchist Kibalchich" at the Astoria Hotel, where she complained of the perks received by Bolsheviks, the better food, better lodging, and better schools than those of ordinary Russians. She asked an old anarchist comrade from America as well as Zinoviev how this could be justified, and "all of them repeated the same refrain: 'What will you, with the blockade around us, the sabotage of the intelligentsia, the attacks of Denikin and Yudenich.'"[14] Though she met with Serge frequently, this is the only mention of him in any of her writings about Russia. She might have remained silent about any comments because at the time Goldman's memoirs were published, 1931, Victor was in a Stalinist camp, and any further accounts of his anti-Bolshevism might well have cost him his life.

11
Why?

Emma Goldman's bitter disappointment with the Russian Revolution when she experienced its somber reality led her to ask an important question: "If the Revolution really had to support such brutality and crime, what was the purpose of the Revolution after all?"[1] In a sense, there is no other question than this one, for if a revolution is fought to make life better, but instead brings the people dictatorship and famine, a famine Serge later described as "organized," then what is its reason for being?[2] Is a revolution considered successful merely by staying in power, if in doing so it has to betray all it stood for, and if it requires the individual revolutionary to betray all his most dearly held ideals? Emma Goldman could pose this question; Victor Serge couldn't, or at least, didn't. This is the matter we must examine.

Deported from her beloved America, Goldman went to Russia, like so many revolutionaries, expecting to find the new world of which she'd dreamed all her life. She was accompanied by Alexander Berkman, who, like Serge, had a Narodnik hero in his family, and he, like Serge, had held the Narodniki up as the *beau idéal* of revolutionism. They saw many, if not all, of the same things Serge did, but there came a point for Goldman and Berkman, the point being Kronstadt and the subsequent general repression, when they could no longer accept Soviet Russia as a valid revolutionary alternative.

What was it that held Serge back? What made a man whose entire past life had been built on individual freedom, and whose future life would return to that theme, unable to say "no"?

That he sincerely felt love for the Revolution despite its failings is undeniable. As he wrote to his friend and comrade Paul Fouchs,

"However tragic the things around me might be, and even more the current moment, I am a fervent, stoically enthusiastic witness of the work of the revolution. And believe me when I say that I remain in all regards a revolutionary, faithful to himself and our common idea."[3] It is, of course, possible that he wrote this letter knowing it would pass through the hands of censors, and that saying anything other than this was risky. But it is nevertheless safe to assume that Serge was sincere in this letter to his old friend. Serge also wrote in 1920 in his article on the anarchists in Russia that, in joining the Communists,

> I soon realized that this attitude imposed real sacrifices on me from the point of view of my freedom of individual action, and important concessions on principles. With complete clarity of spirit I still consent to this. Sacrifices and concessions are imposed on the anarchist militant (if he joins the CP [Communist Party] or not) not before a doctrine or an organization, but in the face of the revolution itself, whose interests are the supreme law. For the revolution it's a question strictly of living and winning.[4]

These notions of party discipline and the need to win are key to understanding Serge's Soviet dilemma.

But we must still square the matter of, as Gaston Leval called it, "Kibalchich versus Serge." Why, knowing what he knew, seeing what he saw, saying what he did in private conversations, did he consider this party loyalty the primary, indeed the only, concern.

Marcel Body, his fellow member of the French Communist Group in Russia, attributed Serge's duplicity to the political atmosphere, but also to his taste as a *littérateur* for fabulation. As Luc Sahagian phrased it in his harshly critical book on Serge, "As he grew older, the scoundrel child continued his misdeeds by giving himself over to the activities of a writer, at first in service to the party, and then in service to his imagination." He concludes, "The liar ends up convincing himself of the truth of his lies from the moment they appear in print."[5] Harsh, but there just might be something to this. Paradoxically, Serge's novels would paint a particularly dark picture of the early days of the Soviet state. His novel *Conquered City*, published in France in 1932, is a far grimmer depiction of Soviet life in 1919 than that presented in a non-fiction work like *From Lenin to Stalin*. In the latter the real heroism of the nascent Red Army and the amazing feats of organization in the midst of the Civil War are front and center. In *Conquered City* dreams are confronted with reality, and come off second best.

But there is obviously more. There is the inescapable presence of fear. Emma Goldman felt that this was the dominant, perhaps the sole reason for Serge's unwillingness to go against the party at the moment of Kronstadt.[6] Serge was now a family man and had to protect his wife and son and his in-laws, the extended Russakov family, who, we will recall, were also returned exiles. Had he crossed the party he might have lost not only his job but also his home, and having no other citizenship than Soviet he would have had nowhere to go. Gaston Leval phrased Serge's dilemma crudely and negatively, but perhaps correctly: "He had to play his role, fulfill the functions assigned to him by 'his boss Zinoviev.' He was paid for it and lived off it."[7] In Soviet Russia, where food and lodging were far from assured, he was relatively well paid and well housed.[8] Goldman's comrade Berkman found there was only one excuse for Serge's duplicity: His fears for his wife and son.

As a party member he was bound by party discipline, and if in 1919 it was still possible to dissent within limits, it would soon be impossible to do even that. After the crushing of Kronstadt and the nearly simultaneous suppression of the Workers' Opposition, called for by Lenin and Bukharin and overwhelmingly supported by the party, it would have been professionally suicidal. So here again he was hemmed in, both practically and politically. As he told Gaston Leval, he could have been arrested or shot at any moment for sympathizing with or aiding the "counter-revolu-tion." Like so many other revolutionaries who came to Russia seeking safety, he was actually at great risk there. In this sense, there is nothing unique in his situation. His silence spared him the fate of hundreds of anarchists and early oppositionists.

Despite his sympathies for many anarchist positions, the time was not ripe for such criticisms. Defense of the Revolution was Serge's primary concern, and if he felt that criticism would weaken it then he would not engage in it. There was enough criticism of the Bolsheviks from outside Russia; joining in made one an objective ally of reaction, and that was simply not an option. And though it's not necessarily a defense, his views were in harmony with the behavior of other rank-and-file Communists at the time, as attested to by the fact that, except for the banned Workers' Opposition, there were few protests within the party for its anti-democratic turn, and for Serge that was the only place where it mattered.

Serge's unflinching defense of the Bolsheviks against anarchist claims that its rule was as harsh as that of the tsar had led to ferocious ad hominem attacks on Serge. That Serge would have felt himself backed into a corner by his former comrades and unable to publicly admit to hesitations is all too natural.

Another reason for his silence about the repression in Russia, and particularly that of anarchists is, ironically, his own anarchism. His openness about his anarchist tendencies and, more impor-tantly, his anarchist past made him suspect. Marcel Body, the French Communist resident in Russia, was quite up front about this: "Of individualist anarchist formation, Victor Serge was, if not suspect, at least considered a doubtful element, but also quite useful for the work expected of him. He didn't delay in rendering the services asked of him."[9] In order to allay any suspicions of his fealty Serge was obliged—in public at any rate—to be more Bolshevik than the Bolsheviks. He couldn't allow the existing suspicions to be confirmed in any way, and if he had supported the Workers' Opposition or the Kronstadt rebels, or defended the arrested anarchists, he would have done nothing but confirm the worst suspicions of him. And so, he remained silent.

In 1937 Serge would present a defense of his failure to do more for threatened anarchists in the pages of *La Révolution prolétarienne*.[10] He noted that anarchists have attacked him over the years for "not having exerted myself sufficiently in the USSR in Lenin's time, against the repression of anarchism." He claims he did all he could "to get it halted or diminished," continuing, "I could not achieve a great deal." Writing in the middle of the Spanish Civil War, when the anarchists were under attack by the Stalinists, he invoked in his defense the ongoing repression of anarchists in Catalonia at a time when the anarchists of the CNT were in the government. "If the CNT could not stop the persecution of the anarchists in Spain, what could be done on that score in the Russian Revolution by an isolated militant." There is undoubted truth in this, but Serge omits what was most culpable in his conduct: his public presentation of a rosy picture of the situation and encouragement of anarchists to support the Soviets and even move there to contribute to the fulfillment of the anarchist dream.

Serge could have tried to leave Russia and join Goldman, Berkman and the editors of *Le Libertaire* in exposing Bolshevik repression from exile in tiny papers that no one read. In his talks with Leval he mentioned the possibility of returning to Spain. He had left Spain willingly and was not under deportation order, as was the case in France. But the job of criticizing the Bolsheviks was already being done by the anarchists, SRs, Mensheviks (and the British secret services), so what would be the point? This is precisely what he said to Borghi during the latter's visit in 1920. With the anarchist movement in disarray, exile—assuming he'd have found a home for himself and his family—would have meant falling into the old routine of pointless meetings held by pointless groups bragging of their pointless purity. No, far better to stay in Russia where something, even if not something perfect, was being done.

Which brings us to what is perhaps the heart of the matter.

Almost all of these reasons for sticking with a revolution he knew had not turned out as he had hoped could have been surmounted. However difficult it is to examine the psychology of a man dead for decades, one can nevertheless hazard a conjecture based on the evidence from that period and later decades. There is a phrase he used in his writings that perhaps reveals the true reason for Victor's standing by the revolution he had told his friends was "a disaster". There was a "new reason for living: to win."[11]

Until his arrival in Russia his life was lived under the sign of failure. There was his failed relationship with his family, his failed membership in the youth branch of the POB, followed immediately by the collapse of the anarchist commune he had lived on, and then the failure of the anarchist group he helped found. He then moved to France, where he experienced the resounding collapse of the individualist anarchist milieu of which he was such an important part, capped off by the ugliness of the Bonnot trial, where his erstwhile comrades disgusted him, and he them.

Jail was yet another dreadful experience, and when he came out, he had to face both the end of his marriage to Rirette, which on his part was truly one of love, and the failure of the Barcelona uprising. The next failure in the series was his inability to get to Russia to join the Revolution, an act that was as much a result of personal desperation as a political one, a way out of the personal crisis he was going through and whose gravity is clear in a despairing letter he wrote on November 10, 1917, to an unnamed correspondent, in which he hints at thoughts of suicide.

And then, at age twenty-eight, he's finally offered a way out and is able to go to Soviet Russia. On the way there he meets the woman he will wed, falling in love not just with her but with her entire warm, accepting, Jewish family. Serge, who had no one, was now part of a family, and when he arrived in Russia was part of a revolution that had, against all odds, taken power and then was able not only to fight off its enemies, but to establish a world center of revolution, the Comintern, in which he played a vital role. Serge was finally on the winning side.

He was playing his last card, and he wasn't going to risk losing, to risk his marriage and his new family when, despite all his reservations, the Bolshevik errors could be justified historically and ideologically. As long as there was a glimmer of hope he would stick by it, though in truth that hope had been extinguished at Kronstadt and the party congress it coincided with, which put an end to any opposition life. He had his reason to live, and he would cling to it until it was no longer possible to hide the fact that the Revolution was hopelessly, irrevocably lost. Then he would take his stand. But until then, against his better judgment, against the attacks of his former allies, he was a Bolshevik, a winner. There was simply no way he could join the anarchists, the losers in the fight, in the trash bin of history.

He spoke of this directly not only in his published writings but also in his correspondence. On May 29, 1921, he wrote to the French syndicalist Michel Relenque of the "dreadful, the indescribable failure of the Russian anarchist movement," mocking their splits into countless tiny groups, as well as the "nuts who invented the language AO."[12]

Far better, then, to stand by the Revolution and write what he didn't necessarily believe. His later notebooks contain a passage that explains his conduct during his early years in Soviet Russia. "We in Russia invented many things, many harmful things, and it wasn't our fault. The state's total control of man was the beginning of our misfortune. Around 1928–30 a new word surfaced in the party, *dvouroutchnitchestvo*, which the French word 'duplicity' doesn't quite capture." In the face of a state intent on squelching any opposition, with "internal reservations" the good Bolshevik says what he doesn't mean "in order to gain time, to serve the party, and to be there (instead of in prison) for history's next turn." Though Serge was proud of his stand in the early Stalin years, of his "Don Quixotism," he recognized that "the naked man disarmed in the face of the machinery of the state has only this pathetic and degrading flight."[13] Though he excepted himself from this syndrome, it in fact perfectly described his actions and writings during the Civil War and the repression that accompanied and followed it and, even more, after the Kronstadt rebellion and the elimination of the anarchists. Serge lived in the hope of history's next turning, one that would salvage the Revolution. Duplicity was a temporary measure, one that would allow him to be there to put the Revolution back on the rails, when his "double duty" would be to openly defend the Revolution from its enemies without and within. That he failed in doing this was not his fault, for history and Stalin were stronger than all.

12

Comintern Agent
in Central Europe

Solidly established as a reliable propagandist, Serge seemed unshaken by all he saw around him. As Sahagian, in his unforgiving study of Serge bitterly put it, "It must be said that he worked, virtually from his arrival, for the propaganda service of the Comintern, thus transforming himself into a professional liar."[1]

In his memoirs, Serge spoke of the period of the early 1920s and its train of "immeasurable calamity."[2] Famine was endemic and millions died. "Authority tottered," he later wrote, but he remained convinced that the Bolsheviks were firmly in control, and "the skeleton hand of famine could not snatch power away from it."[3] At the same time, he admitted decades after the fact, that the party was in a state of "moral crisis" caused by the Civil War, Kronstadt, the NEP, and "the regime's intolerance," leading many of Serge's closest associates to question their choice of the Soviet state.[4] His French Communist comrades resident in Russia scattered, some remaining in Soviet Russia in various posts, some, including his brother-in-law Pierre Pascal, abandoning politics entirely.

Serge describes himself as made of stronger stuff than those who were "disheartened or disoriented."[5] He faithfully wrote prolifically for Communist publications, principally the French Communist Party's Comintern journal *Bulletin Communiste*, and for the independent left (though Communist-leaning) French magazine *Clarté*. Sahagian, in his indictment of Serge, calls his writing "inept," but that was far from being consistently the case. Along with propaganda pieces of little interest today, Serge also turned out work that is still worth reading. His analysis of Bakunin's confession demonstrates a fine sense for the psychology of the imprisoned revolutionary. The excerpts from Serge's study of the files of the tsar's secret police, the Okhrana, are still worth consulting, and are still in print in English.

Serge's articles in *Clarté*, a magazine founded by the novelist Henri Barbusse, were more wide-ranging, more personal, less propagandistic. It was there that he wrote in 1922 on "Intellectual Life in Soviet Russia."[6] He described a life he knew well. During the Civil War, Russia had been cut off from all contact with the intellectual productions of the West, but even so, "people worked in the universities, there were discussions in the workers' clubs, enthusiastic stanzas were declaimed at the club for proletarian culture, ProletKult, people wrote [...]. People lived ardently." The period of intellectual and physical famine came to an end, according to Serge, in 1922, with the beginning of the NEP, "that is, freedom of commerce and business, [thanks to which] intellectual life has returned with intense activity." He depicted a country in which ideas and literature flourished, and where even shortages worked to positive effect. "In Russia, the paper shortage [...] and the need for collective life born of the years of famine and blockade have contributed to giving a particularly intense vitality to groups and organizations." For Serge the writer, there was a confrontation of capital importance in Soviet Russia, that between "the new spirit—revolutionary: the spirit of life—and the old spirit: conservative, reactionary, fighting desperately for survival. For this struggle today constitutes the essential drama of Russian intelligence." In keeping with this he would, over the course of the next few years, write important works on young Soviet writers and the even younger Soviet literature, on proletarian literature, on the great Soviet poet Vladimir Mayakovsky, and on the epic literature of the Russian Revolution.

Serge was at this time a propagandist, a translator (most importantly of Lenin), and a voracious reader of fiction, though not yet a writer of novels. As his writing for *Clarté* shows, he was an interesting critic, and his February 1923 article "New Writers, New Literature" should be read in the light of the novels he would write.[7] After praising a number of writers, including Boris Pilnyak, whom he especially admired, and dismissing Marcel Proust's style compared to that of his favorite Russians, he admitted to a lack in the new literature. "In reading them, one is disappointed to not find in them general ideas. They suffered the difficult times without attempting to explain them [...]. They quite well observed its smallest aspects; they didn't penetrate its deepest laws." Abandoning critical subtlety for political rodomontade, Serge says that "[t]hese great talents are politically limited. The revolutionary accustomed to vast perspectives and the firm architecture of communist thought suffers at the sight of their doctrinal insufficiencies."

As a good Communist and Marxist, Serge attempts to explain the failings of the writers produced by the Revolution. "These men are neither proletarians nor intellectuals assimilated to the proletariat." Being foreign to class ideology, "not being assimilated to the revolutionary class, not having learned to think with it, they remain subject to contrary influences." These writers are the perfect products of the transitional period in which Russia is living, and their literature "will become what Russia will become." If Russia,

as some hope, evolves towards bourgeois democracy, these writers will transform themselves with little difficulty into a Moscow Society of Men of Letters that will cleverly exploit its memories of an adventurous youth. But if the dictatorship of the proletariat succeeds in leading Red Russia to communism, in ten years, increasingly adapted to their environment, they will be in harmony with their era and perhaps truly be revolutionaries.

None of this gives the least hint of the subtle novelist Serge would soon become.

Serge, though, was becoming concerned about the state of the Russian Revolution. His writings of the early 1920s included many pieces in praise of the revolutionary generation, the men and women who "carried out this formidable task: bringing down a society and constituting on its ruins the entrenched camp of the builders of the future and defending this camp for four years against the coalition of all the great powers and all the forces of the past." He wrote a collection of capsule portraits of these fighters, for "knowing them means knowing what it is to be a revolutionary."[8] Just a few years after the October Revolution, Serge saw that Russians needed to be reminded of the glories of the struggle, of the duties of a revolutionary.

In his memoirs Serge wrote that he had come to realize by 1920 that "the Russian Revolution, left to itself, would probably, in one way or another, collapse [...]; that the Russians, who had made superhuman efforts to build a new society, were more or less at the end of their strength."[9] In order to thrive with its revolutionary élan exhausted, the Soviet state needed assistance from the West in the form of revolution, or rather, as he described it, the "build[ing of] a working-class movement capable of supporting the Russians and one day superseding them."[10] He requested that he be granted a transfer to Central Europe, and was offered a post in Berlin by Zinoviev and the rest of the Comintern leadership. Serge, except for a spell back in Russia in 1922, would spend the years from late 1921 to 1925 in Central Europe, in Berlin and Vienna. While there, he would cross paths with many of the most important intellectual figures of the communist movement, among them György Lukács and Antonio Gramsci. Gramsci translated Serge's multi-part series "Lenin in 1917," which originally appeared in *Clarté*, for the Italian Communist review *Ordine Nuovo*. Serge also makes an appearance in Gramsci's prison correspondence.

Gramsci wrote to his sister-in-law on September 13, 1931, of an event that occurred during his time in Vienna, which overlapped with that of Serge. Gramsci had been asked to find an apartment for a member of the staff of the Soviet embassy. He found one at a reasonable price that was owned by a "superstitious petty-bourgeois woman." When he later returned to the apartment the landlord asked if the renter was a Jew, "because she didn't rent to Jews." Gramsci didn't know what to do, since the prospective renter was, indeed, Jewish. He recounted that "I spoke of this to a Frenchman, who explained to me that there was only one solution: tell the landlady that I couldn't, in all decency, ask the new tenant if she was a Jew, but that I knew she was an embassy secretary. [This would work] because as much as the petty-bourgeois hate Jews, that was how much they crawled before diplomats." As the Frenchman predicted, that was just what happened. "The woman heard me out and said, 'If she's a diplomat of course I'll give her the room, since one can't ask diplomats if they're Jews or not.'"[11] According to the late Gramsci scholar Joseph Buttiegieg, "the Frenchman" who offered this sage advice was Victor Serge.[12]

Serge was now one of the heroic breed that would be known as *Cominterniens*, professional international revolutionaries, often living in illegality, though Serge pointed out that his illegality, at least as he crossed Europe to his post, was an "easy" one. The fake Belgian passport he was provided with omitted any mention of his infant son Vlady, but this caused little problem as a comrade distracted the border guards from examining the paperwork too closely by playing with the baby.

In an October 1921 letter to Boris Souvarine, then secretary of the Comintern, Serge criticized the center of world communism for its failure to prepare matters for him. "Though our arrival was known of in advance, and we'd made known their request for the papers required for our legalization, we still lack identity papers." Three weeks into his assignment Serge complained that he only had an "unusable Belgian passport" and his wife, even worse, only had Soviet papers. "We don't think we need to insist about the daily inconveniences of this situation. Inconveniences that at times place obstacles to the carrying out of our work—and its dangers." Serge spoke in his memoirs of purchasing a residence permit in Berlin from the police for a small bribe, using his initiative and resourcefulness to supplement the failures of his superiors.

Serge wrote frequently from Berlin for the communist press on the situation in Germany, living and writing under a variety of pseudonyms, working from a desk in the offices of the Germany Communist Party's (KPD) newspaper, *Die Rote Fahne*.

Serge was in Berlin for the inflation crisis, which he wrote about extensively in Comintern publications. He was there as well for the other great crises of 1923, for Germany's announcement that it could no longer make the reparation payments it owed in accordance with the Versailles Treaty, and the French occupation of the heavily industrial Ruhr region. The French action caused outrage and anger on the right and the left, and it appeared Germany was entering a revolutionary phase.

Strikes occurred in the Rhineland, and the Comintern decided the time had come for the German Revolution, awaited and expected since the days of Marx. From the safety of Moscow, the date was set for it by the International's leadership: October 25, 1923, in honor of the date of the Bolshevik Revolution, which occurred on that date in the old Russian calendar. Serge wrote in his memoirs that Trotsky at this time gave talks in the Moscow Military School on the subject "Can one lay down the date of a revolution in advance?"[13] Serge doesn't give the answer Trotsky offered, but on October 20, in one of the talks in question Trotsky informed his students that "the odds are in favor, and very much in favor, of the German proletariat. The latter can and will take power—everything points to that."[14]

Serge wrote that he had had his doubts about the success, writing to contacts in Moscow that unless the Party's initiative joins with the spontaneous movement of the masses, it is doomed beforehand. Every day I learn of stocks of arms being seized. The tense expectation in the working-class districts seems to be slackening strangely. The unemployed are passing, by swift stages, from an insurgent enthusiasm into weary resignation.[15]

The plans pressed ahead, even going so far as to include "mopping-up" squads that would liquidate counter-revolutionaries after the certain victory.[16] But the plans were derailed. The authorities seized arms and rounded up Communists in advance of the scheduled uprising. The uprising was being led by Germans advised by Soviet military experts. The latter realized that the moment was not ripe after all, and it was called off.

But the comrades in Hamburg, a total of three hundred according to Serge, didn't receive the counterorder and, though they achieved limited success, "the whole of Germany has not moved an inch, and neither for that matter has Hamburg itself."[17] The German Revolution, predicted and hoped for by Marx a century earlier, had again failed to materialize. Who was at fault?

The German Communists, fissiparous as leftists—especially defeated ones—can be, turned on each other. The recrimination began almost immediately. The party leadership, viewed as rightists, was condemned by the party's left, led by Ruth Fischer, Arkady Maslow, Heinz Neumann, and Arthur Rosenzweig. The Comintern, which had been behind almost every move carried out in Germany, joined the party's left in condemning the "rightists" Brandler and Thalheimer. Serge's major contribution to the debate would appear pseudonymously as R. Albert in *Clarté* in February of the following year.[18]

There he demonstrates little patience for the calls for precipitous action. "At this moment we need to remember that social revolutions need, in order to ripen and be completed, not weeks and months, but years." He invoked the examples of the French Revolution and the Russian October Revolution, which required years of preparation. He presented in a positive way the thesis of the defeated leadership, which had "accuse[d] the Executive Committee of the Communist International and the KPD of 'an erroneous estimation of the relative strength of the forces confronting each other.'" Serge even spoke openly of the leaders' accusation that the Comintern (including and especially Zinoviev, Serge's boss, for whom he had little respect) "did not take sufficient account of the observations of the KPD." In short, the Comintern was guilty of the arrogance of thinking it could, from a distance and based on little, incorrect, and tendentious information, determine the how and when of a revolution in a foreign land.

Serge also had little use for the theses of the left of the party, as represented by Ruth Fischer. This group felt that rather than cancel the uprising, "the party should have taken on the struggle, even at the risk of defeat, for this would have given the German proletariat fine revolutionary traditions attached to the name of the KPD, in this way preparing a future victory." Serge had no patience for this point of view, saying that "a Communist rising crushed in Germany by the military dictatorship and the fascist bands would, it seems to me, have provided the German bourgeoisie with a sense of security and victory which it is far from having at present." History provided a solid basis for his opinion. Serge wrote that the defeats that cost the German working-class Rosa Luxemburg and Karl Liebknecht, and the bloodbath that followed the Paris Commune, "weakened [the working-class] for many long years." The lesson of Germany was a significant one. "However convinced we may be of the ultimate victory of the working-class, we cannot maintain that all its defeats are necessarily stages towards victory." This is an interesting modification of the theses of Le Rétif, who dismissed the Paris Commune and all revolutionary struggles as a waste of spilled blood. Spilled blood was now seen to be wasted when it was wasted knowingly and consciously to make a point and little more.

In his memoirs Serge minced no words, remaining true to what he wrote contemporaneously and pseudonymously as R. Albert.

Scapegoats had to be found. Out of defeat came the lying, the suppression, the demoralizing discipline that ruins consciences. Nobody talked about the basic fault. The whole Party lived on the involuntary bluff of functionaries whose first concern was not to contradict their superiors. Misinformation was generated at the base through the personal interest of the poor wretch who, simply to keep his job, assured the *Bezirk* [district] or Central Committee organizer that, yes, he had his fifty men available and that the fifty Mausers had been bought—when in fact he had ten men and was searching in vain to find Mausers for sale. Misinformation ascended stage by stage, through the whole hierarchy of secretaries, so that, at the end of it all, the delegate from the Central Committee of the KPD could tell the President of the International, "We are prepared," when nothing was prepared and everybody in the Party knew it was so, except those who drew up the confidential reports. Now, the International was in fully blown crisis. We could sense that this, in turn, heralded the crisis of the Russian Revolution.[19]

There was another defeat that occurred around the same time as the October Communist uprising, a defeat that, unlike that of the Communists, did lay the groundwork for a victory. On November 8, 1923, two weeks after the Communist fiasco, the National Socialist German Workers' Party, led by Adolf Hitler, carried out in Munich what came to be known as the Beer Hall Putsch. Less than ten years later, Hitler would be installed as Chancellor.

Germany wasn't the scene of the last fiasco in Europe caused by poor decisions by the Comintern under Zinoviev. On December 1, 1924, an uprising of just a few hundred Estonian Communists took place, ending in a rout that saw the revolutionaries slaughtered within just a few hours. For Serge the explanation was simple. "Zinoviev refused to acknowledge the German defeat."[20] For all the focus on Germany, Bulgaria was a country with one of the most militant and well-organized Communist Parties, one of its leaders the soon-to-be head of the Comintern, Georgi Dimitrov. That party carried out assassinations and terrorist bombings that truly shook the kingdom, but which also led to the execution of the perpetrators. As the guide for world revolution the Comintern was proving itself a failure.

In the meantime, on January 21, 1924, Lenin had died, and the battle for succession was engaged. Serge took advantage of the relative respite that life in Europe provided to study Marx (and Freud). He recounted that by 1923 he was already on the side of the Opposition, led by Trotsky. He wrote in his memoirs of his feelings:

> At the time when the date of the German Revolution was being fixed, forty-six old militants warned the Central Committee of two sorts of danger: the weakness of an industry unable to satisfy the needs of the countryside, and the stifling dictatorship of bureaucracy. In the spiritual impoverishment of recent years there had been only two flashes of daylight: two close-written little books by Trotsky, the demands in *The New Course* and the analysis in *Lessons of October*—both works vilified by our official press. We would meet discreetly in some outer district to read and discuss these pulsating pages. Then, bound by discipline, prisoners to our daily bread, we went on endlessly printing our newssheets, with the same insipid, nauseating condemnations of everything that we knew to be true. Was it really worthwhile being revolutionaries if we had to ply this trade?[21]

He felt the International was "rotting from within," for which he had seen much evidence during his relatively brief sojourn in Central Europe. Lukács warned him to be careful, "don't be silly and get yourself deported for nothing, just for the pleasure of voting defiantly."[22] Lukács's prudence, a lifelong trait, was not for Serge. The time had come for him to return to the USSR, and he said that if the atmosphere was too oppressive in Petrograd (now Leningrad) and Moscow he would request a transfer to Siberia and spend his time writing. History would make his decision for him.

13

Opposition

In 1925, while still in Central Europe, as the battle between Trotsky and Stalin was gaining in steam and acrimony, Serge refused to find any fault with the fundamental nature of the Bolshevik Party. In a letter dated June 23, 1925, and published in *La Révolution prolétarienne* in August 1933, Serge described the party as "a great social fact," that was "forged by the hands of the workers for the necessary revolution … a collective being, a new army on the march." Even if in its day-to-day activity it were to fall into the errors of working-class parties of the past, "the theory of the new party would remain no less true." However difficult the times might be, they "don't justify any philosophical pessimism, though they provide ample justification for individual pessimism." His optimism we now know was unjustified, but in a moment of great foresight in the same letter Serge admitted, "We could very well be an entire generation of sacrificial victims." Truer words were never spoken, and Serge would, among other things, be the great memorialist of that generation.

This letter also contained an analysis of the causes of the decline of the Russian Revolution, a theme he would revert to on many occasions. In 1925, seven and a half years after the victory of the October Revolution, Serge sought the moment the Revolution had gone into decline. The Russian Revolution was already in dire straits, Serge says, by the time he arrived there in 1919. "Since 1919 I have foreseen the clear wearing down of the Russians, less and less capable of taking charge with their few truly revolutionary forces both the vast Soviet Union and the global workers' movement, where they are so alone." The failure of world revolution to occur explains the "fierceness of the Russians in holding on to power. Their fervor in holding on to it is legitimate because they feel they are the only revolutionaries." What resulted from this is precisely what Serge and his Oppositional comrades were fighting against: "the bureaucratization of the Russian and international movements."[1]

A state run by a party is dependent on the quality of that party, and Serge was blunt in his estimation of the qualities of the Bolsheviks of 1925. After Lenin's death, the so-called Lenin Enrollment had opened wide the doors of the Communist Party to the masses, expanding its numbers but diluting its ideological strength. He asserted that there were 500,000 members of the Bolshevik Party, submerged in a country with a population of 120,000,000. But even the vanishingly small number that is 500,000 overestimates the party's effectives, for "of these 500,000, at most 30,000 offer guarantees of internal solidity and doctrinal consciousness." But even this reduced number is deceptive, for "every year one or two thousand of the exhausted die."

Despite all this, true revolutionaries must maintain hope. "I see only one thing to do: not throw out the baby with the bathwater; not grow bitter. The moment has come to calmly swim against the tide, as difficult as that might be." Viewing things almost mechanistically, Serge and those like him must "hold out, educating ourselves, hardening ourselves, learning" in order to be ready to take over, a day that will come "perhaps after some frightful crisis, perhaps after many confused struggles, but which will surely come, because it is necessary." The ambient political awfulness must be rejected, and in perhaps the first use he will make of a concept that remained dear to him throughout his life, Serge speaks of the double duty confronting the Opposition. "We are caught between two enemies, that which is within us and the one outside; any clumsiness in the struggle against the internal enemy renders enormous service to the other."

When Serge returned to the Soviet Union in late 1925, he described the atmosphere as "calm, gloomy, oppressive."[2] Given this atmosphere, he'd have preferred being assigned to work in Siberia to returning to either Moscow or Leningrad. The wave of suicides among experienced revolutionaries that would soon become a minor epidemic had already begun. He described the country as living in the grip of a "psychosis" that would grow worse and expand from small political circles to the entire nation.[3]

It's necessary to summarize the stakes and issues of the struggle then under way, and we are fortunate to have a succinct contemporary survey from the pen of Serge himself. His friend the communist-sympathizing Romanian French-language writer Panait Istrati published three volumes on the Soviet Union, the first of which, *Vers l'autre flamme*, will occupy us later. Istrati published two other volumes on the subject of the USSR, where he spent sixteen months in 1927 and 1928. The second, titled *Soviets 1929*, published under Istrati's name, was in reality written in its entirety by Serge. As such, it provides valuable insights into the ideas of Serge and his Opposition comrades.

Serge began his account of the split in the Bolshevik Party in 1923, when "a large current at the head of which could be found a number of old Bolsheviks demanded the democratization of the internal regime of the party." It was, they thought, "necessary to 'demilitarize' the party since the civil war was over."[4] This current, led by Trotsky, was accused of threatening the unity of the party and supporters of this line were transferred to the provinces. Trotsky himself was forced to resign in 1924 from his position as head of the revolutionary council of the Red Army for writing that Lenin had had to confront a right-wing group that included Zinoviev and Kamenev that opposed the seizure of power in 1917. "Trotsky bowed before the decisions of the party, like a 'good soldier,' without abjuring anything."[5]

In 1925 tension grew between Zinoviev and Stalin, the former seeking a rapprochement with Trotsky, who was now calling for a "policy of industrialization, which met with much resistance."[6]

In 1926, at the Fourteenth Congress of the Bolshevik Party, the conflict between Stalin and Zinoviev, that is, between the party organizations of Moscow and Leningrad, was brought out into the open, with Zinoviev attacking both the strength granted to the kulaks—the rich peasants—and "the bureaucratic regime he himself created." Stalin allied with Bukharin in accusing Zinoviev and Kamenev of having caused the failure of the wheat harvest and underestimating the middle peasants. Zinoviev's Leningrad organization was defeated and, Serge wrote, "Stalin's stunning victory was owed to the patient labor he had carried out for years, making use of the prerogatives of the general secretariat of the party to gradually place men loyal to him in all leading posts of local organizations." Zinoviev was now allied (temporarily) with Trotsky, as were Radek and Kamenev, and a meeting of the Central Committee "ended in a terrible uproar. From this moment on, the struggle between the leaders of the party and the Opposition becomes fierce." And as Serge wrote, "it is impossible to follow its twists and turns."

Serge summed up the platform of the Opposition, of which he was a part. For the Left Opposition that was born in 1923, "the nascent new bourgeoisie," made up of kulaks, businessmen made wealthy under the NEP, and bureaucrats, were thriving while "the material and political situation of the working-class worsened." It opposed the bureaucratization of the party and the Comintern, the corruption of its cadres, and demanded the "return to internal [party] democracy" (never noting that such democracy had been banned by Lenin).[7] The Opposition condemned Stalin, calling for the implementation of the terms of Lenin's Testament, which laid out his recommendations for modifications in the party's activity and leadership, and which called for Stalin's removal from his post as secretary. In what would be a long-standing issue, the Opposition stood firm on the matter of internationalism, opposing Stalin's notion of the construction of socialism in one country.

A policy of rapid industrialization was advocated, and the disastrous policies of the Comintern, particularly in China, where the support for Chiang Kai-shek and the Kuomintang doomed "the worker and peasant movement to defeats as demoralizing as they were bloody."[8] We will return to the Chinese Revolution later. The failure of the Comintern and Stalin's policies there were, on top of the German fiasco, proof of its political bankruptcy in the eyes of the Opposition.

The members of the Opposition were increasingly marginalized, transferred to out-of-the-way places, and, in the cases of Trotsky, Zinoviev and Kamenev, three of the historic leaders of the party, removed from the Politburo.

In the midst of these internal battles, the crushing of the Chinese Communist Party in 1927, with the massacre of Communists in Shanghai in April of that year its low point, was added to the disputes over internal policy. For the Opposition, the decimation of the Communist Party by the leader of the Kuomintang, Chiang Kai-shek, was the direct result of a strategy dictated to the Chinese Communist Party (CCP) by the already Stalinized Comintern. In short, the CCP entered into an alliance—in fact became a part of the bourgeois democratic Kuomintang. The Comintern pushed for this, since it viewed the Kuomintang as representing the most progressive elements of bourgeois society, capable of leading China to socialism. The Soviets had, even before Lenin's death, played a role in China. On July 31, 1923, the Politburo sent Mikhail Borodin to lead a Soviet mission in Canton and serve as an advisor to Sun Yat-sen. Stalin, at this time, before assuming power, already set the line that would be criticized by Serge and the rest of the Opposition. Stalin wrote: "Instruct Comrade Borodin that in his work with Sun Yat-sen he should be guided by the interests of the Chinese national liberation movement and should under no circumstances let himself be carried away into schemes to implant communism in China."[9]

So enthusiastic was the Soviet leadership about the nationalist Kuomintang that it was admitted to the Comintern! The policy led to the disaster of 1927 which, for the Opposition, was one sign among many of the utter failure of Soviet Russia's leadership. Trotsky spoke vehemently about the many failings of Comintern policy, which he elevated to an important battlefield in his fight against Stalin. Serge joined the fray, attacking Stalin and the Comintern, not at public or party meetings in Russia, but in the foreign press, in *Clarté*. Serge didn't write just one article, but rather four, in a scathing and detailed indictment of the Kuomintang and the Comintern's role in leaving the CCP disarmed and exposed.

Serge's series of four articles, begun in May 1927, are detailed and masterful. The final article, analyzing the causes of the failure, takes aim at those who caused the defeat of the CCP, though his direct mentions of the Comintern are few. Instead, he picks apart every element in the union of the Kuomintang and the CCP, an analysis that demonstrates that its very foundation was erroneous and that this should have been seen by the Comintern.[10]

Serge asserted that for "economically developed great colonial countries," like China, "in our time [...] there can no longer be bourgeois revolutions in the classic sense of the term." It was because, following the Comintern line, they viewed the situation in this way, that the Chinese working-class is now "defeated and the failure of even the bourgeois revolution is a fact." Rather than defend themselves, the CCP did nothing, for "the proletarians don't have real revolutionary leaders, no cadres capable of leading them to civil war." The main fear of the CCP leadership was "far-left errors" and "a break with the petite bourgeoisie, whose ambiguous role they don't understand." The support that the CCP gave the Kuomintang, even going so far as to condemn peasant uprisings against their landlords, was characterized by the Communist minister of agriculture as a product of "the infantile malady of the left [...] [and] profoundly erroneous."[11]

That this "erroneous" line was that of Moscow and its leadership is demonstrated by Serge in a footnote quoting a May 30 meeting of the Executive of the Comintern, which stated that the government in Hankou, "which is that of the left of the Kuomintang, is not yet the dictatorship of the proletariat and peasants, but is on the road to that dictatorship." For the Comintern, that government is "carrying out a revolution-ary struggle against the imperialists, the feudalists, and now also against an important part of the bourgeoisie of its own country."[12]

Serge paints the darkest of pictures of the outcome of the Comintern's—Stalin's—line, a picture that cannot have pleased the leaders of the International and the Soviet state. His descrip-tion of the situation in China was that of the entire Opposition:

> The comedy is over, the tragedy follows its course. Savage repression in the countryside. Arrests, executions, assassi-nations in the cities. The communists outlawed, the unions dissolved, fascist groupings masters of the streets. The government of a great national movement which in mid-July still feigned representing the anti-imperialist revolution now only represents the bourgeois counter-revolution, natural ally of the imperialists. The proletariat and the peasantry are defeated; the (national) bourgeois revolution as well.[13]

* * *

Quixotically, on November 7, 1927, members of the Opposition demonstrated against Stalin, carrying signs saying, "Remember Lenin's Testament."[14] When the Opposition organized gather-ings to discuss their program and criticisms, workers were told to break them up. The campaign was so vicious that Adolph Joffe, an old Bolshevik and part of the team that negotiated peace with Germany at Brest-Litovsk, committed suicide, the first of what would be a long series of revolutionary veterans who took their own lives. "Strange rumors circulate [and] the leaders of the Opposition were accused of conspiracy and connivance with the White counter-revolution."[15]

"The fight became envenomed" in the fall of 1928 with the approach of the Fifteenth Party Congress. Stalin decreed that only theses presented by him and his followers would be discussed, while the Opposition platform of that year was declared counter-revolutionary, "its publication, distribution, and even reading banned."[16] When they then typed up their documents for distribution and discussion, they were seized and the Opposition accused of "creating underground printing presses."[17] The Fifteenth Party Congress was a "congress of unanimity," and groups of Oppositionists were expelled daily, followed by the deportation of anti-Stalinists.

A wheat shortage and the crushing of the Chinese Revolution resulted in Stalin changing his line, now adopting many of the positions of the Opposition, which he didn't credit with having seen clearly. "The repression of the Trotskyists began immediately after the Fifteenth Congress." It was around this time that Serge had his final meeting with Trotsky, just before the latter was exiled to Alma-Ata. Trotsky, having been evicted from the Kremlin, was temporarily living in the home of a friend. There, they discussed the work being accomplished and to be accomplished by the Opposition, about which Trotsky was his usual optimistic self. Trotsky wished Serge luck and told him to try to move to Europe.

Serge described the situation that confronted the Opposition in 1928, their plans, and his reactions to these plans, in his memoirs:

> The leaders of the now vanquished Opposition hoped to set up a clandestine organization strong enough to achieve rehabilitation in the Party at some future date with freedom of speech and propaganda. I did not share this illusion. I said that illegal methods would fail for two reasons: the unlimited power of the secret police would crush everything, and our own ideological and sentimental loyalty to the Party made us vulnerable both to political maneuverings and, even more, to police provocation. I declared that, rather than allow ourselves to be bundled away into illegality, we should defend, absolutely openly, our right to exist, think, and write. And we should form, also quite openly, an opposition which was completely loyal, being without any organization, but also completely intransigent. It

was all purely academic, since both alternatives were equally impossible.[18]

Serge described the differences among the members of the Opposition during the darkest years of the repression:

[V.M.] Chernykh [former head of the Cheka in the Urals] was (like myself) one of the tribe of revisionists, who maintained that all ideas, as well as all recent history, should be reviewed from top to bottom. On this issue the Opposition was divided roughly into two halves. There were the revisionists and there were the doctrinaires, themselves subdivided into the orthodox, the extreme Left, and the followers of the theory that the USSR was establishing State capitalism.[19]

On January 1, 1928, with the battle against Stalin all but lost, Serge diagnosed the failure of the Revolution based on the quality of the men and women leading it. What has occurred in Russia is "the elimination of one generation by another. Those who made the revolution are eliminated by those who are rising." The rising generation is convinced that victory is won. It didn't experience the Civil War so it's ignorant of real heroism. All that made the first generation (note that the first generation was merely a decade earlier), "the tempering of the militant by devotion and individual effort, the courage of being in the minority, scrupulous theoretical intelligence, and revolutionary lyricism, are foreign to it." In their place, this lyricism is replaced by "official science [...]. [I]t has a simplified mentality, greedy and practical. [They are] parvenus who want to go higher." A revolution doesn't only die from economic failure. A revolution promises a new way of being and living. The old has reappeared. "Since heredity is heavy, since it is a country of small peasants, since the pressure of the capitalist encirclement is enormous [...] we find an entire new virtual, latent—and not so latent—bourgeois-ism that is blossoming and sometimes growing. Though infinitely skilled at disguising itself."

Serge was called to the Control Commission in charge of the Leningrad party on January 15, 1928. Still the good Bolshevik, he declared that he would faithfully carry out the decisions made by the party, but that he considered it to be an "error" to expel the members of the Opposition. At the use of the word "error" the tribunal's members ears perked up and they asked Serge if a party congress or the Central Committee could "err." Commonsensically, Serge answered that "to err is human" and, referring to the German Social Democratic Party, spoke of "great parties" that finally "degenerate." He was immediately expelled from the party.

On April 23, 1928, he received the almost inevitable nighttime visit from the GPU [*Gosudarstvennoye politicheskoye upravleniye*—State Political Directorate, i.e., the secret police]. Though never charged, he was cut off from the outside world and held in a cell designed for one that was now holding Serge and two others.

As Richard Greeman described this imprisonment in his unpublished notes for a biography of Serge,

In spite of the political nature of the arrest, Serge was held as a common prisoner. However, he was denied the rights of common prisoners, like the right to correspond with his wife or to receive newspapers. After twenty-five days, he was questioned again and accused of the crime of belonging to an underground anti-Soviet organization. His reply was to quote the position of Trotsky and the other opposition leaders: that of total loyalty to the Party despite grave differences over policy. Serge added that since Stalin had changed his policy in the months since the Left's expulsion, these differences had lessened greatly and that consequently the continued expulsion of a loyal opposition was all the more senseless. Against this solid front, his captors could do little more than ask him to sign a formal statement disavowing organized oppositional activity. This was easy for him to do, as the opposition had officially disbanded and as, in any case, such activity was impossible to carry on. On the next day, he was transferred to a section for political prisoners and given certain privileges, including a visit from his wife.

He was released after being held thirty-six days.

The revolutionary magazine formerly called *Clarté*, now known as *Lutte de Classes*, published a protest against the arrest, saying that "all our readers, all our comrades, know Victor Serge," who has served "the Russian Revolution and the world revolution since his arrival in Russia." "He is among those who expended the greatest effort to make the Russian Revolution known in the West." There is only one thing held against him: "Victor Serge belongs to the Opposition […]. After the Fifteenth Party Congress he was expelled from the Russian CP, like so many others, simply because of his opinions."

Henri Barbusse, the founder of *Clarté*, had a slightly different take on this first mobilization to free Victor Serge. In the June 15, 1928, issue of the formerly Socialist, now Communist daily *L'Humanité*, Barbusse wrote an article clarifying what he called "a fake petition" in defense of Victor Serge organized by the Committee for the Defense of the Victims of Fascism and the White Terror. Among its signatories were the anarchist Séverine and the human rights activist Bernard Lecache. The Socialist newspaper *Le Populaire* had publicized this petition, which the Communists qualified as a "counter-revolutionary machination." Not only had Lecache and Séverine not signed any such petition, but it was "a maneuver of a clearly political character which, in fact, can do nothing but harm to Victor Serge's interests." In any event, Barbusse wrote, the case was of little importance since "he is today free." He asserted that members of the committee are free to think what they will of the Russian Revolution, but the president of the committee, that is, Barbusse himself, "is concerned [...] exclusively with the defense of victims of fascism and the White Terror and does not intervene in the affairs of democratic regimes and the Soviet regime." This supposedly false petition, according to Barbusse, future author of a hagiography of Stalin, was intended as an attack on the Soviet Union and "to push for the dislocation of the latter and consequently, in the current circumstances, to directly serve fascism."

The period that immediately followed Serge's release from prison was a turning point in his life. He fell ill with an intestinal occlusion and thought he was going to die. Evidently unaware of Barbusse's attitude towards those who defended him during his imprisonment, he wrote Barbusse on July 1: "Barely had I gotten out of prison than I almost died of an intestinal occlusion." On August 4 he wrote Barbusse again, apologizing for not being able to meet the French writer while he was in Russia, explaining that he was "in such a bad way health-wise that [he] needed a cane in order to walk." This personal crisis, combined with the greater crisis facing Soviet society, a period of reaction that he feared would last years, led him to decide to dedicate his life to writing. In his memoirs he places the moment when he decided to change his life as occurring in the hospital. After asking his doctor if he'd live, the physician said he believed so. "The next morning, he told me I was safe. I had taken my decision: that is how I became a writer." He explained in his memoirs that he had abandoned writing when he turned his life over to the Russian Revolution (though he was, in fact, little short of a graphomaniac), describing literature as a "secondary matter." But now, a decade after arriving in Russia, "I felt sufficiently in tune with myself to write."[20]

He embarked on his historical work *Year One of the Russian Revolution*, but also determined to write fiction, and began assembling information for his first novel, *Men in Prison*. Serge was afraid that he couldn't carry out historical research as it needed to be done, and so decided that fiction would be his primary focus. "A certain degree of light can only be cast on history, I am convinced, by literary creation that is free and disinterested, which is to say, devoid of any market preoccupations." This last comment needs to be taken with a grain of salt. Serge's novels were all works whose creation were, to be sure, impelled by an inner necessity. He was, though, as obsessed as any author with "market preoccupations," regularly hounding publishers for his royalties and to have them do a better job promoting his books.[21]

Dismissing those who simply write for pleasure, or "to stock the book trade," Serge expressed his conception of literature in the loftiest terms:

> My conception of writing was and still is that it needs mightier justifications: as a means of expressing to men what most of them live inwardly without being able to express; as a means of communion, a testimony to the vast flow of life through us, whose essential aspects we must try to fix for the benefit of those who will come after us. In this respect, I belonged to the tradition of Russian writing. I knew that I would never have time to polish my works.[22]

This intellectual, who wrote so brilliantly throughout his life of great writers, French and Russian writers above all, dismissed the French novel as too concerned with the life of the individual and the family. "Individual existences were of no interest to me—particularly my own—except by virtue of the great totality of life whose particles, more or less endowed with consciousness, are all that we ever are."[23] Though he said he was influenced by Boris Pilnyak, about whom he wrote frequently and appreciatively, and despite his claim that he was in the tradition of the great Russian novelists, it was the American John Dos Passos whom he claimed as his greatest influence. Not Dos Passos's "impressionism" but his insertion of his characters into a real society, into a reality that existed outside the novels' pages. In the five years between his imprisonments, 1928 and 1933, Serge would write three novels, *Men in Prison*, *The Birth of Our Power* (published by Rieder in 1931), and *Conquered City* (published by Rieder in 1932) before his final arrest in Russia, three novels of revolution that followed his own political evolution from recovering individualist anarchist to syndicalist to Bolshevik. He was not dissimulating, or not entirely dissimulating, when he told his secret police interrogators in 1933 that he had abandoned politics for literature since his first arrest.

If Serge's life was in a parlous state in the late 1920s, so was that of the entire Soviet nation. In March 1929 he wrote to a French addressee describing the difficult conditions that prevailed in Russia, conditions he described as straight out of natural selection as described in *The Origin of Species*:

> For the past two years, living conditions have worsened, there's a shortage of products of general use and the unemployment rate is high. The housing crisis in cities is ever more bitter. In these conditions anyone possessing an overcoat, a room, or a job finds himself surrounded by people who want to take his overcoat, room or job, either because they don't have one themselves, or because the one they have is worn out and they'll soon find themselves without, or because what they have is a form of "wealth" that could become an object of speculation.

Serge's critical stance towards Soviet reality was the explanation for what became known as the Russakov Affair. Alexander Russakov, we will recall, was a Russian-Jewish anarchist Serge had met on the ship taking him from France to Soviet Russia. He'd married Russakov's daughter Liuba, with whom he'd had a son and later a daughter. The elderly man lived with Serge, his family, and three other family members in a former grand-bourgeois apartment, 19 Jeliabov Street, Leningrad.

A dispute in this apartment between Russakov and the other lodgers, led by the party member Sviertseva—who alleged her life had been threatened by Serge's father-in-law—resulted in an almost unimaginable campaign being mounted against Serge's wife's father, an old anarchist who had been involved in the negotiations to end the siege of Kronstadt. It was Serge's friend, the Romanian writer Panait Istrati, who made the issue of a battle over an apartment in Leningrad an international scandal. The *Nouvelle revue française*, France's most prestigious literary journal, published a lengthy essay by Istrati on the case, which Istrati recycled in its entirety and included in his scathing account of his sixteen months in the USSR, *Vers l'autre flamme* (1927). Istrati justified giving such extensive coverage to the affair because, he wrote, "The entire Soviet Union is there: economically, politically, humanely and, alas, above all, morally." Istrati did not measure his words, describing the eviction of the family as "the height of banditry and terror," expressing shock that this could happen in the USSR, "under the regime of the so-called dictatorship of the proletariat."[24]

The incident occurred just a couple of weeks after Serge's expulsion from the Communist Party and three months before his first arrest. These are not coincidences. It's worthwhile quoting extensively from the report of the precipitating incident that appeared in *Leningradskaya Pravda* on January 31, 1928. The tone of the Stalin years can be heard here, and Istrati's claim that all of the Soviet Union is summed up in this minor event is verified.

It is absolutely clear that in the half-darkened corridor of a bourgeois apartment there took place an unmistakable class brawl [...]. [Alexander Russakov] a ferocious enemy of proletarian society, his personal interests offended, he attempted to exercise his hatred against the social militant Sviertseva. Russakov's aggression, armed with his fists [...] constitutes an attempted attack by kulak and NEPman elements against our ranks and our creative labor. Proletarian opinion demands Russakov's immediate arrest. A grand trial is needed, one that must be exemplary [...]. Enemies must be severely punished. Enemies of the proletariat operating on the housing front as well as that of daily life who attack our militants with fists or knives.

This extraordinary call for blood in a dispute over lodging led immediately to factory meetings calling for Russakov to be executed, or at least arrested, along with Liuba and, ultimately, Serge. Though the Frenchman Pierre Pascal, also married to one of Russakov's daughters, thought it was useless to fight back, Serge and Istrati refused to let matters rest. Serge telegraphed the editor of *Leningradskaya Pravda*, protesting against "the ignominious and slanderous campaign carried out in *Leningradskaya Pravda* [...]. This campaign completes a long series of petty provocations emanating from a member of the Young Communists [...] with the sole end of wresting a room, provocations that brought about an attack on my wife in her own domicile."[25]

The climate of fear that reigned is evident everywhere in this tale. Istrati, not satisfied with contacting the newspaper, wrote directly to Mikhail Kalinin, chairman of the Central Executive Committee of the All-Russian Congress of Soviets, and almost immediately heard from the Leningrad paper, which expressed incredulity that he had dared to do something so outrageous. Calling the editor from the hallway of his hotel, Istrati, as he wrote, let loose, "like a man who has nothing left to lose, since faith is lost."

Serge, who witnessed the phone call, was himself horrified by Istrati's conduct, telling his friend in a letter that "that would mean nothing less than Siberia for one of us." Serge and Istrati then went to see the journalist Mikhail Koltsov (later a key Soviet emissary to the Spanish Republic and, shortly after his recall from Spain, a victim of Stalin's purges), who showed them stacks of dossiers similar to that of Russakov and said he could do nothing. They then went to see Kalinin himself, who claimed ignorance of the truth or falsehood of the article attacking Russakov. He ordered a subaltern to arrange matters, though unsurprisingly, the underling did nothing of the sort.

Istrati was shown the resolution passed by the workers in the factory where old Russakov worked, which claimed, "Profiting from the label of worker, disguising himself as a factory worker, Russakov is in reality a vile appendage of the internal counter-revolution, a miserable Black Hundred, a ferocious petit-bourgeois antisemite." Russakov, we should remember, was a Jewish anarchist who had originally fled Russia to escape pogroms carried out by the Black Hundreds.

The trial of Russakov, his wife, and Liuba took place in mid-April where, behind closed doors, Sviertseva, the accuser, admitted she had been placed in the apartment to spy on Victor Serge. The accused were acquitted. Upon appeal by the prosecutor, a second trial took place, and this time government orders were properly followed and the accused were found guilty. Russakov was sentenced to three months imprisonment, his wife to two months, and Liuba to one month, though instead of imprisonment all would be forced to perform unpaid labor.

Istrati's reaction to the affair was the measure of the man and of his disappointment with the revolution he had supported and written in praise of. He now unleashed his rage in no uncertain terms:

> At least Mussolini had had the courage of his crimes. In order to subdue Italy, in order to muzzle it, in order to render it as peaceful as a graveyard, he didn't need to fabricate worker resolutions and declarations of factory assemblies. He said, "It's I who strike, not the masses! It's I who dictate, not the proletariat! It's I who am responsible for all evil!" At least in this way the prestige and honesty of the proletariat remains standing.[26]

Serge, for his part, refused to throw out the revolutionary baby with the Stalinist bathwater. The impetuous Istrati wanted nothing of such caution, asking what will happen to "poor humanity [...] the day this communism will be strong enough to impose its [system of] justice and teach it to live. No, no, a hundred times no. The world is already too wretched to allow its evil to be increased." He went even further, referring to "communist fascism" and asserted that "it is no longer a question of socialism, but of a terror that treats human life like social war materiel put to use for and by a new and monstrous caste." Within a little more than a decade, Serge would be writing in the same tone.

When Istrati's book was published the Communist reaction was, as could be expected, an ad hominem attack on the writer. On October 5, 1929, *L'Humanité* published an article titled "Panait Istrati Agent of the Romanian Police." According to the PCF (Parti communiste français) newspaper, Istrati had met with the Romanian minister of the interior and was assigned by the minister to establish a party "against communist demagogy, i.e., a counter-revolutionary group of Black Hundreds." Istrati's book was not simply the work of one disaffected supporter of the Bolsheviks. "All this mud, this unspeakable campaign of slander is an integral part of the plot that in all capitalist countries imperialism mounts and is leading against communism in order to prepare anti-Soviet aggression." Serge, having access to *L'Humanité* and aware of the scurrilous attack, advised Istrati in a letter not to respond to it, since "it has no impact in the West, and here your response won't be published. You really have no choice but to scornfully let it go."

But Serge was less than pleased with Istrati's actions defending his in-laws. In the same letter in which he advised Istrati to ignore the PCF's attack, he chastised his friend. Admitting that he hadn't been able to obtain a copy of Istrati's article in the *Nouvelle revue française*, he continued:

[A]ccording to everything I saw in several newspapers, I have the impression that your deductions and generalizations are out of all proportion. Your indignation carried you too far.

I infinitely regret that the letters in which I asked you not to publish anything on that affair didn't reach you in time. Neither the USSR nor the Revolution can be judged according to its wounds, which must—in this you are right—sometimes be cauterized. But not having read your article I can't judge it. I only want to tell you that if I fear your exaggerations, I don't doubt and will never doubt your revolutionary faith. That is what matters most.

Even now, in 1929, after having been thrown in prison, after the crushing of the Opposition, after the deportation of Trotsky and the bloodthirsty campaign against his father-in-law, Serge maintained his optimism. Serge offered his advice to Istrati:

My dear old man, don't let the bitterness of this new experience mislead you and eat away at your attachment to the Revolution. We're living in a time when one must occasionally know how to serve it despite itself and often without taking into account how it treats us. It's necessary to look beyond it, at the future and at history.

The atmosphere of harassment weighed more heavily on Serge's wife Liuba than on Serge himself. He recounts in his memoirs that he came home one evening during this period and found her reading the entry on "Madness" in a medical dictionary. "I've just read the article on madness. I know that I'm going mad. Wouldn't I be better off dead?"[27] Though Liuba would join Serge and their son Vlady in their internal exile in 1933, from this point on she was in the constant care of psychiatrists and would spend many years in psychiatric hospitals, dying in one in France in 1984.

Serge's situation worsened with every passing week. He wrote Istrati on December 11, 1929, that "There is [...] a great task to be accomplished affirming the need for intellectuals—and more particularly writers—to have social courage." But his material situation preoccupied him. He worried how "in a week or two I'll know if they'll be cutting off my provisions," as he'd been threatened. "As things are, I'm ¾ boycotted." Though he was a member of the Writer's Union, no writers' organization recognized his existence, and the union didn't back him in 1928 in his attempt to get a passport that would have allowed him to move to France. This was now his goal in life: the hope of finding work in the West, either as a correspondent or doing translations for the Gallimard or Rieder publishing houses.

But he was stuck, and the situation changed little except for the worse as the years passed. Even so, in the depths of his despair he continued to find something positive in the Soviet experience. He wrote to Istrati in January 1930 that things had gotten far worse; the awfulness had been "multiplied a hundred-fold," since Istrati's departure just three years earlier. It was impossible to cook a good meal, but even worse was the general atmosphere: "The atmosphere of a besieged country that rations itself, where the citizens are anxious about public safety, and even more about their own." But all was not lost, for there was also "the sentiment of an immense exploit in the process of being carried out, of the tension of collective energy organized for decisive efforts, the feeling that history is carrying us along almost mechanically." The USSR was on the cusp of enormous events.

Yesterday's newspapers spoke of the total liquidation of the wealthy peasants as a class, i.e., their expropriation and ruin [...]. What's certain is that we are about to live a decisive year of bitter struggles fertile with historic results. What I can't describe is the sentiment of the grandeur of things.

A month later he would write his Romanian friend about being attacked yet again with the aim of taking his apartment from him. Echoing Istrati's claim that this entire affair was emblematic of the general state of the country, where "[m]inds are so embittered that there are virtual tragedies over a liter of milk fought over by three mothers in a doorway." But Serge refused to admit the dream was dead. "And yet, man is not a wolf for other men; this is a great era and I'm happy to see what I see. These times are worth living [while] standing tall, [and] of course without abdicating one's ideas and revolutionary dignity." Serge would constantly go back and forth in his feelings. Soon after this last hopeful comment he would write Istrati that "It's all I can do to hold out from one month to the next," which would be followed soon after by his asserting that "The struggle isn't over and our duty is to have confidence in the revolutionary spirit as long as the least chance of seeing it reborn or triumph remains."

The boycott of his work Serge had mentioned earlier was solidified when he refused to condemn Istrati's *Vers l'autre flamme*, which he claimed not to have read. He was called to Moscow in March 1930 and told that a book of his that was about to go to the printer would not be published after all, due to his refusal to condemn Istrati. Though he'd been asking for and been refused a visa for the West, he told an unnamed official that he would hold out in the USSR,

absolutely refusing to admit that existence is impossible in this part of the world to a Communist like me. On the subject of the author of *Vers l'autre flamme*, I answered that he alone is responsible for his acts, that I haven't read it (which is true and not my fault), that I am ready to express my solidarity with him to the extent he expresses ideas I think correct, but not beyond that, of course, and that I consider him a perfectly honest man.

In February and March 1930, Serge's wavering between gloom and unwarranted hope continued. He wrote to Istrati on February 28 that "It's all I can do to hold out from one month to the next," and followed it on March 14 by saying that "The struggle isn't over and [our] duty is to have confidence in the revolutionary spirit as long as the least chance of seeing it reborn or triumph remains." But in September of that same year, writing to the revolutionary socialist and former Communist Marcel Martinet he described the dark years of 1928–1929 as "now appear[ing] to us as a Golden Age."

In 1932, with his freedom under heavy threat, Serge's novel of the early days of Soviet power, *Ville Conquise (Conquered City)* was published in France. The influence of Dos Passos on the author is unmistakable. Set in Petrograd between 1919 and 1920 (there's a reference in the book to the events occurring eighteen months after the Revolution), the action begins just a couple of months after Serge's arrival. As in the novels of Dos Passos, fictional characters experience real historical events: the famine, the Civil War, meetings in government offices, debates over the military and punitive actions to be carried out. Also like Dos Passos, Soviet society high and low plays a part in *Conquered City*. There are meetings of the Cheka and visits to brothels and illegal doings in factories. Written after Serge's first arrest, it is bold in its description of life in Peter I's invented city under Soviet rule.

Serge doesn't hesitate to expose the country's dark side. Not only are there shortages of all kinds, most seriously of food, but popular discontent with this situation is front and center. Women waiting in line for bread voice their discontent with not only the shortages but also the unfair advantages granted those in high places. Worker discontent is expressed in the most direct way, with theft from factories commonplace, the leadership all but helpless to prevent it. The absurdity of Bolshevik-imposed measures is discussed behind the closed doors of people's homes, and even in the open. "Did you hear [...] that they are nationalizing the news dealers' business, now that there is no more paper, no more newspapers, no more businesses?"[28] Things are going backwards rather than forward: "It takes a week to produce now what was produced in a day last year," a worker says of his factory.[29] Comparisons to great historic disasters are to the detriment of the Soviets: "The death rate in Petrograd this year was higher than in the great plague of 1907!!!!"[30]

The Civil War is going badly, with the Red Army experiencing defeats and desertions. Antisemitism, never far from the surface in Russia, has reappeared. The fear of spies has made the Cheka all the more important and redoubtable; no one is safe from it, since they act unimpeded, with no requirement to actually place any suspects on trial. A simple vote of the local Cheka unit suffices to end a life. To make matters worse, the members of the Cheka commissions are less than exemplary in their character and probity.

Much of the portrait of Petrograd during this dark period of the Soviet regime chimes with what Serge's anarchist friends claim he told them behind closed doors when they visited him during this period. But this is not the entire picture. There are also scenes of heroism, of Red Army soldiers coming from the farthest regions of the Soviet state to defend it against the Whites. And there are men and women of great integrity, like Ryzhik, who will return in Serge's masterpiece, *The Case of Comrade Tulaev*, his integrity ultimately leading him to commit suicide rather than submit to the lies that keep the Soviet state afloat during the Stalin years.

The situation is best summed up by one of the characters, who refuses to lie to himself:

We have conquered everything, and everything has slipped out of our grasp. We have conquered bread, and there is famine. We have declared peace to a war-weary world, and war has moved into every house. We have proclaimed the liberation of men, and we need prisons, and "iron" discipline—yes, to pour our human weakness into brazen molds in order to accomplish what is perhaps beyond our strength—and we are bringers of dictatorship.[31]

The death that is dealt out by the Cheka is done almost frivolously. Did one of their commission members really intentionally allow a suspected spy to escape out of love for a woman, the spy's sister? Did any of them deserve the firing squad at all? And to what end. "Snow covered the fresh graves, which were already forgotten."[32] Technically, Petrograd was not a "conquered city," since the Reds held off the Whites. But a military conquest is not the only kind. The city and its people have been conquered by forces natural and human, dark forces that do evil in order to ensure the good.

* * *

Serge did not content himself with writing three novels and a history of the first days of Soviet Russia, *Year One of the Russian Revolution*. His friend the proletarian writer Henry Poulaille, who worked for the Grasset publishing house, founded the literary magazine *Nouvel Age* in 1930, in which Serge took great interest. The magazine was condemned by the Soviets (one Soviet review claimed that it was run by the anarcho-royalist Georges Valois, who "has taken hold of a tiny clique of proletarian writers who brandish the slogan of an art of ideas nourished by revolutionary-syndicalist tendencies and which, essentially, is fascist") and by French Communists like the writer Louis Aragon, who dismissed it as "very little communist."

Serge sent some of his poems to the review, a translation of Mayakovsky, and a study of the Soviet poet Sergei Esenin, which would ultimately appear in a successor to *Nouvel Age*.

He also wrote Poulaille that "I stubbornly fought to renew contact with the West, to see again new and old friends, but they [the authorities] reject my requests with an unbending, harshly bureaucratic hostility." He told his friend that "I don't at all see how all this will end. We'll see what we'll see."

Much as he liked *Nouvel Age*, he wanted more from it, writing Poulaille in December 1931 that he'd like to see "a section of essays that will deal with the relations between content and form, the tendencies and ideas of authors (ideology), with proletarian literature and the controversies it gives rise to."

Serge would stumble along for the couple of years remaining before his second arrest. On November 1, 1932, he described his mental state in a letter to the Communist novelist Jean-Richard Bloch. Thanking Bloch for an article he'd written on the Russian Revolution, he described it as "a breath of fresh air that reaches me from afar. More than wine and meats, it's the spirit that lacks in this immense tragedy, where the new faith fails like its predecessors. Distrusting, it seems, its own dynamism it wants to be a church, codified, written down, narrow-minded."

In December 1932 he'd end his final letter to Poulaille as a free man by telling him, "For me, no way of getting going. It's as tough as getting out of prison. Which is where I feel I'm housed. Sad." Soon he would literally be in prison.

14
Arrest

As the repression of Oppositionists grew fiercer, Serge later wrote that he considered that he had "a seventy percent probability of disappearing," like so many of his friends and comrades.[1] The opportunity having arisen to contact comrades in France, he wrote a lengthy letter to his friends Marcel Martinet, Magdeleine and Marcel Paz, and the anarchist and free-love advocate Jacques Mesnil, all identified only by their initials on the original of the letter, which has come down to us as Serge's "profession of faith." The recipients were told to publish the essential sections of it in case of his disappearance. In the event, the letter, dated simply "late January 1933" at its head and February 1, 1933, at its conclusion, was published in an abridged form in the May 25, 1933, issue of *La Révolution prolétarienne*, at which point Serge had been held incommunicado for almost three months. The letter contains in germ all of Serge's future thought and provides a foundation for understanding the final decade and a half of his life.

Serge wrote his Paris friends that he had requested a passport to leave the Soviet Union in 1928, after his previous arrest. The request, which had been denied, was for a passport for him alone, not including his wife and son. "Since then," he wrote, "the situation here has gotten so much worse, customs have moved so far in the direction of an increasingly absolute intolerance that at times I have no choice but to doubt for the future."

His solitude, he told his friends, was absolute: "Not a single comrade; all those with whom I was connected [are] deported, imprisoned, dead, lost." Correspondence with others in Russia, and with his friends in France, is impossible, and "a total boycott forbids me any intellectual activity here." His manuscripts are under threat of theft, his letters opened, contact even with relatives of comrades is impossible for fear of further compromising them.

The constant pressure under which he and his family and those around them are living has resulted in his wife now suffering from "intermittent psychosis."

After describing his personal situation, Serge moved on to the political. Serge, the lover of Russia, is forced to admit that what the country is living through in 1933 under Stalin is of a piece with all of Russian history at its worst. As in the past,

[i]t's still the same treatment inflicted on man; the same mortal intolerance, the same incapacity to evolve, the same horror of freedom, the same governmental and bureaucratic fanaticism, the same arbitrariness at all levels of the social hierarchy, the same implacable and shadowy coercion.

In short, he wrote and underlined: "The Revolution has entered a phase of reaction."

He went further, though. "One shouldn't hide from oneself that socialism bears within itself the seeds of reaction. In Russia, these seeds have fully blossomed." Serge then spoke the unspeakable, using a word he claimed to be the first to use—unlikely as that might be—to describe Soviet Russia: "At present, we are increasingly in the presence of a totalitarian state." Stalin's regime was in "total contradiction with [...] the Revolution properly speaking." The heroism of the past still exists in a few brave souls, but "no civic courage is tolerated, no form of disinterest is possible in so bitter a struggle for life."

Serge, for the first time publicly, but not the last, drew stark conclusions from the experience of the Russian Revolution, at least its years since Stalin reached power. "Reaction within the Revolution puts everything into question; it compromises the future, principles, and even the sublime past of the Revolution, giving birth to an internal danger that at the present time is far greater than the external dangers that are so often spoken of."

Employing language that would become habitual with Serge, he warned that "socialism will not vanquish here and elsewhere and will only prove its superiority to capitalism, not by the construction of tanks, but through the organization of social life, only if it offers man better conditions than capitalism: more material well-being, more justice, more freedom, and a higher dignity."

Serge defended all of the positions he took between 1926 and 1933, but admits that, not having read a single book published in Europe in five years, he cannot say that he "is in solidarity with any group." He said he had forsworn political activism and, establishing his political independence, which he would maintain for the rest of his life, he declared:

I am in sympathy with all those who go against the current, who seek to save the principles, ideas, and spirit of the October Revolution. I believe that in order to do this everything must be revised, beginning by establishing between comrades of the most diverse tendencies a truly fraternal collaboration in both discussion and action.

It was in this letter as well that Serge repeated what he had written in 1925 in a letter published several years later by *La Révolution prolétarienne* about the obligation he considered absolutely vital in saving the idea of socialism, what he called the "double duty" that was incumbent upon him to put an end to the "gangrene" of the Revolution. "External defense and internal defense; the latter has become more serious. And those who close their eyes to the evil make themselves accomplices through ignorance, blindness, pusillanimity, or self-interest." It was his fidelity to this double duty, a phrase that recurs throughout his writings, that gave him the strength to hold out against those who betrayed the revolution—capital "R" as in Russian Revolution, and small "r," as in the general idea—as he envisioned it.

Serge outlined three points he called "essential, greater than all." The first was "defense of man. Respect for man. He must be returned his rights, security, and value. Without this, no socialism is possible." His second essential point was "[d]efense of the truth, to which man and the masses have a right." His third point was his insistence on the "defense of thought [...]. I maintain that socialism can only grow in the intellectual order through emulation, research, and the battle of ideas."

These three elements would serve to guide Serge's activities for the rest of his life. All of his points focus on demands that can be described as humanist. Socialism for Serge, in 1933 and for the rest of his life, could not thrive or even survive without recognizing the primacy of the human person.

It is jarring, given his insistence on liberty, to see him cite the example of the founder of the Cheka, Feliks Dzerzhinsky, and the latter's desire, hardly to be taken seriously given the Cheka's record, expressed in 1920, to abolish the death penalty for political crimes. He also brings into his argument in defense of freedom within socialism those Communists who wanted to limit the role of the Cheka to that of investigation.

Serge's vision of the freedom of the human person would remain his first priority, and its presence in his writings and activities would become ever more pronounced, but its accent would shift from this limited one of the ending of political repression to the total liberation of the human person based on a non-Marxist philosophy, Personalism.

Serge signed off expressing the hope to see his friends again soon, and emphasizing the strength of his force of resistance. "I will continue to struggle as best I can. In any case, I am holding out, and if things take a bad turn I will have done all I could, held out as best I could, to the end."

The fear that led Serge to write this letter as a form of testament would soon be borne out. His freedom was about to come to an end.

* * *

The inevitable finally occurred on March 7, 1933. While picking up medicine for his wife at a pharmacy on 25 October Prospekt in Leningrad, he was approached by two men who identified themselves as being from the Criminal Investigation Division. Unable to argue himself out of the arrest, Serge was taken to the new fifteen-story GPU building in Leningrad, where he was questioned by the investigating magistrate for party matters, Karpovich, whom Serge described as a "large, ginger-haired man, coldly cordial, sly, and guarded." In a slight understatement Karpovich told Serge, "We are going to have some long talks together, Victor Lvovich."[2]

Serge told his interrogator that he would answer no questions until his requests were met: the transfer of his wife to the Red Army psychiatric hospital, and that he be allowed to call his twelve-year-old son Vlady when the latter reaches home. Karpovich agreed.

After a quick and accurate recap of Serge's life, Serge's interrogation records reveal him to have been forthright and unafraid to explain his positions. Expressing his sympathy with the Trotskyists from 1927, he nevertheless maintained that he "did not belong to that group." His siding with the Opposition was caused by specific areas of disagreement with the leadership of the Communist Party: "the Chinese Revolution; industrialization; and the peasant question—the attack on the kulaks, the policy of collectivization, and the beginning of the Five Year Plans." There was another issue that mattered to him, one that he said "faded with time": the repression of the Opposition. As he said, "Life went on."

Serge insisted that he supported the general line of the party and its leadership, but doing so "doesn't deprive me of the right to independent theoretical and philosophical thought, which can, in certain cases, take the form of criticism." He told his interrogator, as he had written in his "profession of faith," that he had abandoned political activity.

He told the GPU's Karpovich that because of his abandonment of politics, "I had no occasion nor do I have any occasion [now] to engage in any such criticism," which he must have known Karpovich knew wasn't true. In any event, he continued, he was in agreement with the party's activities in industrialization, collectivization, and on the cultural front, but felt that "distortions and radical turns are taking place and are severely interfering with the development of the revolution." Serge was walking a fine line here, admitting to both criticizing and supporting the party and its leadership, to which he declared his "submission [...] and my readiness to carry out any work in these difficult times."

Serge took great care in accurately describing the literary and scholarly work to which he had decided to dedicate his life, having come "to the conclusion that I would be more useful to the Revolution with my books and my broad life experience, than by everyday party work." He confessed to being "tired" after the factional struggles within the party, the failure of the German revolution of 1923, and the great struggle within the Communist Party in 1927. He concluded this part of his interrogation by telling the GPU agent, "I am now definitively devoting my interests to literature and history."

Serge expanded on his intellectual work, particularly the overseas portion of it, telling of his collaboration with *Europe*, the intellectual journal edited by Romain Rolland and Jean-Richard Bloch, all of whose contributors were, Serge said, "tried and true friends of the USSR." *Europe* was not a minor publication. It was one of the great French intellectual journals in the inter-war period, described by the French historian Michel Winock as "the review of left-wing intellectuals, communist-leaning, hostile to the gratuitousness of art and to the aristocracy of pure thought."[3]

Serge insisted he had no interest in day-to-day matters. "It is completely a secondary question whether the line or the tactics of the party on this or that concrete question is a hundred percent correct." Serge's focus was on higher things: "For me what is important is to develop the problem of transforming man in the revolutionary struggle and to give birth to and develop a new consciousness, the problem of a new man." Skillfully avoiding placing himself outside or against the party and its need to maintain socialism, he offered his services. "I give my sympathy to the proletarian party and I am ready to concretely help it."

And yet, courageously, Serge defended the point of view expressed in his "profession of faith," which most likely would have been known to the GPU through its usual illicit means (he certainly suspected this was the case at a later point). He had no problems with "the politics or the program of the Party." His problem was both larger and smaller: It was with "everyday existence," which he said was "unhealthy and cruel." He expressed his dismay at the lack of free expression of ideas, and here he took a dangerous path, saying it was "wrong to have an intolerant attitude toward dissident thinkers, whether they are syndicalists, anarchists, deviationists or oppositionists of various stripes."

Here we must pause. By 1933 the murderous campaign against "syndicalists, anarchists, deviationists, or oppositionists of various stripes" was already going forward under a full head of steam. Though denying he had any interest in these ideas, the mere fact of defending others' right to hold these ideas and to profess them put his life at risk when he was *not* in the hands of the GPU (that they knew about these ideas already will appear in his later interrogations in Moscow). But to express these ideas while held in the wolf's jaws demonstrates unequalled courage.

Serge did however hedge his bets by engaging in Talmudic hairsplitting. "I think that at the level of ideas, *not political struggle of course*, radical changes are needed. First of all, in the West, and secondly in the USSR" (emphasis added). This point of view, he asserted, again defending his collaboration with Western intellectuals, was shared by those who contributed to *Europe*.

Serge addressed the matter of the construction of socialism in one country, anathema to the Left Opposition but the basis for

Stalin's policies, by engaging in intellectual name dropping. He praised the Bolshevik Party, which (damning with faint praise) "perhaps has achieved some results." But the end goal is "total communism, i.e., a society without classes, without an army, without borders, without a state in the old sense of the word." This was only possible, Serge offered, "if the revolution succeeds in at least the principal countries." This was, according to Serge, the political line of another magazine with which he was involved, *Monde*, edited by Henri Barbusse, the former editor of *Clarté*, which, Serge told his interrogator, saw only one way to solve the problems of the crisis of capitalism: "The revolutionary cooperation or unification of Paris, Berlin, and Moscow." However admirable this goal was, he dismissed it as a "theoretical abstraction," to which he didn't "ascribe great importance." After all, "socialism is being built in one country and is being built successfully." Few would dare deny Serge the right to have stretched the truth as he did here. That socialism could *not* be built in one country alone was axiomatic for the Leninist Serge.

Duplicity, he would later write, was an essential tactic in a totalitarian state, which the USSR was. We have already discussed his resort to duplicity as an explanation for his activities and writings in the early 1920s. Writing in his notebooks on November 3, 1944, and July 5, 1945, in defense of duplicity, he would say "apparent submission is sometimes the final means of resistance; that terroristic despotism leaves room only for duplicity, the ultimate defense through hypocrisy, deception, mental reservations, and secret heroism."[4] The duplicity he spoke of was on a larger scale, duplicity as general political tactic. But it applies just as well under the circumstances of an interrogation by the political police. Saying socialism was not being built would have been signing his death warrant. He was as open as a man could be in his answers to his interrogator Karpovich. But he owed him no debt of absolute truth in the Stalinist war on historical and political truth. He continued to walk the tightrope of utter and justified falsehood and a modified truth-telling that kept him among the living, with the chance to survive and continue to fight for the truth.

His explanation of his point of view on the communist failures in Germany shows that he had decided that on some matters the truth would not cost him his life. The triumph of Hitler was aided, he told the GPU, by the errors of both workers' parties, the Socialists and the Communists. Though he considered the failure of the KPD, led by Ernst Thaelmann, who had just been arrested by the Nazis, to have assisted Hindenburg's election through its tactical refusal to work with the Socialists, he was careful to put the blame on those now absent, who, as the French say, are always wrong. "I remember," he said, "this was a mistake of the leadership of Ruth Fischer and [Arkady] Maslow, condemned by the Comintern." Serge was thus on the side of the angels even in criticizing the Communists: Fischer and Maslow had long since been thrown under the bus of Communist history, a discarding Serge had witnessed when he was assigned to keep an eye on the German revolution in 1923. But the defeat of the left was also proof of the correctness of his own line. "For me the victory of fascism in Germany is only a confirmation of my idea that it is necessary to unite all vital forces in the West and pose the new proletarian question of how we relate to mankind."

Though the formation of a united front between Socialists and Communists would later become the marching orders of the Comintern, defending this position in 1933 made him a premature popular frontist. Serge's position was also that of other figures in the Communist movement, who paid dearly for their stance. Jacques Doriot, Communist mayor of the Paris suburb of Saint-Denis, was a vocal supporter of unity between the Socialist and Communist Parties before this became an accepted or even acceptable position. This led to his expulsion from the PCF in 1934, and his subsequent founding of France's leading fascist party, the Parti populaire français. He would later become an arch-Collaborationist, wear a German uniform, and be killed in the final stage of the war.

In response to his interrogator, Serge returned to his definition of himself above all as a writer, summarizing his then-published works—*Year One of the Russian Revolution*, and the novels *Men in Prison*, *Birth of Our Power*, and *Conquered City*. He described them as "primarily the books of a French writer for the French reader," books that have been well received in the French press. He told his interrogator that "I can say with pride that no one among Western writers who support the USSR and the October Revolution has done as much to popularize and bring to the consciousness of the reading public the saga of the Soviet revolution." In this he was surely right.

The final part of his interrogation concerned his contacts in the USSR and abroad. It is a parade of dead men and women on reprieve, the most significant of the political figures being Alexandra Bronstein and Vassily Chadaev, the latter, he said, the only Oppositionist he considered a friend. Bronstein was Trotsky's first wife, a decades-long revolutionary who was, according to Serge's memoir, one of the few Oppositionists not imprisoned in 1928, and who would vanish in the purges some time before 1938. The literary figures in his circle faced and met the same fate. The flower of Russian literature was among his friends, most of whom would meet death, most prominent among them men like Boris Pilnyak and Osip Mandelstam.

After detailing his acquaintances and friends in Russia, he explained that "almost all my intellectual, i.e., literary, spiritual, and intellectual connections are abroad." Some were Westerners living in the Soviet Union, among them his brother-in-law the Russianist Pierre Pascal and the Italian syndicalist Francesco Ghezzi, a refugee from fascist Italy who would disappear in the Gulag.

Serge provided a full list of the names of his overseas contacts, it making no sense to hide any, since all foreign correspondence was opened and read before being sent on. His list included close friends and allies like Jacques Mesnil and Maurice and Magdeleine Paz, who would be vocal allies during his struggles, as well as important figures in French literary circles like André Malraux, Blaise Cendrars, Léon Werth, Henri Barbusse, Henry Poulaille, and the Belgian Charles Plisnier. If some, like Malraux for a period, and Barbusse for a longer span, were in good odor with the Soviets, others, like Poulaille and Plisnier were marked as dissidents on the left when it came to the Soviet Union, men who shared Serge's point of view and would defend him loyally in the years to come.

More compromising was his admission of friendship with the French Trotskyist Pierre Naville and the Spanish Oppositionist and leader of the Partido Obrero de Unificación Marxista (POUM), Andreu Nin, who would be kidnapped and murdered by the Soviets four years later during the Spanish Civil War. Owing to his experience in Spain—however brief it was—Serge explained that he had been a member of the Spanish-American Society in Russia and had invited Nin to give a report before it in 1929, before the latter's expulsion from the Spanish Communist Party. "It is possible," Serge added, "that since I am his friend I facilitated the organization of this report."

Serge signed the transcript of his interrogation V.L. Kibalchich. The first stage of his calvary was completed. Serge had comported himself with enormous courage and dignity.

The next day, accompanied by two GPU agents in a simple railroad passenger train, Serge was transferred from Leningrad to Moscow. There, on March 9, his major interrogation at the GPU's Lubyanka prison in Dzerzhinsky Square began, headed by the magistrate Bogen. In his memoirs he described his time at the Lubyanka as lasting about eighty days, which matches with the official records.[5] Though originally placed in a crowded cell, Serge was locked up alone between the half-dozen or so interrogations he was made to submit to.

Here, in absolute secrecy, with no communication with any person whatsoever, with no reading matter whatsoever, with no paper, not even one sheet, with no occupation of any kind, with no open-air exercise in the yard, I spent about eighty days. It was a severe test for the nerves, in which I acquitted myself pretty well.[6]

The GPU's attempt to disorient him and increase his fear of the proceedings on the way to his interrogation sessions was described in his memoirs and in his 1936 testimony before the Dewey Commission investigating the Moscow Trials.

They never had me take the shortest route, rather, on the contrary, they took me on lengthy detours through the corridors, so as to give a not always agreeable impression. Sometimes we passed briskly from a dark corridor to one brightly lit, or [...] they made us pass in front of guards and even past the cells which we could presume housed those sentenced to death.

His interrogations, spread out over a couple of months, all of the sessions taking place at night, as he described to the Dewey Commission shortly after his release from the USSR, "began having more the air of a psychological discussion, rather than a judicial examination."

The interrogator, Bogen, told him to simply tell the story of his life and ideas, so that they could "establish the truth in [this] regard." These were not muscular interrogations, though threats were made when he refused to cooperate. He never saw a clerk or anyone taking notes, though he thought it safe to assume someone might have been in the next room, or that the conversations were being recorded.

A summary of the Serge interrogation marked "top secret," and signed by the two agents working on his case, Bogen and Rutkovsky, the latter the chief of the secret political division of the GPU, laid out the questioning and summarized the case against Serge: that he'd been an active Trotskyist since 1926, and that on Trotsky's request he had translated the program of the

Opposition into French. The overseas contacts he had not hidden during his Leningrad interrogation—Pierre Naville, Gérard (obviously Gérard Rosenthal, Trotsky's lawyer and an active Trotskyist), Andreu Nin, and Maurice and Magdeleine Paz and their circle—were considered suspect, if not inculpatory.

The GPU seems to have been confused about Serge's foreign allies and outlets, as his contributions to a supposed Parisian review with the eminently Trotskyist title *La Révolution permanente* were cited, when it was the revolutionary syndicalist *La Révolution prolétarienne*, long a home to his writings, that was intended.

GPU agents had thoroughly infiltrated all Opposition circles, and they had reported to their superiors on Serge's transmission of information on the overseas movement to circles in Leningrad and Moscow. This would feature prominently in his interrogations.

So well implanted was GPU infiltration that it was a GPU agent, Sobelevich, referred to as Zl-l in Rutkovsky and Bogen's secret summary of the Serge case, who was allegedly given a mission by Serge to deliver information on the state of things in Russia for publication in the *Bulletin of the Opposition*.

Zl-l, or Abram Sobolevicius, was also known as Abram Sobolevich, Abram Sobelevich, Senine, and Jack Soble. A GPU agent provocateur and informant, he made his way into the leadership of the Trotskyist movement. He met with Trotsky in his exile in Prinkipo and Copenhagen, and also led the German branch of Trotsky's movement, where he played a key role in its destruction, activities referred to by Serge in the interrogation. Sobelevicius later publicly broke with the Opposition movement that he had been sabotaging. Along with his brother, Ruven Sobolevicius, known in America as the psychiatrist Dr. Robert Soblen, he helped set up a Soviet spy network in the US. Jack was sentenced in 1957 to seven years for espionage. Ever the informant, in 1960 he testified against his brother, who committed suicide while imprisoned. At his brother's trial Jack had insisted that his own espionage duties for the Soviets were mainly the infiltration and exposure of Trotskyists. Jack testified regularly about Soviet espionage after his release from prison in 1962. Sobelevich receives one passing mention in Serge's memoirs, about a telegram from Trotsky's son warning that he is an agent provocateur.[7]

The interrogation report focused on two critical matters that the GPU interrogators claimed Serge spread to the West. The first was that Soviet workers "are discontented and close to open revolt, particularly the Charikopodchipnik factory, who themselves set fire to their factory in response to a decree on the protection of nationalized property." That was not the only sign of worker anger. Serge also wrote of "the open revolt of starving workers [that] broke out in Ivanovo-Voznessensk. It was put down by the army and resulted in deaths." Serge was also alleged to have passed on to the infiltrator Zl-l another piece of information for publication in the *Bulletin of the Opposition*: "There is a split in the Politburo. Molotov, Kaganovich, Postychev and others have formed a bloc against Stalin." Serge is alleged to have told the agent that despite the "crushing" of the Trotskyist organization "faithful comrades remained who could provide Trotsky with information on the situation in the party."

Serge wrote in his memoirs that after a number of night sessions with Bogen he

offered me cigarettes, and explained that my outlook was visibly that of a hardened counterrevolutionary, which was extremely dangerous for me. I interrupted him: "Must I conclude that I am being threatened with the death penalty?" He protested, "Not at all! But, all the same, you are well on the way to destroying yourself. Your only hope for safety lies in a change of attitude and a complete confession. Think it over." I was returned to my cell at about 4:00 a.m.

At this point, Serge wrote, "the interrogation was cut short,"[8] and a new, higher placed agent, Rutkovsky, entered the case, taking over as Serge's principal interrogator. Their sessions began on a distinctly unpromising note for the prisoner. Rutkovsky told him that he was "lost," but that he was offering Serge a "life raft." Alleged accusations made by Serge's sister-in-law Anita were that life raft.

Anita Russakov now got dragged into the mire by the infiltrator, as she was accused of giving the address of a "secret Trotskyist," in fact, a person Serge described in his memoirs as "someone called Solovian, who was quite unknown to me,"[9] and who was also to transmit information to Trotsky. This intermediary was in all likelihood Sobolevich.

In both his memoirs and his testimony before the international commission investigating the Moscow Trials chaired by John Dewey, Serge expressed his anger and disbelief that his sister-in-law Anita had told the GPU that he was involved in any way in Trotskyist activities. In his Dewey Commission testimony Serge says that he had no knowledge of Anita and her "so-called deposition linking him to Trotskyists." He testified that he knew immediately that this evidence against him was forged, but saw great danger in one element of it: One of the Trotskyists he was supposedly in contact with lived in a military city. "This detail, every bit as false as the rest, led me to think that they were aiming at a capital verdict, either against me or my sister-in-law." At this point he "exploded," and refused any further discussion of this matter. Rutkovsky asked him to calm down and, according to Serge's Dewey Commission testimony, offered Serge a glass of water. In his memoirs Serge gives this a slightly different meaning, saying he needed a moment to gather his thoughts, and that at this point

I felt I had to gain a few moments and interrupted him. "I'm very thirsty. Could you get me a glass of water?" There was none there and Rutkovsky had to get up and call someone. I had time to think, and his effect was ruined. He resumed. "So I'm making one last attempt to save you."[10]

Serge soon wrote to the prosecutor demanding that he be allowed a face-to-face confrontation with Anita, which was denied. She was sentenced to three months at this time, but in 1936 would be sentenced to five years in the gulag in Viatka, a deportation Serge believed was decided upon in order to keep her far from him and the possibility of discovering the truth. Anita's five-year sentence lasted twenty years, and she was finally released in 1956.

The interrogation summary signed by Rutkovsky and Bogen covers Serge's crimes as related by GPU informers in detail, from arranging contacts with Oppositionists to providing the passwords needed to make contact with French followers of Trotsky, Naville and Rosenthal in 1932, to passing Trotskyist material to Trotsky's ex-wife A.L. Bronstein.

"Zl-l"—Sobelovich—was not the only informant tracking Serge's and the Oppositionists' activities. Agent "Fedorov" reported that Serge passed on to the Leningrad Oppositionists the news of mass arrests in Moscow. The arrests of more than a hundred persons "are connected to the disavowal of the group of Trotskyists in Germany [which] was corrupted by the agents provocateurs introduced into this group by the leadership of the Comintern and the party." The agent provocateur most involved with this collapse of the movement in Germany was, as we have seen, the key informant against Serge, Sobolevich.

Serge, who had studied the files of the tsarist Okhrana and was the author of *What Every Radical Should Know about State Repression*, based on his research, was not without his own ideas as to how his comrades had fallen. "The affair had gone so far that the agents provocateurs acted even within the secretariat where [Trotsky's daughter] Zina Bronstein worked. Zina maintained contacts within the USSR. Perhaps these 'burned' contacts caused the arrest of [the economist and anti-Stalinist] Preobrazhensky and the death of Zina." Preobrazhensky was executed in 1937; Zinaida Bronstein had committed suicide in January 1933.

On May 13, 1933, Serge wrote a declaration for Rutkovsky that is included in his GPU file. After two months of interrogation, he hadn't budged: "I strongly reject the accusation of taking part in underground Trotskyist work. Among the great number of materials in my writer's work files you can't find one political document written in the last four to five years."

He ended his statement with two requests addressed to the collegium of the GPU. He asked it "1—to give me the opportunity to continue my literary work; 2—to give me an opportunity to support my family both materially and morally; to provide it the support which is essential for its existence, taking into account its exceptionally terrible position, its exceptional defenselessness." He ended his appeal to the goodness of the GPU by invoking his supporters in the West, "devoted friends of the USSR, who will not decline to vouch for me."

By this point his profession of faith had already been published in *La Révolution prolétarienne*, his disappearance from view between March and May taken as the signal for a campaign to make Serge's fate known.

The gravity of Serge's situation cannot be overstated. Espionage of many kinds in Soviet eyes was involved: economic, state, and party. Involvement in any of it, much less all of it, could have made Serge subject to the death penalty. In the end, Rutkovsky settled on the charge of violating Article 58 of the Criminal Code, that of engaging in counter-revolutionary activity, sentencing Serge to three years in the "isolator" of Orenburg in the Urals.

15

Orenburg and L'Affaire Serge

Even in contemporary accounts it was reported that Serge had been sentenced to Siberia. Though this has a certain metaphoric value, Serge would spend his time in an isolator in the Urals, just over 900 miles southeast of Moscow. Before Serge's arrival, up until 1929, Orenburg had been capital of the Kirghiz Autonomous Soviet Socialist Republic, and the year of his departure, 1936, the republic became a full member of the USSR as the Kazakh Soviet Socialist Republic. The winters are cold, with temperatures hovering around zero Fahrenheit, and the summers are mild. He would complain in a May 1934 letter of the things that dominated his life at that time, "heat and famine."

It must be made clear that Serge's sentence was not served in the Gulag, nor did his conditions in any way resemble those suffered by the slave laborers forced to work on the White Sea canal. Though this is the image commonly held of the lot of Stalin's prisoners, Serge never even implies that the conditions under which he was held, though difficult and cruel, were anything like that. Serge's descriptions of life in the isolator of Orenburg very much resemble those of political prisoners sentenced to Siberian exile by the tsar. In his memoirs, in the novel he wrote based on his experiences in the isolator, *Midnight in the Century*, and in his correspondence, we see that social life of a kind was carried on among the internees, who included a group of fellow Oppositionists. His son, Vlady, accompanied Serge not only to Orenburg but also to secret meetings with the other Oppositionists there. These meetings never took place in homes but rather in the woods outside town. Vlady remembered the handful of Oppositionists who met together as *"des durs"*—

the hardcore—men who'd never denied or retracted their beliefs. Vlady explained in later years in a conversation with relatives and the historian and Serge biographer Suzi Weissman that not all were like them, that "there were others who had submitted once, twice or three times. Victor said laughingly that there were some who sent declarations every week, that accumulate at the Central Committee [in piles] that reach the ceiling."

The struggle to survive was as much an economic one as anything else. Vlady would later write, in collaboration with the Mexican Serge scholar Claudio Albertani, that

> In relation to those sent to the concentration camps, we were unquestionably very fortunate. In the first place, legally we weren't considered prisoners, rather exiles, which means we enjoyed a certain amount of freedom. We lived under forced residence and weren't allowed to travel, but were able to maintain relations with the rest of the world, in particular with those overseas, which saved us.

Serge was not a prisoner and so he did not wear chains, nor was he held in a cell. He lived in a house he rented in the town of Orenburg, which he described in his memoirs as "facing the infinite steppes," and had to earn his own living.[1] He had his wife Liuba and son Vlady with him in the early days of his deportation, the former having come out from Leningrad bringing Serge's typewriter and some books that were being returned to him after having been seized by the GPU. Liuba, still suffering from mental illness, stayed with him until October 1934, when she returned to Leningrad and treatment. There, far from Serge, she gave birth to their daughter Jeannine in February 1935. Vlady, who accompanied his father through all his travails, was made to pay for his father's crimes. The fifteen-year-old wrote in a letter on June 7, 1935, that "I have just been expelled from the 24th school of Orenburg ... The reason for this measure is exclusively my father's situation, which has never been officially declared to us."[2]

Serge spoke in his memoirs of his inability to find work due to his refusal to repent and ask for readmission to the party. He lived on small sums he was able to earn and on barter. As was the case everywhere in the Soviet Union, rations of basics like bread were not always available. Occasional work was thrown his way, like a stint as a watchman. We find in his letters sent from Orenburg to his friend Henry Poulaille requests for specific French books that he hoped to translate into Russian to pay his rent and purchase supplies.

Along with Serge in Orenburg were a half-dozen or so other Oppositionists, all, like Serge, veterans of the Bolshevik Party, devoted revolutionaries who had chosen the losing side in the intra-party struggle. Ironically, the sister of the head of the Provisional Government overthrown by the Bolsheviks, Alexander Kerensky, a physician, was among the deportees as well.[3]

Serge suffered illness, deprivation, and the continued deterioration of his wife's mental state, yet held firm. Vlady told the French Serge scholar Jean Rière that, "Our life in Orenburg was very difficult, especially when Maman was there. Her intermittent crises occurred at increasingly shorter intervals, when everything she touched was smashed to pieces. And on days when she was depressed, she would say, feeling guilty, 'I'm of no use to anyone; all I do is cause you harm; I want to leave.'"

Serge not only corresponded with friends in the West, a right that was cut off in 1935, but was able to receive packages of books and medicines from there as well. Henry Poulaille, thanks to his job at the Grasset publishing house, regularly supplied him with reading matter. Magdeleine Paz, according to Vlady Kibalchich's memories of the time, even sent them rice, powdered chocolate, chocolate bars, white flour, and tapioca. Vlady remembered that on a couple of occasions Serge received money from French publishers, which enabled them to go shopping in the restricted Torgsin store, which accepted only Valuta and gold.

None of this is intended to depict Serge's years in Orenburg as time in a dacha. He had to report at regular intervals to the GPU, and though an escape is depicted in the autobiographical *Midnight in the Century*, there's no indication Serge ever contemplated one. He counted on his own inner strength to get him through this ordeal.

He wrote to Poulaille in May 1934, just under a year after his arrival in Orenburg, that "I don't have any idea at all how all this will end. Fate has given me nerves of rope [...] but my family is much less resistant. And yet, let us remain optimistic. One can't be a revolutionary without that, and if you aren't a revolutionary today you are nothing."

The great project of Serge's time in Orenburg was the novel he was writing about his anarchist years, *Les Hommes perdus* (The Lost Men). He finished writing the book in May 1934, and on May 20 sent it via certified mail to the French writer Romain Rolland for it to be forwarded to his French publisher. It was essential for many reasons that it be published in France. As Serge wrote to Poulaille, it is "the sole material foundation for the near future in the horrific destitution that surrounds us." It never arrived.

In his letter to Poulaille of May 28, 1934, Serge provides as full an account of the lost book as we are ever likely to have, as searches in the files of the secret police for the manuscript have been fruitless. Though sent in four envelopes and by certified mail, it never made it to Rolland, having been intercepted by the censors. In certain circles Rolland is held to be at fault for the disappearance of the manuscript of *Les Hommes perdus*, but this is a canard. Rolland laid out the path of the manuscripts very clearly in a letter to Gorky on November 17, 1934.[4] The first manuscript was sent to him directly on May 20, 1934, the second was sent to the censors at Glavlit, the Soviet censorship agency, on July 3, 1934, to then be forwarded to Rolland, as was the third, "heavily insured," on October 1, which was lost along the way. The censors at Glavlit held the manuscript at the Commissariat of Public Instruction, ignoring the authorization to send the book to Rolland issued by the chief of the foreign literary section of the commissariat. Despite all Serge's precautions, none of the copies he sent to Rolland reached their destination. Serge wrote letters of complaint to the authorities about what he described as the "systematic" loss of his works. "They answered me," he wrote in a letter, "that it's quite astonishing and that I'm right to complain." The disappearance of the manuscripts is strictly owed to the actions of Soviet censors. Whatever the later wavering of Rolland in his defense of Serge, he was firm on this matter.

Serge's described the book in his letter to Poulaille:

> It is neither a memoir nor a work of imagination, though having something of both. I define the genre as "testimony." But in general, I hold that the writer is a witness, that all memoirs are largely imaginary, and that nevertheless there is nothing higher than serving the truth [...] I admit that writing this book cost me. Spending months stirring up the memory of rebellions pushed into a dead end and descending into crime, exalting and narrow ideas, absolute and poor, striving to bring to life men lost in the most distressing of fashions, all of it revolving endlessly around suicide, prison, and the guillotine—it's vast.

We can thus be certain that here was the fictionalized tale of the Bonnot Gang, Serge's coming to terms and summing up his youthful experience among the individualists and bandits, which he minimized in his memoirs. This letter is revealing not just in what it says of the lost book, but his admission that "memoirs are largely imaginary." What is certain, as we've seen, is that if his account in his memoirs is not quite imaginary, it's not the testimony that the novel might well have been.

* * *

Serge was not aware that his friends, supporters, and admirers were actively working for his liberation; that unlike almost everyone caught up in the Stalinist purges Serge was able to come out of it alive is a tribute to his fortitude and his allies' efforts.

It's not clear when Serge's sentence was made known to the outside world. The first word any of Serge's friends had of his whereabouts was a postcard dated June 9, 1933, sent from Orenburg to Jacques Mesnil, in which Serge reported that his "morale was excellent."

Well before there was official word of Serge's fate, the non-Communist left, and not only the left, almost immediately protested the arrest of Serge. The context given to their protests varied widely. Some viewed Serge's arrest as a sign of the degeneration of a regime that no longer was worthy of support; others took the tack of appealing to the Soviets on the basis of shared beliefs in the October Revolution from which the Soviets had strayed.

The French Socialist Party published articles in defense of Serge within the first month of his arrest. On April 5 the party newspaper *Le Populaire* published an appeal written by a heteroclite group. The novelist Georges Bataille, close to the surrealists and known for his writings on eroticism and envelope-pushing fiction, was a signatory, along with Serge's friends Pierre Pascal, Lucien Laurat, Jacques Mesnil and his fellow dissident revolutionary, Boris Souvarine. Their appeal focused as much on the mental state of Liuba, who had "lost her reason" as a result of the persecutions the family had undergone, as on Serge. The writers appealed to the conscience of the public, informing them of the then twelve-year-old Vlady's abandonment, "delivered over to the cruelest caprices of chance in a country of destitution and privation." Vlady's and Liuba's sufferings were of a piece with the fate of her family, "driven from Leningrad, condemned to cold and hunger [...] expiatory victims of an atrocious and inexcusable revenge."

For the signatories the fate of the Russakovs and Serge spoke eloquently of the USSR. "These methods of dissimulation and cover-up [are] aimed at spreading fear and giving rise to the worst hypotheses." All of this is "part of a system of government. The presence of such facts, [...] speak for themselves [...] and characterize a government." The appeal called for the release of Serge and Anita Russakov and "humane treatment for the persecuted family."

Already, in late April, the revue *Germinal* issued an appeal for Serge's release, citing the success of the 1928 campaign of Serge's friends and Serge's failed attempts to leave the USSR in 1932. With Serge still under GPU detention, *Germinal* appealed to people of all tendencies and to "all people of good will to [join in] every initiative that will be taken to obtain the liberation of the author of *Year One of the Russian Revolution.*"

That the French Trotskyists were not yet aware of Serge's whereabouts in mid-May is evident from an article in the May 19 issue of the newspaper of the Ligue Communiste. The article, entitled "Still Silence on the Fate of Victor Serge," informed its readers that, "despite numerous articles, despite pressing requests, Stalin has not yet said anything concerning the fate of our friend Victor Serge. Deported? Imprisoned? We don't know a thing. Where? A mystery."

Serge's Belgian comrades joined in early, when the journal *L'Esprit du temps* published in its May 1933 issue a plea from several of its contributors, including Charles Plisnier—the novelist, Oppositionist, and friend of Serge—declaring that, "for the second time, our comrade and friend Victor Serge is paying for his lifelong devotion to the world revolution in a GPU prison [...] He persists in his crime of thinking." The appeal was phrased in unimpeachably revolutionary terms. Serge's arrest was "a violation of the sacred principles of the October Revolution [...] Victor Serge cannot be accused of hostility towards communism. He is a communist. He proclaims it. He proves it."

Serge's profession of faith, written in January and February 1933, was published, as we have seen, by *La Révolution prolétarienne* in its May 25, 1933, issue. This was a few weeks after he was sentenced to the isolator in Orenburg, though at the time his fate was still shrouded in mystery. In its June 10, 1933, issue, when Serge's fate was known, the magazine published the text of a letter Serge wrote to the Central Executive Committee of the Soviets of October 16, 1932, expressing his wish for a passport, the article designed to "make Victor Serge known."

By the end of May 1933, the appeals for Serge's liberation were no longer the work of small left-wing circles. The progressive teachers of L'École emanicipée issued an appeal on May 24, and the Ligue des droits de l'homme, founded in 1898 during the Dreyfus Affair and still active today, issued a statement that appeared in newspapers from all parts of the left (except the Communist Party), from socialists to syndicalists to the the secularist socialists of Action socialiste et de defense laïque. This appeal, too, spoke of the suffering of Serge's wife, a result of the harassment of which her husband was a victim, and didn't mince words about the situation developing in the USSR: "At a time when the universal conscience is rising up against the methods of violence and constraint rampant in Germany, the revolutionary government of the USSR cannot make itself responsible for the same arbitrary persecutions as Hitlerite fascism."

A note in the Parisian daily *Le Temps*, datelined Riga June 21, 1933, stated that the "well-known revolutionary Victor Serge" had been sentenced to two years' deportation in Siberia "for reasons of an administrative order." That a major newspaper published such inaccurate information in the midst of so much pro-Serge activity gives an idea of the secrecy the Soviets imposed.

Intellectual reviews of various kinds spoke out on behalf of Serge. *Esprit*, edited by the philosopher Emmanuel Mounier, who would play a major role in the development of Serge's thinking, stood out among Serge's defenders. It first drew attention to his case in November 1933. Literary figures like Jean Guéhenno, Jean Giraudoux (who directly approached the Soviet embassy in an effort to liberate Serge), and the novelist Léon Werth joined Serge's cause from the very beginning. That Serge was far from the marginal figure he is sometimes thought to have been is amply attested to by just how wide-ranging his support was, and his books were regularly serialized in the daily and monthly press up until the end of his life. Serge was not a minor figure, his writings unknown to the reading public. It was precisely the extent of his celebrity, despite being an unabashed Bolshevik, that saved his life. Not many swept up by the Stalinist state lived to write about it. Certainly not many who were, like Serge, Soviet citizens and subject to Soviet law.

Serge's friends intervened directly in the affair. Henry Poulaille sent an undated letter, likely from June 1933, on behalf of the French Association of Proletarian Writers to the Soviet ambassador in Paris. Poulaille, defending Serge's revolutionary bona fides, requested that he be released and granted what Serge had long requested, "that Victor Serge be able to reside in his country of origin, which has been refused to him." Doing so, Poulaille said, would deprive anti-communists of a weapon against the Soviets: "What do you want us to say," he asked, "to the enemies of Soviet Russia when they claim that a revolutionary is unjustly held in the country of the Revolution."[5]

Among Serge's early defenders was the extremely respectable novelist Georges Duhamel. A physician who had served with honor in World War I, Duhamel would be elevated to the Académie française in 1935, and after World War II was the president of the Alliance française. He was not, in short, a man of the far left like Poulaille or Plisnier. Twice in 1933 he wrote strong articles in defense of Serge, couched in terms quite different from those of writers of a more political bent. Duhamel's demands were phrased diplomatically, appealing to the Soviets' self-interest. These were certainly among the most important articles written on behalf of Serge.

His first article, "The Value of a Man," appeared in the daily *L'Oeuvre* on May 23, 1933. Duhamel had met Serge in 1927 on a visit to Leningrad and been impressed by the intelligence and "broad culture" of the former individualist anarchist converted to

Marxism. Duhamel and his companion on the trip, Luc Durtain, had visited Serge in his fifth-floor apartment, which, he pointed out, would soon be disputed in the Russakov Affair.

Duhamel was clear: "I don't share the political convictions of Victor Serge. It is impossible for me to associate myself with the projects and hopes he formulated at that time." But it was Serge the person who moved Duhamel, and by extension all those who didn't share Serge's beliefs. "I saluted him wholeheartedly, as I always salute sincere abnegation and generous intelligence, even when they work against my personal sentiments."

Duhamel and Serge remained in contact in the intervening years, their correspondence touching mainly on literary matters, though Serge "provided sobering information on the difficulties of his life." Despite his lack of interest in Serge's Bolshevism, Duhamel read Serge's books and considered his then latest novel, *Conquered City*, a work that "grips the heart and touches the depths of the great human abyss."

Duhamel feared that the risks Serge ran mounted with each passing day and that he would disappear forever. Duhamel admitted he couldn't understand why Soviet bureaucrats wouldn't simply give Serge his passport and let him leave. Every attempt to get Serge released had "run up against that Slavic bureaucracy that the revolution has not reduced, but which it has, alas, exalted, enthroned, and I dare say, rendered divine."

Duhamel recognized the difficulties, perhaps even the futility of the steps taken by Serge's defenders, for the Soviet government "has demonstrated that it doesn't attach any value to the opinion of those it calls 'intellectuals.'" Adopting a vague note of hope, Duhamel thought it was possible to "hope all the same for the ultimate success of common sense and, especially of justice." Exercising that same common sense he called for from the Soviets, Duhamel ended his first appeal by saying he "can't see what higher interest there can be for anyone in scorning, without any benefit, this great hope."

Duhamel returned to the Victor Serge Affair on July 18, again in *L'Oeuvre*. Still marking himself off from the bulk of the political defenders of Serge, Duhamel again strived for a more common-sensical and less confrontational approach. He knew of socialist and syndicalist plans to send delegations to the USSR to plead Serge's case, and he thought them a fine thing. But at the same time, he claimed to understand the position of Communists who opposed the fight for Serge, who thought "it wasn't possible, for the salvation of one man, to trouble, to whatever small extent, the experiment and life of a great people confronted by a thousand difficulties." To those who called for public silence so the affair could be resolved quietly, Duhamel said that "silence means forgetting, and we have every reason to believe that forgetting signifies death."

Rejecting silence, then, and citing the success of the Indian poet Rabindranath Tagore in freeing a prisoner of the Italian fascists, Duhamel wondered if "the Soviet leaders understand the harm they are doing themselves with French opinion." No more big words or grand notions:

Let's put aside for the moment justice and even elegance. What we demand today from the masters of Russia is a diplomatic gesture, a gesture in their own interests [...]. If there remains a speck of common sense inside the walls of the Kremlin, within a week Victor Serge will have a valid passport for the West and a railway ticket.

That common sense was lacking, and Serge remained in the Urals.

If there was a figure who might have been able to bring the Soviets to their senses in this matter it was Romain Rolland. Though one feels safe in doubting he is much read now, he was the author of the ten-volume *roman-fleuve Jean-Christophe*, published between 1904 and 1912, which recounts the life of a great composer from birth to death, the main character described by Rolland as "Beethoven in modern times." Rolland was also a wholehearted supporter of the USSR, with contacts in the highest circles, notably with Maxim Gorky. He had also published the work of Victor Serge in his review *Europe*, and Serge had cited his name in his GPU interrogation to demonstrate the high esteem in which he was held by left-wing intellectual circles.

Rolland's correspondence with Gorky contains many refences to Serge, whose case Gorky was familiar with, since he'd been approached by a member of Serge's Frolov family, whom Gorky had known since his childhood.[6] Rolland's letters contain many pleas for his release, but they cast a strange light on Rolland's role. Shortly after Serge's arrest, Rolland wrote to Gorky of "great agitation in Paris around the name of Victor Serge" made by "intellectuals of note. I have to tell you that I don't know Serge personally, except as a writer (and his great talent is not in question)," but Rolland asked Gorky to contact Moscow for information on the case and "to intercede for him, if you judge it possible."[7] In a letter dated November 17, 1934, he tells Gorky of how Serge "vainly sent me *three times* the manuscript of a novel (non-political and dealing with an era other than the present) [...]. None of the three copies reached their addressee. And Boubnov, who I wrote to myself, never answered" (emphasis in the original).[8] Rolland then laid out his real feelings on the case. He had discussed the Serge matter with Jean-Richard Bloch and Henri Barbusse, "who have the same opinion as me on the Serge Affair. Neither they nor I have any sympathy for Serge (though we hold his great talent as a writer in high esteem)." After warning the Soviet writer that "you can't imagine the great harm this Serge Affair has caused among the entire Western intellectual public for the past year," he suggested a solution to the great Russian writer:

We think, Barbusse, Jean-Richard Bloch, and I, that not only justice, but the simplest political common sense demands the opening of the Serge dossier, and if overwhelming charges against him are found there, to make them known. This would help us put a stop to a venomous campaign that makes use of his name. Or, if the charges are light, that we take from Serge any pretext for unjustified complaint and that we allow him, in Orenburg, to earn his living through his profession as a writer (of course, while overseeing him politically). But an end must be put to these postal and other vexations, which "lose" the literary manuscripts he sends and thus deprive him of any means of existence.

Rolland's ambiguous attitude is also visible in a letter to Gorky dated April 30, 1933:

> In my opinion, Serge's overseas friends do him more harm than good through the violence of their demands. But there is no doubt that the agitation created by his arrest is strong and is spreading in circles that are otherwise sympathetic to the USSR. It is in the interests of the USSR that the investigation in the Serge case not drag on and that either he be released promptly if his innocence is recognized, or that public opinion be informed of the facts against him.

And yet, Rolland paid homage to Serge. "Serge is, intellectually, too important a personality to be shrouded in silence."[9] Rolland throughout the early days of the affair was concerned that Gorky keep him up to date so he would be able to answer letters he will receive in support of Serge, hoping to find a defense of Soviet actions.

L'Humanité, the PCF's newspaper, put Rolland to use in the anti-Serge cause in their May 26 report of an interview with the great novelist, one that very much matches the private sentiments he expressed to Gorky. After stating how much he wished his old age didn't prevent him from joining in the construction of socialism, the Communist paper reported that Rolland "scornfully waved off the 'Serge story,'" which he claimed was concocted by Panait Istrati against the USSR and had "become a machine in the hands of all counter-revolutions against the USSR."

Shortly after the appearance of this interview, Rolland wrote to the editors of *La Révolution prolétarienne* to clarify what he'd said, which appeared in the June 25, 1933, issue. His clarification does not redound to his honor.

The interviewer for *L'Humanité* misunderstood him, Rolland wrote. Rolland instead claimed that what he actually said was that "Istrati, through his publication [*Vers l'autre flamme*], in which Serge collaborated, was the person mainly responsible for the problems of which Serge has since been the object." Rolland continued that, if he had been correctly informed, he believes Serge himself had tried to prevent Istrati from publishing his account. In this Rolland was partially right. In the unpublished sections of his profession of faith Serge wrote that in Istrati's account of the Russakov Affair the Romanian writer had "written many foolish things, understanding nothing of politics or the great tragedy of the revolution." But whatever Serge's hesitations and unhappiness with Istrati's impetuosity, far from regretting Istrati's publication of the facts of the case, Serge wrote to his friends that Istrati, in doing so, "perhaps saved all our lives."

Istrati was clearly not in anyone's good graces. Rolland condemned him, and the Communists despised him for the harsh criticisms contained in his *La Russie nue*, the overall title for the three volumes on the USSR published under Istrati's name. The Communists lumped Istrati together with Serge in the writing of this unquestionably critical view of the USSR, condemning the two of them equally. But *La Révolution prolétarienne* defended Serge against this charge by comparing the personalities of the two men. The editors of the revolutionary syndicalist magazine wrote that "The bitter critique it demonstrates is the expression of a temperament totally different from [Serge's]." If Istrati is accused by the Communists of "degrading the Russian revolutionary effort in the minds of intellectuals," Serge, on the other hand, is of a "moderate and prudent turn of mind, always seeking the positive aspect of things. Victor Serge always places his confidence in men of good faith."[10] This abandonment of Istrati, whose book showed great courage and clear-sightedness, is not pleasant to read.

But Rolland was also concerned with the way the affair had developed into an anti-Soviet campaign. He accepted the good faith of *La Révolution prolétarienne* and Serge's friends, but "all sorts of people, for whom saving Serge was the least of their concerns, had latched on to his affair, and their way of making use of it for their own ends thwarted our efforts in his favor."

In fairness to Rolland, he said that he wrote a letter to the Communist paper requesting that they correct their report of what he said, which they failed to print. He had also written Gorky twice asking for his assistance in liberating Serge.

At around the same time, Rolland wrote an article for a little magazine, *Le Huron*, in which the balancing act between saving Serge and defending Stalin features prominently. Duhamel's moving defenses of Serge and Giraudoux's contact with the Soviets were criticized by Rolland in this letter. The actions of the two writers "unfortunately conferred on the Serge Affair a bothersome importance for those who want to intervene without great display."

Rolland's hesitations represent the weakness, hesitations, and even cowardice of many left-wing intellectuals of the time. In his letter to *Le Huron*, Rolland said that

> Serge is a great revolutionary writer. But I don't know him personally and I don't know the reasons for his arrest. It is thus not possible for me to judge, either for or against. It is unjust to go to war against the USSR before knowing anything. One doesn't judge through an act of faith. One must know.

But how? Is Rolland ready to believe the evidence provided by the Soviets, this after tens of thousands of arrests and executions on charges that only the most naïve could believe?

The crisis of conscience Serge's deportation caused can be seen in the reaction of the independent revolutionary magazine *Masses*, edited by René Lefeuvre, who would remain an ally, publisher, and friend of Serge's until the latter's death. In the June 1933 issue of *Masses* Lefeuvre wrote an article titled "Victor Serge Is Deported," the bulk of which was taken up with the section of Serge's profession of faith already published in France, as well as Romain Rolland's letter to *Le Huron*. For Lefeuvre there is no question of Serge's innocence: "We refuse to accept that [Serge's] deportation can be justified by the political position and divergences with the Soviet government that Victor Serge expressed in his profession of faith."

This opinion resulted in a split in the magazine and the departure of several members of its staff. They did not go quietly, writing to *L'Humanité*, which published their statement on July 14, 1933.

The dissident staff wrote that they

> no longer have anything in common with [*Masses*], which was created as a revolutionary review of Marxist culture that had committed, in its first issue, to defend against bourgeois calumny the USSR's effort to construct a classless society by opposing truth to lies. The repeated publication of certain notes (the Victor Serge case), [...] against the expressed will of all the members of the editorial committee, with the exception of the editor-in-chief [Lefeuvre], seems to the signatories incompatible with the principles posed at the start.

For them, writing and publishing in defense of Victor Serge signified one thing and one thing alone. Those resigning from the magazine "warn the readers that the review *Masses* is destined to become an instrument in the hands of counterrevolutionaries."

No less than that! The departing writers reserved the right to the use of the name *Masses Nouvelles—New Masses—*for a new magazine, which never saw the light of day.

There is no biographical information in the encyclopedia of the French working-class movement edited by Jean Maitron for any of the signatories of this mass resignation letter, save one, Léon Limon. His dissidence in this matter shows that the cleavages caused by the Serge Affair were not simple. Limon was a member of the PCF in 1933, and seems to have left the party in 1938, when he joined Marceau Pivert's Parti Socialiste ouvrier et paysan (PSOP), where he served on its press committee, headed by ... René Lefeuvre.

Serge's supporters were unstinting in their calls for his release all through his detention. No forum was too small or too big. At the conference of the Unitary Federation of Teachers in August 1934, an organization riven by pro- and anti-Stalinist factions, two collections were taken up: one by the anti-Stalinists for Serge, the other for the leader of the German Communist Party, Ernst Thaelmann, in a concentration camp since 1933. The former garnered 1400 francs, the latter 700.

The most resounding moment in the campaign resulted in scandal, pitting Stalinists and anti-Stalinists against each other on an international stage.

From June 21 to June 25, 1935, writers from over thirty nations gathered in Paris for the International Congress in Defense of Culture. Largely Communist-organized, with the tenor of the speeches leaning towards the Communist position on all matters, the primary focus of the gathering was the suppression of freedoms in fascist lands, particularly Germany. The silencing of dissent in the USSR was not on the agenda. Present were many of the greatest literary figures, some not particularly noted for their leftism, like the philosopher Alain and the novelist Jean Guéhenno, as well as many who were, at least at that time, Communists or close to them: Paul Nizan, Louis Aragon, Anna Seghers, the American Mike Gold, André Malraux, and André

Gide. Gide, who knew Serge's work and was fully aware of his situation, was expected by Serge's supporters to air the matter openly. He didn't, though he privately addressed the case in discussions with Soviet attendees and permitted pro-Serge speakers to take the podium. He deserves some little credit for allowing the issue of Serge's deportation to be discussed in so hostile an environment, but as he said, "The greatest proof of love we can give the USSR is to have confidence in it in this affair." André Malraux as well, already famous for his first two great novels, *Les Conquerants* and *La Condition humaine*, also remained silent. Discomfiting the Communists was simply not the done thing. As the historian and critic Roger Shattuck wrote,

> This was the most thoroughly rigged and steamrollered assemblage ever perpetrated on the face of Western literature in the name of culture and freedom [...]. There sat some of Europe's most distinguished men of letters presiding over a meeting that systematically swept into a corner any dissent from the prevailing opinion that the true revolutionary spirit belonged to the Soviet government.[11]

The afternoon session of June 24 was presided over by Malraux. Speakers included Emmanuel Mounier—whose later relationship with Serge we will examine in greater depth below—the Dutchman Jef Last, and the German philosopher Ernst Bloch.

Magdeleine Paz then spoke, her speech rescheduled from the previous day's evening session. Her talk was almost exclusively about Victor Serge. Despite the reduced attendance at the afternoon sessions, she did not disappoint.

Paz told the assembled writers that she was there to address one of the five points that constituted the basis of the congress: "The dignity of thought. Freedom of expression. Indirect and direct forms of censorship. The writer and exile." She would address all this through the case of Victor Serge.[12]

Knowing that by 1935 the image of Serge had been thoroughly deformed and tarnished by the Communists, Paz began with a lengthy, admiring, and at times exaggeratedly positive biography of Serge. Tracing his political path from his youthful anarchism through its various stages until reaching Russia, she touched on all the highlights, particularly stressing his accomplishments in the USSR, his work as a loyal propagandist, his role in establishing the Museum of the Revolution, "which every tourist has visited in Leningrad." Kronstadt didn't shake him in the least (though we know it did), she said. He loyally carried out all missions assigned to him and his writings were an "excellent summary of revolutionary thought and tactics on a world-wide scale." Paz described him as "the most educated, the most orthodox of communists." We can forgive Paz her overreach here, given her need to reach an audience predisposed to be against Serge precisely for his lack of orthodoxy.

On the other hand, Paz was forthright on a matter that could only enrage most of the attendees. In the dispute that arose in Russia after the death of Lenin between Trotsky and Stalin, Serge "thinks that Trotsky is right." Paz was careful not to make Serge appear too dangerous a Trotskyist, saying, "Let us not waltz around the crime: deep in his heart he is a Trotskyist." But he is not a dangerous one: "He gave no speeches, wrote no articles, engaged in no agitation; everything was limited to private conversations, to discussions among friends, and letters to foreign friends."

Here was finally a chance to tell those on the other side what really happened, and Paz described his arrests of 1928 and 1933, his deprivations between the two events, his inability to earn a living, and the suffering of his family. She spoke of his courage during his detention in Orenburg, of his refusal to sign a statement, saying, as she phrased it, "I don't think what I think." But nothing wears him down, and even there he has completed a novel, which has disappeared into the maws of the GPU.

To an assembled crowd familiar with Serge's case mainly through the Communist press—or who, knowing the facts hid themselves from them—Paz read sections of Serge's profession of faith.

After laying out her case, Paz called on the writers to

Be revolutionaries to the extent—which is immense—that writers can be. Flee the conformity of a dying society (it's easy, everything incites us to do so) but also, what is more difficult, flee the conformity established within the Revolution itself, which brings with it glory and honor and lulls independence and numbs the critical sense.

Paz ended with a cry of anger and hope: "There are voices that can't be silenced! There are forces that can't be broken."

Le Populaire, the Socialist Party newspaper, covered Paz's speech in great detail and with great sympathy.[13] The reaction to what it called an intervention "in favor of the true dignity of thought" was, as it described, "violent." There was "loud applause mixed with hostile exclamations cast at Serge."

Charles Plisnier spoke about Serge, as did the Italian anti-fascist Gaetano Salvemini. When Salvemini spoke, *Le Populaire* reported that his mentions of the Serge Affair "provoked varied reactions in the hall."

Soviet writers in attendance defended their government against Paz's attacks. Nikolai Tikhonov declared that Serge had

become a Soviet citizen at his own request; he ate our bread and knowingly submitted himself to the laws adopted by the entire working population of the USSR. A state functionary, Victor Serge [...] took an active part in the counter-revolutionary activity of the Trotskyists, which ended in the assassination of Kirov. By virtue of a legal decision, the Soviet government exiled him to Orenburg, where he lives and incidentally remains a functionary of the translation bureau. The rumors concerning his misfortunes are false.

Ilya Ehrenburg, the semi-official face of Soviet culture in the West, insisted that "In order to defend itself and to limit the damage the enemies of the Revolution might cause, it has the right to take all necessary measures, like those taken in the case of Serge." Even foreign Communists, like the German Anna Seghers, stepped up to defend the Soviets, engaging in what-aboutism. She asked, "Why, if Magdeleine Paz claims to fight fascism and defend the USSR, does she not speak of [the victims of the Nazis] Ludwig Renn and Eric Muhsam, whose fingers, before assassinating them, the Nazis cut off."[14]

André Gide then took the podium and closed the debate. At least the in-person part of it. The Communists were far from finished, and they covered Paz and her comrades' defense of Serge and freedom of thought in their short-lived cultural journal *Commune* the next month.

"The pettiness of a few Trotskyists, the bourgeois spirit of a few surrealists, were in the eyes of all an object of scorn and pity. We will mention here the attempts of Mme Paz and Plisnier to sabotage the unity of the writers of thirty-five nations on the pretext of defending the counter-revolutionary Victor Serge. For any who doubt the use made of his case as a machine of divisiveness, [Paz's position] clearly shows who Victor Serge serves," listing a variety of fascist newspapers, as well as the Socialist *Le Populaire*, which had spoken so glowingly of Paz's speech.[15]

On July 7, 1935, Gide wrote to Magdeleine Paz directly about the Serge Affair, assuring her he hadn't abandoned the deportee. Paz had made several requests on Serge's behalf, which Gide addressed directly:

Obtaining for Victor Serge the authorization to send [texts] to French publishers for publication (as long as these polemical tracts aren't against the Soviet regime) was precisely the object of my long discussion with the Soviet ambassador two weeks ago. I also gave him a letter on the subject of this thorny affair, one I requested he forward to the higher spheres.

Three months after the congress, on September 12, 1935, Gorky announced to Romain Rolland that Serge was to be freed. He had to spend seven more months in Orenburg, though. The release of Serge and his family, which now included the infant Jeannine, born in 1935, finally occurred on April 12, 1936. His destination was Belgium, where the socialist Emil Vandervelde, having been approached by the indefatigable Plisnier, had arranged for Serge to have a visa legalizing his stay in the country.

On April 14, Serge reached Warsaw, but not before further harassment by the Soviets. Soviet customs officers at the Polish border took from Serge yet another copy of the manuscript of *Les Hommes perdus*, as well as the novel *Le Tourmente*—a novel he described in a letter to an unidentified recipient as "a psychological novel, the continuation of *Conquered City*, painting an epic tableau of the Revolution in 1920"—and unpublished poems. Also left behind in Moscow in the hands of a Mrs. Piechkova, head of the organization Aid for Political Prisoners, were two trunks, for which the promised authorization for shipment to the West had also not materialized. The trunk contained "personal relics" and documents dating back to the beginning of his political life in 1907.

From Warsaw, where the ever-faithful Magdeleine Paz had sent Serge 420 zlotys, as indicated by a receipt in the Victor Serge archives at Yale, the Serge family caught a train for Brussels. Reconnecting with a segment of his past, he was met in Brussels by Plisnier and the Russian émigré anarchists Nicolas and Ida Lazarevich.

On April 22, he wrote to his faithful friend Poulaille in Vanves, France: "I've been free for several days. I owe it strictly and solely to those who defended me with such noble stubbornness.

The Stalinist regime *never* forgives anyone who resists it, like me, by non-consent and abstention."

For the first time, Serge would now be able to fight openly against Stalin, to act on the double duty he had imposed on himself, opposing enemies of the Revolution from within and without. He would not stint in this.

16
Return to the West

With Serge's right to residence in his native country now assured for three years, thanks to the socialist leader, government minister, and bête noire of his youth, Emil Vandervelde, he and his family settled in Brussels. Their first lodgings after their arrival on April 17, 1936, were split between the home of the Belgian anarchist of Russian background, Nicolas Lazarevich and that of Charles Plisnier. Serge roamed the streets of his childhood neighborhood of Ixelles and visited Vandervelde to thank him for his assistance. He quickly found work writing for the Liège-based socialist newspaper *La Wallonie*.

Serge reports in his memoirs that friends advised him against writing about Russia: "[P]erhaps you might be too bitter… We are just at the start of a movement of popular enthusiasm. […] We are allied with the Communist Party, which is winning over wonderful masses of people; for them Russia is still an untarnished star. Besides, no one would believe you."[1] This was advice Serge would not take.

An open letter to André Gide was among his first writings published after his arrival in the West, and it goes right to the heart of the matter of the Soviet Union. This open letter actually appeared twice, once in a small Trotskyist sheet, *Le Service d'information et de presse*, in May 1936, and then again in *Esprit* in its June 1936 issue. Writing as a self-confessed "communist," Serge speaks of the effects of reading in Gide's published journals that the reason for the latter's adherence to communism was "Because it ensures the free development of the personality." Serge admits to reading this with mixed feelings: "I was at first happy to see you come to socialism […]. Then again, I was saddened by the contrast between your assertions and the reality in which I was plunged." After speaking of "the revolution ravaged from within by reaction," he recounts the litany of Stalin's crimes, the murders, the violations of human rights, the Soviet leader's scorn for international law, all of which would become leitmotifs in Serge's writings.

Not forgetting the main enemy, Serge wrote Gide, "We are confronting fascism. How can we bar the road to it with so many concentration camps behind us?" Gide's support for the USSR alarms Serge and disqualifies Gide as a supporter of the workers' cause and of human rights:

> Your courage has always been that of living with your eyes open. You cannot close them today on this reality, or you will no longer have the moral right to say a word to workers for whom socialism is much more than a concept: it is the work of their flesh and spirt, the very meaning of their lives.

Serge ended with a *cri de coeur*:

> No one better represents that great Western intelligentsia which, if it did much for civilization, has much reason to ask forgiveness of the proletariat for not having understood what the war of 1914 was, for having underestimated the Russian Revolution at its beginnings, in its grandeur, for not having defended the freedom of the workers. Now that it is finally turning sympathetically towards the socialist revolution embodied by the USSR, it must choose in its heart between blindness and lucidity. Permit me to tell you that one can only serve the working-class and the USSR in total lucidity. Permit me to demand of you, in the name of those who are the most courageous, to have the courage of that lucidity.

Serge wrote in his notebook in November 1936 that Magdeleine Paz felt that publishing this open letter was a mistake, "as it looks like I'm putting him on the spot." Serge rejected the criticism, saying that "Great intellectuals are too fond of parading under the shelter of noble phrases. I hold Gide in too high esteem; I don't have the right to handle him with kid gloves." In fact, the letter didn't seriously damage their relationship.[2]

Serge had set the tone for the years left to him. His task would henceforth be that of imposing the facts that would encourage the West to adopt the lucidity he asked of Gide. The latter, after visiting the USSR in 1936, wrote *Retour de l'URSS* (Return from the USSR)—published in November 1936, a classic volume on that visit. It was largely positive, though it contained criticisms of what he saw. Gide was, as a result, pilloried by the Communist world. His period as a fellow traveler was relatively brief.

Serge was invited to Gide's apartment on rue Vaneau in late 1936. There he espied a copy of his pamphlet *Seize fusillés à Moscou* (Sixteen Executed Men in Moscow) laying open, facedown, obviously being read. They had a frank and friendly conversation, during which Gide spoke of his failure to recover Serge's missing manuscripts. He condemned new anti-homosexual legislation in the USSR and spoke of his forthcoming book on that visit, which would permanently end his relationship with the Communists. They spoke of "the disaster of communism [...] of the Moscow Trials. [Gide has] no illusion concerning that villainy and cruelty. I carry away the impression of an extremely scrupulous man, troubled to the depths of his soul who wanted to serve a great cause and no longer knows how."[3]

Their relationship was close enough that Gide a few years later wrote Serge with his opinion of *S'il est minuit dans le siècle* (*Midnight in the Century*) in a letter dated December 18, 1939. Gide had mixed feelings about the book: "What a horrible nightmare, what fear. Unrelenting, from page to page one wonders: Is this possible? And yet, there is no doubt that all you say is true." But he then expressed his reservations. "How, with such a subject, is it that you don't more firmly grip the reader? It's that [there are] remarkable pages (the various interrogations, above all), [where] you paint powerfully, but without concerning yourself with logic, and often propose (to the imagination) things that cannot be realized."

Serge found work as a proofreader while a regular columnist for *La Wallonie*. Though Belgium and France were passing through turbulent times, with general strikes, the French Popular Front government's rise and fall, and the growth of Leon Degrelle's fascist Rex movement in Belgium, Serge wrote mainly on two subjects. The first was the continued decline of the USSR and the horrific repression that was underway. The second was an event that would join the Stalinist purges on the front page in July 1936, the Spanish Civil War.

From this point on in his writings as a journalist, commentator, and essayist Serge turned away from the places in which he lived as a topic for serious analysis and focused his gaze and intelligence elsewhere. Belgium and France do not figure in his writings between 1936 and 1941 to any great extent. Similarly, once he was out of Europe and living in Mexico City, it was Europe and the Soviet Union that were his main concerns. One would look in vain in the final years of his life for any serious analysis of Mexican political reality, except insofar as it affected him and his fellow exiles.

His first article for *La Wallonie*, "Retour à l'Occident" (Return to the West), from the June 12–13, 1936, issue, is significant for its optimistic tone, regarding both the East and the West. Serge presents his reflections of the trip from the USSR to Brussels, and notes that despite the vast gap between them economically, "one is at once struck by the task begun [in the USSR] and of the even vaster scope of what remains to be done." He quotes Lenin on the irony that the task of building socialism fell to "the most backward, the least prepared of people," but insists that if the task of transforming man "will be more difficult to initiate, it will be all the easier to continue." At the same time, he holds out great hope for the West. Having seen France and Belgium, and knowing the vast movements then sweeping them both, he wonders, "how can one not be struck by the maturity of these countries for socialism?" It's a sign of how degraded life was in the USSR that Serge can write that "A kind of diffuse socialism fills the very atmosphere [in the West], whether it's to do with relations between men, based on clear notions of right, or the so rich system of distribution of products, of the improvement of public services, of material bases. In a word, of human life." Clearly speaking of himself, Serge continued:

An observer coming from the Russian Revolution [...], even taking into account the arrogant might of capitalism and the dangers of reaction it harbors, feels disposed to optimism. One finds that most of the work that had to be done after the revolution is already made here in all fields, and it even seems to me that appreciable progress has been realized since the war.[4]

One can't help but wonder why Serge didn't draw the conclusion that revolution is not in the cards in this West he was discovering anew. If the benefits of a revolution like the Russian one were to bring backward Russia not even up to the level of the West at an incalculable price in blood, death, and suffering; and if "most of the work that had to be done after the revolution is already made here in all fields," why make a revolution? The time had not yet arrived for Serge to ask these questions, but that time would come.

Hope existed for Serge because the memory of November 7, 1917, remained strong. The hard times would pass.

In order for the history of November 7, 1917 [...] to be totally renewed, [...] it's necessary that in Russia itself and elsewhere, there be a great awakening of the socialist masses, that it be victorious, that we leave the dark times behind us. The entire past is a guarantor of such a future.[5]

Whatever hope he had, there was no arguing the reality of Russia during this period, and Serge, who knew the players intimately, was able to explain the whys and wherefores of events there. How and why did men who'd dedicated their lives to the cause of the revolution abase themselves during the show trials, admitting to crimes against a state they'd given their lives to founding and keeping alive. Why this "total political suicide?" that went beyond anything imagined by Dostoevsky in his novel of nineteenth century political conspirators, *The Possessed?*

> The explanation is clear for anyone who knows these men. It can be summed up in a few words: devotion to the party and usefulness [...] Founders of the old party of Lenin, not able to conceive that it is possible to live outside the party, Zinoviev and Kamenev professed that it was necessary to remain in the party, whatever the cost, even in denying one's ideas, even by feigning to bow before the officially adored Leader, considered in their heart of hearts to be the wrecker of the revolution.[6]

Serge would be one of the most important analysts of Soviet politics and policy for the remaining years of his life. His analyses rarely appeared in widely circulated newspapers and journals, though he did often appear in the influential review *Esprit*. His articles would often be gathered in pamphlets published by small left-wing houses, like Spartacus in France, run by the courageous anti-Stalinist revolutionary René Lefeuvre. These opuscules, like *Seize fusillés a Moscou*, and his investigation of the murder of the Trotskyist Ignace Reiss, contain important information and unequaled insights. But they only very occasionally made it outside the realm of the convinced.

Safely out of the USSR, that nation's authorities continued to make his life difficult. On July 16 he wrote to Maurice Wullens, editor of the magazine *Les Humbles*, for which Serge would write until breaking with Wullens for publishing an article sympathetic to the "accomplishments" of Hitler, that

Two pieces of news reached me at the same time. 1—The censor categorically refused to authorize the departure of my manuscripts from the USSR, after having formally promised to do so. This is illegal, extremely illegal, but what can I do? 2—Through a recent measure taken without my having been heard or accused of anything at all, a measure with no basis that I know of, I have been outlawed and stripped of Soviet nationality. The legation is keeping our passports.[7]

Serge was again stateless and would remain so for the rest of his life. His connections continued to work in his favor, and in September 1936 he was able to write a friend that he would soon have papers and would be free to travel. Shortly after that, Serge submitted an application for a tax break granted to writers by the Belgian government. Belgian life wasn't as bad as all that, but France was his true goal. On January 27, 1937, the French minister of the interior, René Marx Dormoy, annulled Serge's 1917 expulsion order, and on February 25, 1937, he was given a French visa valid for six months, renewable at the end of every six-month period. He benefited from this until his departure for Mexico in 1941.

Serge was working on a book then titled *Destin de l'URSS*, later *Destin d'une Révolution* (The Fate of the USSR/The Fate of a Revolution), which he hoped would soon be ready to go to press; in the end, publication, as is often the case, dragged on for a frustratingly extended length of time. Serge was deeply involved in the cause of defending the freedom of expression. He figures among the sponsors of a Committee for the Investigation of the Moscow Trials and for the Freedom of Opinion in the Revolution, in which he was joined by figures like André Breton, the historian and schoolteacher Maurice Dommanget, the revolutionary syndicalist Alfred Rosmer, and his friends Poulaille and Magdeleine Paz. Their appeal stated:

We defend socialism because it can neither live nor vanquish without a living idea that controls it through self-criticism [...], and because it will only triumph if it brings the workers more well-being and freedom. We defend the revolution of October 1917, because it assigned itself the goal of establishing in Russia the broadest workers' democracy.

Serge expressed unhappiness with his ability to have an impact on events, to spread the word about Stalinist terror. As he wrote Henry Poulaille in August 1936:

A more than painful rage grips me when I think that I've not managed to shake up people. On the one hand, [I've failed] to wrest the sectarians from their stifling doctrinal quarrels, and on the other hand [to move] the rest so they would mount the energetic campaign in support of the imprisoned there [in the USSR] that could have prevented the massacres under way, for it's not over.[8]

In December 1936 the editor of the Parisian magazine *Le Crapouillot*, Jean Galtier-Boissière—also a member of the committee investigating the Moscow Trials—commissioned a lengthy piece by Serge on the USSR, "De Lénine à Staline." The article covered sixty-eight magazine pages and was a thorough and brutally critical examination of the Stalinist rise to power. The editor described working with Serge. After having requested an article on "the true history of the Russian Revolution," he reported that "[e]very two days for a month I regularly received about thirty pages of copy, with nothing crossed out and that I immediately handed over to the compositor. I never had a collaborator so punctual ... He kept strictly to his commitment and the issue appeared on its scheduled date."[9] It appeared in the January 1937 issue of the magazine and was later published in book form.

It was no coincidence that following on the heels of this article, on February 2, 1937, Serge's former French comrade in Moscow

Jacques Sadoul published an article in *L'Humanité* that counts among the most scurrilous ever written attacking Serge. It is all too typical of the Communist press and representative of the atmosphere in which Serge and his anti-Stalinist comrades lived.

Headlined "Trotsky's Advocate," the article is an attack on the campaign being mounted against the Moscow Trials. Sadoul claimed that for every sector in France, from the working-class to the middle class and intellectuals, "the confessions of the defendants no longer leave any room for ambiguity concerning their horrific guilt." Despite the obviousness of the defendants' guilt, a campaign has been launched against these "unambiguous" cases by a "handful of Trotskyists connected to the bands of [the far-right nationalist] La Rocque and [the fascist] Doriot." "The principal artisan of the new campaign is a base Trotskyist adventurer, Victor Serge." Speaking of Serge's article in *Le Crapouillot*, Sadoul says that unlike other attacks on the USSR by "aesthetes" like André Gide and Louis-Ferdinand Céline, "the 'communist' indictment by Victor Serge risks troubling the conscience of many good people whose political equilibrium is not all that solid."

Sadoul thus felt the need to undercut whatever influence Serge—"so mediocre, so vile"—might have by denigrating him, a task to which he bends himself with unmistakable glee.

People must know that "the great revolutionary, the hero of the Civil War," whose physical cowardice is legendary, never participated in the Civil War and never occupied any responsible political post in the USSR, where he only arrived in the winter of 1919. He was only ever employed in subaltern positions, working in secretariats and at literary labors. He never knew Lenin, indeed never met him. Lenin categorically refused to receive this suspect individual [...]. He never in any way participated in the leadership of the Communist International.

Serge's sole political claim to fame was that of "a troubled past of so-called anarchist banditry." Sadoul wrote of "Victor Serge Kibalchich's [...] undeniable complicity in a long and bloody series of thefts, burglaries and murders perpetrated in France by the sadly famous criminal gang 'the Tragic Bandits.'" Ignoring the fact that Serge was, in fact, not accused of complicity, but of possession of stolen weapons, Sadoul speaks of his "pitiful and idiotic attitude in criminal court," which earned him "many years of imprisonment." Sadoul is not entirely incorrect when he points out that Serge's banishment from France was not officially for political crimes but for his criminal condemnation while stateless.

Sadoul paints the worst picture of Serge imaginable. The explanation for his name change to "Serge?" Ashamed of his political past and anxious to start life anew, he dropped the name Kibalchich, "a name however, made famous in the history of Russian revolutionary history by other Kibalchichs." Casting the facts aside, Sadoul asserts that assuming the name Serge was a way of entering the Soviet Union, "the only country where the right of asylum, pardon, and forgiveness allow the regeneration of the refuse of bourgeois societies to change their ways." According to his erstwhile friend, Serge attempted to hide who he was under his pseudonym, and "in its clemency, the USSR welcomed the criminal, generously gave him (as it always does in such cases) every possibility to reeducate himself, to regenerate himself through labor." A labor that was never any more important, according to Sadoul, than that of the pen.

Throughout his years on "the honest and social road," Serge was never more than an opportunist, and all who saw him "deplored worrisome material needs in the ex-Tragic Bandit, which always led him to stubbornly beg, with a mix of bitterness and humility, for more elevated functions." Serge was such an opportunist that Sadoul felt free to say with certainty that "this vain person would not have gone over to the counter-revolutionary camp if the USSR, as clear-eyed as it is generous, hadn't refused him the political confidence and abundant resources to which he thought he had a right." Sadoul concludes by expressing gratitude that Kibalchich has fallen back on his "own kind." "The Trotskyists will find in him an instrument worthy of them. This unrepentant criminal was never anything but a valet of the pen [...]. It is logical that after having sold his pen to Bonnot's Tragic Band he has sold it to Trotsky's."

Serge did not take this attack lying down, taking to the pages of *La Révolution prolétarienne* a mere week after Sadoul's article appeared. He defended himself against the specific charges against him, saying, accurately, that he had not taken part in any of the Bonnot Gang's acts, and slightly less accurately that he was sentenced simply for having said he alone—and not Rirette Maîtrejean—was the editor of *l'anarchie*. He denied hiding his true identity in the USSR, which was absolutely true, saying he'd taken the name Victor Serge in Spain in 1917, because his collaboration on the anarchist *Tierra y Libertad* could have cost him his life. He reminded Sadoul that he fought during the Civil War in a communist battalion (he was "doubtless wrong to survive thanks to chance"), and spoke of the missions he later carried out in Germany and Austria on behalf of the Comintern. Countering the accusation of careerism, he wrote of the posts and offers he'd turned down. Serge then accused Sadoul of errors and missteps of his own, of his taste for women and fine food—tastes which led him to prefer survival to a principled stand in the battles between Stalin and Trotsky—and of hypocrisy, since Serge had in his possession letters from Sadoul that were "friendly and affectionate."

But Sadoul's insults were secondary to Serge. Sadoul has lied about and to himself. "I often heard you deplore the excesses of the Terror, or Russia's Asiatism." Sadoul is not someone he hates; rather he feels pity for him. The two of them had worked to prevent the spilling of blood in 1922 in the trial of the Social Revolutionaries, and now Sadoul bays with the hounds against the accused in the ongoing trials. "What inexplicable lack of courage has broken you in this way?" It is with sorrow that he wrote the final paragraph of his defense, with the comprehension and lack of rancor that appears in Serge's finest pages:

> As for me, I knew full well that in defending the proscribed and the executed, defending the strangled revolution against the gag and the executioner, in fighting for communism against what dishonors it, I was fated for insult and slander, for perhaps worse, since the Bois de Boulogne is no longer safe in broad daylight. Your sad example confirms me in the conviction that the Stalinist nightmare opens before us an era of horrific demoralization. If you're not capable of becoming yourself again, [then] continue to lie and insult. I will continue, in these dark times, to do my duty, which is that of speaking the irrefutable truth. The workers will judge.[10]

Trotsky had learned of Sadoul's attack through French comrades, and on March 5, 1937, wrote a letter of support to Serge. Sadoul, Trotsky wrote, was not only a "liar" now, but "Over his whole life has been a cowardly parasite on the working-class movement." Sadoul had denied that Serge ever had any dealings with Lenin, and Trotsky countered by writing that "Lenin viewed Sadoul with contemptuous irony." Trotsky was mortified that Sadoul should have called Serge "a valet of the pen" and accuse him of careerism. "There is nothing," Trotsky wrote Serge, "more repulsive than a servile philistine whose powerful bosses have told him 'Everything is permitted.'" Trotsky felt there was a lesson for the young in this sad tale. "A single article by Sadoul is enough to enable a sure diagnosis: Stalinism is the syphilis of the working-class movement. [...] So let's teach the younger generation how to despise this fungus on humanity."[11] There are moments when Trosky's near-constant vituperations are a tonic. This is one of them.

Serge was defended by some, none of whom had the audience of Sadoul in *L'Humanité*. One of them was Gaston Bergery, advocate of a doctrine called Frontism, in his journal *La Flèche*. His defense led Sadoul to return to the attack, on Bergery, for refusing to accept the guilt of the Moscow defendants and for defending Serge, and Serge himself. Sadoul, in his second attack on February 14, 1937, connected the Bonnot Gang to Trotskyism:

> The other day I evoked the exploits [of the Bonnot Gang] who, two or three years before the war, terrorized France, accumulating—they, too, for their personal gain—thefts, burglaries, bombings and murder under the flag of anarchism, and not yet Trotskyism. How can one contemplate the deeper meaning of the fact that, twenty years later we again meet precisely one of the most dangerous of the Tragic Bandits, Victor Serge Kibalchich, discreetly camouflaged as Victor Serge, in the skin of the Trotskyist leaders, closely connected to the Moscow defendants.

Sadoul reminds his readers that Serge used to edit *l'anarchie*, "a rag aimed essentially at 'ideologically' legitimizing burglary and murder committed by the repugnant bandits [...] in the same way the abundant 'literature' of the parallel Trotskyist center serves to hide the purely personal shady designs of its great leaders." The headline of Sadoul's second piece said it all: "Victor Serge is not a political figure. He's the fence of the Bonnot Gang."

Serge feared that the manuscript of his novel on the Bonnot Gang, *Les Hommes perdus*, had it finally turned up, would be turned over by the Soviets to the French Communists so they could dig up further grounds for attacks.[12] At the time, he planned to rewrite the lost book, and even had a contract with Éditions Sagittaire for the new version, which sadly was never written.

* * *

In the summer of 1937, Serge was a bit player in one of the many tragedies of the era, the assassination of Ignace Reiss. He wrote about the killing in his notebooks and in a pamphlet written jointly with Maurice Wullens and Alfred Rosmer, *L'Assassi-nat politique et l'URSS* (Political Assassination and the USSR). Reiss's murder was a potential template for the fate Serge feared for himself.[13]

Ignace Reiss was a Polish Communist, but also a member of the Soviet Communist Party and of its secret service. He was a holder of the Order of the Red Flag and had been charged with missions in France and Holland by the GPU. He was, in short, at the heart of the Soviet repressive machinery. The judicial killings of Kamenev and Zinoviev shattered him, and on June 27, 1936, he sent a letter to the Soviet Central Committee resigning his post and returning his decorations. He all but signed his death sentence by writing:

> In order for the USSR and the international workers' movement not to succumb to counter-revolution and fascism, the working-class must have done with Stalin and Stalinism. This mixture of the worst opportunism, lacking in any principles, combined with lies and blood, threatens to poison the world and the last remaining strength of the working-class. Merciless struggle against Stalinism![14]

Though aware of the danger he ran, as Serge recounted, Reiss didn't seek asylum "from a democratic country; he attempted to hide from his executioners by his own means."[15] Reiss warned the Dutch Oppositionist Henk Sneevliet and Serge that terrorist acts against the Opposition abroad were in the works. In August, Serge communicated this threat in a talk he gave in Paris, hosted by the progressive teachers of the École émancipée. Later that same month, Sneevliet arranged a meeting with Reiss, who had sent a statement on his decision to turn his back on the USSR, which was published by the Committee for the Investigation of the Moscow Trials. That month, Sneevliet arranged a meeting between himself, Reiss, Serge, and Trotsky's son Leon Sedov, which Sedov had to cancel. The meeting was rescheduled for

September, and when Sedov canceled again, Sneevliet and Serge went to meet Reiss in Reims, where they arranged to meet Reiss at the train station on September 5, at the station's snack bar. Reiss failed to appear on September 5 and 6. The two men saw in the newspaper that a man named Eberhard, who had Czech papers on him, was found riddled with bullets near Lausanne. The victim had a ticket for France in his pocket. Serge and Sneevliet suspected the victim was actually Reiss, and Sneevliet traveled to Switzerland, where he was able to confirm this.

The investigation was quickly carried out, and the assassins were all Soviet agents who had carried out a close surveillance of their prey and had been in hiding in Switzerland. The brazenness of the Soviets was underlined by Serge. "The GPU had just killed a man virtually beneath the windows of the League of Nations, at the very moment when [Soviet delegate] Litvinov was in Geneva studying the proposed international convention against terrorism."[16]

Serge lists the names of the participants in the murder in his notebook, an international collection of Communists and GPU agents, but the true guilty party was much more highly placed. Reiss had left detailed notes behind of other crimes of the Soviet state, including the undermining of an Opposition figure named Grilewicz in a campaign in which Stalin personally intervened. Serge wrote that "[k]nowing the extreme centralization of the secret services acting abroad, this note allows us to assert that Ignace Reiss's assassination was organized under conditions exactly like that of the machination against Grilewicz, i.e., on Stalin's personal order."[17]

The importance of Reiss's death was far greater than that of the murder of one man. "[T]he bloodthirsty corruption of the Stalinist regime is winning over the working-class movement and progressive intellectuals of the West. The shadow of Ignace Reiss, who died for his socialist faith, serves to warn us of an immense danger."[18]

* * *

Serge, as we saw in his responses to his GPU interrogators, maintained that his political activities as an Oppositionist had long since ceased when he was arrested in 1933, and that he had dedicated himself solely to literary work. This is not strictly true, and Serge paid for his support for Trotsky with his three years in Orenburg. It didn't take long after his arrival in the West on April 17, 1936, for disillusionment to set in with the movement he, his friends, comrades, and family had dedicated their lives to.

In May and June 1936, after the election of Léon Blum's Popular Front government, a wave of strikes and factory occupations swept France. In response, Trotsky famously announced, "The French Revolution has begun." Serge wrote the Old Man—as Trotsky was known to his followers—that he had it all wrong. "Not at all," Serge wrote. "It's only the recovery of the French working-class that's begun." Serge also advised Trotsky not to get his hands dirty intervening in the affairs of his rivalrous disciples, divided into a number of tiny groups, and expressed doubts about the viability of any new International: "We can't found an International without parties. One cannot build an International when there are no parties ... One cannot build parties out of rotten political behavior and with a Russian ideological language that nobody understands." Trotsky's response was to the point: "You're an enemy who wants to be treated like a friend."[19]

Shortly after this, still in the summer of 1936, Serge was visited by the American A.J. Muste, then a Trotskyist, later among the leaders of the pacifist War Resisters League, who extended an invitation from Trotsky to participate in the Bureau for the Fourth International, Trotsky's replacement for the Stalinist Third International.

Serge quickly experienced firsthand the dogmatism and sectarianism of the movement when he learned that Trotsky's son Leon Sedov had said of the anarchists in Spain that they were "destined to stab the revolution in the back." Serge disagreed strongly and advised Trotsky to support the anarchists as an allied non-Stalinist revolutionary force. As he wrote Trotsky on August 10, 1936, the Trotskyists should issue an appeal saying, among other things, "We consider you, the anarchists and syndicalists, to be our class comrades and dedicated revolutionaries. We offer you our fullest cooperation along with uncompromising criticism and ideological struggle, carried out in a fraternal atmosphere."[20] In a letter to POUM leader Andreu Nin, Serge explained his reasons for the need for an anarchist presence in the revolutionary camp in Spain. If the anarchists of the CNT and FAI are able to impose discipline on their men "in time of revolution, their influence will constitute a precious antidote to statist and bureaucratic tendencies of the workers' movement [and] their presence will vivify worker freedom." Trotsky responded on August 19 saying, "What you write about Spanish, or rather Catalonian anarchists is absolutely true, and I am extremely glad about our unity on this principal question of the present moment."[21] Serge thought instructions would be given to the movement to back this position, but no such instructions were given. Instead, in Trotsky's 1938 essay "Their Morals and Ours," which would be a cause of the final split between Trotsky and Serge, the former wrote: "The democratic Philistine and Stalinist bureaucrat are, if not twins, brothers in spirit. In any case they belong politically to the same camp. The present governmental system of France and if we add the anarchists of republican Spain, is based on the collaboration of Stalinists, social-democrats, and liberals."[22]

Serge seemed to have swallowed all this for the moment, but matters reached a head in January 1937, when the Fourth International gathered in Amsterdam at the home of Sneevliet, who had proved his revolutionary bona fides as a Comintern agent in Indonesia and China, and who would be executed during the war by the Germans. The subject of Spain came up at the Amsterdam gathering and, as Serge wrote, "the Trotskyists were already directing all their fire at POUM." He defended the Spaniards' positions, particularly regarding participation in the government of Catalonia, which he said would strengthen their presence and lead to the arming of the masses. The leading voices of Trotskyism, a minuscule movement suffering absurd splits, men like Pierre Naville, Trotsky's lawyer Gérard Rosenthal, and Rudolf Klement, spoke against Serge's position.

Serge returned home devastated by the meeting, feeling he was dealing with a "sect," suffering from "authoritarianism, fractionalism, intrigues, maneuvers, close-mindedness, and intolerance." All this in a movement where, in England and France, there were no more than a hundred members in each section, more likely only dozens, split into opposing groups engaged in mutual sniping. They even marched separately in demonstrations, including at the funeral of Trotsky's son Leon Sedov, who died in a clinic in Paris in 1938 under suspicious circumstances.[23]

From 1937, Serge separated himself from the abortive Fourth International, writing to Sneevliet, "This isn't a beginning, it's an end." "Sickened" by what he saw, he wrote that "The great and noble movement to which we had given so many lives in Russia thus degenerated overseas in impotence and sectarianism." Serge, still and always an admirer of Trotsky, continued to serve as his French translator and defended the Old Man as and when he could.

Among the works he translated was "Their Morals and Ours," about which Serge wrote an essay he never published in his lifetime. It is a central document in tracking Serge's shift away from the Bolshevism he publicly espoused for twenty years, expressing grave doubts about the moral, political, and personal underpinnings of the Russian Revolution.[24]

For Serge, Trotsky's work is an expression of "the Bolshevism of its great years," but also of its "decadence." Though Serge says, "the modern world owes [Trotsky and the Bolsheviks of the October Revolution] a great deal, [and] the future will owe them even more," he warns against the impulse to "blindly imitate them."

Serge points out that the book's "tone" is significant, for it is "domineering," typical of the Bolsheviks' speech of the time, and of Marx's before them. Chosen at random, a typical example of Trotsky's tone is his comparison of Bolsheviks and social democrats:

> Compared to revolutionary Marxists, the social-democrats and centrists appear like morons, or a quack beside a physician. They do not think one problem through to the end, believe in the power of conjuration and, hoping for a miracle, cravenly avoid every difficulty. Opportunists are peaceful shop-keepers in socialist ideas, while Bolsheviks are its inveterate warriors.[25]

Serge was spot on when he said that the tone "is something of great importance, for this tone is essentially one of intolerance." Trotsky's tone in this work "implies the claim to the monopoly of truth, or, to speak more accurately, the sentiment of possessing the truth."

The sources of Serge's later disputes with his comrades in Mexico, of his fallings-out with old friends, of the development of his ideas on society and social struggles were already present in germ in this essay, as he writes that

> The truth is never fixed; it is constantly in the process of becoming and no absolute border sets it apart from error. The assurance of those Marxists who fail to see this is quickly transformed into smugness. The feeling of possessing the truth goes hand in hand with a certain contempt for man, of the other man [...]. This sentiment implies a denial of freedom, freedom being, on the intellectual level, the right of others to think differently, the right to be wrong. The germ of an entire totalitarian mentality can be found in this intolerance. Respect for the human person, toleration, nay acceptance of other opinions as legitimate, must be the guiding principles of a reborn socialist movement.

Serge here again gives a hint, more than a hint, of his future development, when this lifelong revolutionary accepts the role of reformist socialists:

> Would it not be wiser and more in conformity with Marxism, which above all is awareness of social reality, to admit that these men and these parties have a mission to fulfill in the workers' movement and to grant them the esteem they unquestionably deserve, being at the head of a combat that grows daily more difficult? The discussion would be made considerably easier, and discussion remains one of the methods by which thought progresses.

The solidity of the social democratic parties, despite the attacks and jeremiads of Stalinists and Trotskyists alike, is not the result of misleadership. Serge views it as the natural outcome of a simple fact:

> Since my return to the West, I have become convinced that the old communist manner of proceeding, which consisted in claiming to rescue "the masses" from the pernicious influence of "the corrupt reformist leaders," "agents of the bourgeoisie," rested on false premises. The reformist masses remain remarkably faithful to their leaders, despite the campaigns mounted against the latter, especially when these are campaigns of insults, because these leaders represent them perfectly, and in most cases are sincere men of conviction.

The working-class simply wasn't buying what the Communists were selling.

The real question, one that Trotsky refused to ask, and that his followers denied was relevant, was this: "[H]ow can we not ask if the Bolshevik regime didn't have several weaknesses, several foundational or functional vices that facilitated the bureaucratic usurpation? The question cannot not be posed." The founding of the Cheka, which occurred during Lenin and Trotsky's reign, and the crushing of Kronstadt, which Trotsky never ceased defending: Here were the seeds of the degeneration of the Soviet state. For Trotsky, "the regime that in reality was suffering from an extremely serious illness, remained irreproachable and unassailable."

Serge's clear-eyed vision of the weaknesses, political and, even more, personal, of Trotsky lead one to ask, would a Soviet Union led by him have been any better than Stalin's? The dogmatism, the refusal to listen to or tolerate others, and the certainty that he held the truth in his hands forces us to wonder if the principal difference between Stalin and Trotsky is that the latter never got a chance to establish a dictatorship that would have been equally repressive.

In August 1939 Trotsky fired his final blast against Serge, attacking him in the *Bulletin of the Opposition* for the promotional material for Serge's French translation of "Their Morals and Ours." Serge wrote to Trotsky explaining that he had nothing to do with it, and Trotsky could easily have asked his French lawyer,, Gérard Rosenthal, to find out who did write it. "I hope you will take it to be necessary to publish this letter of mine in the next issue of the *Bulletin of the Opposition*. I have every moral right to this satisfaction."[26] Serge's rectification was not published. Trotsky instead mentioned its contents and then continued to attack Serge for having "fallen under the influence of petty-bourgeois skepticism."

Serge and Trotsky also dealt acrimoniously with the issue of the Kronstadt uprising of 1921. It should be recalled that Serge wrote in his memoirs that at the time of the revolt of the sailors "After many hesitations, and with unutterable anguish, my Communist friends and I finally declared ourselves on the side of the Party."[27]

A year after the revolt, as we have seen, Serge made a public statement of support for the crushing of the revolt, writing in *La Vie ouvrière* that the rebels possessed

"The peasant, petit-bourgeois mentality," which doesn't aspire to socialism and whose sole ideal is the peaceful enjoyment of a plot of land cultivated for the profit of the individual, the lucrative commerce of regional fairs, and the free speech of a rural democracy that, if it were realized, would, through its obscurantism and conservatism be a powerful force for reaction.

Serge also parroted the opinions of his boss Zinoviev that the demands for free soviets were being "exploited by the Social-Revolutionaries, the Mensheviks, the anarchists, [and] even by communists carried away by the storm, who lacked clear-sightedness or were embittered by even more suspect elements, foreign espionage agents, and former officers."

Kronstadt was an issue that continued to cause controversy a decade and a half and even longer after the event. Trotsky never had a moment's hesitation about the correctness of the suppression of the revolt. He wrote the American journal *The Socialist Appeal* that the sailors' ideas, which were "deeply reactionary," "reflected the hostility of the backward peasantry toward the worker, the self-importance of the soldier or sailor in relation to 'civilian' Petrograd, the hatred of the petty bourgeois for revolutionary discipline."[28] Serge, in response, accepted that those at Kronstadt "formulated a demand that was, politically, extremely dangerous at that moment, but which was of general interest, disinterested, and sincerely revolutionary: 'Freely elected soviets.'" As for their economic program, it was "so far in reality from being counter-revolutionary, and so easy to grant, that in the very hours when the last of the mutineers was being shot, Lenin implemented the same demands by getting the New Economic Policy, or NEP, adopted."[29]

Serge returned to the issue of Kronstadt on several occasions, as we have seen, at times seeming to find justification for the government's actions, at others condemning it as a premonitory sign of the future degeneration of the Revolution, and at others still using it to justify his own failings at the time by remaining silent. In an article in *La Révolution prolétarienne* in October 1937, he spoke of Kronstadt as being a "red-hot topic" that needed to be confronted twenty years after the victory of 1917, when "[w]e all feel ourselves to be vanquished." Serge told his readers that "Out of a magnificent workers' victory we have seen the rise, on the basis of the socialist ownership of the means of production, of an inhuman regime, profoundly anti-socialist in the way it treats human beings."

Trotsky, as was his wont, seasoned his defense of Kronstadt with invective, in one case dismissing Serge's contribution to the discussion by saying Serge is "trying to manufacture a sort of synthesis of anarchism, POUMism, and Marxism."[30] Note the separation he implies between POUM and Marxism, of which he is the sole arbiter. Defending the storming of Kronstadt and the executions that ensued, Trotsky flippantly says that "Under similar circumstances only people like the Spanish anarchists or POUMists would have waited passively, hoping for a happy outcome. The Bolsheviks, fortunately, belonged to a different school."[31] A school from which Serge would now firmly demarcate himself.

Serge's "Once More Kronstadt" was published in the April 1938 issue of *The New International* and marks a step forward in Serge's analysis of the Bolshevik Revolution, its failings, and its failures. Trotsky had dismissed support of the sailors in 1921 by denying they were the same sailors as those of 1917, who helped the Revolution to emerge victorious. Serge turned the tables on Trotsky, asking if "the party of 1921 was that of 1918? Was it not already suffering from a bureaucratic befoulment which often detached itself from the masses and rendered it inhuman toward them?" Serge here again pushes back the beginning of the degeneration of the Russian Revolution to Lenin's lifetime. But he continues to seek the seeds of collapse, citing the criticisms in 1920 against the Workers' Opposition, and of the "evil practices that made their appearance during the discussion of the trade unions in 1920." Still in 1920, Serge points out the "monstrously false claim" made by the Cheka that the Mensheviks and Social-Revolutionaries were engaging in "intelligence with the enemy." Again in 1920 the Bolsheviks reneged on their promise to legalize the anarchists and instead arrested them (which Serge was silent about at the time). "The revolutionary correctness of a policy cannot justify, in my eyes, these baneful practices."

Serge is not done, though. The Revolution's downfall was in progress virtually at its birth, as Serge asks, "Has not the moment come to declare the day of the glorious year 1918 when the Central Committee of the party decided to permit the Extraordinary Commission [i.e. the Cheka] to apply the death penalty *on the basis of secret procedure, without hearing the accused, who could not defend themselves* is a black day" (emphasis in original). Serge found and spoke aloud the root cause of Stalinism, which dates to Lenin's heyday. Even so, he would spend the rest of his life defending Lenin and calling for a return to workers' democracy, a workers' democracy he had established never existed, or at best, momentarily.

Let us leave the final word on Kronstadt and all that surrounds it to Serge:

> By not recognizing old errors, whose gravity history has not ceased to bring out in relief, the risk is run of compromising the whole acquisition of Bolshevism. The Kronstadt episode simultaneously poses the questions of the relations between the party of the proletariat and the masses, of the internal regime of the party (the Workers' Opposition was smashed), of socialist ethics (all Petrograd was deceived by the announcement of a *White* movement in Kronstadt), of humaneness in the class struggle and above all in the struggle within our classes. Finally, it puts us today to the test as to our self-critical capacity.[32]

Serge's post mortem on his relations with Trotsky and Trotskyists is sad and clear:

It would have been so simple to say "There's a great disagreement between us on this or that point," but the Old Man and his partisans had become completely incapable of speaking such straightforward language. The terrifying environment of persecution in which they—like me—lived inclined them to persecution mania and the exercise of persecution.

Perhaps nothing defines both men better than a late exchange between them that began with the death of Trotsky's son Leon Sedov on February 16, 1938. Serge wrote to Trotsky and his wife Natalia on February 18, 1938, to offer his condolences, saying, "I want to tell you that in these black days, I and numerous other comrades known and unknown to you, who have considerable and yet secondary disagreements with you, all of us deeply and wholeheartedly share your grief."[33] Serge displayed great naivete when he referred to these differences. Trosky, even in his grief, remained the stern teacher, the unforgiving, unbending leader of a tiny—but in his eyes pure—sect. He responded on April 15, 1938.

In your letter you touched upon our disagreements and called them "secondary." Unfortunately, I cannot agree with this at all. If the differences between Bolshevism and Menshevism are secondary, then what is meant by the word primary? *Révolution prolétarienne* is an utterly reactionary organ which only distracts a number of people from the working-class movement. If your disagreements with us are secondary, why do you contribute not to our publications but to the publications that are mortally hostile to us through the very nature of their program?[34]

All this in response to a letter of condolence! As Max Eastman would write about Trotsky in a volume of reminiscences, "[H]is social gift, his gift of friendship, is actually about on the level of a barnyard fowl."[35]

Their correspondence would continue for several more letters in a painful dialogue of the deaf. Trotsky, unforgiving, finally admitted that the letter Serge sent was "very friendly in a personal sense, but demonstrates to me again that you are passing through a prolonged ideological crisis." Trotsky psychoanalyzed Serge from a distance. "You are turning your dissatisfaction with yourself into a dissatisfaction with others."[36]

That Serge should have made his differences with Trotsky over Spain a major issue is not surprising. Though his stay in Spain in 1917 was relatively brief, it was a decisive one. Serge wrote with great hope of the role of Spain and its fight against fascism in *La Wallonie*. "It is [...] the destiny of Western civilization, best represented by international socialism which is today being defended by the worker militias there. The fate of all of us is in a way tied to theirs. Never has the most total and active solidarity been demanded of us for more elevated interests."[37]

In August 1936, a month after Franco's uprising against the republic, Serge wrote a heartfelt letter to his close friend and fellow Oppositionist Andreu Nin, founder and leader of the Partido Obrero de Unificación Marxista (POUM). It was a party to which he would remain attached virtually until his death, and even beyond (he is buried among POUM exiles), though differences arose between him and the party's exiles in Mexico in Serge's final, contentious years.

Serge wrote his old comrade that reading POUM writings "brings me a bit of the tonic air of a revolution in which I've believed for almost twenty years." Serge even assigned the Spanish workers a messianic mission: "It seems to me that since 1917 an exceptional mission has been assigned you in the infirm West." Serge then expresses a doubt that will grow over the next decade about the working-class in general. The rise of fascism was caused by the "weakness of the working-class." "Nowhere," he continues, "except in Russia for a few years, has it been up to its task[...] [I]t allowed itself to be led by charlatans, naifs and cowards, and its revolutionary deficiencies made the historic fortunes of Mussolini and Hitler." These failings were a product of the bloodletting that was World War I, which explains the hopes he placed in the working-class of Spain. Not having been involved in the war, "it maintained all its vital force," and so it is the class "destined to emerge victorious."

It was in keeping with this vision that Serge wrote to Nin and offered his opinion of the question of power as it was posed after Franco's attempted coup. The military uprising revealed the real nature of the enemy and the futility of fighting only to protect the republic. Should the uprising fail,

> The generals [...] will have rendered you an immense service by removing their masks and annihilating illusions and finally forcing the proletariat to take a decisive step forward towards another republic, where democracy will be the freedom and might of the workers instead of a compromise with the counter-revolution hidden in ambush, sheltered behind laws for which it has no use [...]. Only the working-class can defeat fascism; it alone can construct a republic worthy of its name.

Serge gives Nin a lesson in revolutionary tactics, reminding the Catalan that the working-class should be armed and remain so. Surrendering arms after what seemed a victory meant surrendering the revolution to the bourgeoisie. "But one can have immense confidence in you [i.e., the Spanish working-class]. Your salvation lies within you. It depends on your firmness and clear-sightedness. There is no power more legitimate than that of a people in arms." The Spain Serge saw POUM fighting for was one where the working class "must, though its own organizations and the initiative of all, control everything: power, production, the army, supplies, and communications. It can only count on itself."

Serge's support was welcomed by POUM, for whose newspaper, *La Batalla*, he occasionally wrote. In January 1937 Serge wrote an article, censored upon publication, "Against

Slander," warning of the growing menace of the "campaign of discredit and insane accusations begun against you and [which is] already enormous overseas." We can surmise that it was the Communists who did the censoring by the fact that there is a blurred space in the newspaper in every place where the word "Communist" or "Stalinist" can be assumed to have been written. It is unquestionable that it was to the Communists in Spain, France, and elsewhere that Serge is referring when he speaks of the "slanderers" who accuse the POUM of causing the governmental crisis in Catalonia. Serge wrote that POUM had one way to fight back, that of telling the truth.

Serge, speaking from his Russian experience, poses at the end of the article the main question raised by the slander of POUM. "Do [the Communists] intend, within the closed field of the proletariat, to suppress the freedom of opinion? To suppress the freedom to criticize?" The campaign against POUM does indeed aim at this, Serge wrote, for it means that "those who don't think like [them] are enemy agents, means they deserve to be jailed or executed." The rest of the article in censored.

At the same time as this latter article, in January 1937, Serge also wrote the Executive Committee of POUM, the letter apparently delivered by hand by someone Serge knew in France, since it mentions being sent in such a way as to avoid the "Stalinist" postal censors.

In this admonitory letter Serge warns his comrades that the "campaign begun against you will never end." The reason is clear: "Given the current state of affairs, the Stalinist bureaucracy can in no way tolerate political formations that escape its influence and that know it well," both excellent defining characteristics of POUM. Serge shows great foresight, telling them to "Prepare yourselves for a long and very dangerous struggle, for they will stop at nothing." The underhandedness and dishonesty of the Communists was not to be underestimated. "Beware not to commit the unpardonable mistake of believing deals to be possible or to believe that moderation and loyalty on your part will force your adversary to a minimum of honesty." The ten years the Opposition spent trying to come to an agreement with the Stalinist bureaucracy by showing themselves "faithful and disciplined at demonstrating revolutionary virtues" were fruitless when dealing with men "who in reality led us to physical extermination, because this is the political necessity for the class of parvenus who took power there over the proletariat."

The Stalinists, Serge correctly saw, planned to "isolate red Catalonia, form a bloc of the liberal bourgeoisie, the petite bourgeoise, and a part of the working-class (reformists and official Communists) against it, and crush Barcelona by force."

Serge optimistically and unrealistically saw Soviet involvement in the war as a way of propagandizing among members of the Soviet military, advising POUM to prepare leaflets in Russian that could be given to Soviet sailors who disembarked in Spain, leaflets that would make the Opposition case in Spain that it was not possible to make in their homeland.

Despite Serge's difficulties with Trotsky and Trotskyists, whose "sectarianism" he condemned, he asked POUM to find a "place for Trotskyist left communists, even if they're doctrinaire, as long as they accept fraternal discipline." Citing Lenin in support of his position, "the Spanish Revolution must be Spanish [...] a revolutionary movement in a given country must have its own character and follow its own development." This, of course, was exactly the contrary of the orthodox Trotskyist position.

Serge also asked the embattled Spaniards to add a campaign for those imprisoned in Soviet Russia for their opposition to Stalin to POUM's already heavy charge. In doing so, in offering asylum to these anti-Stalinist fighters, "the Spanish Revolution will be stating an important principle: The Spanish Revolution calls for the freedom of working-class thought and openly defends it." Serge, faithful to his friends in Soviet prisons and camps, provided the POUM leadership with a list of names of political prisoners in Russia, including native and foreign socialists,

Trotskyists, and anarchists. Most, if not all, ultimately met the fate one would expect.

Serge ended by explaining all that depended on POUM. "I think that POUM can give the workers' movement a great example by its unity and spirit of free criticism, and that at this time it is the natural gathering point of everyone in the world who sincerely desires socialist revolution."

POUM would meet the fate of the Opposition in Russia, and in short order. On May Day 1937, fighting broke out in Barcelona between the Stalinists on one side and POUM and the anarchists on the other. The Stalinists drove POUM underground, kidnapped the party's leader Andreu Nin, and killed him in June 1937. Serge wrote a moving memorial to Nin in the August 14–15 issue of *La Wallonie*, titled "Farewell to a Friend." Serge eulogized Nin in this final tribute. "Adieu my friend. Your great, brave life remains with us, filled with accomplishments and actions. Your horrific death remains with us as well. Like you, it is to the bitter end that we must hold out so that socialism can be free."[38]

In 1939 and 1940 Serge signed a series of articles for the popular daily *L'Intransigeant*. The articles are focused almost exclusively on Soviet policy and practice and the ways in which it impacted the conduct of communists in other countries. His crystal ball lacked clarity in this case. Writing on October 22, 1939, Serge dismissed the possibility of a German attack on Ukraine, saying that that would mean Germany confronting "an army capable of supporting with redoubtable energy a short war."

The failure of the Soviet invasion of Finland was further proof of the incapacity of the Soviet state, the difficulties it encountered in its aggression due not only to the strength of Finnish resistance, but to the utter unpreparedness and poor planning of the Soviets. But these failures were only to be expected in Serge's opinion. An early article in the series, published on October 5, 1939, asked the question in its title: "The USSR: Can It Really Make War?" The answer was an unambiguous no.

Serge presented the dire situation of the USSR in unvarnished terms. "No country has lied about itself, lied as much to its own citizens, and spread beyond its borders so many waves of lies." But the situation in all fields is hopeless: "The state of transport is extremely worrisome," supplies of all kinds are lacking, and the country is demoralized from the forced collectivization. "A regime whose portrait is sketched out in this way, cannot without exposing itself to the risk of a rapid disintegration, engage in a real war."

* * *

Liuba has all but disappeared from this tale. As she took her final descent into madness, which would see her institutionalized for the rest of her long life (she died in 1984), Serge began his final romantic entanglement. In the spring of 1937, in April or May, he noticed Laurette Séjourné in a museum. She was wearing black, with a flower-patterned blouse. Either that evening, or shortly thereafter, he gave a talk in a hall near the Bastille, and saw her in the audience. At the conclusion, as he was leaving, as Serge described it, "she suddenly turned around, very close to me. It seemed like I silently called out to her. She smiled joyfully. That was it."

These details of Serge's meeting with the Italian-born Laura Valentini Séjourné, twenty-three to his forty-six when they met, are contained in a small notebook diary Serge kept, written with a novelist's eye and pen.[39] The heightened security of recording their affair in Russian can certainly be explained in part by the fact that Laurette was married to the French film editor Bernard Séjourné, with whom she'd had a son, René. She was making her way in the world of French film, also as an editor, her name appearing as Laura Séjourné in the credits of three French films she worked on before World War II and one she edited in Mexico in 1944. Around the time of her meeting with Serge, Laurette also frequented figures like André Breton and Jean Cocteau.

Serge must have thirsted for romance, and as was always the case when he fell in love, he threw himself into the affair heart and soul. In late June of 1937 Laurette appeared at his door one morning, and he wrote, "It was as though she had answered a call from within." Their age difference, or at least Serge's relatively advanced years, were on his mind. One rainy night, as they walked towards the Seine near the Louvre, Serge spoke to her of his fatigue and age. Laurette replied, "I would gladly give you my youth." Serge "wanted to reply jokingly, 'Then give it to me.'"

There were moments of imprudence in the early months, with Serge attempting to arrange rendezvous in her husband's presence. There were mishaps: Laurette standing him up, then he standing her up. It was only on March 17, 1938, that she paid her first visit to his lodging, and only then that she mentioned the existence of her son. They made "involuntary confessions" to each other, Serge telling her of a married friend who boasted of many lovers, Laurette telling him that "I imagine you to be completely different." They looked forward to spending time alone when her husband left for America, and spent every day together, strolling, working together, dining, going to the cinema, sitting in cafés.

Finally, on May 20, at his apartment, he stepped away so she could undress,

And then it was wonderful and agonizing; there was boundless joy and sadness to the point of tears. There was a long, quiet, uniting conversation—about everything. We lay there for several hours. I caressed her a lot. She was wearing a pink nightgown. Her breasts covered. I caressed her whole body— she gave herself completely. Twice I wanted to rise above her—"No," she said, "let's stay like this a bit longer—it feels so good!"

I lay on her. Desire came and went from this blissful state. She opened up—completely ready. I almost took her—and

couldn't. "Stay like this, stay," she said. And I lay on her—
open and surrendered—for a long time.

We rested. She rose above me, as if she wanted to be on top of
me, her face wondrous… Everything was repeated. I caressed
her, loved her—it was wonderful and painful—and I couldn't.

Suddenly, she turned over and lay on her stomach. I kissed her
neck. My hand began to caress her till she moaned. Warmth.
Flesh. And suddenly—desire. "Give yourself to me." She
immediately turned over—opened up. "Help me…" And
there was wetness, warmth, everything… all of her. "I love
you, love you, love you, do you love me…" she repeated,
excited, with a joyful half-moan.

I moaned.

Afterwards, "We talked about our life together, which is
inevitable. 'If only you won't stop loving me. B[ernard] would
agree to me having a lover, but I can't. Our love is so much
deeper, I can't. I don't know what to do about him….'"

Several days later, on May 28, they succeeded in consummat-
ing their relationship. A week later Serge went to visit Liuba in
the hospital. When he returned to Paris, he and Laurette threw
themselves into each others' arms.

She was still dressed. I began caressing her body, hesitated,
and suddenly she unbuttoned herself, saying, "I'm making it
easier for you." With gentle, fiery affection, I appeased her
longing completely. She moaned. She opened her eyes: "I
want…"—she didn't dare to finish—"I want to do something
for you."—What? "Well, a cup of tea…" She shied away
from offering herself to give me pleasure. Instead, she quietly
said, "Take me." I replied, "I can't, it wouldn't be wise."

They loved each other frantically. "At home I caressed her whole
and satisfied her twice."

After the joy, she spoke with a clear face—searching for the right words. "It's hard for me to put into words... I'll find them sometime. There's something new, something I'm feeling for the first time. I thought I can just live near you, happily, without this. But now we've enriched ourselves, and it's better this way—wonderful. But what is this feeling? I want to do something for you." "Do you surrender yourself?" "Yes, but it's not that... I feel under your power. How can I say it?"

They admitted their love for each other, and finally, on June 20, she asked what was to be done? "Will we live together?" Serge doesn't reveal the answer, but Laurette later that day said, "The decision is made, irreversibly. If I continue living with B. for a little while longer, as a companion whom I love—what is it for you? Nothing can separate us. I don't like that you see some danger for us in this."

The notebook ends abruptly the next day, saying, "We didn't see each other." But she left her husband and, finally, her son. Serge and Laurette would wed, the marriage a miserable failure. Laurette later told Serge biographer Suzi Weissman that "[s]he considered her marriage to him 'an error,' she was too young, and his life too full of tragedy and darkness for her to understand."[40]

* * *

Serge was not exclusively a political figure, nor was everything in his life politics. He was a novelist, and even if all of his novels revolve around history and politics, he was a literary figure, and was respected as such. The variety of his contacts can be seen from an examination of his address book. It's undated, but covers the years 1936 to 1940, since it contains almost none of those he knew in Mexico, nor any Mexican phone numbers, with only a couple of exceptions. It is a marvelously and fascinatingly revealing piece of evidence of Serge's life, of the circles in which he ran, of their scope and importance. The entries in the address book cover politics, literature, and the arts.

Some of those who appear in it are unsurprising. We find the visiting card of the aforementioned Marcel Body, like Serge a member of the French Communist group in Soviet Russia, who opposed Stalin and was expelled from the French Communist Party. Felicien Challaye, whose *carte de visite* describes him as a "teacher at the Lycée Condorcet," was a pacifist and anti-colonialist writer whose political activities began during the Dreyfus Affair.

The Autant-Lara living on rue Lepic is certainly the filmmaker Claude Autant-Lara; Colette Audry was a polymath who, among other things, was a screenwriter who, like Serge, supported POUM during the Spanish Civil War, writing for the group's French organ; Robert Aron, who later entered the Académie Française, was a film critic. The presence of so many people involved in cinema is likely explained by Serge's connection to Laurette. André Breton, the Pope of Surrealism, who would flee France on the same ship as Serge in 1941, was then living in the ninth arrondissement, and was also a friend of Séjourné.

Otto Bauer, a dissident Marxist and later companion in exile in Mexico, lived in what was then known as Brunn and later Brno. The great revolutionary Angelica Balabanoff is listed with her residence at the Park Plaza Hotel on West 77 Street in Manhattan, and C.L.R. James resided in London at 9 Heathcote Street. Somewhat surprisingly, the reformist socialist Harold Laski is here, living in Devon Lodge in Fulham. The writer Blaise Cendrars was an acquaintance, while André Gide on the rue Vaneau and the novelist Jean Giono were more than acquaintances; Gide, as we've seen, having participated in the movement to liberate Serge, while Giono later offered Serge shelter during the exodus from Paris at the time of the German invasion. René Vauthier, author of a scathing book on Belgium's depredations in the Congo, is listed, and Jules Romains, one of France's most famous writers, was also a friend. The Croatian Ante Ciliga, like

Serge, was a foreign communist sentenced to a Soviet isolator who lived to tell the tale, and was living in the heart of the Latin Quarter on rue du Cardinal Lemoine, while Francesco Ghezzi, an Italian anarchist who fled fascist Italy for Russia, is listed with his Russian address, from which he would be taken by the secret police and never heard from again. Serge fruitlessly dedicated himself to locating Ghezzi. Another Italian exile appears, one who achieved international fame, Ignazio Silone, living then in Zurich. Another foreign listing was that of POUM at Pizarro 14 in Madrid. It is not surprising to find Georges Duhamel in these pages, who defended Serge during his imprisonment in Soviet Russia, nor the offices of *Esprit*, for which Serge wrote, which he read religiously, and whose philosophy of Personalism he claimed as his own. The review's founder and editor, Emmanuel Mounier, whose correspondence with Serge we will come across later, is listed at his temporary Brussels address.

Perhaps the most surprising person in the address book is Jacques LeRoy-Ladurie, who later served as France's minister of agriculture under Pétain's collaborationist government and who, though he would eventually go over to the Resistance, was, before the war, very close to fascist circles. The presence of the leader of Belgian socialism Emil Vandervelde is not surprising, as he played a central role in getting Serge a Belgian visa after his release from the Soviet Union, despite the young Serge having called him a "slave trader."

Serge's first wife, Rirette Maîtrejean, living outside Paris in the Seine-et-Oise, is in his address book, and his third wife, Laurette, also appears, living on rue de l'Atlas in Paris. The French Trotskyist Pierre Naville was living in the fifth arrondissement, and we also find Trotsky's French lawyer Gérard Rosenthal. The dissident American communist, Max Schachtman, who would attempt to assist Serge in his flight from France after the Nazi conquest, was living in New York's Greenwich Village. At the same time, the address of the moderately right-wing newspaper *L'Ordre* on rue Tronchet had a place in Serge's book.

Serge's close friends and allies the novelists Charles Plisnier and Léon Werth and the left-socialist Marceau Pivert, who, like Serge would flee to Mexico City and would become embroiled in political differences with Serge, are listed. Mexico finally features with the address of Diego Rivera and Frida Kahlo at Londres 127 in Coyoacan, though Rivera has a second listing as well in Altavista, Mexico City. Trotsky's son Leon Sedov is listed as living at the same address as Rivera and Kahlo in Coyoacan.

Serge wrote about Antoine de Saint-Exupéry in his notebooks, but the author of *Le Petit Prince* isn't in his address book. Instead, we find his wife, the El Salvador-born Consuela, who suffered through a stormy marriage to the writer, punctuated by frequent affairs on the part of both the husband and wife. She, too, was a friend of Laurette's. Serge was in many ways a left-wing Zelig.

17

Flight from Europe

The German invasion of France on May 10, 1940, and Germany's rapid victory, certified by Marshal Pétain on June 22 with France's surrender, led to a massive flood of refugees from Belgium and France fleeing south ahead of the Germans, what became known as the *exode*, the exodus. Serge, Vlady, and Laurette, accompanied by the Spanish exile Narciso Molins y Fabregas, were part of this mass flight. We can date their flight to around June 9 or 10, since Serge mentions leaving Paris right after the Germans set Rouen ablaze. It would seem Serge had foreseen the need to flee. He had obtained a "collective safe conduct" authorizing travel from Paris to Pau in the south of France, valid from May 28 to June 28, 1940, the reason for travel listed as "evacuation." Serge subsequently received another safe conduct for himself and Vlady, who was described as an "artiste peintre," valid July 26–30 from Agen to Manosque.

Serge had about 4000 francs in his possession, about $100, and described his state of mind in his memoirs, written just a few years later:

> Our flight is accompanied by a sense of release bordering at times on gaiety. All our possessions have been reduced to a few bundles. Only the other day I was peeved at not being able to find a brief jotting among my papers, and now, lo and behold, books, personal objects, documents, manuscripts, all disappear at one stroke without effecting any real emotion.[1]

Serge, like many, if not most, viewed the French defeat as not only military but also political and moral, the collapse of the French Third Republic, which, after weathering storms and scandals aplenty in its seventy years of existence, had finally lost the will to live. "All the revolutionaries, together with the whole French population, would gladly have fought against fascism and for a Third Republic determined to survive, if this had been possible. But only a living society can be defended and this one had reached a stage of decomposition that was too advanced." But the defeat was also a reflection of the softening of the French working-class, which he described in terms reminiscent of those used by his youthful persona of Le Rétif. "Nobody believed in anything anymore, because nothing in fact was possible anymore: certainly not a revolution, with this working-class gorged on fresh Camembert, pleasant wine, and ancient ideas which had become mere words."[2]

Serge had an advantage over many: He had a personal mythology to fall back on as a support through seemingly hopeless times. He carried with him the putative revolutionary past of his parents, which he exaggerated in his description of the role of their memory at this time:

> I grew up among Russian revolutionary exiles who knew that the Revolution was advancing towards them, inexorably, out of the depths of the future. In simple words they taught me to have faith in mankind and to wait steadfastly for the necessary cataclysms. They waited for half a century, in the midst of persecution.[3]

As we have already seen, there was no half-century of persecution or political activism on the part of his parents. He was born into a shabby broken home, one he left when still a child. But psychologically this myth was a foundation of Serge's personality, one he transmitted to his son.

Also on the road south was Serge's ex-comrade, ex-companion, and ex-wife Rirette Maîtrejean. She had settled into a life of anarchism and proofreading, the latter a trade that had long been—and would continue to be for many decades—the fiefdom of anarchists and other leftists. She was not alone in her travels. Accompanying her was a young writer from Algiers she had befriended, and whose ideas she greatly influenced. Her traveling companion was Albert Camus.

Serge stopped in several towns along the way south to Marseille, and had received attractive promises of aid from Jean Giono, the great novelist and a dedicated pacifist. He received two undated letters from Giono, in the first of which the latter told Serge of how he already had fifteen comrades and several children with him in his home in the countryside. In a second letter Giono wrote Serge, "in late September I can put at your disposal a three-room apartment in Banon," in the Alps of southern France. Giono was generous: "I will help you in your stay by giving you vegetables, potatoes, and everything I can. I will also help you financially." This offer was not the only one of its kind Giono made. A December 23, 1940, letter from Galy Malaquais, wife of the thirty-six-year-old writer Jean Malaquais, with whom Serge would have a violent falling out in 1943, described Giono's generosity towards her and her husband in Banon. In the end, Giono's offer couldn't be taken up. When Serge got to Giono's home "a pretty little house surrounded by flowers," the door was locked. "Giono has gone to the hills to meditate." The refugees were arrested but allowed to depart.[4]

Serge reached Marseille sometime in September and, along with so many others, was assisted by Varian Fry and his Emergency Rescue Committee, also known as the American Rescue Committee. So well-known and courageous was this group, so vital were they in rescuing thousands from occupied France, that they were the subject of a Netflix series, *Transatlantic*. The series was wildly inaccurate in too many regards to be enumerated here, but the series at least made the name of Varian Fry famous. As Serge wrote about the man and his staff: "If it had not been for Varian Fry's American Relief Committee [*sic*], a goodly number of refugees would have had no reasonable course open to them but to jump into the sea from the height of the transporter bridge, a certain enough method."[5]

But in a very real sense it was the kindness of strangers—or at least friends he'd never met—who helped Serge flee France. No two individuals were more ferocious in their defense of Serge, in their persistence on his behalf, than Dwight and Nancy Macdonald. Though it is Dwight, the formidable editor and critic, whom Serge usually thanks most effusively and whom he praises in his memoirs, it was Nancy who did most of the running around in a failed effort to get Serge an American visa and who assembled documentation for him.

An example of her tirelessness on his behalf can be found in a letter dated July 20, 1940. Nancy wrote to the American consul in Marseille, saying, "I am extremely anxious to make it possible for my friend Victor Serge to leave France and come to this country to live with my husband and myself." She pledged full support of Serge and even sent the consul a report of their resources, including a listing of their stock and bond holdings (which were significant). Her husband's salary at *The New Yorker* was shown to be $40 weekly, which makes the $50 they sent to help get him through his struggles around this time all the more significant. "My husband and I have known Victor Serge for several years and have the highest regard for him both personally and as a literary man." Serge calls the many letters from Macdonald "breathtaking" and how Macdonald and the Swiss poet J.-P. Samson "seem to clasp my hands in the dark."[6]

The following month, according to documents quoted in Serge's FBI file, obtained by Serge biographer Suzi Weissman and graciously donated by her to the Yale Serge archive, Serge wrote to an unnamed friend asking for financial assistance, help in getting a visa, and "for contacts with and addresses of Jewish aid groups." Preparing for his future, he was transporting manuscripts of books with him he wished to have published and so bring in income. He also at the same time wrote to the writer Max Eastman and others asking for help and, according to the

FBI summary of the letter, "he maintains that he is one of the last refugees of the Russian Revolution. He expresses a conviction that a better time is coming after the dark period we are in." A sign of Serge's desperation is evident in his sudden mention asking a friend about the possibility of receiving a Venezuelan visa, and later of one for Ecuador, as well as his expectation that he would be receiving aid from Jewish groups (perhaps owing to the fact that Vlady, with his Jewish mother, was technically a Jew). Shortly after this he learned that Eastman, who had contacted the Jewish group, discovered it was no longer in existence, but he, too, sent Serge a small amount of money. At various points Serge discussed the possibility of crossing to Portugal via Spain, and even wrote to an Argentine editor asking about the possibilities of writing for her review. The editor, in answer to a query about the possibility of Serge receiving a visa for Argentina, told him that "the doors are becoming increasingly closed against immigrants and especially against those whose names are well known, as in your case." The correspondent, whose name is redacted, wonders if it "would[n't] be easier to get a visa for North America?"

Serge's greatest desire was to obtain an American visa, at the very least an American transit visa, which he hoped he'd be able to convert into one allowing him to stay in the US. Toward the end of 1940 he wrote that another possibility would be to go to Mexico and, once there, cross the border into the US. This was the great hope of the Macdonalds as well, but as Serge would write in a letter in March of 1941, a Russian refugee has no particular right to an entry visa to the US.

The matter of an American visa appears frequently in his correspondence. Serge often felt he wasn't receiving the assistance he could have hoped for, complaining in September 1940 that this was because he wasn't the leader of any group. He also alleged that he was being kept from the US by Communists who were working in the State Department, writing in a letter summarized in his Freedom of Information Act (FOIA) records that "there are a goodly number of reactionaries and some friends of the USSR [in the State Department] who are discreet but do their duty."

More striking still was a letter read by the FBI dated October 7 addressed to "Dear friends": "I imagine that by now you realize what great obstacles I am up against...." That obstacles existed to entry to the US was a fact that frustrated many. Serge, though, placed the blame for his inability to get a US visa on unexpected villains:

Through certain information which we now have I know that the Stalinist work is being done in the United States on a large scale by a goodly number of journalists and Stalinist intellectuals who have arrived there. They even have a certain amount of support in the Administration and without doubt among certain aliens of the Bourgeoisie. Their action is and will be camouflaged [...]. They would do anything if they could get all their personnel installed in the United States. They will be able during a certain period of time, at least, to close the door to me.

Around this time, in frustration, he expressed the wish that groups on the left and far left would set up their own refugee aid groups, since no one was seeing to the needs of the militants of these groups.

Though Serge was surrounded in Marseille by refugees waiting for visas, in March 1941 he complained that the treatment he was receiving was "exclusive" to him, and that there exists information in files in Washington "that will soon be turned over to the enemy just at a time when the United States claims to be working in favor of the political refugees of Europe." In fact, his file was not yet constituted but would be once he left France, and at no time did the US claim to be working in favor of the political refugees of Europe. Serge was like thousands of others, some in far more dangerous situations, blocked by US immigration policy.

Finally, in a September 1940 telegram to Serge, Dwight Macdonald cabled that "President Cárdenas of Mexico recommended your visa we telegraphed Cárdenas intervene locally you should visit the Mexican consulate." This was far from the end of Serge's travails. Even the Mexican president's recommendation didn't impel the bureaucracy to work with any great haste. It wasn't until November 12, 1940, that the Mexican government officially notified its agencies that Serge, Vlady, and five-year-old-Jeannine, "who are currently to be found in a [French] concentration camp," had been granted visas. It wasn't until January 13, 1941 that the Mexican consul in Marseille certified that Serge, "Vladimiro," and Jeannine had been accepted by Mexico; Serge was described as "stateless" and traveling on a Belgian passport. This authorization later had to be extended, a letter dated June 10, 1941, explaining that "given the difficulties of the period [he] wasn't able to leave France until March 24, arriving in Ciudad Trujillo [now Santo Domingo] in the Dominican Republic on May 24." Serge writes in his *Memoirs* how tens of thousands of Spaniards owe their lives to President Lázaro Cárdenas.

The mention of Serge's daughter Jeannine is worth a momentary halt. Jeannine is always something of an afterthought in Serge's private and public writings, an unwanted child at birth who never received a fraction of the attention her older brother did. It was assumed that Jeannine would travel to Mexico separately from Serge and Vlady, accompanying Laurette, whose visa application was experiencing many delays, though she was a French citizen and qualified for an entry visa to Mexico and even the US on the French quota.

The writer René Vauthier, living in Lyon, wrote Serge in February 1940 that Jeannine is very happy now that she is going to school and that it would be wrong for Serge to think of taking her overseas when there will doubtless soon be as much danger and disturbance overseas as there now was in Europe. Jeannine had clearly been with Vauthier for some time, since in January Vauthier wrote Serge to tell him about Jeannine's Christmas, and how Vauthier took Jeannine to see the town's Christmas tree. Vauthier praised Jeannine's "good temperament," telling Serge of Christmas morning when her wooden shoes—the French version of Christmas stockings hung from the fireplace—were filled with gifts.

> She reflected all morning, contemplating how this good old man had fulfilled the wishes of every member of the family and everyone in the village. When we sat down to eat, she confided in us that she would love for her part to give something to Santa Claus, but she had to know what.

Her stay with the Vauthiers was a long and apparently enjoyable one. The five-year-old girl sent her father a handwritten note from Pontarlier, complete with drawings, informing Serge that "Jeannine is going to go to Lausanne tomorrow by bus." After some other news she signs off, "Jeannine gives her papa a kiss."

Nancy Macdonald wrote to Serge on December 24, 1940, that Laurette should

> write for a French quota number if she still wants to get an American visa [...], and I hope to go to Washington on Thursday (26th) to try to get a transit visa for you and to make a last plea for a faster visa. I cannot write you of all the negotiations that have taken place, of telegrams and letters and telephone calls that have been written and made.

Around the same time that the Mexican government was officially informing Serge that the visas for him, Vlady, and Jeannine were approved, Laurette cabled Nancy Macdonald that "visas arrived invalid under pseudonym with a nationality error necessary to rectify to Mexico City for Kibalchich Victor and child of Russian origin (signed) Sejourne." An issue that appears and quickly disappears is a November request, accepted almost immediately by the Mexican government, to add Laurette's eight-year-old-son René to her visa application.

Serge and Vlady had passage booked on January 22, 1941, on the American Export Lines, the carrier informing Serge that they'd received $927 to cover the costs, paid for by—of course—the Macdonalds. Serge and his friends in New York were still hoping for an American visa, though Serge felt that the American consulate was predisposed against him. The Macdonalds continued to work mightily on Serge's behalf, pulling strings, contacting friends, writing what they described as "strong" letters to the State Department. All to no avail, though the French government, on February 12, issued a safe conduct authorizing travel to the US. Varian Fry, for his part, joined the effort to assist Serge in obtaining American transit visas, writing to the American [Joint] Distribution Committee and presenting Serge as a respectable figure. Serge, Fry writes, was the author of a book on life in prison that is "a classic of its kind and which is read by thousands of social workers as part of their training." However trite it might be to call Serge's situation so, his Kafkaesque nightmare continued to deepen. In order to pass through Martinique, a French overseas department, Serge needed a visa from the Dominican Republic.

Finally, on March 25, 1941, Serge wrote of his "eight-month battle for a visa," complained of people who might have helped him but failed to do so, who in fact did the opposite. That same day he joined the passengers aboard the *Amiral Paul Lemerle*.

Also on board were cultural figures of great importance. André Breton, the painter Wilfredo Lam, the German Communist writer and sworn enemy of Serge Anna Seghers, and the French anthropologist Claude Lévi-Strauss. The latter was on his way to Brazil, which would provide him with the material for his classic *Tristes Tropiques*. In it, he mentions his fellow passenger Serge:

As for Victor Serge, I was intimidated by his status as a former companion of Lenin, at the same time as I had the greatest difficulty in identifying him with his physical presence, which was rather like that of a prim and elderly spinster. The clean-shaven, delicate-featured face, the clear voice accompanied by a stilted and wary manner, had an almost asexual quality, which I was later to find among Buddhist monks along the Burmese frontier, and which is very far removed from the virile and superabundant vitality commonly associated in France with what are called subversive activities. The explanation is that cultural types which occur in very similar forms in every society, because they are constructed around very simple polarities, are used to fulfil different social functions in different communities. Serge's type had been able to realize itself in a revolutionary career in Russia, but elsewhere it might have played some other part.[7]

The voyage took months, and the bureaucratic nightmare never let up. Proof of vaccination was needed and provided on May 19 in Fort-de-France, Martinique. There were delays in the return of customs documents in that same place. On May 29, Serge was forced to write to the Mexican ministry of foreign affairs for an extension of his entry visa due to the many delays he'd experienced. While in Ciudad Trujillo, now Santo Domingo, Serge registered for a reader's card at the library of the university. He also sent Nancy Macdonald an account of the mental state of the refugees.

The militants of the old socialist parties, completely worn down, were nothing but fugitives who underhandedly fought over places on the last boat. Among them, solidarity had been reduced to a group egoism (if I survived the crisis of July–August 1940 it was by chance, through natural optimism, and thanks to you). As for the old Russian socialists of all tendencies, with whom I maintained courteous relations. [They] behaved towards me in an unspeakable manner simply in order to keep visa and assistance funds for themselves. "Comrades" did the same. Friends told me despairingly, "We're fighting for men who are done for, who are no longer worth a thing, who will be nothing but dead weight."

In August they reached Havana, where he and Vlady were held at Camp Tiscornia, and where Serge received $50 from Dwight Macdonald. This seemingly small sum was the equivalent of $1087 in 2024 dollars.

As his arrival in Mexico grew nearer, the Mexican Comite pro-ayuda a las victimas del fascismo wrote the authorities informing them of the imminent arrival of Serge, saying, "Given the personality of said writer we would like to request [that] the [executive] secretariat [...] issue the necessary orders so there are no impediments to his landing." On the same paper and with the same typewriter on the same date Serge's Mexican publisher Ediciones Quetzal made the same request.

Finally, on September 3, 1941, Serge and Vlady arrived at their final destination. Serge's registration papers, dated October 13, are for Victor Serge Kibaltchiche Poderevsky, in keeping with Spanish naming practices. His height was 1.66 meters; his native language was French, but he also spoke Russian, Spanish, English, and German; his religion was Orthodox; and he was authorized to stay a year.

Serge and Vlady were now safely arrived, but Laurette was still delayed. On October 10 her entry to Mexico was authorized, but two weeks later Nancy Macdonald wrote Serge to tell him her ship had been delayed until November 4, and that she risked missing even that one. Nancy was clearly frustrated with the Emergency Rescue Committee. She took it upon herself to visit their offices to ensure they had Laurette on board that ship, and she planned to send Dwight to see them the following week, since they needed to be "goaded" into action. On November 5, Martin Temple of the committee wrote to the Mexicans asking that they add Laurette's son René to her visa, which they agreed to do four days later. In the end Laurette's son remained with his mother's family in Italy, her country of origin, to which he had earlier been sent. He finally made it to Mexico in later life, where his mother lived out her days. He was, reputedly, "full of hostility for his mother" for her abandonment of him.[8]

Also on November 9, Nancy wrote saying she still had no news of Laurette's departure, but held out hope for the December boat, saying that "Fry seems to think that she will get on that one." Of Fry, to whom she had spoken the previous week, she said that "he has a really charming and fine manner." Having expressed discontent with Fry's organization, Nancy said of this meeting, "I am so used to being snubbed by the Emerescue that the experience of having a leisurely and interested conversation with one of their people impressed me." The Macdonalds' generosity was limitless. After saying that Fry seems to think that Jeannine will be traveling with Laurette, she made an astounding offer:

If you do not have enough money we can always send you what is lacking until you can take care of the two of them yourself. Or you can send Jeannine to us if that seems preferable and possible. Please let us know if you need some money and don't live too Spartanly.

Perhaps it was a formality, but the final document in this lengthy dossier was a note dated February 20, 1942, stating that the Mexican government had received funds to cover Laurette's possible repatriation.

18
Liuba

Serge left someone behind.

His second marriage, to Liuba Russakov, as we have seen, was lived through terrible times. The Soviet government's war on her husband and her family destroyed Liuba and led to decades of mental illness and residence in psychiatric hospitals in the Soviet Union and France. A cousin of Serge's, Irina Gogua, whom we heard from describing Léon Kibalchich as a "gambler" and casting doubt on the legend of his political heroism, was a witness to the marriage and described it and Liuba's state straightforwardly to Suzi Weissman and Vlady. Irina, like so many around Serge, was sent to the camps, in her case in Ufa, Vorkuta, and Ukhta for twenty-one years, from 1935 to 1956, charged with belonging to a—in her words—"Trotskyist-Bukharinist-Zinovievist right-left-SR, Menshevik, anarchist bloc."

Liuba, according to Gogua, adored Serge, but, she added, "he was too strong for her, and it bothered her." Liuba had many pregnancies and many abortions when they were living in Leningrad, the abortions explained by Serge's opposition to having a large family. Though the persecution she and her husband suffered played a role in her descent into madness, this conflict over children seems to have played a role, too. Gogua told Vlady and Weissman that Liuba asked her, "Can you hear those voices? They are the cries of the babies I had to get rid of. Victor didn't want me to have many children, and now they are following me." For Gogua, it was the difference in strength between Serge and Liuba that broke her. Again, according to Gogua, when Liuba discovered she was pregnant with the future

Jeannine, she hid the fact—and herself—from Victor so the pregnancy could be carried to term.

Liuba's mental state was treated dismissively by her son Vlady. As far as he was concerned, as he wrote in an article with the Mexican Serge scholar Claudio Albertani, "his mother abandoned him in order to withdraw into madness and to no longer participate in his future." Since then, and until Liuba's death at eighty-six in 1984, a half-century later, "he felt [for his mother] a strange sentiment of tenderness mixed with resentment." Serge, for his part, "felt great bitterness about the situation, but in his relations with Liuba was able to maintain a gentle and tender expression."

Despite Vlady's insistence that his mother's madness was a form of evasion, some of her psychiatric records have been preserved, and they graphically demonstrate her harrowing condition. Graphs of her mental state while she was interned in 1933–35, with the high points representing "great excitation" and the lowest the degree of depression, show periods of "normality" that last weeks, broken up by manic fits, followed by depressive fits. There is, unsurprisingly, no pattern to her suffering. In December 1933 she was in deep depression from December 13 until December 22, when she went into a manic fit, followed the next day by the darkest of depressions, a manic day, ten days of normality followed by two weeks of depression interrupted by one day of manic behavior.

The photo on her Belgian identification card, issued on September 12, 1936, is that of a haunted woman, staring at the camera apprehensively, far from the stunningly beautiful woman at the time she met Serge. Shortly after the family's arrival in Belgium, where they were living at 134, rue Joseph Bens, Serge wrote a medical history of his wife, apparently for the information of her psychiatrists. It is a remarkably frank document, laying out the past and present of its author's unfortunate spouse.

Serge establishes a case for a hereditary tendency towards mental illness. She was described as the "[d]aughter of Jewish workers." There were no organic causes for mental illness in the past, like syphilis. But her father was "subject to accesses of violence, and over the course of his life went through a crisis of nostalgia that reached the level of psychosis, having been separated from his family." As for Liuba's mother, she "presented signs of hysteria." Liuba's sisters, who all suffered terribly because they were related to Victor, had no mental illness, but "tended toward egocentrism."

Serge explained that her first memories were of a pogrom in her birthplace, Rostov, and the emigration to France that followed it. She lived thirteen "calm" years in France and then had to confront the experience of the Russian Revolution in Petrograd. "From 1928, [she lived through] a period of constant traumatization due to the persecution of her father and her husband in the USSR." When she was around eighteen, which would have been in 1916, since she was born in 1898, she "suddenly began to waste away, thought she was going to die and suffered a moral crisis," which she was able to surmount with a little bit of rest. She suffered a relapse caused by jealousy when her younger sister married.

Liuba was, according to her husband, an "active, hardworking, gentle, honest woman," but she always had a tendency to look at the dark side of things. "If we go out, she says it's going to rain; if we undertake something [she] thinks we'll fail." Childish and meditative, she "regrets that she's not a believer, and would like to become one." Though she had several abortions, she has two children, the younger, Jeannine, was premature, born during the seventh month. "The patient very much wanted to have this child in order to obtain a hold on life."

Liuba's first serious crisis struck in 1930, when she was thirty-two, during a trip to Moscow. "Insomnia, persecution mania, limitless fear…" She recovered when she reached her home, but after fourteen peaceful months she suffered a crisis that lasted two weeks. That was followed by six months of peace and then another crisis. Her bouts of madness would strike her every couple of months after that. In Leningrad she was diagnosed as manic depressive (as the graphs of her care demonstrate). Her husband's arrest in 1933 and her father's death paradoxically returned her to health, but by the end of 1933, while she was living in Orenburg with her husband, "her illness took a terrible form."

Serge spares nothing in his description.

> The patient became hyperactive, happy, sang a great deal, became talkative, smiled for no reason. This lasts a day. The next day, sudden jags of sobbing, laughing, and tears. Insomnia. Third day an increase in inner violence. She paces as if in a cage, is exasperated, nasty, hateful. Smashes and rips objects she loves.

Liuba suffered fits of jealousy, of eroticism and despair. "Twice she tried to kill herself, but in a childish fashion (struck herself in the neck with a dullened knife). She spoke frequently of suicide: 'I'm good for nothing; I can't do anything for my son or my husband. I'm nothing but a weight on them. I should die." After a year of biweekly crises, she was admitted to a psychiatric hospital in Leningrad, where she was diagnosed with schizophrenia, "but the doctors were not pessimistic about her situation."

Her situation had slightly improved in Leningrad, but now, in Belgium, her cycles of madness returned, and, "in two months, [May and June], there were four very bad days (three violent paroxysms) and, on June 29, a terrible depression, with headaches and a desire to commit suicide; the next day was excellent, and seven or eight perfectly good days." Due to "lack of funds," she was currently not being treated.

In May 1937 she was a patient at the Hôpital Henri-Rousselle in the fourteenth arrondissement and was prescribed a number of illegible medications.

In 1938, Serge sent Liuba the annex to his will, dated October 11, 1938, relating to her. Though labeled "testament," it has nothing of a will, as it informs the hospitalized Liuba that he has written a will "in favor of the friend who helped me [obviously Laurette Séjourné, his future third wife], and naturally Vladi, to live." The full letter is perhaps the most moving and touching document in Serge's abundant correspondence, a letter written from the bottom of the man's heart.

After telling Liuba that Laurette, who is never named in the letter, "never wanted to take anything from her," he continues:

> If I were to die, I want you to know that I have always felt infinite affection for you. I infinitely thank you for having given me so many luminous years. I deeply wish you will find your memory again and that you find me there still at your side, forever. I haven't left you and have never accepted the idea of this. It was inexorable circumstances that broke you and, wearing you down, separated us. After years of solitude, I loved another woman with all my soul, without your ever ceasing to be my companion for life. This is how things truly and definitively are. I want both of you to know this. I ask that you never forget it. Get better, regain your strength, live for our children, and don't forget me, darling Liuba.

By September 1939 she was living with a Mme Kogan in the town of Le Vaudoue, where she was given a safe conduct pass on May 9, 1940, with a destination of Paris. Her specific destination appears to have been the Sainte-Anne Psychiatric Hospital, for a notice was sent on May 18 saying that "the director of the Sainte-Anne Psychiatric Hospital has the honor of informing Monsieur Kibalchich that, in conformity with the instructions of the prefect of the Seine Madame Kibalchich Lubov Rossakov [sic] was transferred on May 18, 1940 to the Maison Blanche Psychiatric Hospital," located in the Parisian suburb of Neuilly-sur-Marne. M. Kiblachich paid the prefecture 975 francs for her hospital expenses. She was evacuated in 1944 to the psychiatric hospital of Puy.

Several of Liuba's letters have survived, and they are as heart-breaking as her mental history. The first dates from February 6, 1936, when she was still in the USSR. She had just left a mental hospital and was staying with her mother. She complains of Jeannine, of how "heavy she is to carry," that she has to be vaccinated. Liuba's situation was already a bad one. "I count on assistance, but from who? I hope for a clearing in your life, and a bit of our past life will also brighten my sad lot."

In July 1939, while a resident at the Villa Les Bruyères in Le Vaudoue, she wrote her husband, "I want to finally go see a bit a Paris and go to the movies. Tell me when this will be possible. Can you give me permission to come?" The letter is signed off, "your wife, Liuba." On March 24, 1940, Serge wrote to tell her he'd finally received authorization to come visit. On April 2, 1940, she thanked Victor for his "little letter" and for the portrait of Jeannine. But she wonders, "Why doesn't Vladi [sic] write me. I'd so like to hear from him." Liuba signed off, "I'm waiting for you. Don't delay. A big kiss." She wrote to her husband on April 23, after his departure. "What sorrow after your departure. You stayed so short a time." She hoped to leave the pension for good and asked that Victor tell her when he reached home. "I absolutely want to spend some time with you."

Serge promised in reply that Vlady would visit her and spend twenty-four hours with her, but later in the year, in September, Liuba wrote from La Maison Blanche, imploring her husband, "When are you coming? I so want to leave the clinic and take up a normal life again." She was also disappointed in her husband's infrequent contacts: "I'd like to hope that I'll soon hear from you. I'm also hoping you'll visit soon."

Serge never saw Liuba after 1940, and the next letter we have from her dates from 1946 and was sent to her physician, Dr. J.D. Martinet. She accepted an offer he made and asked for "some Nestlé's milk, some cookies, a small comb and a serious book." But she had another serious matter to discuss. "I want to work. I'm a stenographer/typist and would love to straighten out my life by working." She asked if Dr. Martinet could find her a post in a hospital and that she be notified in the event his response was a favorable one. Her return address was the Montperrin Psychiatric Hospital in Aix-en-Provence.

The last letter in her hand dates from September 15, 1947, just two months before Serge's death. He had not been in contact with her in any way, as Liuba writes that she "was very happy to learn his address," six years after his departure for Mexico. As she wrote, "So here it is seven years that I haven't seen you; perhaps we'll see each other soon." Still interned, she tells her husband, long since remarried, their children viewing another woman as their mother, "I really want to get out, to breathe the free air, to make another life."

She told her ex-husband that she loves her doctor, "a very interesting woman." She continues to place her romantic hopes in Serge, speaking of her wish that "we will again take up our life together." Her final words to Serge, after stating, "I'd like to pay a little visit to my country and see [sic] my religion" (demonstrating Serge's 1936 description of her attraction to faith), were, "A hug and a kiss for my children. My best wishes to the three of you, Victor, Vladi [sic] and Jeannine." She signed the letter, "Liuba your wife and their mother." She survived her former husband by thirty-seven years.

19
Finally Mexico

Serge and Vlady arrived in Mexico on March 25, 1941. The years he spent in Mexico City until his death in 1947 were difficult and unhappy ones. He was far from Europe and great historical events, yet mentally he never left there. Mexico was where he lived, yet reading his notebooks, articles, and correspondence, aside from his accounts of the thuggery and dishonesty of the Mexican Communists, Mexico is mainly an exotic backdrop. He wrote stunning passages in his notebooks about trips into the countryside and about ancient sites. He produced a novella, "Le Séisme," the outgrowth of his experience of an earthquake in Mexico City, one of "the 2000 *temblores* yearly" reported Mexican seismologists.[1] His notebooks also contain analyses of *lucha libre* and the Mexican comic actor Cantinflas. But of Mexican politics and society outside of the ways in which it effected Serge and his comrades, there is little.

This is somewhat surprising. Though he didn't do so often, among his articles published in *La Wallonie* after his return to the West were pieces demonstrating his appreciation and understanding of the radicalism of the current phase of the Mexican Revolution under President Lázaro Cárdenas. In 1938, the year Cárdenas nationalized foreign oil companies, Serge wrote in "Honor to Mexico":

Three times in less than two years Mexico has earned a place of honor. It offered asylum to a great outlawed revolutionary driven from all the countries of Europe, Trotsky. It openly provided weapons to the Spanish Republic. Finally, it has just demonstrated to the international oil trusts that their power will not last forever.

Serge didn't stop there. Making abundantly clear his disenchantment with the Russian Revolution, he made the heretical claim that the Mexican Revolution had accomplished more than the Russian:

> One may conclude that from the point of view of the workers, the Mexican Revolution has been more fruitful than the Russian Revolution. There is certainly no more poverty in Mexico than in the USSR, but freedom of opinion, freedom of the individual, freedom to organize unions, freedom of asylum exist in Mexico. Fertile with tragedies and even atrocities, the Mexican Revolution was by far the more humane of the two. It did not invent secret executions, nor thought control, nor fabricated show-trials. Threatened by a powerful imperialist neighbor, Mexico did not opt for ultra-militarism.[2]

Just as Serge saw glimmerings of socialism in the Belgium he traversed upon leaving the USSR, in this article he proposes an alternative form of revolution. Mexico is both revolutionary and democratic. Within this article is a refutation of the notion dear to the supporters of revolutionary dictatorships that you can't make omelettes without breaking eggs. Mexico had been changed without a bloodbath. It took no small amount of courage to see this and praise it.

Laurette's departure from France had been delayed, as we saw previously, and sometime after her arrival accompanied by Jeannine, in either late February or early March 1942, after a brief foray back into the world of cinema, she took up the study of anthropology, which would occupy her the rest of her life. But things went poorly for the couple, and they lived a simulacrum of a marriage, carrying on separate lives while together. The polymath Serge began immersing himself in pre-Columbian anthropology and archaeology, and felt confident enough in his learning and abilities to make conjectures on the nature of the ancient Mexican societies. Serge's account of his visit to the Toltec ruins of Tula on April 30 and May 1, 1944, show him making connections between the pre-Columbian structures and the statuary in Tula to other locations in Mexico, in Vera Cruz and Tabasco, as well as to European and Mongolian statues, and even to the Greeks and Gothic architecture. He hazarded conjectures about the Mexican *calavera*, points out the similarities between the Mexican *calavera* and Christian symbology, saying that "it brings together two symbolisms, that of pre-Columbian civilization and that of Christian death." He even wandered into linguistics, pointing out similarities between Aztec names and the West: "Teotihuacan"—in Aztec "The City of God," and "theo": God. He even brings together the names Teotihuacan and Tarascon and the Mexican Tula with the Russian Tula.[3]

Serge intended to write several books about Mexico, and completed three unpublished papers in 1945 on pre-Columbian societies, "The Tomb of Civilizations," "Ritual Cannibalism," and "The Splendor and Destruction of Tenochtitlan." Decades later the French academic Michel Graulich praised Serge's work, saying that "he comments on, critiques and takes positions, often with remarkable penetration." It is worth pointing out that Serge, who, as we will see, did not show much concern for post-war anti-imperialist struggles, had positive things to say about the conquistador Cortez, while Séjourné, according to Graulich, "would later speak of 'an unexampled genocide' carried out by the Spanish conquerors." Archeology, in which Serge was an intellectual tourist, was an area in which his opinions were opposed to those of his wife; a field in which "he refused to take dogmatic or partisan positions." He was also, Graulich maintains, "more rigorous" in his methodology than Séjourné.[4]

Mexican art can also be considered an area where Serge avoided "dogmatism." He has little of substance and even less that is positive to say of Mexico's greatest muralists, Diego Rivera and

David Alfaro Siqueiros. Rivera, after having been a Communist then a Trotskyist and host of the Old Man and his wife when they came to Mexico, had returned to the Communist Party; Siqueiros participated in an assassination attempt on Trotsky and was expelled from the Communist Party, an expulsion Serge described as "strictly formal [and intended] to shield the Communist Party."[5] On the other hand, Serge wrote appreciatively of the politically unsavory painter Dr. Atl. Born Gerardo Murillo, Dr. Atl was a most curious character. Once a figure of importance on the far left of the Mexican Revolution, he had converted to antisemitism and the far right and was an embezzler, adventurer, archaeologist, and many other things, not least a Nazi sympathizer. He preferred to live atop volcanoes and obsessively painted Mount Popocatépetl. Serge visited him in August 1943, at which time Dr. Atl expounded on his philosophy: "The worst thing in the world is order. Once you allow yourself to impose order within, you're lost. It was disorder that saved me. Nothing is more beautiful than disorder." Serge was shown paintings by the artist, which he admitted to finding "luminous, deserted, no living being is ever seen in them, nothing but the harsh mountain with its lines of terrestrial energy." Serge was charmed by the man, his work, and his mode of living. "I feel myself forgiving him for something unforgiveable, anti-Semitism: He has no choice but to hate men, at least in the abstract for he is all benevolence [...]. He needs to believe he is hating deliriously in a disordered way, thinking he has unmasked the universal conspiracy."[6] There is something both admirable and unsettling about this open-mindedness. This largely positive description of his visit should be placed alongside Serge's disdainful description of his first visit to Diego Rivera on September 25, 1941. Rivera, according to Serge, is "an overgrown child (mental age twelve), crafty, with a delirious imagination that applies itself to social affairs, goes from exaggeration to paradox, ceaselessly outlining complicated frescoes of conspiracies, tales of vast corruption, international perspectives painted with a broad brush."[7] He spent time with surrealists who were living in Mexico City, making acerbic yet perspicacious remarks about Leonora Carrington, who was "clearly schizophrenic."[8] He had travel companions, like the wealthy philanthropists the John de Menils and his future enemy, the writer Jean Malaquais.

But all in all, his Mexican period was a train of miseries. He was living in poverty, with mere pesetas to his name. He often couldn't pay his rent and Laurette was unable to contribute her share of their living expenses.[9] Worst of all, he was far from the Europe—no, the Paris—he loved. Suicide had haunted Serge at various times, and he admitted to feeling suicidal urges in the winter of 1941; in February 1945 Laurette attempted suicide.[10] Her recovery did nothing to bring them closer together, and Vlady, an aspiring artist, was now a young man and breaking away from his father politically, taking a more uncompromisingly left-wing line.

* * *

Serge considered *The Case of Comrade Tulaev*, largely written in Mexico and published posthumously in 1948, his best novel, and few would question that characterization. It does, though, suffer from some of the faults of all of his fiction: a tendency to lose himself in the adjectival along with occasional lapses in pacing due to overly literary digressions (particularly in the Paris scenes in the chapter on Xenia Popova). But as Serge wrote in an unpublished note, this is in the nature of the language in which he wrote, "the French style being rich." Above all, though, from a psychological point of view it contains some of the most stunning pages Serge ever wrote. In *Tulaev*, Serge enters the minds and lives of characters for whom he has little sympathy—including Stalin!—and enables us to understand their paths and motivations. Written between 1940 and 1942—as he was leaving France—in Paris, Agen, Marseille, Ciudad Trujillo, and Mexico City, Serge presents the world of the Stalinist purges that he left the USSR just in time to miss. The madness of the purge trials, which were the subject of so much of his polemical writing, is here the ground for a brilliant work of fiction. In an unpublished note aimed at obtaining an American publisher for the book, he explained that "The sole intention of the writer has been to serve the truth by means of art, that is to say, of literary creation."

Serge had other titles in mind for the novel, his handwritten notes—mostly in Russian—containing the suggestion *Le Crime de Kostia* (Kostia's Crime), the name of the actual assassin of Comrade Tulaev, an ordinary citizen who kills Tulaev during a chance encounter and is never suspected by the authorities. Serge also planned to call the novel *La Terre commençait a trembler* (The Earth Began to Quake). In a one-page summary of the novel Serge described the novel as "revolving around a chance crime—in the event, the assassination of the Communist leader Tulaev—in which we witness the preliminary stages of a trial that does not take place, but in which several characters are involved, including old revolutionaries, functionaries, and the Chief himself." As for its nature, "On a whole the work takes on the tone and scope of historical testimony presented objectively. It is extremely dramatic and extremely varied and ends neither optimistically nor pessimistically, in expectation of the war. Life goes on."

The titular Comrade Tulaev is an important figure in the Communist Party who is assassinated on the streets of Moscow by a passerby who sees him getting out of his official limousine. Though angered by the state of the country, Kostia, the killer, is not a member of the Opposition or a figure of any political importance: he is the average Russian. He happens to be carrying a gun, and after failing to fire on Stalin, whom he had seen earlier, he shoots and kills Tulaev, fleeing the scene on foot.

Kostia evades arrest, and the security forces turn their investigation from a search for the actual guilty party to placing the blame on opponents of Stalin. What follows is, chapter by chapter, an account of all those who will become the victims of this process. Those who are accused are a mixed bag, with little or no connection to each other, nor any serious connection to the Opposition. The killing by a random passerby will lead to a random group of men and women losing their posts, their freedom, and some their lives as the Stalinist machine crushes people it considers suspect or disloyal.

In an accurate reflection of those who would fall in reality, it is both Trotskyists and loyal Stalinists who will pay the ultimate price. The former for obvious reasons, the latter as a result of expressing doubts about the leader, or failing to meet the insane and unrealizable targets set for them in their field of responsibility, or for simple mistakes, or for no reason at all. Serge's cast includes modest men who simply want to do the right thing, and opportunists whose opportunism fails to save them. The glory of the revolution is there in the case of Makeyev, elevated from a simple worker in the fields to a post as head of a region. Makeyev's glorious ascent is accompanied by megalomania, hubris, and his downfall. Only Ryzhik, a convinced Trotskyist previously encountered in *Conquered City*, and who is foreign to the entire Tulaev affair, acts heroically from beginning to end, refusing to cooperate in any way with the security forces, choosing instead to starve himself to death rather than submit. Those who submit and why they do so—the treacheries, petty and great, that were the stuff of Stalin's USSR—are the core of Serge's novel. Who were the victims? What were their pasts? How did their pasts turn them into defendants who accused themselves of crimes they didn't commit?

Serge's accounts of these men, of their reasons and rationalizations for their acceptance of their fate, very much resemble the actions of Rubashov in Arthur Koestler's *Darkness at Noon*, published in English in 1941, and in French in 1945. It is unlikely that it in any way influenced Serge, and the similarities in the insights of the two books are easily explained. Like Serge, Koestler had been a Comintern agent. The Bolshevik mindset had once been his as well. It was thus easy for him, as it was for Serge, to understand why a lifelong Communist would debase, degrade, and sully himself for the good of the cause. For Serge and Koestler, the tragic fate of devoted Communists during the Stalinist purges was a result of two elements aside from the torture they were subjected to: The acceptance of the idea that the party is always right, even when it is wrong, and the certainty that the individual is nothing and must accept the party's dictates. On top of that, denying the charges, accusing the Soviet state of fabrication, meant playing into the hands of the bourgeoisie, of participating in the Trotskyite-fascist plot. Better to die than to aid the bourgeoisie.

Serge often claimed that his books failed to receive their due, or that Communist influence prevented them from being published in France. The relative fates of *Darkness at Noon* and *Comrade Tulaev* puts this claim in question. Published in 1945, *Le Zéro et l'Infini*—as *Darkness at Noon* was called in France—was an enormous bestseller, a book extensively talked and written about. If the Communists had the power Serge claimed they did, if they could block a book's publication, this was one to block. And yet they couldn't and didn't. Serge's novel was published in 1948 by an excellent house, Éditions du Seuil, yet did not have the impact of Koestler's book at the time of publication. The reason isn't hard to understand, and it had nothing to do with PCF interference. Koestler's book is a straightforward anti-communist tract, though Rubashov is a sympathetic character, and the reader feels the same fascinated horror for his GPU interrogator as we do for the evil characters in a Dostoevsky novel. *The Case of Comrade Tulaev*, on the other hand, refuses to fit in with standard anti-communist schemas. It's unstinting in its depiction of the lies and criminality of the Soviet state. At the same time, its victims, the main characters of the book, are mostly presented as men of integrity, and the socialist state viewed as something worth defending, despite the crimes committed in its name. As the faithful Trotskyist Ryzhik explains, and as many Trotskyists in the decades that followed the purges maintained: "Despite its internal regression, our state remains a factor of progress in the world because it constitutes an economic organism which is superior to the old capitalist state." Even the repression descending on him and his comrades is a secondary factor:

> [D]espite the worst appearances, there is no justification for classifying our state with fascist regimes. Terror is not enough to determine the nature of a regime, what is basically signif-icant is property relations. The bureaucracy, dominated by its own political police, is obliged to maintain the economic regime established by the Revolution of October 17.[11]

In true revolutionary fashion, this depressing analysis leads to an optimistic conclusion. "[I]t can only increase an inequality which, in its own despite, becomes a factor in the education of the masses." The masses that are developing are an entirely new people "a new proletariat, of peasant origin, is developing in new factories. It needs time to reach a certain degree of conscious-ness and, by its own experience, to overcome the totalitarian education it has received."[12] A man who can maintain hope in such dire circumstances as those of the Soviet Union in 1936 is not one who will willingly deny the truth in the face of his inquis-itors, and Ryzhik doesn't. His death as a result of his refusal to acquiesce and his hunger strike are necessary steps in ending that totalitarian education.

Serge, by the time he wrote *Comrade Tulaev*, no longer saw the USSR as a factor of progress in the world. But it is proof of his ability to enter the skin of those he doesn't agree with that he can present ideas like Ryzhik's—which he once held—with such sympathy and insight.

Nothing better exemplifies this than Serge's portrait of Stalin in the novel. The assassin Kostia passes him briefly early in the novel, so we are made aware that he is not only an image hung on every office wall, not only "The Chief" invoked on all occasions, but a real person, buffeted like everyone else, by the winds of history. "The Winds of Defeat," the novel's fifth chapter, shows us an unexpected Stalin. Ivan Kondratiev, who recently served in Spain as an agent of the Soviets, had been sickened while there by the conduct of the Communist-led secret services of Spain and the Soviets, particularly in their kidnapping of an anti-Stalinist militant. Kondratiev has been recalled to the Soviet Union. This was usually a death sentence, but Kondratiev is received by Stalin himself almost immediately after his return. The two men had been comrades and companions in the days of struggle, before the October Revolution, and even now they call each other Iossif and Vania. Stalin is presented as a product of the revolution, a maker of the revolution, and not just its gravedigger. And he also acts like "The Good Tsar," to whom common folk turn to redress ills caused, not by him, but by the tsar's underlings.

The novel's Stalin stands apart from his henchmen, craving honesty, telling his old comrade Kondratiev,

> You know, brother, veterans like you, members of the old party, must tell me the whole truth… the whole truth. Otherwise, who can I get it from? I need it, I sometimes feel myself stifling. Everyone lies and lies and lies! From top to bottom they all lie, it's diabolical… Nauseating. I live on the summit of an edifice of lies.

This Stalin, who we can almost believe is sincere, admits the government's economic statistics are all lies, the very statistics used to justify claims of success and, when they're poor, are used as evidence in trials leading to the execution of the "saboteurs" who are at fault for the failures. "The plans lie, because nine times out of ten they are based on false data." Kondratiev himself doesn't know if he should believe what his old comrade is saying, and asks, "Isn't it a little your fault?" Rather than find himself in the cellars of the Lubyanka with a pistol held to his neck, Stalin gives him a "warm smile," and explains his own plight:

I'd like to see you in my place old man—yes, that's something I'd like to see. Old Russia is a swamp—the farther you go the more the ground gives, you sink in just when you least expect to... And then, the human rubbish! ... To remake the hopeless human animal will take centuries. [...] I haven't got centuries to work with, not I.[13]

The conversation will continue, Kondratiev criticizing the quality of Soviet tanks, condemning the "liquidation" of Bukharin, "which [t]he Chief took without flinching, his face stone," though maintaining he was a traitor.[14] After over an hour of harsh but comradely criticism, Kondratiev is given a choice of new posts. He will survive when so many others haven't. A later conversation with Stalin goes less well, but Serge has given voice, and not unfairly, to the Stalinist justification for the abandonment of world revolution, for the retreat that is "socialism in one country." There was no one Serge blamed more for the destruction of the ideal he had once believed in than Stalin. But Serge the novelist could not help himself when turning him into a literary character. The man who in his autobiographical, journalistic and political writings is the very personification of evil is here a human being who justifies his actions to himself and others. In Jean Renoir's masterpiece *The Rules of the Game* one of the characters, Octave, says that "The thing in life is that everyone has his reasons." Serge applies that axiom here, and does so brilliantly.

Serge engages in a more profound, more essential analysis of the descent of the Russian Revolution into totalitarianism, of its rejection of the revolutionary path traced by Lenin and Trotsky. The problem goes deep, far deeper than Stalin's superior skills at using the bureaucracy, though it is also that. Kiril Rublev, an intellectual caught in the security force's net, has kept a notebook while imprisoned, which, read by one of the investigating attorneys, provides us with the thoughts of a man very much like Serge. The notebook contains praise of Trotsky and his revolutionary intuition, his sense of Russian reality, his "sense of victory," his reasoned intrepidity; and deplored his "pride as a great historic figure," his "too self-conscious superiority," his "inability to make the mediocre follow him," his "offense tactics in the worst moments of defeat," his "high revolutionary algebra perpetually cast before swine, when the swine alone held the front of the stage."

Rublev recognizes that, at bottom, what made the revolutionary generation impotent twenty years after victory was that "we demanded the courage to continue our exploit, and people wanted nothing but more security, rest, to forget the effort and the blood." The tragedy was that "we bear witness to the fullness of a victory which encroached too far upon the future and asked too much of men."[15] Revolutions are demanding things, requiring a constant effort, a constant striving. Serge, writing as Le Rétif, doubted that the masses were capable of this long-term effort. That persona reappears in these pages in the form of this disabused Old Bolshevik. He is asking if it might be the case that the just society, one built on human brotherhood, that demands permanent consciousness, is within the grasp of only the few. This is the question Kiril Rublev and Victor Serge are forced to confront as Rublev prepares to meet his death.

* * *

Serge was not an old man when he arrived in Mexico, only fifty-one, but his peripatetic life, combined with living in Mexico City, situated at an altitude of 7349 feet above sea level, was wearing on him. A passage in his notebooks, recounting a visit on December 3, 1944, to his fellow exile Michael Fraenkel, neatly sums up Serge's mental and physical states, and how the former impacted the latter. "Spoke of the incredible difficulty of working: shortness of breath [...]. I think that the altitude of Mexico City diminishes me greatly by causing endless crises of breathlessness." Fraenkel thought there was more to it, though. "M.F. shares this opinion, but he insists on the lack of an intellectual environment: the vast, sad city of business and Indian poverty, the real inexistence of ideas, Europe's silence." Nostalgia completes his misery: "We recall the unimaginable tonic the streets of Paris were for us. We're on a diet of shortness of breath in a desert."¹⁶

Serge lived in that desert, really more an island in the middle of a desert, of some 10,000 exiles admitted by the Mexican government. Shortly after his arrival in Mexico, Serge joined in the forming of a group of independent leftists, Socialismo y Libertad. It was an amalgam of various currents of the anti-Stalinist left, with members of POUM like Julián Gorkin, and Enrique Gironella; Marceau Pivert, founder and leader of the French Parti socialiste ouvrier et paysan; the revolutionary surrealist poet Benjamin Peret; the Polish-Jewish French-language writer Jean Malaquais; the Italian Leo Valiani (alias Paul Chevalier), who had left the Italian Communist Party after spending time in Spain and would later be elected to the Italian Constituent Assembly; and the Gustav Regler, who had quit the KPD after the signing of the Hitler–Stalin pact in 1939. This group would be the target of a vicious Communist campaign throughout the war years and beyond.

Serge wrote to Dwight and Nancy Macdonald about his new group on November 2, 1941:

We are in the process of forming, not a group, but a small milieu of trustworthy and nonsectarian comrades who have decided to collaborate in socialist studies. There are several intelligent Germans, an Italian who seems quite good. (Among others, Gustav Regler, the writer, returned from the International Brigades in Spain.) The general feeling: It is necessary to avoid the stagnation among the demoralized exiles, to avoid at all costs becoming cripples and the stragglers of defeat, to get beyond ready-made formulas, as the bulk of what Marxism and socialism has established is alive and powerful, but must be audaciously and steadily put back in touch with reality—to prepare for the future that is at hand. Julian [Gorkin] is clear-sighted about this. He sees especially in the POUM—which still exists in Spain and has some small but good nuclei over here—elements of a future formation that will be entirely different. By contrast, M. is as conservative as you can get and thrives on a kind of romantic exaggeration of a party that has in reality dissolved. The various Fourth Internationals are the incarnation of this intellectual paralysis to an astounding degree.

The path outlined in the letter, of reexamining the very basis of socialist activity, was one that Serge would carry out over the six remaining years of his life, a path that would leave him isolated and alienated from the "non-sectarian" grouping he placed such high hopes in.

Serge wrote frequently in his notebooks and his correspondence of threats to his life. A typical example is a letter to Dwight Macdonald of February 8, 1942, telling of a visit he'd paid to "an extremely cultivated Mexican personality," who'd requested to see him urgently. This anonymous individual told Serge that "a meeting had <u>recently</u> been held in which was studied the technique for our suppression, me first, but the others as well" (underlining in original).

There was a fairly important Communist emigration in Mexico City, particularly the German-speaking one. It included Anna Seghers, Egon Erwin Kisch, Ludwig Renn, and an individual known as André Simone who was, in reality, Otto Katz. Katz was a *cominternien* who traveled to countless countries carrying out Comintern missions, even working in Hollywood to strengthen the communist presence there. His fidelity to the cause did not save him. He would be hung as a defendant in the antisemitic Slansky Trial in Prague in 1952. The large Communist emigration in Mexico was, according to Serge, not accidental. In another letter to Dwight Macdonald, dated February 17,

1942, Serge provides his American friend with the names of two men who, working with left-wing Mexican labor leader Vicente Lombardo Toledano, saw to it that Stalinists were granted visas and "[w]e know there is a directive to concentrate active agents here, and that even some who have visas for the U.S. were invited to remain in Mexico."

The Stalinist campaign against the independent socialists in Mexico City, which had begun in earnest in October 1941, with articles attacking them in the Communist Party newspaper, became particularly worrisome in January 1942. A plenum of the Mexican Communist Party's Central Committee described them as the "shock troops of the Fifth Column." Their meetings had been attacked and seven deputies of the Mexican Chamber of Deputies demanded the expulsion of Serge, the POUMists Grandizo Munis and Julian Gorkin, former Communist commissar in Spain Gustav Regler, and Marceau Pivert. Serge wrote to the Macdonalds on January 19, 1942, that

> [w]e receive confidential warnings (there are quite a few people sickened by Stalinist methods but who don't dare break with the CP because they're living on [their] assistance or work they give them). I was told last night that my assassination has been ordered and set for soon. The words of a well-known Communist were quoted: "I wouldn't give a penny for V.S.'s skin."

Serge pointed to the true culprit: "The violence and the systematic character of these attacks prove that they're ordered by the GPU and probably on the orders of Moscow itself."[17] Serge, all too familiar with the techniques of the GPU, even outlined the possible methods to be used against him, Pivert, and Gorkin:

> I think that the things most to be feared are: 1. A mysterious "heart attack," but it's relatively easy to protect oneself

against this; 2. A villainous denunciation supported by false documents—but this could in no way have serious or lasting effects; 3. An attack on the street by "angry young people" (the press campaign looks to be preparing this), but it poses the same problems as an assassination.

The trio of potential victims wrote to the president of Mexico protesting the maneuvers and threats of the deputies, and his office forwarded the complaint to the relevant authorities for investigation. Despite this, Serge continued to receive warnings that his assassination was imminent and that an assassin was already present in Mexico City to carry it out. His neighborhood was infested with Communists, he feared, and he was certain that a recent ship carrying German refugees included thirty GPU agents. If this was a form of paranoia, it was one based in the climate of fear that followed the assassination of Trotsky in August 1940. Serge's inside information was so detailed that he claimed to know that there was a team of four killers, two Spaniards and two Germans; the Spaniards, though, questioned the wisdom of killing Serge, Pivert, and Gorkin, fearing the negative repercussions that had struck the Communists in Spain after the killing of Andreu Nin, while the Germans were anxious to press on with the assassinations. Serge claimed to have the names of the men who discussed the killings openly at a Mexico City café. Sloppy work, if true.

The Macdonalds, as always, sprang into action, informing Gorkin that a petition had been sent to President Cárdenas's successor Manuel Camacho supporting the exiles, and encouraging them to share the task of contacting American press agencies and journalists in Mexico City, and that they do so immediately.

The Communists continued to slander the anti-Stalinists. The February 28, 1942 issue of the left-wing American magazine *The Nation* included as a letter to the editor a telegram signed by a group of Mexican legislators—presumably those who had condemned Serge, Regler, Pivert, and Gorkin—but also signed by political exiles like Anna Seghers, Ludwig Renn, Egon Erwin Kisch, and the Chilean Pablo Neruda, Communists all. The letter stated that "A representative committee of the Mexican Congress has made serious formal accusations against Serge and his partners, charging that it has proof of their connection with the Nazi Fifth Column in this country. None of the members of the committee belong to the Communist Party, some even being well-known anti-Communists." After citing the anti-Nazi work done in Mexico by an ally of the Communists, the telegram claimed that "Mr. Serge and his partners have never done this type of work, dedicating their efforts exclusively to the slander of the Soviet Union and its government," in which they were following "the official Trotskyite line." The signatories explained their motives: "We are addressing you in the hope that the true information submitted herewith will help you to understand the Mexican situation with regard to foreigners posing as leftists who are really undermining the anti-fascist struggle." *The Nation*, in an editor's note attached to the letter, expressed doubt that Serge or, even more, Regler were guilty of being members of the Fifth Column, but their demurral was hardly wholehearted. They also said, "We shall waste no sympathy on Nazi agents. If the legislative committee mentioned in the protest has proof that Serge and his partners are actually guilty of such connections, we believe and hope that they will be dealt with severely by the proper authorities."

Almost immediately upon publication of this exchange, the Mexican-based American writer Bertram Wolfe wrote an angry personal letter to Freda Kirchway of *The Nation*, asking her, "Do you not comprehend that you are playing with the reputations of men whose lives are actually in danger? That there has been an OPEN campaign of incitement to murder them? [...] That merely to descend to the level of answering such charges is debasing and degrading?"

Wolfe denied that the seven deputies who had attacked Serge and his comrades were "a representative committee of the

Mexican congress." They were, instead, acting on their own, not as a committee of the Chamber, and all of them were allied in one way or another with the Communist Party, if not members of it, contrary to the claim of they were independent. Wolfe reminded Kirchway of a sad fact: Despite the charge that Serge, Pivert, Gorkin, Munis, and Regler were agents of the Fifth Column, "only the attackers, or rather organizers, of the attack on them, have been in cooperation with Nazi agents during the Hitler pact period." Wolfe hoped *The Nation* would publish a correction. It didn't.

The force of Serge's anger can be felt in his response to a November 1941 letter from the Mexican writer Eulalia Guzman inviting him to speak at a meeting of Mexican PEN. He angrily rejected her invitation. Not because of anything she'd said, but because, as he wrote, "I see in the newspapers that you spoke at the so-called Congress of Democratic Action, [which] basely slandered us at its first meeting because it was conquered and maneuvered by the Stalinist totalitarians." Serge, Pivert, and Gorkin had missed the meeting, and he informed Guzman of the threats to their lives, saying that because the three men are "irreducible adversaries of <u>all</u> totalitarian regimes and are convinced that it is impossible to defeat one set by serving the other, for years we have been hunted down by the Stalinist organization at its disposal in all countries, of millions of secret agents and fanaticized groups" (underlining in original). Serge told Guzman that he had been told that a Communist had been overheard saying that "I wouldn't give five cents for Serge's life. These are the people who were cynical enough to expel us from the congress in our absence, without hearing us [...]. These are the people who used your words and your renown to cover their unspeakable task."

Simply by attending the meeting Guzman was complicit. "My duty is to request that you take a position in the face of slander and the preparation of murder of which we are the victims. By your presence at a tribune where the 'communists' made the law your name was engaged."

The overt violence long feared finally occurred on April 1, 1943. Henrykh Ehrlich and Victor Alter were two leaders of the Polish-Jewish socialist Bund. They had taken refuge in the USSR in 1939, and were murdered by the Soviets in 1941. News of their killing, however, did not get out until 1943, and Serge's independent socialists, joined by several other anti-Stalinist leftists, held a commemorative meeting in their honor, as well as that of Carlo Tresca, murdered by the Mafia in New York on Mussolini's orders on April 1. Serge recounted the events in his notebooks.[18]

The meeting was held at the Centro Ibero-Mexicano, and before it could start, 200 Communists attacked the hall, seeking first to attack the scheduled speakers. Serge, though he called the attackers Communists, also wrote they were "shock troops recruited on the streets, probably paid." They sacked the hall, tore up books, and beat up and seriously injured Julian Gorkin and Enrique Gironella. They also took the time to call the Mexican press to say they'd broken up a fascist rally, where the audience had shouted "Viva Hitler, Viva Franco, Viva Mussolini." The police finally brought an end to the disorder and the scheduled meeting took place after all. Despite the Communists' efforts, the Mexican press covered the attack factually. Serge described the night's events as a "pogrom."

A couple of days after the Communist attack on the Alter–Ehrlich commemoration, Serge composed a desperate entry in his notebooks. He feared "liquidation" at Communist hands, friends telling him to take taxis instead of buses. Publication in the US, he said, was "impossible" (this, we will see, was not the case), his books unpublished, and "Stalinist penetration" so thorough that "they have agents on every newspaper, even those on the right." In America, increasingly the land of his hopes and dreams, publishers "understand nothing of the problems I pose." The situation was hopeless, with bourgeois publishers afraid of his writings and "[l]eft-wing publishers are all Stalinized." "The socialist émigrés don't like me: for them I'm a 'Trotskyist' (it's a handy word) and at bottom, most of them fear intellectual competition. There and here, the Trotskyists denigrate and detest me because they detest heresy." It required but two words to describe his life: "Completely stuck."[19]

20
Revising the Revolution

Speculation as to where Victor Serge's political journey would have ended is futile. Where he actually was politically in his final years is, however, there for us to see. Unfortunately, many significant documents necessary for determining Serge's actual positions are buried in archives in the form of correspondence and drafts of unpublished articles. Many others, though, are hiding in plain sight, in his published notebooks and articles in small—and even not so small—but prestigious publications.

What is certain, from Serge's notebooks, his correspondence, and his published and unpublished essays, is that, for all their variety of origins, the political exile circles of which Serge was a part clung firmly to a vision of political action in the present and future that owed much to the revolutionary schemas of the first decades of the twentieth century. Serge at this time made his final and, in many ways, most interesting turn. Personal freedom, or as he regularly called it, "respect for the human person," became his primary focus. His insistence on this respect intensified his hatred of Stalinism and, more broadly, of Communism, which, as we will see, he came to exclude from the socialist movement. Communism and Communists were incompatible with the democratic values he came to prize. These concerns inevitably led him to view the composition of the movement that would midwife the new post-war world in a way that contradicted the precepts that guided the revolutionary left. The Serge who had already revised his worldview several times, changing not out of opportunism or weakness, but in keeping with the ways in which the world had changed or that movements had failed. The teenager who left the reformist socialism of the POB because it was no longer a vehicle of change now, in the last years of his life, made the bold move of eschewing self-satisfied political purity in order to ensure a more just, safer world, and, more specifically, a unified Europe.

On October 10, 1941, Serge wrote in his notebook about the death of the Austrian Marxist economist Rudolf Hilferding. While doing so, he took the opportunity to expand on the topic of the German economist's "martyrdom." Hilferding, a Jew, had been tortured by the Nazis, which led to his death. Serge took the opportunity to describe the socialism of the men of the Second International like Hilferding and the Belgian socialist Emil Vandervelde, men he had once scorned. "The socialism of these men is a bourgeoisified socialism, but it's the most elevated product of the consciousness of an era." Their failing was that they were unable to see things in a harsh enough light.

> What they are unable to conceive of is the sentence hanging over a society of which they are the best, the most noble representatives, and the necessity in certain struggles for hardness, a destructive hardness, in practice inhuman and thus regressive, something that those energetic men belonging to less cultivated and organized peoples understand spontaneously: Bakunin, [the Spanish anarchist] Durruti, the Russian revolutionary Marxists.

The hatred revolutionary leftists felt for these socialists was a result of a category error, one that Serge fails to mention he had shared until recently. The social democratic leaders of Germany, of Austria, of Belgium, or of France were men of a different stripe, brought up in a different world.

> In accusing them of "treason" the Communists committed both a psychological error and a moral mistake. Reformism was a betrayal of the interests of socialism strictly from the perspective of the revolutionary class struggle, which could

neither be the perspective of these men nor of the mass working-class they so well represented.[1]

Defense of the morality and, even more, the ideas and activities of social democrats, as Serge does here, though at this point it's mainly a matter of understanding the leaders of social democracy, was anathema to most of Serge's fellow exiles, particularly some of the members of POUM and Marceau Pivert, himself an ex-socialist now moved further to the left. Serge's later break with his fellow exiles' dogmatic revolutionism is limned here, months after his arrival in the New World.

In an undated manuscript entitled "Trotskyism," Serge applied his critical views to the movement that was once his, one that he had long since separated himself from. As he had already done in the late thirties, he dismissed the new Fourth International, about whose practical legitimacy he had his doubts, as a "sect whose possibilities of development are extremely limited." Among its foundational sins was that it "employs a 'Bolshevik-Leninist' language out of the Russian past in countries where this theoretical language is necessarily unintelligible." Nowhere does it play an "appreciable role." Like the people around Serge in Mexico, Trotskyists "mechanically apply to the Second World War the analyses and propaganda slogans formulated at the time of the war of 1914–1918." Trotskyism, for Serge, bears a fatal mark: "Its organizational methods, its way of carrying out polemics, the very language of its militants have shown themselves to be stained with the failings of decadent Bolshevism, i.e., of the totalitarian spirit."

Two years later, on December 6, 1943, Serge would write a lengthy response to a questionnaire sent by the British Independent Labour Party on the subject of "a new socialist movement." In it he would deepen his analysis of the current state of affairs of the left and its future course. In the first instance, he dismissed the appeals for a new International. The current state of the socialist movement in Europe, the Americas, and in scattered exile communities was too weak for such a thing to be considered feasible. He didn't tiptoe around the facts, speaking of "the defeat of the working-class," which had many causes, none of which featured the left's hobby horse of poor leadership. Serge ventured into new regions, blaming the left's defeat on the "generally bourgeois psychology of the Western European labor aristocracy." That was not all that had led things to such a sorry pass. Technological progress, mass unemployment which had "degraded' millions of workers in Europe and America," and yet another new factor: the formation of "a new middle class, active, growing and dynamic." Much if not all of this escaped standard Marxist strictures and structures.

Serge also noted a factor he'd mentioned in passing in his notebook entry on this proposal. For half a century the working-class of Europe had "maintained a stubborn fidelity to their old parties of the Second International." Implicitly criticizing the very foundation of the revolutionary left in Europe, the Third International, the fruit of the splitting of the parties of the Second International, he took the next logical step. Serge believed that in post-war Europe the old-style reformism would no longer hold sway, and that "revolutionary militants must seek contact, collaboration, and union with the great socialist formations, and not isolate themselves in order to perpetuate divisions belonging to the past."

This could be viewed as the Trotskyist tactic of entryism, revolutionaries participating in mass socialist parties in order to sway them to adopt revolutionary positions, or even the return of the Popular Front. But in this 1943 document Serge's intent is quite different: He genuinely seeks full unity of all socialists, including in this almost every tendency, and calling on the new groupings to support, in the face of Communist totalitarianism in Russia, all socialists, "including anarchists, social democrats, Georgians, Armenians, and Zionists." Openness must be absolute, with one significant exception. "No socialist international can, [without] betraying its mission and dishonoring itself, accept within it totalitarian communists... led by secret bureaus provided with secret funds and subject to a discipline that annihilates the critical spirit." The same exclusion, Serge insists, would apply to any international labor organization, since Soviet labor unions are nothing but organs of the totalitarian state. This latter anti-communist element of Serge's analysis would grow in importance until it all but dominated his political vision. We will return to the subject.

It was important to Serge that the charters of parties of any future new International be "clear and intelligible to all." But that wasn't enough. "The notion of socialism is now inseparable from the respect for the human person, from the spirit of freedom, and from truly democratic institutions."

His enterprise of critiquing the socialist movement from within was the road that must be taken by all. "Socialist ideology demands a severe auto-critique, an updating of theories that takes into account the scientific gains of the last fifty years." The difficulties of both carrying out this self-criticism and of getting it accepted were soon made clear to Serge.

In an undated essay that is likely from 1944, titled "The Europe of Tomorrow: Neo-totalitarianism or Democracy," he continued on his futurist track. It is not only the future that will see planned and administered economies: That future has already arrived. The one thing Serge viewed as improbable was a "social solution for Europe [that] is a return to the past." Foreshadowing his later interest in European unity, planning will not be national, but continent-wide, the continent including the soon-to-be-defeated Germany and Russia as far east as the Urals. The planned economy he envisioned was not the totalitarian version that a planned economy under the old ruling classes would entail, or one established under Soviet rule. Rather it "requires freedom of investigation, of initiative, and criticism."

Serge feared that a "dictatorial power" might take control of this planning process at the war's end. This could not be even temporarily allowed, since it would lead to full-blown totalitarianism. Socialist movements must intervene immediately and take control of the process in order to ward off the risk of totalitarianism; they must be "the irreducible defenders of traditional democratic institutions [...] which can become revolutionary in the new historical circumstances in order to guarantee freedom." Serge's support for "traditional democratic institutions," which had always been dismissed as defenders of bourgeois rule, could only set off alarm bells among the ardent leftists in Serge's circle.

The proximate cause of blow-up in Serge's relations with the exiles in Mexico was a meeting reported in his notebooks on September 13, 1944. The theoretical differences expressed in the programmatic works above here took on great personal acuity, for now he was directly contradicting and criticizing those with whom he dealt daily.

The discussion involved a political document prepared by Marceau Pivert, Wilebaldo Solano and Enrique Gironella, all of them hardened veterans of the anti-Stalinist revolutionary left. The document they presented was the very type of analysis that Serge had risen up against. Dismissing it as "a sort of *Communist Manifesto*, very rudimentary, recycling all the old phrases of the genre," he proceeded to carry out an indictment of the document and the school of thought it represented, which he listened to, he said, "with interest and suppressed hostility." The basis for his opposition to the document was that "every term, every idea must be revised in the face of new realities and launched in the middle of a hurricane," which the three authors failed to do. If POUM was barely holding on to a tenuous overseas existence, Pivert's Parti socialiste ouvrier et paysan had been swept away with the debacle of French defeat. This statement, however true, could not but wound the party's founder, Pivert, who insisted Serge was wrong and that the party "exists and is a force." It seems safe to assume Pivert did not forget this insult to his political formation in the months intervening between this meeting and Serge's definitive falling-out with his comrades.

But Serge was not concerned with the petty matter of the strength of this party or that; it was all the work of the Marxist left that needed to be rethought. Serge's attack goes to the very roots of socialism, asserting that "It's false to write that in a bourgeois democracy the working-class has only its chains to lose [when] it enjoys—in Europe enjoyed—real well-being and real freedoms." Not content with this, Serge made the point that the notion dear and even essential to Marxists that the state was the "armed band of one class for the domination of another," as Engels said, was no longer true. Or rather, it is, but only in one country: the USSR. The state, as Serge saw it, has a positive role now, in fields like education and communications. Everything but everything must be reexamined.

The colonial question did not play a significant role in Serge's late writings, though liberation struggles were in progress in many places by the time of his death in November 1947. The document under discussion took a firm anti-colonialist stance; Serge dismissed the language employed in this regard as well. The sovereignty of colonial peoples, the need to provide them with assistance of all kinds, moral, economic and armed, is dismissed by Serge as "comical incoherencies." His position is a more modest one, "that the emancipation of the peoples of the colonies can be the result only of close collaboration with the socially reorganized industrial countries—the metropoles on the march towards greater justice and humanism." It is hardly surprising that this point of view was, as Serge wrote, "coldly received." Lest we think Serge's equivocation on colonial matters was a one-off expressed before a small group and in his private notebooks, this is not the case. In a pamphlet published in 1946, *Le nouvel imperialisme russe* (The New Russian Imperialism), he downplayed the threat and even importance of Western imperialism. In that publication he insisted that the British Empire, led by the Labour government, "is evacuating from Egypt and offers India its independence. The old methods of colonial exploitation are exhausted." As for the exemplar of the new form of imperialism, the United States, Serge claimed that he knew Americans sufficiently well to know that they "don't contemplate imposing tyrannies on the five continents and on the contrary desire a sustainable reorganization of international relations." No commentary is required here.

There was almost nothing upon which Serge was in agreement with his comrades. These men, who had been at the heart of social struggles in France and Spain, in Germany and Austria, felt that academic discussion was not the key: They were men born to act. But Serge had a more realistic idea of their possibilities. Without saying it directly, he knew that action from Mexico was not going to sway events on the European continent. Instead, he asked, "aren't correct viewpoints also acts in a certain sense?"

Serge felt unmoored in time sitting there. He experienced the same frustrations he'd felt in 1927 at meetings of Oppositionists as they were about to be engulfed. Serge described his comrades and what he realized was his position among them in stark terms: They are "idealists hemmed in by the sclerosis of doctrines and circumstances, and dominated by their convictions and their emotional attachments; in short, by fanaticism. Under such conditions the person who disturbs the inner security of the others is a hateful heretic." Unlike them, he is willing to question things.

Unfounded optimism based on the grasping at tiny straws of hope was also at play among Serge's comrades. He saw that their blindness was based on

their extremely optimistic and schematic conviction that the Russian Revolution will soon be repeated in Europe. "The workers will occupy the factories (Pivert), they'll take power (Gironella), etc." So deluded are they that the POUMists think that they'll be back in a free, socialist Spain in six months, and Pivert speaks proudly of the potential for the formation of a Red Army in France!

Not only is this an absurdity, but Serge claims that this plays into the hands of reaction and the Stalinists.

His theses are those already outlined in earlier texts which he will expand on.

> That this war is profoundly different from that of 1914–1918, of which it is the continuation, and that it entails elements of international civil war. (Strong protests by M.P.)—That the economic structure of the world has changed, traditional capitalism making way for a planned and controlled economy, thus collectivist in tendency, which could be that of monopolies and totalitarian parties—or of democracies of a new type, if the latter succeed in being born. (Strong protest by M.P.)— That the defeats of European socialism cannot be imputed solely to the failures of leaders, though this counts, but are rather explained by the decadence of the working-class and of socialism as a result of modern technology (chronic unemployment, declassing of the unemployed, immense increases in the productive capacity of machinery with less need for workers; increased influence of technicians). (M.P. rejects these views as a whole without attempting to refute them), and to speak of a weakening of the working-classes as a class seems to them all to be a sacrilege.

Serge's defense of his theses is simple: "I can't help it if it's the truth." There won't be a repeat of the Russian Revolution; there will not be a proletarian dictatorship, but rather a new Europe that must include everyone in whom "a socialist-leaning consciousness" is burgeoning. None of this is possible without democracy, and democracy must be on the alert. The largest anti-Nazi resistance movements are actually a danger. "Stalinism, which molded and nourished the armed resistance movements in France, Yugoslavia, Greece, and elsewhere, constitutes the worst danger, a mortal danger which we would be mad to aspire to fight on our own." Notice that Serge considers the Communists "the worst danger," not "a danger." The French Communists would form a pole of opposition to de Gaulle; Tito would make Yugoslavia a socialist state; ELAS, the Communist-led Greek People's Liberation Army, would be opposed by British imperialism after the war, but in 1944 was fighting the Nazis. Yet for Serge it was the Communists who were the greatest danger to the new Europe. Note should be taken of this when reflecting on Serge's post-war writings.

He left the meeting distressed and disgusted. "Whatever I might say, agreement is impossible and discussion difficult and sterile. Those possessed of inner flexibility will change beneath the cudgel blows of events; the rest will vegetate in tiny groups on the margins of life (which offers many satisfactions), or will be crushed."[2]

Later that same year he returned in his notebooks to the tenacious grip of the old on the left, which was living as if it was still 1917 or 1918, "and even 1871."[3] Serge says what is almost too obvious to need saying, yet it was and still is. Fragmentarily there might be some returns of the old, but "the entire context being different the big picture will be profoundly different." There is a paradox that Serge draws out. Revolutionaries, who in the words of "The Internationale" want to make "tabula rasa of the past," are hindered by, of all things, tradition, whose power is so great it "attain[s] to blindness." Psychological factors enter into this fear of shaking off old schemas, Serge recognizing "the painful difficulty of mastering a new situation, full of pitfalls and disappointments; the spirit of objective investigation retreats and gives up rather than advancing towards discoveries it is not certain of being able to master and which, it foresees, may put in question the former foundations of its faith."

There are no longer two forces facing each other, but three: "conservatism, socialism, and Stalinist totalitarianism, engaged in a fight to the death." Democracy is essential and must be at the heart of the socialist movement, which has one main enemy: "Its worst enemy, the most destructive one at this moment, is the totalitarianism of postrevolutionary Russia, Bolshevism transformed into absolute totalitarianism of a type analogous to that of reactionary totalitarianisms." If the Soviet Union is now the main enemy, who is the only ally upon whom socialists can count? "The sole natural allies of socialism are among the democratic masses of the countries where bourgeois democracy lives on with traditions predating big capitalism, England and the United States." This assertion is still a shocking one, one that can only have confirmed the doubts his comrades had developed about Serge.

For all these reasons the revolutionary movement that followed World War I is an impossibility, "except to bring about results immediately worse than those of the revolutionary victory in Russia and the defeat of European socialism." There are no revolutionary parties "there are neither large parties nor cadres nor an ideology capable of reproducing them." The only hope is one that again still sounds shocking: "I'm inclined to think that Europe's fate can only be decided when Stalinist totalitarianism has been limited or destroyed in the new conflicts that it necessarily begins."[4]

In an essay from January 1945, "The Time of Intellectual Courage," Serge repeated many of these arguments, but continued his critique of Marxist—and not only Marxist—doctrine. Returning to the nature of the state, Serge asserts that "the anarchist thesis of the destruction of the state and the Marxist thesis of the withering away of the state through the natural functioning of a socialist democracy [...] have shown themselves to be equally unreal." The world of 1945 demanded intellectual courage, the ability to change ideas with the times, in keeping with new realities. Despite his privately expressed disappointment and pessimism, this essay ends on a note of hope:

All the elements of an action program and an ideology look to be within our grasp at a time when history on the march demands that we have the courage to become conscious of new facts and to recognize that the syntheses and doctrines of the last century no longer suffice. And nothing would be more dangerous for us today than to follow the path of intellectual routine.

During his Mexican years Serge, who was not a theoretician, laid out the blueprint for a new path for the socialist left. This blueprint is in a more or less straight line from some of the ideas already expressed in the few years he spent in Western Europe before his flight to North America, and constitutes as significant an epistemological break as did his rejection of individualist anarchism after his condemnation in the Bonnot trial. In both cases he drew the conclusion that his previous worldview had run into a dead end: anarchism with the Bonnot Gang, revolutionary Marxism with Stalin and an opposition that remained tied to a view of reality long out of date. His latest conversion was a more radical one, in that it was not a change that affected Serge alone. Serge was now trying to change the entire course of the left. That doing so from Mexico, far from the political centers of the world, while writing for small journals in the US, France, Mexico and Chile, was quixotic didn't stand in his way. That the people he addressed them to in Mexico, his supposed comrades, rejected these ideas didn't deter him.

But there is something striking about Serge's revision of Marxism, something missing from it: any mention of Marx or Marxism. As was the case in his anarchist days, Serge seldom employs the argument from authority: Citing Stirner in his individualist days, or citing Marx in his socialist period, is not something he does or considers necessary. An argument is valid for what it says, not who said it. Marx and Marxism is a stepping stone for him. But even this statement must be qualified. He dismissed the programmatic document by Pivert and Co. as "a kind of Communist Manifesto," clearly not intending that in a positive sense. He dismisses the central Marxist thesis of class versus class, pointing out that there are no longer two classes but several. The state is no longer a means of class oppression. It has a positive role to play in the modern world, and in a democratic state it is not an oppressive tool at all. Only in the one socialist state is the state a means of crushing the people. The state is also not something that will wither away in time but rather will take on an ever-greater role through its planning functions. It will be a more democratic state than those now existing, but will very much resemble them. And as for Lenin, though he admired the man till the end of his life, nothing of Leninism is left, either. The Leninist party doesn't meet the needs of the day and would only lead to isolation: Broad-based parties including all tendencies are what are needed. Lenin in *State and Revolution*, attempting to steal the thunder of the Russian anarchists, had seen the socialist state as withering away. Not Serge. Finally, if for Lenin imperialism was the highest stage of capitalism, Serge, as we have seen, viewed its end in the capitalist world optimistically. The real imperialist threat came from the USSR, which he denied was socialist any longer but did not claim was capitalist. Serge's revision of Marxism is in many ways a jettisoning of Marxism. That his analyses are largely correct is undeniable. That they should have angered his diehard Marxist purist comrades is hardly surprising. The logical end of this was expressed by Serge in July 1945: "The ideas of the Revolution are dead. The hammer and sickle have become emblems of despotism and murder."[5]

In February 1945 Serge wrote an essay, "Socialisme ou totalitarisme." It was later included in his pamphlet *Le nouvel imperialisme russe*. In this essay he did cite an authority in support of his campaign for the revision of left-wing doctrine: the Catholic philosopher and former French ambassador to the Vatican Jacques Maritain. Maritain had written of the French people's loss of confidence in its former leading classes, and how people are considering a second French Revolution that will grow out of the Liberation. Serge explains that when Maritain speaks of a "revolution" he is speaking euphemistically.

M. Maritain thinks that the French people should put off till later a revolution that it can't make immediately, and he perhaps isn't wrong. The world of today is too dangerously complex to set too quickly to the task, and the socialist-leaning masses in Europe have more common sense than people think.[6]

If there could be more heretical ideas to oppose to Marxism than one borrowed from a Catholic philosopher, it's hard to imagine what it might be.

But this citation is in fact not as strange as it might seem. The basis for Serge's intellectual shift, particularly his increasing concern for the defense of the human person, has its source in Serge's avowal of the now unjustly forgotten philosophy of Personalism, a philosophy rooted in Catholicism. Its seeds had been planted well before his Mexican years, but were now in full bloom.

Victor Serge had arrived in the West in 1936 still calling himself a communist. In a May 1936 letter to Magdeleine Paz, who played such a vital role in keeping his case before the public eye, he spoke of himself as an "Opposition communist, free writer, and troublesome witness." But over the course of his final decade Serge's focus would shift. The victim of the Stalinist apparatus spoke against it vehemently and regularly, in 1936 already writing of concentration camps in the USSR, doing so in the name of a revolutionary socialism represented by the revolutionaries of POUM.

In this he was in the direct line of many anti-Stalinist revolutionaries. But increasingly a new concern became essential to Serge. It was no longer enough to defend the Revolution from its enemies within and without, his famous double duty. Starting in the late 1930s, a new phrase enters his lexicon, one that he would use and reuse as a leitmotif in his final years. What was important for Serge was "the defense of the human person." The phrase sounds fairly banal and unexceptional, a part of his discontent with the dictatorship in the land of the Revolution. But nothing could be further from the truth. The "defense of the human person" was not a phrase he threw about lightly with no intellectual content. These five simple words are the summary of the philosophy that Serge adopted as a supplement to the Marxism that he came to feel needed to be totally revised. Serge's final years can only be understood within the context of his adoption of the philosophy of Personalism as developed by Emmanuel Mounier, the Catholic intellectual and founder and editor of the review *Esprit*, a journal which supported Serge's cause while he was in Orenburg, and in which Serge's writings frequently appeared. Serge would write some of his most important articles for this left-wing Catholic review, and maintain a correspondence with Mounier up until his death. It is impossible to understand the last Serge without understanding the role Personalism played in his activities. Richard Greeman, in his introduction to the New York Review Books Classics edition of Serge's *Memoirs of a Revolutionary*, describes Serge as "on his own confession, personalist,"[7] but in his extensive writings about Serge, Greeman never discusses the importance of Mounier's ideas to Serge.

That Serge was a Personalist is not a simple conjecture. His "adherence" to the doctrine, as he phrased it, was something that he spoke about openly. It is only because of our unfamiliarity with this vital school of thought, and our insistence that Serge was always and only a revolutionary socialist, that we miss the signs he left of his beliefs.

The most striking and incontrovertible proof of Serge's Personalism can be found in the least obscure of locations: his memoirs. There he says that "I do not think of myself as at all an individualist: rather as a 'personalist,' in that I view human personality as a supreme value, only integrated in society and in history."[8] In this context it seems to be some kind of loose descriptive term, not the very specific, vigorous and rigorous school of thought it was.

Serge avowed his Personalism in his correspondence. In a 1938 letter to Maurice Wullens, a longtime acquaintance of

Serge's from his anarchist years, he wrote defending Mounier and his review against an attack by Wullens in his publication *Les Humbles*. Serge wrote that *Esprit* "carries out with honesty and tenacity an excellent work too little known by our comrades." He goes on to speak in the highest terms of Mounier and Personalism: "His doctrine, postulating above all respect for the human person, a priori deserves the respect of the workers' movement whose militants are, except for the Stalinist totalitarians, 'Personalists' without being aware of it."[9] He praised the team at *Esprit*: "The openness of [their] views, the sincere desire to see clearly, and [their] intellectual probity are truly remarkable in a time where intellectuals are customarily abandoning themselves to so many profitable infiltrations." Serge had more to say on the topic to Wullens. In another, undated letter from 1938 (which might have been a draft for the previous one, or vice versa) Serge wrote that "I am unreservedly with the Personalist movement when it above all affirms respect for the human person." Serge then makes an important admission, moving up his attachment to Personalism by several years:

I defined my Personalism long ago, before knowing the word, in a message you perhaps know, where I notably wrote this (February 1, 1933): "Defense of man, respect for man." He must be given his rights, security, [and] value. Without this there is no socialism; without this everything is false, a failure, polluted. Man, whatever he may be, if he's the worst of men, "class enemy," son or grandson of a great bourgeois, I don't care, we must never forget that a human being is a human being. This is forgotten every day right in front of us, everywhere. It's the most revolting and anti-socialist thing there is.

Emmanuel Mounier himself could not have expressed the essence of Personalism better than Serge did in this last letter.

In a letter to Mounier, Serge made matters even clearer. On September 10, 1945, Serge wrote to his friend:

For me it is an absolute that the respect for man, for all men, and consequently for the democratic institutions that are to be renewed, purified, recreated for the Europe that is gestating; that this respect be at the very foundation of socialism, as for any forward-looking movement. In this sense, I definitively maintain my implicit and clear adherence to Personalism and I feel, in so doing, that I am in the great socialist tradition.

What then was this doctrine that Serge claimed as his own? Though Personalism was not "invented" by Emmanuel Mounier, it was Mounier's left-wing version of it that Serge adopted as his own.

The phrase *der Personalismus* was first used by the German theologian Friedrich Schleiermacher in his influential book *On Religion* in 1799, and in America it was introduced by Walt Whitman in 1868, who wrote an essay by that name on "the single solitary soul." The twentieth-century version of Personalism was largely the work of Mounier. He was born in Grenoble in 1905, and studied philosophy at the university in his hometown. As described by the French historian Michel Winock in his fine study of *Esprit*, "the young Emmanuel burned with an uncommon faith in God."[10] Mounier also burned with a hatred for what he appositely called, quoting the Catholic socialist poet and philosopher Charles Péguy, "the established disorder." He and a group of young people who shared his ideas established *Esprit* in 1932. In their pre-war incarnations *Esprit* and Mounier were opponents of both the bourgeoisie and Marxism, though finding some good in the latter and none in the former. In the post-war years, as we will see, Mounier's relationship with communism became entirely positive.

In the October 1936 issue of *Esprit*, Mounier published his "Manifesto in Service to Personalism," in which he summarized the essential points of his philosophy. It began with a definition: "We call Personalist every doctrine, every civilization, that affirms the primacy of the human person over material necessities and the collective apparatuses that sustain their development."

Mounier's Personalism was not a contemplative doctrine, but a philosophy of action. He insisted that "we be judged by our acts." Mounier sought to refine the notions of action and act: "Not every action is an act. An action is only of value and effective if in the first instance it has taken the measure of the truth that gives it its meaning, and of the historical situation which gives it its scope and its conditions for realization." Personalism was politically optimistic, for "there is no doubt that we can already considerably renew the visage of most lives by freeing man from all the servitudes that weigh on his vocation as a man." Moreover,

Personalism does not announce the constituting of a school, the opening of a chapel, or the invention of a closed system. It testifies to a convergence of wills and puts itself at their service without impinging upon their diversity, so as to assist them in their search for the means to effectively weigh on history.

There was no necessary contradiction, then, between Personalism and Serge's existing ideas. When he discovered Personalism, it was mainly a form of anti-bourgeois non-conformism, which suited Serge's temperament. Freshly released from the *univers concentrationnaire* of the Soviet Union, he could not help adhering to a doctrine that sought to define, as Mounier wrote, "all the forms of mutual consent capable of establishing a civilization devoted to the human person." Serge had learned the hard way that communism was a doctrine sorely lacking a focus on the individual. It was all of humankind, instead, that was to be transformed. Personalism, by contrast, represented a refutation of such lethal abstraction. The group putting out *Esprit* impressed Serge in a way that few did. "They sensed sharply that they were living at the end of an era; they loathed all lying, especially if it formed an excuse for murder, and they said so outright. In their

simple teaching of 'reverence for the human person' I felt immediately at one with them."[11]

Serge's correspondence with Mounier began in the late 1930s
and was interrupted by the war and Serge's departure for Mexico.
His final note to Mounier before its temporary suspension was
written while he was en route to Mexico in 1941. He again
referred to the philosophy that he shared with Mounier:

> My dear friend, I remain a faithful friend of *Esprit* and will
> strive to remain in contact with you. I will be happy to be
> of use to you (without currently being fully in agreement
> with you [a reference to Mounier's suspected support for the
> Revolution Nationale in Vichy France]). But I believe that our
> agreement on Personalism is much deeper than any circum-
> stantial disagreements.

Four years later, however, the circumstantial disagreements
would become fundamental disagreements. When they were
able to pick up their correspondence at war's end, Mounier
provided Serge with his view of the post-war situation, and
though his hopes chimed with those of Serge, his analysis was
radically different. Despairing of the dream of a renewed France,
Mounier asserted that, owing to the strength of the right and
to the weakness of a Socialist Party that was lacking in "men,
energy, and historical imagination," and which had an "increasingly slim working-class base [....] it is necessary to speak a truth
that will be hard for you to hear: apart from the Communists
there is nothing." Like so many left-wing intellectuals in France,
most famously the circle around Jean-Paul Sartre at *Les Temps
modernes*, Mounier and *Esprit* had made a choice that Serge
abhorred. Mounier explained to Serge that

> outside of a small Trotskyist minority there is only one way to
> explain the situation: the workers are Communist. As a result,
> the problem is a tragic one. One must both bear witness for

everything that is dear to us, while not setting ourselves apart from the only remaining revolutionary force in France.

Serge's disagreement with Mounier's stance could not have been stronger, and he expressed it from the Personalist standpoint that he felt Mounier had abandoned. "Our era of grief is also that of the decline of all values, since the primordial values, human life and the truth, hardly count anymore." Responding to Mounier's observation that there is nothing outside the Communists, Serge castigated his friend, saying that he and those like him had

committed an enormous error in seeking to delude themselves about the latest totalitarian peril, which is immense. It would have been necessary, it is necessary, to remain firm by delineating the differences between even disguised totalitarianism and freedom, maintaining the right to speak the truth on the most inhuman regime in the world.

Serge was moved to write angrily to Mounier in January 1946 after reading his article in the November 1945 issue of *Esprit*, in which Mounier made an unambiguous case for support of the Soviet Union and the Communists, writing that "without the vast infusion of humanity that could come from the East, the West will continue to die its little death. Without the decisive lessons the USSR offers us, the European revolution will be bogged down in the social democratic swamp." Serge was enraged and didn't hide it:

I think you are wrong, just as my executed friends and I were wrong for more than a decade, and for the same reason: a profound confidence in man. The civilized individuals that we are refuse to believe the worst. You demand "more precise knowledge [...] of the contemporary reality of the Soviet Union." You certainly cannot be expecting it from official sources. Other information slips through, but they form a picture so horrifying that whoever would publish them in France (where I believe this would be practically impossible) would immediately be accused by the PCF and men of good will of infamy à la Goebbels.

Serge then cited figures taken from *The New Leader*, which was among his favorite American publications. (*The New Leader*, which lasted in print until 2006 and for four more years online, was founded as a socialist weekly in 1924, and between 1936 and 1960, when it was edited by Sol Levitas, it was an uncompromising liberal anti-communist journal.) Serge informed Mounier that there were five million deportees in concentration camps in Siberia, and that one and a half million of them were sent there between 1937 and 1940.

As far as Serge was concerned, Mounier would never be able to get at the truth with his current attitude.

Unless totalitarianism is denounced, honest information is impossible. And if we renounce this, we have no choice but to say that this totalitarianism has become strong enough to silence consciences and impose a general complicity with its official lies. My conviction, based on too much experience, is that no compromise is possible with this totalitarianism without abandoning Christian, humanist, and socialist values and without inevitably disastrous consequences.

If there were a real hope for a useful meeting between Russia and America, I would be with you—despite what I am saying here. But I don't see any sign of such a hope. If totalitarianism sustains itself, which is possible, there will be no democratic renewal in the West (by which I mean one ensuring the truth and the rights of man); [there will be] a permanent state of crisis exploited by the Communist Parties and, in the end, a Third World War [...]. If, as is also possible, the USSR changes its appearance and once again becomes even an imperfect socialist democracy, all hopes are permitted for it and for Europe, and the nightmare of a Third World War will be avoided. But I see no third possibility, if not stalling for time. In a word, your position seems to me utopian. I think that at bottom it is that of the best minds of France, and I understand the psychological motivation for it. And yet, as concerns you it disappoints me, because your starting point is the healthiest of doctrines, the one most capable of rallying all those who are honest, the one least compatible with the camouflaging of reality.

Serge's disappointment with *Esprit* and Mounier would only grow, and he bluntly summed up his objections in a letter to Mounier in March 1946, about the most recent issues of the journal:

I must say to you, with all the rigor that it seems to me that we, as men of good will, owe each other, how disappointed and distressed I am to see the review take the wrong road, and so badly deviate from the willingness to defend man and truth as to enter into contradiction with itself and engender its own negation. *Esprit* leaves the clear impression of being a pro-totalitarian, pro-Communist publication that wants to ignore the crushing of man and the annihilation of the truth by an essentially inhuman regime.

The correspondence with Mounier ended in July 1947, in the same disappointed and agitated spirit:

I remain in profound disagreement with *Esprit* concerning the very singular pro-Stalinism of the journal, which I consider the gravest of intellectual errors—and a moral failure. When will the journal decide to finally take account of the colossal and irrefutable documentation published on the concentration camps in the USSR and on their ten or fifteen million pariahs.

21
Anti-communist?

As we can see from the account of Serge's relationship with Mounier, the common assumption that Serge, despite his firm anti-Stalinism, never became an anti-communist, requires closer examination. A reading of Serge's writings after his liberation from the Soviet Union shows a drift from revolutionary anti-Stalinism to a hatred of Stalin and Communists more generally that can't be called simple anti-Stalinism. Serge went beyond this and became an anti-communist. Of a socialist variety, like Orwell and many American intellectuals of his time, but anti-communist all the same.

During Serge's lifetime, anti-communism was the view that the primary enemy faced by humankind was communism, represented by the USSR, which had its tentacles everywhere, opposed democracy, subverted democratic governments and institutions, and was more to be feared than the Western powers. Communists, wherever they were, were agents of a foreign power, that is, the USSR, carrying out its designs to destroy Western civilization. Anti-communism aimed at preventing the spread of communism and, if possible, rolling it back from those lands it ruled. In the post-war world divided into two camps, for an anti-communist there was only one camp to side with: that of the US-led West, seen as a benignant force at worse, a positive one at best.

There were attempts, particularly in France, with the short-lived Rassemblement démocratique révolutionnaire, which included Jean-Paul Sartre among its leaders, to establish a third way between the anti-Soviet West and the USSR and the powerful Communist Parties that emerged from the war and the Resistance. Serge chose the West, and viewed everything touching on the

Soviet Union as criminal and poisoned. As we've noted, Serge wrote in his notebooks on September 13, 1944, "That Stalinism, which molded and nourished the armed resistance movements in France, Yugoslavia, Greece, and elsewhere, constitutes the worst danger, a mortal danger."[1] Viewing Communism as *the* danger is the very definition of anti-communism.

Decades later, with communism long dead and buried, it's hard for many people, the young in particular, to imagine there ever could have been a case for supporting the USSR. That case was filled with lies and blindness, yet it was accepted by millions. That looking east to Moscow could have given hope to anyone seems impossible, yet it wasn't. Unlike the Russia of today, the USSR was a real power, representing a pole of opposition to capitalism and imperialism, the primary ills confronting humanity as far as the left was concerned. Serge downplayed the role of Western imperialism. He complained in his correspondence that "Leftist organizations are indignant about Indonesia and comprehensive about Indochina, but silencious [*sic*] or worse about Poland." Serge was absolutely right, and the pro-Communist left's failure to condemn Stalin's final round of crimes after World War II, to acknowledge the camps, cannot be excused.

But Serge, for his part, right as he was to condemn Soviet crimes, had his own blind spots. He placed far too much faith in the European powers when it came to their colonies. He never mentioned the massacres in Sétif, Algeria, on May 8, 1945, and believed the end of colonialism would come from the natural beneficence of the Western powers. He dismissed the threat posed by America's drive for international hegemony, saw capitalism as evolving towards democratic planning, and thought all of this was imperiled by the Soviet Union. To say Serge would have evolved in the same directions as his comrade in anti-Stalinism Boris Souvarine, who eventually supported the US in Vietnam, might be going too far. But it's hard to deny, given the positions he took and the language he employed in expressing his opinions (he was not averse to using the word "commies"[2]), that Serge agreed with the point of view of ex-communist anti-communists like Arthur Koestler.

We have already seen that in his correspondence with Mounier and in his notebooks and articles Serge believed that the improvement of the lot of the working-class was more effectively implemented in the countries of the West and Mexico than in the Soviet Union. The West was Serge's political and social horizon, and communism was no longer even necessary, having proved its failure in the Soviet Union. The human person received no protection in the USSR or from Communists. In all these ways it was humanity's enemy, and Communists adored a murderous mirage.

Serge has his defenders against the charge of anti-communism, and they deserve to be taken seriously. In a 2003 letter to the Trotskyist historical journal *Revolutionary History*, Ian Birchall, a translator and scholar of Serge's works, and an open and perspicacious writer, criticized Alan Wald's article in the journal *Critique* on "Victor Serge and the New York Anti-Stalinist Left," which proposed that Serge was moving towards a vision of the world in which the USSR was the "main enemy."[3] Though he considered Wald's account to be "balanced," Birchall rejected Wald's conclusion, citing in defense of Serge's rejection of anti-communism a letter Serge wrote—and perhaps never sent—to his longtime comrade and supporter, René Lefeuvre.

The letter, which Birchall conjectures is from 1946, presents three points which he considers crucial in defending Serge from the charge of anti-communism.[4] In the first instance, "Serge is highly critical of reportage on Russia which is not adequately documented." Birchall asserted that

Serge sees the danger of war as lying rather more on the American side than on the Russian, since Russia is still exhausted from the Second World War. Most crucially, Serge recognizes the double nature of the Stalinist parties as courtiers outside the Russian bloc. Despite their Stalinist politics, they are working-class parties and part of the working-class movement.

Birchall concludes that "given the orientation spelt out in this letter, I find it hard to imagine Serge succumbing to stalinophobia." Trotskyists have always walked the fine line between condemning the USSR and anti-communism, and Birchall sees Serge as having done this as well. Sadly, Birchall is wrong on all counts.

Serge's letter to Lefeuvre contested the writings of a ferocious anti-communist, Walter White, on many counts, including White's "constantly resorting to a comparison between the standards of living in the USA and in the USSR, when the two countries are at very different stages in their evolution, and when the latter has been sorely tried by the war." Serge also condemned "warmongering propaganda against the USSR, which in certain circles in the USA has become the Number One Enemy, replacing Nazi Germany." He ended this short letter by saying,

If the Soviet regime is to be criticized, let it be from a socialist and working-class point of view. If we must let American voices be heard, let them be those of sincere democrats and friends of peace, and not chauvinistic demagogues; let them be those of the workers who will one day, we hope, succeed in organizing themselves into an independent party.

The sentiments expressed here would seem to protect Serge from charges of anti-communism. But there is a problem: The preponderance of his actual writings run counter to everything he wrote to Lefeuvre. Serge, we will show, did view the USSR as the "Number One enemy." He *did* negatively compare the economic performances, both real and potential, of the US and Russia. Is that not what his praise of Belgium and Mexico constitute? He frequently denied any socialist character to the Soviet regime. He even went further down a road that can only be described as anti-communist, advocating for everything from blacklisting to informing on Communists.

Serge's anti-communism did not just sprout up between 1941 and 1944. Hatred of Communists and attribution to them of occult powers had entered Serge's worldview even before his departure from France. His FBI file contains a previously quoted letter from October 17, 1940, addressed to "Dear Friends"—perhaps the Macdonalds—in which he discusses his visa problems, including his inability to get a transit visa for the US. "I imagine," he wrote,

> that by now you realize what great obstacles I am up against, since through certain information which we now have I know that the Stalinist work is being done in the United States on a large scale by a goodly number of journalists, and Stalinist intellectuals who have arrived there. They even have a certain amount of support in the Administration and without doubt among certain aliens of the bourgeoisie. Their action is and will be camouflaged [...]. They would do anything to get all their personnel installed in the United States.

We find here in Serge allegations that would become common currency just a few years later at sessions of the House Committee on Un-American Activities.

By the time World War II entered its European-wide phase, as we have seen when examining his reinvention of socialist doctrine, Serge was calling for the banning of Communists— or "totalitarians" as he called them—from any new socialist movements that might spring up in the post-war world. "No socialist international can, [without] betraying its mission and dishonoring itself, accept within it totalitarian communists [...] led by secret bureaus provided with secret funds and subject to a discipline that annihilates the critical spirit." Long before there was a Cold War, Serge was advocating for a backlisting of Communists from the left. Moderate left-wing groups, especially in the US, would implement just such a ban. A generation later it would be a basis for the rejection of their elders by the young founders of Students for a Democratic Society.

The New York review *The New Leader* published many articles by Serge in the final years of his life. The articles are of interest, to be sure, but included with every submission was a personal letter to its editor, Sol Levitas, in which Serge laid out behind the scenes information he claimed to be privy to. These letters are replete with accusations against and suspicions of the USSR and Communists. His involvement with *The New Leader* very much displeased Serge's most consistent American supporters, Dwight Macdonald and his wife Nancy. Though they never met Serge, they were, as we've seen, of enormous moral and material support during the period when Serge was attempting to flee Europe. Macdonald provided Serge with an outlet in his magazine, *Politics*. The extent to which Serge had swung to a basic form of anti-communism is revealed in an April 21, 1945, letter he sent to Dwight.

Serge had been inspired to ire by Macdonald, who'd written an article in the April issue of *Politics* rejecting what Macdonald viewed as the error of "regard[ing] Stalinism as an all-powerful Principle of Evil that operates independently of concrete historical circumstances." Macdonald had concluded that "I cannot believe that any man-made organization can be so perfectly effective, whether for good or for evil."

Serge responded to this with barely contained anger. "Comm[unist]-totalitarianism is, in fact, a principle destructive of human values that are essential for us, a principle, to be sure, that is not 'all powerful,' but at this time <u>extremely powerful because it is acting in favorable historic circumstances</u>" (underlined in original).

Contra Macdonald, Serge believed that totalitarianism had in fact achieved a degree of perfection and effectiveness (so have [*sic*] been "perfectly effective" [this phrase in English in the original French-language letter], sufficiently so in Russia to extermi- nate entire generations of elite men in Central Europe [and] to exterminate millions of Jews: The GPU and Maidenek [*sic*] demonstrate the perfect efficacity of the man-destroying total- itarian organization.

Adopting the idea that there was an equivalence between Com- munism and Nazism, Serge wrote Macdonald that it is wrong "to forget that the Communist Parties are to the same extent as the GPU part of totalitarian machinery, and that for the past while the camp at Maidenek [*sic*] is used by the GPU."

Serge accused Macdonald (in English) of "wishful thinking," his ideas contradicting "all observed facts for over twenty years." Serge then made a curious observation. He wrote of the Zinoviev-led opposition in 1927 to Stalin's leadership that "all the oppositions led to political suicide, and millions of brave Russians to physical extermination." Any attempt to reform Communist Parties was futile and was "inexorably and easily destroyed." Opposition movements "were destroyed in times of social peace and in times of civil war." Serge, who for decades took such pride in being a part of the generation that made the Revolution and tried to put it back on the rails, now tells Dwight Macdonald, "I was already against [this course] at that time," that is, in 1927. Serge, the Opposition activist who spent three years in the isolator and was an international face of opposition to Stalin, was claiming that even in the time of Zinoviev he opposed active oppositional activity. He never made this claim to the GPU, but he now made it as a way of projecting into the past the idea that there never existed a possibility to save communism from its natural totalitarian fate.

Serge continued along this line, saying that the fight to change communism is hopeless because hopelessly unequal. "The explanation for this fact resides in the superiority of the industrial organization, rationally organized, from a police and terroristic point of view over any political amateurishness, over any disarmed democracy." In the end, "the least complacency towards it is the first step to suicide; it can only be resisted by rejecting it straightaway, completely, and en bloc: its influence, its maneuvers, its masks and its faces." Anti-communism cannot be more total than this.

Serge's opinions worried Macdonald, and he noted in a February 27, 1945 letter that "our political views seem to be diverging rapidly." He gave Serge his unvarnished opinion of both the *New Leader* and Serge's line:

> [T]he New Leader has no political ideas or principles except anti-Stalinism. The only reason I can see for someone like yourself, with your past record and your fine moral and intellectual sensitivity to the real needs and interests of the masses, to accept such a political milieu is that anti-Stalinism is becoming your own basic political principle.

Most of what Serge wrote over the remaining years of his life supported Macdonald's critique.

The war was not yet over when, in a June 18, 1945 letter to Levitas, Serge informed him of the political line of the left-wing Latin American trade union federation, the Confederación de Trabajadores de América Latina (CTAL), the largest labor federation in Latin America, which Serge considered communist controlled. The CTAL, Serge warned, was inflaming its members and supporters by falsely claiming that the anti-Roosevelt right was on the rise, aiming "to sabotage San Francisco [i.e., the founding of the UN], [and] the decisions taken in Moscow, Teheran, Yalta, [and] Bretton Woods [...] [CTAL] utilize[s] slander and conflict to destroy the soviet-english-american [*sic*] unity." Despite Serge's claims that this was nothing but anti-West fear mongering by the Communists based on falsehoods, we know all of this to have been true: The Cold War and the rise of the right in the US was, indeed, already in progress at the time of Roosevelt's death and Truman's assuming the presidency. Serge spoke dismissively of the "tone of argumentation diffused in the Latin American workers' movement," viewing it as the propagation of "a strongly adopted 'line', well-coordinated and dangerously significant. The comm[unist] apparatus is preparing the rank and file for an ambiance of far-reaching conflict." For Serge, it was a given that if there was fear of a war started by the West, then it was artificially cooked up by an international Communist campaign, not by real threats made by real Western politicians.

On January 8, 1946, Serge wrote Levitas that the "general situation" called for two things: "the reestablishment of a healthy democracy […] and the combatting of totalitarian influence." The Communists are all-powerful in France, according to Serge, posing a threat to people's livelihoods and the freedom of the press. He wrote in the same letter:

In all circles the pressure of the P[arti] C[ommuniste] and its parallel camouflage org[anizations]. is terrible. Many times, a civil servant or worker who permits himself a few critical remarks about Stalinism is risking his job and tranquility […]. Generally, it is not permitted to qualify USSR totalitarian [*sic*]; information about the Russian regime is not published.

Though the Communist Party was powerful, it did not rule in the areas of hiring and firing (except in Communist-run cities), and did not have the ability to quash anti-Soviet news from being printed, which could be found daily in countless newspapers and journals.

In Serge's eyes no one was sufficiently bold in confronting the Communists. The Trotskyists, a minuscule formation in France (and everywhere else) were, according to Serge, now succumbing to Stalinism, for they "write about the encirclement of the USSR by the US." Even more, they promote "a PS-PC-CGT government." His pique with everyone around him even reached POUM, who though "very valiant in the past adopt a new orientation vis a vis the comm[unists]. Russian power (My best old friends publish a daily and a review—but they fear my name and don't asked [*sic*] me for collaboration)." Serge's accusation that POUM was soft on communism is a hard one to swallow, and his claim that "his best old friends" don't ask for his collaboration because they are afraid of him is a distortion, at the very least. In a dispute with the Mexico City-based émigré newspaper *Mundo* in early 1944, which we will discuss later, he had complained that they weren't running his articles with sufficient regularity. He had been told that they were spacing his articles out, as they did with all their writers, in order not to appear to be the journal of one man, tendency, or party. Serge, recounting this to Levitas, a New York magazine editor innocent of any knowledge of the internal doings of a small group of foreign exiles in Mexico City, was attempting to solidify his self-image as a martyr of the anti-Communist cause.

He wrote to Levitas of French resentment of the GIs' "privileged material standards [and] for their role in the black market," as well as for the "insufficient economical [*sic*] help of the US." Serge denies these feelings any spontaneous, independent existence. "I suspect that these feelings are encouraged by the PC propaganda." Communist malevolence perverts things big and small.

Serge wrote regularly for *The New Leader* about Spanish matters, almost always pointing out Communist control of the Republican Government in exile. In a letter written on July 24, 1946, he took his hatred of the Communists to its most extreme point, informing on "partizans [*sic*]" fighting Franco. He wrote Levitas,

I am informed, from the best sources, that [Spanish Communist leaders Modesto and Lister] are in France at the head of an important military organization, chiefly concentrated in the south and near the Sp[anish] border. This organization, tied with the sp[anish]. partizans who are receiving from Russian officers dayly [*sic*] instructions by radio, counts with several thousand od [*sic*] armed men and seems to be formed in order to assume after the fall of Franco a police job in Spain. This is a very important and dangerous fact. It appears that in spite of the opposition of the Soc[ialist] Party and many others Republican [*sic*], Modesto and Lister have obtained the approval of the sp/Gov-t.

That the Spanish Communists, unlike the rest of the anti-Franco forces, were continuing to fight fascism was not praiseworthy. Because it was a Communist undertaking, it was a danger that had to be feared.

The occult powers of the Comintern (dissolved in 1943) are not only immense now; they had long been so. Included with his article "The Substance of the Comintern," published about a month before his death, was a letter dated October 24, 1947, telling Levitas that "I was informed in Moscow in 1929–30 that, from this time, some three hundred influential Rumanian generals and politicians (e tutti quanti) were under the occult control of the stalinist Secret apparatus." That such high numbers of generals should have been suborned by the Soviets seems unlikely on the face of it. The claim seems all the more unlikely in that bloody repressions of mine and railway strikes occurred during that period. If there was an unstoppable Soviet apparatus at work it failed miserably. This was also the period that saw the rise of Romanian fascism, in the form of the Romanian Front and the Iron Guard, murderous antisemites all. Was the Iron Guard the work of the Soviets as well?

Communist omnipotence was one of its greatest strengths, its sources well placed and Soviet ability to put them to use undoubted. As Serge wrote to Levitas in this same October 24 letter: "Since 1936–37 we can consider that from the point of view of personnel the Comintern is strictly and solely made up of men belonging body and soul to the political police. More precisely, to the secret service." The Comintern Central American bureau is "better informed on the economic structure of Cuba than is the government of that republic." The European bureaus in France and Italy "possess on the majority of politicians of these countries, and even of on modest working-class militants and many well-known intellectuals detailed files and dossiers." "If we were to conceive a debarcation [sic] of Stalin's forces in Costa Rica the agents of the NKVD [the then-current acronym for the secret police]-Comintern would immediately know who must be suppressed, which others it can likely corrupt, and which worker militants it can count on." It's hard to call these statements anything but those of an anti-communist.

One of Serge's final collections of his writings, published by René Lefeuvre at Spartacus, appeared in January 1947 with the title *The New Russian Imperialism*. It's a varied collection, of which we have already spoken, and not all of the essays it contains deal directly with the Russian imperialism of the title (note the use of "Russian" and not "Soviet").

Serge compares the relative threats posed by the various victorious powers and their empires, and there is no question who Serge considers "the Number One enemy." "If danger and failure there is in postwar Europe, it comes from the East." "I note that the total failure of reconstruction—which would necessarily have been socialist—of Eastern Europe is owed to invasions, occupations, spoliations, and aggressions of the totalitarian USSR."[5]

Standing up to the Communists is the primary duty of all people of good will. As we saw in Serge's relations with the Personalists, particularly with Emmanuel Mounier, Serge came to view as soft on communism. In the opening essay of *The New Russian Imperialism*, he attacks a May 1946 article in *Esprit* for its attitude towards the USSR. The review and its followers have failed their cause:

I remember a time when the Personalist review *Esprit*, a propos the Moscow purges and the purge of the old leaders of the true Red Army, employed quite a different language. The contradictions between respect for the human person and the destruction by the state of the human person then appeared [...] what it is: obvious and monstrous.[6]

Serge dismisses the Soviet claims that it needs to ensure its security. "Who doesn't see the shocking falsity of this argument?" Germany and Poland are not threats, Serge says. What dictates Soviet actions is that "Central and Eastern Europe, reconstructing themselves under democratic governments, [and] necessarily influenced by socialism, would be—without any bombers— very dangerous for the absolutist government of a great country destined for poverty and deprived of freedom."[7] Serge failed to hear the sound of sabers rattling in the West, while hearing them very clearly from the East.

The situation in Europe is a disappointing one, the disappointment all caused by the Communist role. Contrary to the hopes for the post-war world of people like Serge, "it's not the European socialist movement that exercises a liberating influence in the USSR, it's the totalitarian machinery *born of the Russian Revolution* which clearly tends to dominate the socialist-leaning masses of Europe, and even the reborn Socialist Parties, as we can see in Italy, in France, and in Greece" (emphasis added).[8]

For Serge the two arguments—or rather what he calls "myths"—that elevate the USSR in the eyes of the working masses are easily dismissed. The first is that the USSR represents a new form of worker democracy. In this he was absolutely correct. The other is that

It seemed reasonable till now to maintain that from the economic point of view the completely planned and directed system of the USSR, with its (in principle) rational centralization in the field of production, represented considerable progress in relation to the more or less anarchic capitalist system. The degree of planning attained in several capitalist countries [...] diminishes the value of this argument. The possibility of attaining in a few European countries social-ist-tending economies in a democratic regime, without insisting on either terroristic intolerance or abolishing the rights of the individual, seems to us totally real. From the moment it becomes to a certain extent a reality, the countries that have taken this road will become progressive countries, even in relation to the totalitarian USSR [...]. This is perhaps the principal reason that the industrially developed countries with a deeply rooted democratic tradition will not enter the path of totalitarian collectivism unless they are violently pushed to it by mightily armed minorities.[9]

Battling his fellow exiles in Mexico, who were demonstrating, in his mind, weakness towards communism, Serge found a home in a certain liberal but anti-communist press in the US. Anti-communism was not only a political ideology. It brought with it a mindset, one that saw the Communist hand everywhere. Serge certainly saw the world in that light. As Emmanuel Mounier said of Serge in his obituary published in January 1948 in *Esprit*: "Since the end of the war his letters were polarized around one single concern: the Soviet dictatorship and the camps in the USSR [...]. Far from France, he spoke inaccurately of realties he didn't know. But we forgive him this, for men of his mettle and humanity are few."

Far from France, as Mounier said, Serge failed to see what was actually occurring on the ground. Missing the West, yearning for America, he idealized them both, failing to see that they were imperfect carriers of the antidote to communism he hoped for. He was an exile, and suffered from the inability of the exile to know what was truly happening in the world—in Serge's case worlds—he was cut off from. A fitting way to explain Serge's politics at the end of his life was that they were those of a New

York intellectual. He wrote for two of their reviews, *Politics* and *The New Leader*, and, like many of the New York intellectuals, he had passed through a Communist and/or Trotskyist phase. He was still a man of the left, but of the anti-communist left of reviews like the *Partisan Review* or the later *Dissent*. Had he lived longer, his articles would have fit in the *Commentary* magazine of the early 1960s.

All of the arguments Ian Birchall made defending Serge against the charge of anti-communism are thus reduced to naught. That he had more than enough reason to hate both Stalin for what he'd made of the Revolution, and the world Communist movement for backing him, can't be denied. But those who condemn the language of the unquestionably anti-communist Koestler or Whittaker Chambers can only deny Serge that title by ignoring what Serge actually wrote.

And yet, even as an anti-communist Serge was unruly. In his final decade Serge's hatred of Stalin, the USSR, and the world Communist movement was boundless. At the same time, unlike the common run of anti-communists, even those who were former Communists, Serge never wavered in his belief that the Bolshevik Revolution was at its outset a positive event and that Stalinism was a perversion of Leninism, not its continuation. His posthumously published 1947 article, "Thirty Years After the Russian Revolution," is proof of this.[10]

Most opponents of communism saw the Bolsheviks as an insignificant minority in 1917 who attained power through a coup d'état in pursuit of their dictatorial aims. Serge, on the contrary, wrote that "The Bolsheviks took power because, in the process of natural selection that took place among the revolutionary parties, they showed themselves the most adept at expressing in a coherent, far-sighted and determined manner the aspirations of the mobilized masses." Once they'd risen to power, they were able to hold on to it, not because they banned and murdered opponents but because "the masses supported them from the Baltic to the Pacific." Serge asserted that "until the end of the civil war, in 1920–21, the Russian Revolution took on the aspect of an immense popular movement, to which the Bolsheviks provided a brain and nervous system in the form of leaders and cadres." Far from being focused solely on their own power, Serge wrote that "the Bolshevik Party sought and obtained the collaboration of the Left Social Revolutionary Party," though he excepts Lenin and Trotsky from those Bolsheviks who desired a coalition with other, more moderate, left groups. Whatever authoritarian tendencies the Bolsheviks had were not unique to them, for "all the Russian revolutionary parties, from 1870–1880 on were in fact highly authoritarian." At the start Lenin did not want full government control of industry, but rather worker control. "[O]nly in July of 1918 did the outbreak of civil war force complete nationalization as a defense imperative." The Bolsheviks were in the direct line of the Russian character and their times.

Did the early Bolsheviks commit errors? Serge does not deny they did. First among them was the founding of the Cheka, the predecessor of the GPU and the NKVD, whose target was counter-revolutionaries. It was, Serge admits, a flawed organization, "which judged the accused, and mere suspects, without hearing or seeing them," and which "finished by exterminating the entire revolutionary generation." Serge, again in a very uncommon fashion, grants extenuating circumstances for the founding of Bolshevik state terror, which "in fairness to Lenin's circumstances," he enumerates. Lenin's hand was forced because "the republic lived in mortal peril," and so had no choice but to take the authoritarian path it did: The Revolution's survival depended on it. But they were basically humane, and in 1920 capital punishment was prohibited, on paper. In that same year things took a turn for the worse, and again it was not the fault of the Bolsheviks. External and internal circumstances, like the war with Poland and Britain's recognition of the Whites, were the motive forces behind the supposed repressive shift. The Red Army's failed attempt to overthrow Pilsudski and the ongoing civil war left Soviet Russia exhausted. Serge explains that "there was no longer any question of abolishing capital punishment or beginning the reconstruction of the nation upon the basis of Soviet democracy." The result was that "[m]isery and danger paralyzed the party-state in an economic regime intolerable to the population and doomed from within." The Kronstadt rebellion was the final nail in the coffin: "The errors and mistakes of power are all tied in with Kronstadt 1921." Among other things, "the truth about the conflict was hidden from the party and from the country as a whole by the press which—for the first time—lied shamelessly." One feels confident in doubting this last assertion, since the Soviet press had been largely triumphalist—and so, false—from its inception, in which Serge himself played a part. The Bolshevik monopoly on power was solidified, even codified after Kronstadt. The primary reason for this, according to Serge was that "during crucial moments, the Bolsheviks trusted no one but themselves."

Another crucial extenuating circumstance in Serge's defense of the Bolshevik dictatorship was the failure of the Western proletariat to seize power. Had that occurred, had the German workers in particular won out, their revolution "would have been infinitely fertile for the social progress of humanity as a whole." This, of course, didn't occur, and it was Soviet misjudgment and mismanagement that assured this outcome. Serge, in defending the Leninist leadership that was in place, presents this counter-history of a world ruled by the proletariat as a battle against the "claim that history is nothing but a chain of fatalistic, mechanical occurrences and not the unfolding of human life in the flow of time." But history is an account of what happened, not what should have happened.

Serge, in the final year of his life, spoke of his erstwhile comrades, most of them murdered by Stalin, in terms never found in the pages of anti-communist literature. Bolsheviks and their fellow Communists around the world were not dupes, nor were they tools of dictatorship. Rather, they "were moved by a great will to liberation. Anyone who ever rubbed shoulders with them will never forget it. Few men in history have ever been so devoted to the cause of man as a whole." But that was then. He tenaciously holds to the insistence that there was a rupture between the Leninist and Stalinist periods, which he had maintained at length in almost everything he wrote on the subject. At the same time, he makes clear that the seed of the demise of the Bolshevik dream was planted during its first decade, during most of which Lenin was alive and the leader of the party and state. Thirty years after the storming of the Winter Palace, nothing was left of the Soviet Russia Serge admired and still cloaked in an aura of revolutionary purity. Among anti-communists his position is a unique one. For most opponents of communism the ideology was flawed and false by its very nature. Serge still carried within him the cult of an idealized past, while his vision of the present was uncompromisingly negative. Actually existing communism was the enemy of humanity, a betrayal of a past that would never return.

22

Fisticuffs

Serge's insistence that everything must be revised did not sit well with his fellow members of Socialismo y Libertad. Differences of personality and politics and matters of pride were a dominant feature of the discord, which blew up in 1944. From our historical distance the issues involved are petty ones, but they speak eloquently of the fractures on the exiled left. They do much to reveal Serge's personality and character, something in the exile too often ignored in descriptions of his truly courageous political battles. We've seen that in the 1930s Serge was considered an intellectual of tremendous importance, respected even by those who didn't share his beliefs. His release by Stalin would not have been possible without this respect and admiration. By 1944, three short years after arriving in Mexico to what he thought would be a non-sectarian and open-minded anti-Stalinist left, he had alienated almost everyone around him, including his wife. Rumors continue to circulate to this day that Laurette was having an affair, and the rare mentions of their relationship in his notebooks leave that impression. This stubborn and unruly revolutionary had isolated himself among the isolated European radicals in Mexico.

This isolation even included strained relations with his son Vlady. The young man had chosen art as his field, and had not, like his father, moved on from the idea that revolution was possible. Testimony to this appears in the Italian novel *The Fugitive*, written by the former autonomist Massimo Carlotto. Carlotto, fleeing from arrest in Italy as a member of the far-left group Lotta Continua, had, inspired by Serge's memoirs, chosen

Mexico as his place of exile. While in Mexico City, Carlotto met and came to know Vlady Kibalchich. He described Serge's son as

> a man who was tormented by his own past. Following his father, he had already experienced, as a child, the pain of exile, Siberia [sic], and the long voyage by ship to Mexico, the only country willing to accept Victor Serge. Ideological disputes that followed the death of Trotsky had separated them, and had obliged Victor to live the last years of his life in an unjust and painful state of isolation. Whenever Valdy spoke of his father, it was clear that he was plagued by a sense of guilt for their separation during the last years of Victor's life.[1]

Serge battled all of his closest allies and friends, starting with the leadership of POUM, then with other exiles. On January 29, 1944 Serge had written to POUM about the status of the Commission on International Relations of their exile organization, whose functioning it was decided was to be put on hold. Serge disagreed with the decision, thinking it should either be dissolved or its activities carried on as before. He submitted a document laying out his vision and requested that a meeting be called. It wasn't, and it was only in April that he received a response from the secretariat, admitting his letter had been completely forgotten. He was invited to a meeting where his proposals would be entertained. On June 15, Serge wrote an angry letter complaining that, contrary to what he thought had been the plan for reorganization, POUM, Pivert, and two German comrades had presented him with a series of "faits accomplis." His wishes and plans had been cast aside, and work he had already been engaged in with a group of Polish socialists was to be discontinued. Other groups in which he participated had issued resolutions in which he had played no part, and "comrades with whom I have been connected by long years of struggles excluded me from any participation in a labor they are correct in considering the most important: The elaboration of a platform destined to become that of our common tendency." None of this should have been a surprise to Serge, for in May he had been told to his face by Gorkin that "the comrades of POUM [...] and Marceau [Pivert], Stein, and Jacob unanimously consider that, for ideological and political reasons, collaboration with you is impossible." Serge wrote in response that "I consider it profoundly wrong that in an International Commission containing six active militants five militants should constitute a fraction to the exclusion of the sixth."

Serge accepted that there were serious political divergences between him and his comrades, since some seemed to be aiming at the formation of a revolutionary socialist international uniting POUM, the British Independent Labour Party, and Pivert's Parti socialiste ouvrier et paysan, "in short the old groups of the far left."

Serge's letter did little to mollify the exiles. Pivert wrote to Serge that "you must, dear Victor, courageously beat your breast and say a mea culpa." Pivert refused to believe that Gorkin had said that it was impossible to collaborate with Serge, since everyone had agreed with a statement from the German members of the need for the group to stay together.

Serge, sounding very much like his former mentor Trotsky, wrote to Pivert that "[y]our letter confirms my impression that close collaboration between us would be quite difficult to achieve." The members of POUM were just as little pleased, writing Serge on June 27 that "the form in which you sent the [June 15] letter demonstrates an evident lack of confidence in the [executive] committee, democratically elected by all of us." Serge had to have the last word, writing four days later: "Since this is how things are, I can only regret that the POUM group has a conception of collaboration and camaraderie very different from mine and very little defensible."

This was not his only dispute with the exiles. In February 1944 he had resigned from the organization's newspaper *Mundo*, claiming that articles he'd written weren't published. Gironella, its editor, responded they'd only been delayed. Serge replied, claiming that pursuing serious ideological work wasn't possible if his articles only appeared every three months. Mounting a personal attack on Gironella, he said that by preventing him from appearing more frequently "at a time when I am more boycotted than ever [...] Gironella is lacking in camaraderie." Gorkin wrote to Serge explaining that *Mundo*, in order not to seem to be the journal of a party, man, or tendency, imposed a discrete "periodicity" on the appearance of articles by its writers. There was nothing against Serge intended, and he was assured that if he needed extra space in issues of the review it would be given. Serge stood by his resignation, while criticizing articles he disapproved of that had appeared in *Mundo*.

Serge, it is clear, was not a humble man. He was unhappy that he couldn't appear with greater frequency because *his* theoretical work was of primordial importance. No one denied his importance; what was denied was his primacy. It is unquestionable that he was in profound disagreement with most of the exile organization's members and almost all of its leadership. It's impossible to deny that the political disagreements played a role in his difficulties. But it's also impossible to deny the arrogance of his refusal to accept no for an answer, and his insistence that people and things be bent to his desires. The final brouhaha of the year was unmistakably a follow up to its predecessors.

Things reached their nadir in October 1944 as a result of a dispute with Jean Malaquais, a francophone Polish-Jewish writer, a former or perhaps even current Trotskyist, who had arrived late in Mexico. Their dispute is a sad one on many levels, but it's a significant one and worth exploring for two reasons. First of all, it is revelatory of the man Victor Serge, of how he viewed himself and how he was viewed by his peers. It also, and unsurprisingly, demonstrates the ways in which personal differences among exiles who are far from their normal field of struggle can be magnified out of all proportion. Serge's group of independent socialists, a relative handful of men in Mexico City, could have virtually no effect on events in Europe. But among exiles as among academics, the fight was all the more vicious in that the stakes were so small. All that was left them was personal honor, and that had to be defended at all costs.

In his notebooks, Serge wrote on October 17, 1944:

Break with Jean Malaquais, inexplicably stupid and violent. An incident at a meeting, his wife's insults, his incredibly insulting letter. Herbert Lenhoff, reading the document, says: "It's a remarkable example of the rationalization of a subconscious impulse [...]. He wrote this while in a strange state and one could conclude that he hates you because he loves you."[2]

The incident Serge refers to was undeniably "stupid and violent." The facts, as laid out in the correspondence between Serge and Malaquais that followed the incident, are not in doubt.[3] At the October 13 meeting of the International Socialist Commission, in response to a remark of Serge's, Malaquais interjected, "Given Com. Victor's position, I think I understand that he places his hope in the English Tories and Liberals." Serge, in response, told Malaquais that he was of "a rare dishonesty," for which Serge was called to order. As they left the meeting and were going down the stairs to the street, Serge confronted Malaquais and told him that he—Malaquais—knew "full well that it wasn't true" that Serge sided with the Tories. Malaquais clarified his accusation, telling Serge that he wasn't with them "in the formal sense" of the word but that "I think that politically you've become a right reformist, like so many illustrious dead, like [German reformist socialist Edward] Bernstein and [the father of Russian Marxism Georgi] Plekhanov." Insults were then exchanged on the subject of comparisons to Plekhanov (!!). Galy, Malaquais's wife, added some insulting remarks to the conversation, at which point Serge told her she was "an impertinent little woman."

Things deteriorated completely when they reached the street. Malaquais told Serge that though Serge had described him as dishonest, "you are yourself [dishonest] in your relations with your comrades…" at which point Serge "pale and trembling," in Malaquais's words, grabbed him by the lapels, telling him "You dare claim I'm dishonest in my relations with the comrades? You're a little bastard." Galy, who Malaquais elsewhere admitted had a temper, told Serge, "You have the nerve to call Jean a 'little bastard'? What are you then?" Serge then apparently grabbed Galy and told her, "If you weren't a woman I would have slapped you." Galy, responded in kind. "If you weren't so old I'm the one who would have slapped you."

This is an exchange in which no one emerges unblemished. Malaquais's juvenile analysis of Serge's politics was, indeed, insulting. Serge could hardly accept being called a supporter of the party of Churchill. But Serge's reaction—grabbing the Malaquais, threatening Mme Malaquais, and calling Malaquais a "little bastard"—was certainly not acceptable, which Serge recognized in his notebook, writing, "Disquiet and difficulty of reacting to J.M.'s aggression. The insults gave rise in me to a violent reaction which I have trouble controlling."

Apologies were called for on both sides in what was, after all, a personal difference. That is not how things developed, though. Tensions had been building between the two men for some time. A month before, during discussion of a political document written by Marceau Pivert, which, as previously discussed, Serge considered to be "a sort of *Communist Manifesto*, very rudimentary, recycling all the old phrases of the genre [… Of a kind that] can do nothing but discredit the handful of men who take responsibility for them."[4]

Almost immediately after the argument, in what Malaquais considered a step towards reconciliation , he unleashed a barrage of attacks, not on Serge's beliefs but rather on how Serge presented himself, or as Malaquais perceived Serge's self-presentation. Serge, Malaquais informed him in a letter written on October 14, is so domineering, so sure of himself, so haughty, that the other exiles "call [him] The Pope behind [his] back."

Serge is also a hypocrite. The great advocate of comradely discussion fails to live up to his words: "You forcefully demand the greatest correctness in argument, as if others had the flagrant habit of insults, as was the case [with you] yesterday."

Malaquais lamented that Serge couldn't see himself as others see him, because "your behavior in meetings would cause you to blush, if you could." Unconsciously, Serge expressed his attitude towards others even when listening to them: "When you listen to others you can't imagine the air of ineffable superiority on your face."

Speaking for the other exiles, Malaquais informed Serge that "the comrades simply cease to take you seriously when you coldly assert, without batting an eyelid, that you are the last survivor of the Old Guard, that you represent a pyramid of corpses." Indeed, Malaquais continued, all of Serge's mentions of his role in Soviet Russia are aimed at making it sound like he was there in October, that he was "in the circles of Russian leaders." All this, in Malaquais's eyes, is a form of condescension, for "all of us have fifteen to twenty years of militant life behind [us]; all of us more or less know the history of the Bolshevik Party [...] [I]t is truly superfluous [...] and has a disastrous effect to constantly bring up your past." Not only is Serge haughty, but also a backstabber who has terrible things to say about his fellow exiles behind their back, including people to whom he is as close as he was to Pivert and Gorkin.

Serge the humanist doesn't escape Malaquais's indictment. "For a long time, I considered you benevolent and generous towards all of humanity, as you constantly say, and that's doubtless true. But as soon as it's a question of your person, your pride, your vanity, your ideas, I've learned to see that no one is less benevolent than you."

Malaquais wrapped his letter up by describing what he had once considered "one of the most beautiful friendships of my life." But after Serge called him "a little bastard," can he "reasonably expect [Malaquais] to come to him?"

Every element of this letter was intended to wound, written when the insults exchanged were fresh. But it almost certainly expresses Malaquais's real thoughts, which had been simmering within the young man in the face of the experienced revolutionary. One can't help but feel that some of the accusations and some of the sentiments Malaquais attributes to others were truly felt by them. Serge's reaction was swift and merciless.

In a letter written on October 15, saying he's only "skimmed" Malaquais's missive, Serge immediately set the tone, telling the younger man that he "comes through in it just as you are in your novels: systematically viewing things from their darkest side, in a profoundly denigrating fashion."

Serge didn't deny Malaquais's version of the events of the fight. As for the negative comments Serge is claimed to have made behind people's backs, he condemns Malaquais for omitting the positive things he also says. But Serge does address the political issues at hand, and here we are given insight into Serge's difficulties with his comrades in Mexico, and not only them.

"Quite often," Serge wrote, "even with Trotsky, I was accused of adopting positions on the right. This is an old story. I consider that we can't always walk on the left [...]. In keeping with historical circumstances, Marxism is sometimes led to be 'moderate' and sometimes 'rev[olutionary],' with many other more complex variants." Reflexive political positions are ruled out by Serge. "As for the systematic extremism that you seem to unreflectingly advocate, I see nothing in it that is seriously defensible."

Serge cogently sums up his politics and his political life. His past "is not that of a conformist, a 'reformist' (in the negative sense of the word, which also has an excellent one)." And in any event, Serge wonders, who is Malaquais to criticize him? The younger man's political life "till now is not that of a militant who has provided the proof needed to permit himself lapidary judgments on Plekhanov and myself."

Here was the true heart of the matter. Serge, unlike many of his comrades, was willing to accept that there is such a thing as an "excellent" sense of reformism. Frozen in the schemas of the post-World War I world, expecting World War II to produce the revolutionary wave that followed the Great War, Malaquais's "systematic extremism" was not his alone; it was shared by all of the comrades, save Serge. This was the real battlefield. This was where Serge should have remained and where, in his writings, published and unpublished, he made significant contributions that are valid to this day.

Sadly, it's not where he let this matter rest.

Serge continued in his letter by calling Malaquais's wife Galy "a primitive" whose "upbringing must have been woeful and who never received the imprint of an environment which is based on mutual understanding and tact."

Malaquais is diagnosed by Serge as suffering from "an inferiority complex, which easily makes you wicked, belligerent, envious, and aggressive, without any objective reason." But that's not enough for Serge. He told Malaquais that "you're a Jew and hide it [...]. You're Polish and don't want to be so. In all this there's a denial of yourself which is a proof of illness."

This is all unpleasantness between two proud—not to say prideful—men, and should have been resolved or abandoned and the men gone about their lives. But Serge now proceeded to make allegations that resulted in involving their entire community. He accused Malaquais of having written for a Collaborationist magazine, *Aujourd'hui*, which Serge considered especially awful "in a writer who had passed through Trotskyism and was a Jew to boot." This matter, though, had already been adjudicated by the exiles' commission in June 1944 and the charge dismissed. But this was not all. Malaquais went to Spain during the Civil War, not to fight, "but out of pure curiosity, sponsored by Stalinists in the company of Ehrenburg," that is, Ilya Ehrenburg, the voice and face of Soviet literature to the West, and widely regarded as a stooge of Stalin's.

Round one of this disgraceful incident ended with Serge saying, "Ah, so much bile... So much bile. You should be pitied, but I no longer have the courage for it."

The worst was yet to come. Serge discovered that Malaquais's letter to him had been leaked, and he accused Malaquais of having been the source. Writing on October 22 to Marceau Pivert, who Malaquais had claimed Serge bad-mouthed, Serge described his adversary as "a psychopath," claiming "I am the object of an attempt at calumny comparable to that of the Stalinists."

On October 26, the leaders of the International Socialist Commission informed Malaquais that Serge had requested the Commission investigate the leaked letter and censured Malaquais based on Serge's information. Malaquais replied on October 30, defending himself against Serge's charges of collaboration with Stalinists, and saying it was Serge who had spoken to Michael Fraenkel, an American friend of theirs, about the contents of their correspondence, forcing Malaquais to share the actual letters in order to set the record straight. Fraenkel wrote to Malaquais that he told Serge that "it seems a pity to me that at this stage in the world's affairs, men like you should be up to the ears in a personal squabble." Would that anyone involved had heeded these words of wisdom.

Fraenkel's intervention convinced the leadership of the Commission, including Pivert and Serge's friend Gorkin, to withdraw their censure of Malaquais. Obviously hoping the matter was at an end, the organization's leaders wrote that they were sending letters to both men "requesting that you put an end to this conflict, without making any further public case of it."

Their hopes were cruelly crushed. Serge continued to send a flood of letters to his fellow émigrés, including one nine-pages long, containing nineteen numbered points, rehashing the events, contradicting the words and explanations of others, condemning the Commission for failing to censure Malaquais, and condemning Malaquais's wife for her conduct. It also contained a mini-auto-biography defending his entire past political life, going back to his teen years in Belgium. Continuing to demand action against the Malaquais, he wrote, "We cannot allow baseness, slander, and division to be cultivated among us." The pot was certainly calling the kettle black.

On November 14, the Commission decided to open formal arbitration between the two men, a proposal Malaquais accepted. But on November 18, Serge was still asking for an inquest, though he said there was no longer any dispute between him and Malaquais, "who I definitively ignore." No arbitration hearing would be acceptable to him. Serge now went off on another line of attack. He had already several times questioned Malaquais's bona fides as a leftist; he now went for the jugular. "M. Malaquais is a member of no socialist organization and is not an activist in any serious way. He is a Jewish refugee rather than a political refugee. I want neither to waste my own time nor that of the comrades in studying his attacks."

Serge is not saying that this Jew has no right to attack him, in an antisemitic sense. Rather Serge here gives voice to a syndrome that was very common among exiles communities, discussed extensively in Jean-Michel Palmier's *Weimar in Exile*. Political exiles tended to consider themselves to be in a more exalted position than that of ethnic or economic exiles. The misfortune that had befallen Serge and the other exiles was the fruit of their political choices, and so somehow more ennobling than that of a Malaquais, forced to flee Europe because of his birth as a Jew, for which no credit can be taken. It is an unattractive argument, and among the ugliest sentiments expressed in Serge's voluminous correspondence.

Serge having refused arbitration, the Commission leadership declared the matter closed. But it wasn't for Serge. He issued another blast on November 29, informing the commission members that it had given its "assent" to Malaquais's insults, as well as Malaquais's insulting of the Commission. "I can't but note this stupefying lack of dignity, which makes impossible any camaraderie [between] any people who adopt this attitude and myself."

Serge wrote that his falling out with the International Socialist Commission dated back to July of 1943, since at least which time, "I have allowed myself to express opinions divergent from [the commission's] on the reconstitution of the international socialist movement and perspectives on the end of the war."

The movement of which he was a member had failed to meet his demands for "loyalty in discussion and free and healthy discussion, excluding insult and slander." He complained that an article criticizing the French Socialists in their newspaper, *Mundo*, had elicited a response from Serge and some socialists, which the editors had failed to publish. The time had come for Serge to draw a line under his relationship with the International Socialist Commission. "Proceeding in this fashion only continues the demoralizing morals of the Comintern. I've had more than enough, and I withdraw, convinced that I've done everything I could to honestly and cordially maintain a collaboration that has shown itself to be impossible."

Having taken this blow, the commission got the last word, and it was a scathing one that confirmed much that Malaquais had said about how Serge was viewed. Accepting his resignation, on December 12 the leadership wrote to Serge that he "has the right to believe in the name of his egocentric sentiments, his infallibility and omniscience, that Reason always assists him against all." Politically he was within his rights to propose "bourgeois reformist 'democratic fronts' that blame Marxism for all the ills between the two World Wars." He also "has the right to prefer snobbish intellectual gab sessions where great psychological and even spiritual problems are discussed, where all the participants believe themselves among the Chosen." All of Serge's accusations against Malaquais were dismissed, and Serge's general attitude, as well as his entire conduct during this affair, excoriated. As for the accusation that the Commission was adopting the methods of the Comintern, Serge needed to look in the mirror. "On the contrary, [the Commission] opposed one of the typical practices of the Comintern, into which Serge had attempted to drag it." The authors of the letter held nothing back. Serge had done nothing but "cause ill-feeling and spread discord." The years of exile had shown work and collaboration between various parts of the left were possible, but that "Serge's presence and collaboration in this work has constituted a source of near constant dispute and conflicts."

After almost two months, it was all over: "With this resolution we consider liquidated the case of Victor Serge in reference to the International Socialist Commission."

On September 25, 1945, Malaquais wrote to his friend and comrade Marc Chirik summarizing the dispute, minus any of the personal details. "I broke with Serge," Malaquais wrote, "over political questions. He has become a vulgar opportunist, envisaging 'democratic' concentrations that would take in all 'socialist-leaning' tendencies (the word is his; the terms 'socialism and revolution' never appear in his language), democratic, Christian and even conservative-liberal."

A friend of all the parties involved weighed in on this affair sometime later. In March 1945 Dwight Macdonald wrote Serge a letter that included his response to a letter from Malaquais, which "I show [...] to you so that you may not feel I am discussing things behind your back." Malaquais accurately informed Chirik in Paris that Serge had "unleashed incredible maneuvers to expel me from the political emigration in this country." There is no disputing Malaquais's final words: "The result is that [Serge] finds himself completely isolated; everyone, without exception having broken with him."

Macdonald wisely remarked that the quarrel and its "bitterness is the natural result of all of you being forced to live in an unnatural (to you) and isolated milieu." But he adds that "despite my long admiration for Serge and my warm personal affection for him [...] if the reports I have had are to be trusted, the fault—though I dislike talking in such terms, which are not at all adequate or just—lies more with him than than [*sic*] you." Macdonald had heard accounts from people he admired and trusted, like Bertram Wolfe and Marceau Pivert. That these men he knew to be "most upright and amiable people [have] been forced to break with Victor seems to me significant."

Macdonald addresses the political matters at issue and manages to get at the nub of the problem. The American admits to being more optimistic than Serge and is "more hopeful than [Serge] of some revolutionary good to come out of the present European situation, and in any case, less preoccupied with fighting Stalinism from any political point of view, and more sympathetic to the present European Resistance movements even if they are (as they are) tainted by Stalinism." But for Macdonald this was part of a general disturbing shift in Victor Serge's politics. He was a regular contributor to the anti-Communist *New Leader*, and "As I have written Victor, I am somewhat disturbed by what seems to be a tendency of late on his part to accept allies from any quarter (including the American *New Leader*, which I consider politically rightwing and opportunistic) in the fight against Communism." Dwight Macdonald, one of the most perceptive and subtle of American cultural critics and political analysts, saw in this seeming tempest in a teacup, which he considered "regrettable and necessary," a much larger question and matter, one we have discussed at length: Had Victor Serge become consumed with anti-Communism?

Malaquais got revenge as only a writer can, putting Serge in a novel. In his 1947 *Planète sans visa* Serge appears as Ivan Stépanoff. In Marseille, among revolutionaries and Jews waiting for visas to leave Europe, Stépanoff, unlike the novel's hero Marc Laverne, based on the uncompromising ultra-leftist Marc Chirik, has descended into reformism. Malaquais's distaste for Serge's ideas is searingly expressed:

Stépanoff wasn't for the war, but for the victory of the democracies. Hell was no longer capitalism as such, but its brown variant [...]. Laverne let him blather on [...] seeing in him nothing but the ghost of what he'd once been, a ghost that at times still gave the illusion of being alive.[5]

Stépanoff ultimately commits suicide, dying as a result of a hunger strike. Malaquais's final word on Serge/Stépanoff was one of grudging respect: "Like him or not, the fact remained that his broad shoulders bore a past of uninterrupted struggles, of indomitable honesty that made of him a giant."[6]

23

The Final Interview

Combat was a newspaper that grew out of the French Resistance, a paper that proudly said on its masthead, "De la Résistance à la révolution": from the Resistance to the revolution. Edited by Albert Camus, it was close enough to Serge's beliefs that it serialized Serge's *Memoirs of a Revolutionary* when it originally appeared. It also published Victor Serge's final interview in its issue of November 16–17, 1947, the second date the very day of his death.

Serge's interviewer could hardly have been a more sympathetic one. Victor Alba was part of the same exile community as Serge in Mexico City. Victor Alba was the pen name of Pere Pagès (his pen name was borrowed from a character in a novel he wrote), a prolific writer throughout his long life, dying at eighty-seven in 2013. A veteran of POUM, he had spent eight years in Franco's jails after the Civil War before going into exile in Mexico. He remained a member of the POUM leadership until 1950 and wrote extensively on the party and its leaders. Unlike many leftists, Alba was admitted to the US and was a professor at Kent State University in Ohio. His time in the US earned him the suspicion of some of his former comrades that he was a CIA agent.[1]

Serge could not have suspected that this interview would be his last words to the public, and had he set out to issue a final "profession of faith," a codicil to that of 1933, it perhaps would have been different from his conversation with Alba. But Serge knew he was addressing Europeans, the audience that mattered most to him, and the direction he gave the interview is, taken in context with all we have seen of him in his final years, perfectly consonant with his ideas of the time.

It is certainly significant that in the interview Serge explains his many exiles not as caused by his revolutionary activity, but because he "defended values that are essentially French (and so European), such as freedom of thought [and] the rights of individuals."

Europe is the source of all that is good in the New World, Serge told his friend. It is "to our old Europe, today cruel and crippled [...] to which the Americas owe everything." According to Serge, if Latin America was then suffering from a shortage of intellectual and artistic life, it was due to the collapse of Europe.

Defining himself as an "anti-totalitarian," he saw Europe—which did not, as many people thought, end at the Urals—as facing only two alternatives. "Europe's rebirth, in which I have faith, will be that of man's essential and superior rights, i.e., a society organized for and by the freedom to create [...] or it will not be." Europe, along with the East and the Middle East, all face the same choice: "Rebirth, or the stifling of man."

A Third World War was entirely avoidable, but what was truly important was that the new Europe not seek to reestablish the mastery it maintained over the previous century. "I hope," Serge told Alba, "that its imperialisms are coming to an end." Given his confidence that the imperial powers were ceding their rule, this would seemingly not require wars of liberation.

Serge had a mission, and it "can and must give the next generation [...] the example of a humanist society, rational in its organization, just, stable, and penetrated with a feeling of justice." To the accusation that this was all idealistic verbiage, Serge asserted that, in fact, all that was left in Europe were "idealists, those who've resigned themselves, and totalitarians." He proudly placed himself in the first group.

If Serge had for the past few years expressed his disappointment in intellectuals, especially in France, for their willingness to join hands with the Communists, he now broadened his criticism of their conduct, siding with the reigning school of Soviet literary criticism. Clearly speaking about the dominant existentialists, he said it was the duty of all thinkers "to reject the philosophies of despair which only express a feeling of discouragement." Despair was not for him. "I choose the side of living." If life seemed a "nightmare" in much of contemporary literature, that nightmare indeed existed, and in "superabundance." "The real problem is not to die from it or to feed on it, but to confront and defeat it." Serge almost returns fully to the demands made on Soviet writers: "From the writer's point of view, what I see as imperative is the return to a certain bravery, taking clear positions on day-to-day combats."

Victor Alba ended the interview asking Serge for his solutions to the problems of building a new Europe. For Serge, the new Europe would be based on "economic planning, the just division of the products of labor and—to start with—the shrinking of national borders." This new Old World would include Germany and even Russia, "after disasters or after having avoided disasters."

The old revolutionary, whose first writings burned with rage and fury, who had spent almost his entire life on the barricades, ended by painting a picture of a world that has turned its back on any form of Manicheanism. Europe, and thus all that was best in humanity, more than anything else, needed reconciliation.

What I'd like to call for, along with lucidity and boldness of action, is the reconciliation of victims. Nothing is more natural [to man] than rancor after such vast slaughters, but nothing more diminishes or divides him, either. The reconsecration of victims demands a great moral effort, and it is precisely this that will make it fertile. All peoples were ground up by the machinery that dominated them. In order to heal this psychological block, they must recreate a fraternal soul, keeping in sight a fraternal future.

On November 17 Serge died in a cab taking him home. He was in ill health, a fact that appears in his notebooks, where he complained of exhaustion and shortness of breath. Pictures of him taken in his final years show a portly man, looking far older that his fifty-six years. It was determined that he died of a heart attack, though conspiracy theories about his death arose. Was he killed by the GPU, which delivered a poison that was disguised as heart failure? Was it "killer gangs" of taxi drivers organized by the Communist Party? Vlady Kibalchich suspected his stepmother, Laurette. He told Suzi Weissman of his suspicions, and she wrote that "[a]pparently Laurette was never emotionally committed to Serge, and months after his death married a prominent Mexican Communist and joined the Communist Party herself." Laurette admitted it was possible her husband had been poisoned but thought it unlikely.[2]

Julian Gorkin, the POUM leader with whom Serge had collaborated and battled, went to the police station where Serge's body was being held. He left a detailed description of what he saw:

> In a room with gray walls, bare and wretched, he was laid out on an old operating table. The soles of his shoes, worn down to nothing, had holes in them. He was wearing a workman's shirt. His mouth, that mouth that no tyranny had managed to gag, was held shut by a bandage. The body could have been that of a hobo, picked up out of charity. But hadn't he been an eternal wanderer of life and his ordeals? On his face there remained an ironic and bitter expression of protest, Victor Serge's final one, a man who, throughout his life, had protested against human injustice.

Serge was buried in an unmarked grave among Spanish exiles. Forty-five years later a stone was placed over it.

Epilogue

Controversy followed Serge beyond the grave.

On January 31, 1948, the Gaullist newspaper *Le Rassemblement* published a letter Serge wrote to André Malraux after the victory of the Gaullists in the October 1947 municipal elections. De Gaulle's newly formed party, the Rassemblement du peuple français (RPF), overtook and passed the Communists, who in the immediate aftermath of the war had become the largest party in the country. The RPF, in which Malraux was a prominent figure, took 38 percent of the vote to the Communist's 30 percent, displacing the Communist mayors of Marseille and Nantes, and Socialist mayors in Paris and Bordeaux. The RPF tidal wave was immense, sweeping Lille, Strasbourg, and Rennes as well.

The elections took place towards the end of a year full of conflict. The Communists had been part of the government until May 1947, when their ministers were dismissed. They had pursued a policy that encouraged the growth of French industry, and thus were at best lukewarm towards any kind of strike movement. But they had changed their line, and strikes were widespread across France, touching all major industries, the railroads, and the public utilities, with all the attendant inconvenience. Post-war rationing was not only maintained but even made harsher, with daily bread rations cut from 300 grams to 250. Chaos was widespread and would continue until the end of the year. It was in the midst of all this that the municipal elections were held. On the international front, the Cominform—the Information Bureau of Communist and Workers' Parties—had been founded in October 1947, a kind of mini-Comintern with member parties from all of the newly established socialist states and only two member parties outside the Soviet bloc, those of Italy and France.

When Serge's letter was originally published in January 1948, emotions had not calmed. The letter was re-published in April 1948 in *La Révolution prolétarienne*. Serge wrote to Malraux, the former supporter of the Communists, now a Gaullist militant:

> I would like to tell you that I find both brave and probably reasonable the political position that you have adopted. If I were myself in France, I would be among the socialists partisans of collaboration with the movement in which you participate. I consider the electoral victory of your movement a great step toward the salvation of France, which I predicted but whose size surprised me. True, more long-term salvation will depend on the way you and many others will be able to accomplish what I call the double duty: That of combating the enemy of a European rebirth and that of mastering the threats we bear within ourselves.

If the Gaullists celebrated the letter, it caused shock and dismay on the left. *La Révolution prolétarienne* wrote in an unsigned note accompanying the letter of its "surprise at the letter's content," since "in the many letters he sent from Mexico to revolutionary friends in France, Victor Serge never spoke, to our knowledge at least, of the sympathy towards the RPF we so sadly find in the letter to M. Malraux."

Serge's assertion that Malraux was "brave" was rejected out of hand. "Passing from Stalinism to Gaullism means nothing more than leaving one totalitarian camp for another." Stalin and de Gaulle were not merely totalitarians. The only acceptable attitude towards them both was one of "hostility" in the face of "these two movements whose organization and methods invincibly recall Hitlerism."

The revolutionary syndicalists criticized Serge's understanding of the Gaullist victory in the elections, which was far from being "a great step towards the immediate salvation of France." Gaullism had done right in ridding itself of its alliance with

Stalinism, "whose game it had complacently played since August 1944," but the RPF's victory in 1947 "signified the resurrection of social reaction." Serge was wrong as well in implying there were many more socialists like him who felt as he did, since "that variety of socialist [...] has not yet asserted itself publicly."

Nowhere did *La Révolution prolétarienne* question the reality of the letter or consider it a fabrication. Serge was clearly wrong in their eyes, but they made no attempt to explain or excuse the source of the error.

The matter did not rest there, for the following month Serge's son Vlady responded. Expressing his "indignation" at the magazine's interpretation of the letter to Malraux, Vlady insisted that it was intended as a means of "reestablishing courteous relations, justified by the active part Malraux had played in the liberation of Serge (during a trip to Moscow after the scandal of the Cultural Congress, he spoke of the Victor Serge case to Stalin personally)." Such a reestablishment was necessary because, according to Vlady, Serge and Malraux had had a "stormy" conversation in Marseille after the French defeat in 1940, during which Serge had bitterly attacked Malraux for his pro-Stalinist activities. But "Victor Serge's attitude towards Gaullism was never one of sympathy, and even less of identification." Serge's son admitted that "In observing the events from afar he might have been led to rejoice at the development of an opposition to Stalinism, but that never signified approval." That there was confusion as to what Serge meant was caused by the "ambiguity of certain remarks made by Victor Serge."

Vlady admitted he had certain disagreements with his father towards the end of the latter's life, due to what he called his father's failure to draw "concrete conclusions," and he spoke of the disagreements Serge had had with his fellow exiles concerning what would follow the war, which in their eyes, but not Serge's, was revolution.

Kibalchich wrote:

I assure you there was no untoward turn, nor any pro-Gaullist encouragement on the part of Victor Serge. If that had been the case, we would all be there to condemn him. But doing so would mean misunderstanding the profoundly revolutionary spirit of a man who had never ceased to give proof of it. I am prepared to defend the sole property of a man to whom, like so many others, I owe so much.

Several months later, on June 3, 1948, *Combat* reported that Kibalchich had called the letter "a falsification, subject of a lawsuit." If the suit was followed up, there is no sign of it.

In its response to Serge's son, the editors of *La Révolution prolétarienne* said that they "drew no conclusions from the two letters." They were clearly not convinced by Vlady's response; but they did not, for all that, cross Serge off:

Let us leave to the Gaullist journalistic cannibals these ten lines of Serge's. What is left us is the life he lived for the past thirty years. This is where we can find the Victor Serge we loved, the Victor Serge who was faithful to our RP; the Victor Serge for whom socialism was essentially respect for man.

The letter had also appeared in, of all places, the *New York Times*, on February 14, 1948, in an article by C.L. Sulzberger datelined Paris headlined "Europe's Anti-red Trend Inspiring Strange Tie-Ups." Sulzberger, the *Times*'s foreign correspondent, admitted that "the gradual development of anti-Communist fronts in Europe is making for some curious ideological combinations and strange political bedfellows."

Malraux, in the course of an interview with Sulzberger, showed his visitor the letter. Ever the political chameleon, Malraux told Sulzberger that if Trotsky would have defeated Stalin, "he would today be a Trotskyist Communist." And so, Sulzberger continued, "It is not surprising that Mr. Serge felt the same way." Sulzberger's article outlines many of the steps then being taken in France and Greece to counter Communist Parties, and though his knowledge of the left is inadequate, the context in which he places Serge's letter, which clearly exists since he saw it, is the appropriate one.

Bill Marshall, in his compact but thorough and thoughtful study of Serge, explaining the letter, wrote: "Serge was out of touch with certain French realities, and might not have been so indulgent towards the RPF if he had known of some of its more thuggish elements." He is correct in stating that Serge "was more concerned about the role of the PCF in French politics than that of the RPF."[1]

In my many conversations with Richard Greeman about this letter, he told me that according to Vlady the letter was written at the latter's behest in order to encourage Malraux to help Serge obtain a visa for France. Serge, then, risked being exposed as a hypocrite for a visa we have no reason to believe he wanted, for he told the press of the period he didn't want to return to Europe. Given his attachment to things European, this might seem unlikely, but what is certain is that his wife Laurette had settled into Mexican life in a way that Serge hadn't, becoming a recognized specialist in Mexican anthropology. She had no desire to leave the new life she had built and in which she would thrive. As we previously wrote, shortly after Serge's death his wife would join the Mexican Communist Party, the arch-enemy of Serge's final years. Make of that what you will.

Serge's letter was certainly written based in part on a misunderstanding of the situation in France. Mounier, we will recall, attributed Serge's anti-communism to his condition as an exile and his lack of understanding of events on the ground in France. As Bill Marshall says, it's unlikely that Serge still thought Gaullism was in its heroic World War II phase. The de Gaulle of 1947 could not be confused with the de Gaulle of June 18, 1940, the general who refused the French surrender.

There was a recent precedent for the ideas expressed in his letter to Malraux. On January 8, 1946, Serge had written to Sol

Levitas at the *New Leader* of his admiration, despite it all, for *Esprit*. He recommended to the American, "You can ask for exchange with this review. It is the organ of my friends, leftist intellectuals of the MRP, a very honest intellectual group who in the past had taken a firm position against Stalinism." The MRP (Mouvement républicain populaire) was a Christian Democratic party led by the former Gaullist ally Georges Bidault. Those who wrote about the Malraux letter at the time and since, who have said they don't know of any left-wing support for de Gaulle, will find it in this passage from his letter to Levitas.

Finally, Serge saw clearly that France's economic revival would owe much to the US. In his letter to René Lefeuvre supposedly condemning anti-communism, he wrote that though he opposed France being "dragged into either camp," it was necessary to "resist any Soviet interference in the political life of our country. But, as one of our comrades writes, France's economic recovery cannot be ensured without American aid." A Communist victory in elections would make such assistance impossible. De Gaulle might be a prickly character, but with him at the helm France could develop without Soviet interference. All the more reason to support him.

Serge very correctly saw de Gaulle for what he was: the primary countervailing force barring the road to the PCF. Only de Gaulle had the prestige and the record to oppose to that of the Communists, who presented themselves as the *parti des fusillés*: the party of the executed, the party of the armed Resistance and the fighters who gave their lives for France. The Communists in power meant the implantation of Stalinism in Paris, the heart of Europe. Ensuring their inability to assume power in France was Serge's primary goal.

There's another reason to assume the letter to Malraux was entirely sincere. The dual duty that Serge had lived by since the 1930s was, as he explained in his final interview with *Combat*, no longer a duty towards socialism. In that interview, discussed in the previous chapter, it is Europe that must be protected from enemies within and without. The Europe he no longer lived in, that had formed him, that he had loved and still did, was endangered by the extension of Soviet power, by what he called "The New Russian Imperialism," which is how Serge viewed a Communist electoral victory.

In January 1946, writing to the far-left writer Daniel Guèrin, Serge expressed similar sentiments. He asked Guèrin for his opinion on the situation in France, which he described as "unstable, full of obscure and worrying points." He described what he felt was the essential tasks of the day: "[T]he reestablishment of a healthy democracy—which can only be regenerative—and the combat against totalitarian influences." De Gaulle was not the "totalitarian influence" he had in mind. As always, it was the Communists who must be kept from the seat of power.

Stalin had already laid waste to the socialist ideal Serge believed in and fought and suffered for. It was a united Europe that would be a vivifying force in a continent struggling to rise again. A Socialist Party still led by the cultivated Léon Blum could have represented a chance for that new Europe in Serge's eyes, but it lacked the moral force and electoral effectives of the Gaullists. And so, writing Malraux that "if I were myself in France, I would be among the socialists partisans of collaboration with the movement in which you participate" was not a sign of personal interest, an exile sucking up to a highly placed person for help. It was a sign of the real fear Serge felt that a Communist France was possible and had to be prevented at whatever cost.

Those who are offended by Serge's stance do so based on a notion of socialist action Serge would have rejected, and did reject. Serge, in this stance and at this time was acting very much in the great French socialist tradition of Jean Jaurès. For Jaurès, there could be no socialism without the Republic, which provided the basis for democracy, which in turn provided the basis for socialism with freedom. Soviet totalitarianism was the major roadblock to socialism as Serge envisioned it, a socialism that respected the human person, as he often said. De Gaulle, for all his failings, was not, for Serge, a Hitlerite, as his comrades at *La Révolution prolétarienne* claimed, proving that being in France didn't guarantee that an analysis would necessarily be more accurate than one made from afar. De Gaulle victorious meant it was still possible for a real left to develop and win in the future, a possibility that a Communist victory would exclude, since a PCF win meant the installation of totalitarianism in France. De Gaulle, despite himself, by defending democracy, opened the way for socialism. Serge's letter to Malraux was neither a fake, a ruse, a fiction, nor an aberration. It was the final expression of an eternal rebel's search for a way to defend the human person.

Conclusion

In the preface to this volume, I spoke of the problems inherent in a reader saying that they admire Serge. There were many Serges, or at least many positions he adopted across the forty-plus years of his political life. Which one counts? Which is the one by which he should be judged? How can we define him politically?

What is certain is that he had rejected the idea of proletarian revolution in his final years. It's impossible to be clearer than Serge was in his 1947 article "Thirty Years After the Russian Revolution," which was published posthumously in *La Révolution prolétarienne*. In its concluding section he wrote:

> I do not think the "dictatorship of the proletariat" will reappear and be viable in the struggles of the future… I am convinced that the role of the workers' movement will be to maintain its democratic character, not for the benefit of the proletariat alone, but for the benefit of all workers and even nations. The proletarian revolution is not, in my eyes, our goal. The revolution that we are planning to serve can only be socialist, in the humanist sense of the word, more precisely socialist-leaning, carried out in a democratic and libertarian fashion.[1]

In 1947 Serge could still justify the October Revolution, but gone was his hope of its spreading anywhere in the West in any recognizable form.

That he was a revolutionary in his youth can no more be questioned than the fact that he no longer was one at the end of his life. To attribute this change to the natural conservatism of aging is to grossly underestimate Serge. It is precisely his ideological shifts, which follow a definite pattern and share a common basis and motive, that make him so important a figure An examination of his course allows us to see that Serge's rejection of dogma and his insistence on looking reality directly in the face, unencumbered by fealty to ideas that no longer squared with reality, made him the restless and unruly character he was. The lesson of his life and what makes it admirable can be found in this, not in the revolutionism he left behind.

Serge began his life as a member of the youth branch of the POB, and it was not just the fire of youth, but rather real principle that led him and his friends to leave it. The annexation of the Congo that the POB called for was a violation of socialist principles. To abandon social democracy was an entirely justified position for any consequent radical to take, and he did so.

His shift to the radicalism of individualist anarchism was an understandable reaction to the tepid social democracy he had experienced, and Serge lived his anarchist period to the fullest. If social democracy was all about compromise with the existing order, about meliorism, Serge would, for five or so years live the life of the total rebel. No party or group could properly represent or bring about revolutionary change, mired as they were in the system they claimed to oppose; only the free individual could fight as he or she chose against every aspect of capitalist society. His writings and talks from this period support rejection of mass action, carried out as he felt it was by the herd of sheep that was the working-class, in favor of a revolution in the everyday, up to and including killing police and engaging in crime. This was Serge's most radical period, and one whose importance he spent the rest of his life minimizing. This minimization was dishonest and obscured an important matter. It was the period in which both his elitism and his insistence on freedom as an essential element of political struggle make their first appearance. Through the rest of his twists and turns Serge's quest for the proper means of ensuring the right of the individual to live as he or she willed would be the red thread that ran through his life. It was sometimes submerged, sometimes open; by the end of his life, it would be all that mattered to him.

However deeply Serge felt this, the Bonnot Gang made him realize that the unfettered individual was dangerous, and he reconsidered the question from top to bottom. This reconsideration did not constitute the overnight and clear-cut break with individualism he claimed it was, but it did occur. During his brief period in Barcelona in 1917 he saw the possibilities of mass action, while still keeping a foot in his individualist milieu. His syndicalist contacts in Spain allowed him to see that liberty combined with radical mass action was, after all, possible. The Russian Revolution in its earliest phases didn't dispel his skepticism, but the Bolshevik phase inspired him as a mix of anarchism and revolutionary socialism. That he totally misread the true situation is clear now, and was so at the time. That he did so willfully and knowingly cannot be doubted. That he finally saw the error of his ways is also undeniable. He perfectly summed up the reasons for both his enthusiasm and his disappointment in an article written in 1938:

It is easy to explain—and even to justify—by the mortal perils it faced, the magnificently energetic policy of public safety of Lenin, Trotsky and Dzerzhinsky. It is simple and correct to recognize that in the first instance it ensured the victory of the workers, a victory obtained amidst truly unheard-of difficulties. It is only proper to recognize that it then led to the defeat of the workers by the bureaucracy.[2]

The rise of Stalin led him to question his Bolshevik orthodoxy, leading to his next ideological shift. His optimistic vision of Bolshevism, some of which he never shed, surrendered to the reality of the seizing of power by Stalin and the party bureaucracy. Whatever the truth of his claim at the time that his role in the Opposition led by Trotsky was minimal, and his later claim that he was against any oppositional activity at all as futile, he did stand up against the final descent of the Russian Revolution into ignominy. Knowing Soviet ways from the inside, he was aware this was a risky path to take, and he paid for taking it. He didn't suffer the worst consequences, death or the Gulag, which perhaps backs his claim that his role in the Opposition wasn't a major one, but he certainly showed great courage, whatever that position was. In 1933, before his arrest, Serge wrote a document, his so-called "profession of faith" that, with modifications, can serve as a programmatic statement for the rest of his life. The human person will henceforth be at the center of Serge's concerns. The questioning of the basis of socialism that would dominate Serge's final years was expressed in this document, which recognized that the revolutionary movement had left behind what should have been the center of its concerns: the actual people it claimed to want to free.

If Trotsky was the figure who represented opposition and resistance to Stalin, and so earned Serge's support, that did not mean the Old Man was owed eternal fealty, and Serge, shortly after being freed from the isolator at Orenburg and deported from the USSR, saw that the reality of Trotsky and his movement was deeply, even fatally flawed. Dogma is one of freedom's most ferocious enemies, and Trotskyism had quickly hardened into a dogma and sectarianism that violated both Serge's notions of freedom and his sense of political reality. His admiration for Trotsky was profound, but it was far from blind, and it enabled him to stand apart from the movement and ultimately leave the Old Man's ideas behind. Trotsky's tendency to take his revolutionary wishes for reality held no attraction for Serge, who upon seeing the West after his release in 1936 quickly saw that the categories that had ruled his life and the beliefs of leftists needed to be looked at more closely. In the end, he would decide they needed to be revised, if not jettisoned.

This was the result of Serge's final mutations. The primary element of this was his rejection of the notion of the inevitability or even possibility of revolution in the post-World War II world. Serge's fellow exiles in Mexico were tied to a vision of the world and a doctrine—classical Marxism—that reflected their hopes, and not the world that was out there for all to see, if they chose to do so. A corollary to this was another shift that is hard for admirers of the Serge myth to accept, though the evidence, as we have laid it out, is clear. His focus on democracy and protection of political freedom and democracy, for pan-European unity, for respect for the human person turned him into an uncompromising enemy of communism. The deaths at Stalinist hands of so many of the loyal Communists he had known profoundly shook him; the show trials that occurred around the time of his death receive scant mention in his writings, but they hadn't yet taken on their full scope. The Slansky trial in Czechoslovakia, with its judicial killing of loyal Stalinist servants in an antisemitic show trial, would almost certainly have been confirmation that the fiery anti-communism he had adopted was not fiery enough. Communism was the enemy of anything decent in socialism and was, even more, a threat to humankind that must be contained. We find him accused by the ultra-leftist Malaquais of Toryism in 1944, but it would be more accurate to say he had become the reformist social democrat he had refused to be as a teenager. We've quoted him speaking approvingly and with understanding of Belgium's social democratic leaders in the 1940s. *Their* decency was not in question, since it was social democrats who saw to his obtaining visas to live in Belgium and France while communists were threatening his life.

Tying his final ideas together, as we have seen, was Personalism, which was more important than Marxism in his worldview at the end of his days. Serge was certain that he was right and that his reading of Personalism's application to the politics of the post-war world was correct, even in the face of its main exponent, virtually Serge's *maître à penser*, Emmanuel Mounier. His anger with the latter was caused by what Serge viewed as his failure to see the threat to the human person posed by the Soviets, who no longer represented a socialist alternative to capitalism.

Serge's apparent mutability was, in fact, a search for an effective way to ensure true freedom and democracy. His internationalism had been modified, but not jettisoned. Now it was focused not on world revolution, but on a Europe without borders, which would ensure freedom and the growth of the individual. The world had changed since the days of the October Revolution, and Serge's idea had changed with it. The crimes of Stalin had placed the defense of the human person at the center of Serge's concerns, and only democracy as it existed in the West could ensure a socialism that would respect the individual. At the end of his days Serge returned to his beginnings: He sought a more just society in which the individual would flourish. The means of achieving his goal had changed since his teen years, but even if his path was a solitary one, he stayed the course.

Acknowledgments

This book would not have been possible without the generosity and lifelong dedication to the life and works of Victor Serge of Richard Greeman. Richard's doctoral dissertation in the late 1960s was on Serge, and he began work on a biography at around that time. He spent years assembling remarkable documentation covering every facet of Serge's life, a task that took him decades to accomplish, while also translating most of Serge's novels into English. Over a decade ago he asked me to help him finish the biography he had dedicated his life to, but we discovered that collaborating on such detailed work with an ocean between us—Richard lives in Montpellier, France, and I in Brooklyn—was simply impossible. When I finally asked if I could write the biography on my own, using the material he had gathered, Richard gave me permission to do so. Without this gracious consent I couldn't have written these pages. This is not the book Richard would have written, but even so, it is an act of gratitude to a remarkable scholar.

I owe much to people with whom I discussed my findings while writing this, and they, thanks to their insights and occasional disagreements, played a vital role in helping me clarify my ideas. Andy Blunden, Matan Ben-Moreh, Dan LaBotz, and Leon Wieseltier served as goads in bringing this work to completion. Suzi Weissman was always there to lend her point of view on a subject she loves.

Sofia Kleiner of Tel Aviv stepped in at the last minute and brilliantly and rapidly translated Russian documents that were closed books to me.

About a third of the way through the writing of this biography I became legally blind. As a result, more than most biographers, I was dependent on the kindness of strangers. The staff at the

Beinecke Library at Yale provided scans of hundreds of primary sources that I was able to enlarge and make use of. Shirley Wong-Li and the accessibility staff at the New York Public Library scanned rare publications by Serge that I also was able to read thanks to their work. And when my eyesight made my work impossible, Rita Langhirt of the New York State Commission for the Blind came to the rescue and purchased assistive devices for me that allowed me to continue my research. My gratitude to all of these people is immeasurable.

Finally, my wife, Joan Levinson, spent years listening to my tales of woe and arguments with myself over what I was writing, encouraging me to go on when my condition seemed to make it impossible. Unlike the others I've thanked here, I give her not just my thanks but my love.

Notes

PREFACE

1. Pierre Bayard, *Enquête sur Hamlet*, Paris, Minuit, 2002, Kindle edition loc. 2129.
2. Ibid., loc. 2144.

CHAPTER 1

1. Serge's father is sometimes referred to as Leonid. I have adopted his name as it appears on all official documents in Belgium, England, and Switzerland.
2. Victor Serge, *Memoirs of a Revolutionary*, New York, New York Review of Books Classics, 2012, 3.
3. Ministère de l'Intérieur (Russie), *Chronique du mouvement socialiste en Russie (1878–1887)*, St. Petersburg, 1890 in Richard Greeman Collection of Serge papers.
4. Richard Greeman Collection of Serge papers, op. cit., 33.
5. Franco Venturi, *Roots of Revolution*, Chicago, University of Chicago Press, 1960, 720.
6. Ibid.
7. Richard Greeman, "Myth and History: Victor Serge's Russian Heritage Part II," *The Massachusetts Review*, vol. 53, no. 2 (summer 2012), 495.
8. I owe this information to Sofia Kleiner, a Russian-Israeli translator who assisted me with Russian sources.
9. Pierre Semnome, "Masques et visages," *La Revue anarchiste*, no. 17 (February 1932), 66–67.
10. Okhrana files F 102, 1889 D 33, p. 13.
11. Serge, *Memoirs*, op. cit., 5.
12. Ibid., 7.
13. Loc. cit.
14. Notes from conversation between Suzi Weissman, Vlady Kibalch-chich, and Vera Frolova in Richard Greeman Collection of Serge papers.

15. Serge, op. cit., 5.
16. Serge, op. cit., 11.
17. Serge, op. cit., 11–12.

CHAPTER 2

1. Serge, op. cit., 9
2. Émile Michon, *Un Peu de l'âme des bandits*, Paris, Dorbon-Ainé, n.d. [1914]. 195.
3. Serge, op. cit., 16.
4. Michon, op. cit., 196.
5. Jan Moulaert, *Le Mouvement anarchiste en Belgique*, Ottignies, Editions Quorum, 1996, 298–299.
6. See translation at the Marxists Internet Archive, www.marxists.org/ archive/serge/1908/05/emile-henry.htm.
7. www.marxists.org/archive/serge/1908/06/illegals.htm.
8. Le Rétif, "Noël," *l'anarchie*, December 25, 1908.
9. Le Rétif, "1909," *l'anarchie*, January 1, 1909.
10. Moulaert, op. cit., 299.
11. Brussels police, confidential report 16974, dated February 22, 1890.
12. Serge, op. cit., 19.
13. Brussels police, report 11908, dated May 19, 1908.
14. *Le Peuple*, June 17, 1909.
15. Bureau des Étrangers, report 16779, dated June 22, 1909.
16. *Le Peuple*, June 19, 1909.
17. Ibid.
18. Ibid.
19. Serge, *Memoirs*, op. cit., 20–21.
20. Ibid., 21–22.
21. Ibid., 22.
22. Richard Parry, *The Bonnot Gang*, London, Rebel Press, 1987, 37.
23. Victor Serge, *Mémoires d'un révolutionnaire et autres écrits*, ed. Jean Rière, Paris, Bouquins, 2001, 988.
24. Rirette Maîtrejean, *Souvenirs d'anarchie*, Paris, Éditions La Digitale, 2005, 27.
25. Serge, *Memoirs*, op. cit., 22.

CHAPTER 3

1. Serge, *Memoirs*, op. cit., 29.
2. Ibid., 32.

3. Jean Maitron, *Le Mouvement anarchiste en France*, vol. 1, Paris, Gallimard, 1992, 421.

4. Maîtrejean, *Souvenirs d'anarchie*, op. cit., 73.

5. Cited in a police report dated February 8, 1912.

6. Maîtrejean, *Souvenirs d'anarchie*, op. cit., 28.

7. Yves Pagès, "Les premières armes de la critique," nos. 226–227 (July–October 1991), 300.

8. Serge, op. cit., 32–33.

9. William Archer, *The Life, Trial and Death of Francisco Ferrer*, New York, Moffat, Yard and Company, 1911, 298–300.

10. *L'Humanité*, October 13, 1909.

11. *L'Humanité*, October 14, 1909.

12. *Le Figaro*, October 14, 1909.

13. Serge, op. cit., 33–34.

14. *L'Humanité*, October 18, 1909.

15. Serge, *Memoirs*, op. cit., 34.

16. *Le Matin*, January 9, 1910.

17. Loc. cit.

18. Serge, *Memoirs*, op. cit., 35.

19. *L'Humanité*, January 9, 1910.

20. *L'Humanité*, January 10, 1910.

21. *Le Matin*, January 10, 1910.

22. *Le Matin*, May 5, 1910.

23. Benjamin Ivry, *Maurice Ravel*, New York, Welcome Rain, 2000, 200.

24. *La Guerre Sociale*, June 7, 1910.

25. *La Guerre Sociale*, June 22, 1910.

26. *La Guerre sociale*, June 28, 1910.

27. *L'Humanité*, July 1, 1910.

28. *L'Humanité*, July 2, 1910.

29. Loc. cit.

30. Le Rétif, "La Haine," *l'anarchie*, September 9, 1909. See also Victor Serge, *Anarchists Never Surrender*, ed. and trans. Mitchell Abidor, Oakland, AK Press, 2015, 32–35.

31. Le Rétif, "Les Hauts-Criminels," *l'anarchie*, January 25, 1912. See also Serge, *Anarchists Never Surrender*, op. cit., 111–113.

32. Le Rétif, "Par l'audace," *l'anarchie*, October 6, 1910. See also in Serge, *Anarchists Never Surrender*, op. cit., 68–71.

33. Le Rétif, "Notre antisyndicalisme," *l'anarchie*, February 24, 1910. See also Serge, *Anarchists Never Surrender*, op. cit., 38–42.

34. Le Rétif, "Une Expérience Révolutionnaire," *l'anarchie*, March 30, 1911. See also Serge, *Anarchists Never Surrender*, op. cit., 81–85.

35. Le Rétif, "L'Illusion Révolutionnaire," *l'anarchie*, April 28, 1910. See also Serge, *Anarchists Never Surrender*, op. cit., 43–47.

36. Le Rétif, "Une Expérience Révolutionnaire," *l'anarchie* March 30, 1911. See also Serge, *Anarchists Never Surrender*, op. cit., 81–85.

37. Le Rétif, "Les Fédérés," *l'anarchie*, March 28, 1912. See also Serge, *Anarchists Never Surrender*, op. cit., 120–122.

38. Le Rétif, "Une Expérience Révolutionnaire," *l'anarchie*, March 30, 1911. See also Serge, *Anarchists Never Surrender*, op. cit., 81–85.

39. Le Rétif, "L'Individualisme facteur du Progrès," *Par delà la Mêlée*, no. 16 (1917). See also Serge, *Anarchists Never Surrender*, op. cit., 132–134.

40. Le Rétif, "L'Individualiste et la Société," *l'anarchie*, June 15, 1911. See also Serge, *Anarchists Never Surrender*, op. cit., 80.

41. Le Rétif, "Je Nie," *l'anarchie*, February 17, 1910.

42. Serge, *Anarchists Never Surrender*, op. cit., 23.

43. Le Rétif, "Révolutionnaires? Oui, Mais Comment?" *l'anarchie*, December 14, 1911. See also Serge, *Anarchists Never Surrender*, op. cit., 101–103.

44. Le Rétif, "L'Individualiste et la Société," *l'anarchie*, June 15, 1911. See also Serge, *Anarchists Never Surrender*, op. cit.,78–80.

45. Le Rétif, "Deux Russes," *l'anarchie*, December 29, 1910. See also Serge, *Anarchists Never Surrender*, op. cit., 72–77.

46. Le Rétif, "Une Tête va Tomber," *l'anarchie*, May 12, 1910. See also Serge, *Anarchists Never Surrender*, op. cit., 58–62.

47. Max Stirner, *The Ego and His Own*, New York, Libertarian Book Club, 1963, 238.

48. Le Rétif, "Un Honnête Monsieur," *l'anarchie*, June 15, 1911.

49. Le Rétif, "Le Bon Example," *l'anarchie*, January 27, 1910. See also in Serge, *Anarchists Never Surrender*, op. cit., 51–54.

50. Le Rétif, "Les Illegaux," *Le Communiste*, June 20, 1908. See also in Serge, *Anarchists Never Surrender*, op. cit., 15–17.

51. Le Rétif, "Anarchistes et Malfaiteurs," *l'anarchie*, February 1, 1912. See also in Serge, *Anarchists Never Surrender*, op. cit., 114–116.

52. Le Rétif, "Les Bandits," *l'anarchie*, January 21, 1912. See also Serge, *Anarchists Never Surrender*, op. cit., 104–107.

53. Le Rétif, "Contre la Faim," *l'anarchie*, September 21, 1911. See also Serge, *Anarchists Never Surrender*, op. cit., 92–97.

54. Quoted in Jean Maitron, "De Kibalchiche à Victor Serge," *Le Mouvement Social*, no. 47 (1964), 50.

55. Le Rétif, "Émile Henry," *Le Communiste*, May 13, 1908. See also Serge, *Anarchists Never Surrender*, op. cit., 18–20.

56. Georges Palante, *La Sensibilité individualiste*, Paris, Alacan, 1909, 105.

57. Palante, op. cit., 106.

58. Quoted in Jean Maitron, op. cit., 49.

59. Jean Grave, *Le Mouvement libertaire sous la troisième république*, Paris, Les Œuvres représentatives, 1930, 193.

60. Serge, *Memoirs*, op. cit., 28.

61. Maîtrejean, "De Kibalchiche à Victor Serge," op. cit., 39.

62. Police report, dated April 13, 1911.

63. Jean Maitron and Alain Droguet, "La Presse anarchiste française de ses origines à nos jours," *Le Mouvement Social*, no. 83 (April–June 1973), 11.

64. Serge, *Memoirs*, op. cit., 39.

65. Police report, dated August 27, 1911.

66. Pagès, op. cit., 300.

67. Police report, dated November 3, 1911.

68. Police report, dated November 28, 1911.

CHAPTER 4

1. Maîtrejean, *Souvenirs d'anarchie*, op. cit., 44.

2. Victor Méric, *Les Bandits tragiques*, Paris, Simon Kral, 1926, 18.

3. Maîtrejean, *Souvenirs d'anarchie*, op. cit., 29.

4. Gilbert Guilleminault and André Mahé, *L'épopée de la Révolte: Le roman vrai d'un siècle d'anarchie*, Paris, Denoël, 1963, 194.

5. Ibid., 202.

6. Méric, op. cit., 38.

7. Maîtrejean, *Souvenirs d'anarchie*, op. cit., 48.

8. Police report, dated February 8, 1912.

9. Police report, dated March 8, 1912.

10. Police report, dated March 14, 1912.

11. Méric, op. cit., 55.

12. Méric, op. cit., 57–58.

13. Police report, dated June 6, 1912.

14. Police report, dated September 8, 1912.

15. Police report, dated September 6, 1912.

16. Michon, op. cit., 50.

17. Maîtrejean, *Souvenirs d'anarchie*, op. cit., 59–60. Unless otherwise noted, the account of the trial is drawn from the daily press and the *Gazette des Tribunaux*. Slight variations in the quotes occur, but the sense is maintained across the different accounts.

18. *L'Humanité*, February 4, 1913.

19. Méric, op. cit., 166.

20. Police report 143316, dated August 27, 1911.

21. *Gazette des Tribunaux*, February 5, 1913.

22. *Gazette des Tribunaux*, February 8, 1913.

23. *L'Action Française*, February 13, 1913.

24. M.J. Dhavernas, "Les anarchistes individualistes devant la société de la Belle Époque 1895–1914," Université Paris X Nanterre, 1981, 217.

25. Ibid., 232.

26. *La Guerre sociale*, February 19, 1913.

27. *L'Humanité*, February 27, 1913.

28. Maîtrejean, *Souvenirs d'anarchie*, op. cit., 62.

29. *La Guerre Sociale*, May 4, 1912.

30. *L'Humanité*, February 28, 1913.

31. Méric, op. cit., 153.

32. Maitron, *Mouvement anarchiste*, op. cit., 439.

33. Serge, *Memoirs*, op. cit., 51.

34. Maîtrejean, *Souvenirs d'anarchie*, op. cit., 62–63.

35. Serge, *Memoirs*, op. cit., 53.

CHAPTER 5

1. Victor Serge, *Men in Prison*, Oakland, PM Press, 2014, 178.

2. Serge, *Memoirs*, op. cit., 55.

3. Ibid., 57.

4. Ibid., 53.

5. Serge, *Men in Prison*, op. cit., 175.

6. Loc. cit.

7. Loc. cit.

8. Loc. cit.

9. Loc cit.

10. Loc. cit.

11. Ibid., 177.

12. Ibid., 178.

13. Ibid., 248.

14. Ibid., 249.
15. Michon, op. cit., 104.
16. Loc. cit.
17. Ibid., 104–105.
18. Ibid., 105.
19. Loc. cit.
20. Ibid., 106.
21. Loc. cit.
22. Ibid., 108.
23. *L'Excelsior*, October 14, 1917.

CHAPTER 6

1. Serge, *Memoirs*, op. cit. 62.
2. Loc. cit.
3. www.marxists.org/archive/serge/biog/subscription.htm.
4. https://www.marxists.org/archive/serge/1917/12/nietzsche.htm
5. Victor Serge, *Birth of Our Power*, Oakland, PM Press, 2014, 21.
6. Ibid., 31.
7. Ibid., 33.
8. Ibid., 31.
9. Ibid., 37.
10. Loc. cit.
11. Ibid., 37–38.
12. Ibid., 57.
13. Ibid., 38.
14. Murray Bookchin, *The Spanish Anarchists*, Oakland, AK Press, 2001, Kindle edition, loc. 2934.
15. Ibid., 2935–2938.
16. Serge, *Memoirs*, op. cit., 65.
17. Ibid., 54.
18. Bookchin, op. cit., 2978–2979.
19. Serge, *Memoirs*, op. cit., 63.
20. Rirette Maîtrejean, "Une mauvaise action," *La Revue anarchiste*, July 1, 1931, 113–114.
21. Victor Serge, "A propos de Naissance de Notre Force, " *La Revue anarchiste*, February 1, 1932, 65.
22. *L'Excelsior*, October 14, 1917.
23. Serge, *Memoirs*, op. cit., 74.
24. Ibid.,78.

25. Ibid., 79.
26. See, for example, *Le Temps* of February 16, 1927.

CHAPTER 7

1. Serge, *Memoirs*, op. cit., 92.
2. Victor Serge, *From Lenin to Stalin*, New York, Pioneer, 1937, 31.
3. See in this regard, "Les tendances nouvelles de l'anarchisme russe," *Bulletin Communiste*, nos. 48–49, November 3, 1921.
4. Alexander Skirda, *Les Anarchistes dans la Révolution Russe*, Paris, Editions Tête de Feuilles, 1973, 23.
5. Serge, "Les tendances nouvelles de l'anarchisme russe," op. cit., 808.
6. Victor Serge, "Les anarchistes en Russie," *Bulletin Communiste*, January 27, 1921, 57.
7. Serge, "Les tendances nouvelles," op. cit. 812–813.
8. Ibid., 811.
9. Serge, "Les anarchistes en Russie," op. cit., 58.
10. Serge, "La pensée Anarchiste," *Le Crapouillot*, Janvier 1938.
11. Serge, "Les anarchistes en Russie," op. cit., 58.
12. Serge, "Les tendances nouvelles," op. cit., 812.
13. Skirda, op. cit., 25.
14. Paul Avrich, *The Russian Anarchists*, Oakland, AK Press, 2005, 161–162.
15. Emma Goldman, *Living my Life*, vol. 2, New York, Dover Publications, 1970, 725–726.
16. Quoted in Avrich, *The Russian Anarchists*, op. cit., 197.
17. Ibid., 201–202.
18. Ibid., 196–197.
19. Peter Kropotkin, *Revolutionary Pamphlets*, New York, Dover Publications, 1927, 253.
20. Paul Avrich, op. cit., 211.
21. Serge, *Memoirs*, op. cit., 140.
22. Anatole Gorelik, *Les Anarchistes dans la Révolution Russe*, in Skirda, op. cit., 68.
23. Serge, *Memoirs*, op. cit., 144.
24. Gorelnik, op. cit., pp 70–77. Avrich, op. cit., 222–227.
25. Emma Goldman, *Living My Life*, vol. 2, New York, Alfred A. Knopf, 1931, 485.
26. Serge, *Memoirs*, op. cit., 145.
27. Ibid., 146.

CHAPTER 8

1. Paul Avrich, *Kronstadt 1921*, Princeton, Princeton University Press, 1970, 14.
2. Victor Serge, *Conquered City*, trans. Richard Greeman, New York, New York Review Books Classics, 2011, 7.
3. Paul Avrich, *Kronstadt*, op. cit., 59.
4. Paul Avrich, *The Russian Anarchists*, op. cit., 229.
5. Victor Serge, *Memoirs*, op. cit., 147.
6. Pierre Pascal, *Mon Journal de Russie, 1918–1921*, Lausanne, L'Age d'Homme, 1977, 218.
7. *Kronstadt Izevestia*, vol. 1, March 3, 1921, www.marxists.org/history/ussr/events/kronstadt/izvestia/01.htm.
8. Serge, *Memoirs*, op. cit., 147.
9. Serge, *Memoirs*, op. cit., 160.
10. Emma Goldman, *My Disillusionment in Russia*, New York, Dover Publications, 2003, 198.
11. Isaac Deutscher, *The Prophet Armed*, New York, Vintage Books, 1965, 512.
12. Victor Serge, *Memoirs*, op. cit., 160.
13. Paul Avrich, *Kronstadt*, op. cit., 213–215.
14. V. I. Lenin, "Preliminary Draft Resolution of the Tenth Congress of the RCP on Party Unity." *Collected Works*, vol. 32, Moscow, Progress Publishers, 1965, 241–244.
15. Victor Serge, *Memoirs*, op. cit., 155.
16. Victor Serge, "La Tragique d'une Révolution, " *La Vie Ouvrière*, March 31, 1922.
17. Victor Serge, "Five Years' Struggle," *The Communist Review*, May–October 1923.
18. Gaston Leval, "Kibalchich contre Victor Serge," *Le Libertaire*, March 3–10, 1922.
19. Gaston Leval, "Réplique à Victor Serge," *Le Libertaire*, April 14, 1922.
20. Victor Serge, "Once More: Kronstadt," *New International*, July 1938.
21. Victor Serge, *Notebooks (1936–1947)*, New York, New York Review Books Classics, 2019, 124.
22. Victor Serge, "La Défense de Trotsky. Réponse à Trotsky," *La Révolution prolétarienne*, October 26, 1938.
23. Undated, unpublished document in Richard Greeman Collection of Serge papers.

24. Victor Serge, *Memoirs*, op. cit., 150–151.
25. Ibid., 149.
26. Ibid., 153.

CHAPTER 9

1. Rhillon, "L'Avenir de la Révolution Russe," *Le Libertaire*, July 13, 1919.
2. Sebastien Faure, "Mon Opinion sur la Dictature," *Le Libertaire*, April 15, 1921.
3. Gaston Leval, "Réplique à Victor Serge," *Le Libertaire*, April 14, 1922.
4. Le Rétif, "Des Moyens," *Le Révolté*, no. 24, November 14, 1908.
5. Rhillon, "Un Révolutionnaire vertueux," *Le Libertaire*, October 28, 1921.
6. Maurice Wullens, "Kibaltchitche," *Le Libertaire*, November 4, 1921.
7. Gaston Leval, "Réplique à Victor Serge," *Le Libertaire*, April 14, 1922.
8. Gaston Leval, "A Propos de la répression Bolsheviste," *Le Libertaire*, February 24, 1922.
9. Louis Lecoin, "La Commune de Paris en Russie," *Le Libertaire*, April 7–14, 1922.
10. Victor Serge, "Quelques mots personnels," *Le Libertaire*, March 11, 1921.

CHAPTER 10

1. Branko Lazich, *Lenin and the Comintern*, Stanford, Hoover Institution Press, 1972, 314–315.
2. Marcel Body, *Un Piano en bouleau de Carélie*, Paris, Hachette, 1981, 157.
3. Serge, *Memoirs*, op. cit., 122.
4. Serge, "L'Expérience de la révolution russe," in *Mémoires d'un révolutionnaire et autres écrits politiques*, op. cit., 132.
5. Branko Lazich, op cit., 315.
6. Armando Borghi, *Mezzo Secolo di Anarchia*, Naples, Edizioni Scientifiche Italiane 1954, 234.
7. Ibid., 234–235.
8. Marcel Body, *Un bouleau ...*, op. cit., 295–296.
9. Maurice Vilkens, "Les opinions privées de Kibalchiche," *Le Libertaire*, February 11, 1921.

10. Maurcius, *Au Pays des Soviets*, Paris, Eugène Figuière, 1922, 196–197.

11. Gaston Leval, "Victor Serge contre Kibaltchiche. Kibaltchiche contre Victor Serge," *Le Libertaire*, March 3–10, 1922.

12. Serge, *Notebooks*, op. cit., 151.

13. Maurice Vilkens, "Les Opinions privés de Kibalchiche," *Le Libertaire*, February 11, 1921.

14. Emma Goldman, *Living My Life*, New York, Dover Publications, 1970, 732.

CHAPTER 11

1. Goldman, *My Disillusionment in Russia*, op. cit., 118.

2. Victor Serge, *From Lenin to Stalin*, New York, Pioneer, 1937, 32.

3. Letter to Paul Fouchs, dated Petrograd, August 23, 1921, Richard Greeman Collection of Serge papers.

4. Victor Serge, "Les Anarchistes en Russie," op. cit.

5. Jean-Luc Sahagian, *Victor Serge: L'Homme Double*, Paris, Libertalia, 2011, 122.

6. Goldman quoted in Sahagian, op. cit., 2011, 82.

7. Gaston Leval, "Victor Serge contre Kibaltchiche," op. cit.

8. Marcel Body, *Un bouleau* ..., op. cit., 283.

9. Marcel Body, *Les Groupes Communistes Françaises en France 1918–1921*, Paris, Alia, 1998, 35–36.

10. Victor Serge, "Les écrits et les faits," *La Révolution prolétarienne*, no. 257, October 25, 1937, 9–10.

11. Serge, *Lenine 1917*. In Serge, *Mémoires d'un Révolutionnaire et autres écrits politques*, op. cit., 167.

12. Letter to Michel Relenque, dated Petrograd May 29, 1921, Richard Greeman Collection of Serge papers.

13. Serge, *Notebooks*, op. cit. 551–552, November 3, 1944.

CHAPTER 12

1. Sahagian, op. cit., 122.

2. Serge, *Memoirs*, op. cit., 181.

3. Ibid., 182.

4. Loc. cit.

5. Ibid., 183.

6. Victor Serge, "La Vie intellectuelle en Russie des soviets," *Clarté*, no. 25, November 15, 1922, 6–8.

7. Serge, "Le nouvel écrivain et la nouvelle littérature," *Clarté*, no. 31, February 15, 1923, 158–160.
8. Serge, "Vie des révolutionnaires," *Bulletin Communiste*, March 1, 1923, 135.
9. Serge, *Memoirs*, op. cit., 183.
10. Loc. cit.
11. Antonio Gramsci, *Lettere dal Carcere*, ed. S. Caprioglio and E. Fubini, Turin, Einaudi, 1975, 488.
12. Email from Joseph Buttigieg August 13, 2013.
13. Serge, *Memoirs*, 198.
14. www.marxists.org/archive/trotsky/1922/military/ch26.htm.
15. Serge, *Memoirs*, op. cit., 199.
16. Ibid., 200.
17. Ibid., 201.
18. R. Albert [Victor Serge], "Au seuil d'une révolution," *Clarté*, no. 53, February 15, 1925.
19. Serge, *Memoirs*, op. cit., 204.
20. Ibid., 207.
21. Ibid., 224–225.
22. Ibid., 226.

CHAPTER 13

1. Serge, "La correspondance de Victor Serge," *La Révolution prolétarienne*, no. 158, August 10, 1933, 4–15.
2. Serge, *Memoirs*, op. cit., 227.
3. Ibid., 240.
4. Panait Istrati, *Soviets 1929*, Rieder, Paris, 1929, Kindle edition, loc. 877–878.
5. Ibid., loc. 893.
6. Ibid., 673–674.
7. Ibid., 868.
8. Ibid., 924–925.
9. John Sexton, *Red Friends*, Brooklyn, Verso Books, 2023, Kindle edition, loc. 368–370.
10. Serge, "La lutte des classes dans la Révolution chinoise," part IV, *Clarté*, no. 13, September 15, 1927, 382–388.
11. Ibid., 382.
12. Ibid., 383.
13. Ibid., 384.

14. Istrati, op. cit., loc. 968.
15. Ibid., loc. 952.
16. Ibid., loc. 938–939.
17. Ibid., loc. 941.
18. Serge, *Memoirs*, op. cit., 283.
19. Ibid., 359.
20. Ibid., 303–304.
21. Ibid., 304.
22. Loc. cit.
23. Ibid., 304–305.
24. Panait Istrati, *Vers l'autre flamme*, 1929, Paris, Rieder, 205.
25. Ibid., 228.
26. Ibid., 260.
27. Serge, *Memoirs*, op. cit., 321.
28. Victor Serge, *Conquered City*, New York, New York Review Books Classics, 2011, 17.
29. Ibid., 27.
30. Ibid., 30.
31. Ibid., 36.
32. Ibid., 195.

CHAPTER 14

1. Serge, *Memoirs*, op. cit., 326.
2. I have used as the basis for Serge's interrogations the transcripts made by the GPU at the time, as well as Serge's 1936 testimony at the Dewey Commission. These, unlike Serge's memory of the questioning, are not widely available and have the added advantage of being written almost immediately after the events.
3. Michel Winock, *Esprit, des intellectuels dans la cité*, Paris, Seuil, 1975, 17.
4. Serge, *Notebooks*, op. cit., 514–515.
5. Serge, *Memoirs*, op. cit., 336.
6. Loc. cit.
7. Ibid., 380.
8. Ibid., 339.
9. Ibid., 338.
10. Ibid., 339.

CHAPTER 15

1. Serge, *Memoirs*, op. cit., 353.
2. "Correspondance inédite Victor Serge–Henry Poulaille," *Cahiers Henry Poulaille*, nos. 4–5, Paris, Plein Chant, 1990, 98.
3. Serge, *Memoirs*, op. cit., 366.
4. Jean Pérus, ed., *Correspondence entre Romain Rolland et Maxim Gorky*, Paris, Albin Michel, 1991, Kindle edition, loc. 6490–6507.
5. *Cahiers Henry Poulaille*, op. cit., 180.
6. Response to request by M. Van Den Bruk for information from secret police files of Serge dated April 28, 1995, no. 10/14-10354.
7. Pérus, Kindle edition, loc. 5732–5739.
8. Ibid., loc. 6490–6507.
9. Ibid., loc. 5779–5787.
10. Jacques Mesnil, "L'Affaire Victor Serge," *La Révolution prolétarienne*, no. 154, June 25, 1933.
11. Roger Shattuck, *The Innocent Eye*, New York, Farrar, Straus, and Giroux, 1984, 28–29.
12. "Liberté pour Victor Serge," *La Révolution prolétarienne*, no. 202, July 10, 1935, 227–229.
13. *Le Populaire*, June 27, 1935.
14. "Correspondance inédite," *Cahiers Henry Poulaille*, op. cit., 214–215.
15. "Pour la culture," *Commune*, no. 23, July 1935, 1202.

CHAPTER 16

1. Serge, *Memoirs*, op. cit., 379.
2. Serge, *Notebooks*, op. cit., 3.
3. Ibid., 4–5.
4. Victor Serge, "Retour à l'occident," *La Wallonie*, June 12–13, 1936, in Richard Greeman, ed., *Retour à l'ouest*, Marseille, Agone, 1–4.
5. Serge, "URSS il y a vingt ans," *La Wallonie*, November 6–7, 1937.
6. Serge, "Explication d'un suicide," *La Wallonie*, September 5–6, 1936, also in Greeman, ed., *Retour à l'ouest*, op. cit., 25–28.
7. Published in *Les Humbles*, no. 8, August 1936.
8. Letter dated August 31, 1936, in *Cahiers Henry Poulaille*, op. cit., 110.
9. Jean Galtier-Boissière, *Memoires d'un parisien*, vol. 2, Paris, La Table Ronde, 1962, 326–327.
10. "Insulte à grand tirage," *La Révolution prolétarienne*, no. 240, February 10, 1937, 6–7.

11. David Cotterill, ed. and trans., *The Serge–Trotsky Papers*, London, Pluto, 1994, 102–104.

12. Letter to Henry Poulaille, March 10, 1937, in *Cahiers Henry Poulaille*, op. cit., 62.

13. Serge, *Notebooks*, op. cit., 20–26.

14. Victor Serge, Maurice Wullens, and Alfred Rosmer, *L'Assassinat politique et l'URSS*, Paris, Les Humbles, 1938, 34.

15. Ibid., 11.

16. Ibid., 12.

17. Ibid., 17.

18. Ibid., 42.

19. Cotterill, op. cit., 190–191.

20. Ibid., 91.

21. Ibid., 95.

22. www.marxists.org/archive/trotsky/1938/morals/morals.htm.

23. Serge, *Notebooks*, op. cit., 42–45.

24. www.marxists.org/archive/serge/1940/trotsky-morals.htm.

25. www.marxists.org/archive/trotsky/1938/morals/morals.htm.

26. Cotterill, op. cit., 111–112.

27. Serge, *Memoirs*, op. cit., 150.

28. Cotterill, op. cit., 162.

29. Ibid., 164.

30. Ibid., 168.

31. Leon Trosky, "The Hue and Cry over Kronstadt," in Cotterill, op. cit., 168–170.

32. www.marxists.org/archive/serge/1938/04/kronstadt.htm.

33. Cotterill, op. cit., 106–107.

34. Ibid., 107–108.

35. Max Eastman, *Great Companions*, New York, Farrar, Straus and Cudahy, 1959, 161.

36. Cotterill, op. cit., 111.

37. Serge, "Destin de L'Occident," *La Wallonie*, August 16, 1936, in Greeman, ed., op. cit., 16–20.

38. Serge, "Adieu à un ami," *La Wallonie*, August 14–15, 1937. See also Greeman ed., op. cit., 110–113.

39. This thirty-seven-page notebook was translated for me by Sofia Kleiner of Tel Aviv.

40. Susan Weissman, *Victor Serge: The Course Is Set on Hope*, Brooklyn, Verso, 2001, 183.

CHAPTER 17

1. Serge, *Memoirs*, op. cit., 418–419.
2. Ibid., 418.
3. Ibid., 419.
4. Ibid., 420.
5. Ibid., 424.
6. Ibid., 423.
7. Claude Lévi-Strauss, *Tristes Tropiques*, New York, Atheneum, 1975, 25.
8. Weissman, op. cit., 263n.

CHAPTER 19

1. Victor Serge, *Le Tropique et le Nord*, Paris, Maspero, 1982, 7.
2. Serge, "Le Mexique à l'honneur," *La Wallonie*, April 10, 1938. See also, Greeman, ed., op. cit., 175–178.
3. Serge, *Notebooks*, op. cit., 408–410.
4. Michel Graulich, "Le couple Kibaltchiche et la civilsation mexicaine," in Victor Serge vie et oeuvre d'un révolutionnaire, *Socialisme*, nos. 226–227, July–October 1991, 380–385.
5. Serge, *Notebooks*, op. cit., 531–532.
6. Ibid, 320–321.
7. Ibid., 91.
8. Ibid., 325–327.
9. Serge, *Memoirs*, op. cit., 243.
10. Serge, *Notebooks*, op. cit., 212.
11. Victor Serge, *The Case of Comrade Tulaev*, New York, New York Review Books Classics, 2004, 239.
12. Ibid., 238–239.
13. Serge, *Notebooks*, op. cit., 161–162.
14. Ibid., 168.
15. Ibid, 358–361.
16. Serge, *Memoirs*, op. cit., 466.
17. Serge, *Notebooks*, op. cit., 137–138.
18. Ibid., 241–245.
19. Ibid., 244.

CHAPTER 20

1. Serge, *Notebooks*, op. cit., 93.
2. Ibid., 433–436.

3. Ibid., 454.
4. Ibid., 460–463.
5. Ibid., 522.
6. Serge, *Le nouvel impérialisme russe*, Paris, Spartacus, 1947, 13.
7. Serge, *Memoirs*, op. cit., xxiii.
8. Ibid., 438.
9. Undated letter to Maurice Wullens in Victor Serge, *L'extermination des Juifs de Varsovie*, Claudio Albertani, ed., Paris, Joseph K., 2022, 80.
10. Michel Winock, *Esprit*, op. cit., 36.
11. Serge, *Memoirs*, op. cit., 389–390.

CHAPTER 21

1. Serge, *Notebooks*, op. cit., 436.
2. Letter to Sol Levitas, dated October 5, 1945.
3. Alan Wald, "Victor Serge and the New York Anti-Stalinist Left," *Critique*, vol. 28, no. 1 (2000), 99–117.
4. www.marxists.org/history/etol/writers/birchall/2003/xx/serge.html.
5. Serge, *Le nouvel imperialisme russe*, Spartacus, Paris, 1947, op. cit., 3–4.
6. Ibid., 10.
7. Ibid., 7.
8. Ibid., 15.
9. Ibid., 17.
10. Included in Victor Serge, *Year One of the Russian Revolution*, Chicago, Haymarket, Kindle edition, loc. 9183–9554.

CHAPTER 22

1. Massimo Carlotto, *The Fugitive*, New York, Europe, 2007, 94.
2. Serge, *Notebooks*, op. cit., 445.
3. I've drawn from the file (File One) on this dispute at the Malaquais papers at the International Institute for Social History, which contain a hundred pages of letters and other documents on this matter.
4. Serge, *Notebooks*, op. cit., 443.
5. Jean Malaquais, *Planète sans visa*, Paris, Phebus, 1999, 329.
6. Ibid., 151.

CHAPTER 23

1. See obituary in *The Guardian*, March 23, 2003.
2. Weissman, op. cit., 183.

EPILOGUE

1. Bill Marshall and Victor Serge, *The Uses of Dissent*, New York, Berg, 1992, 29.

CONCLUSION

1. Serge, *Mémoires d'un révolutionnaire et autres ecrits*, op. cit., 867. See also in Victor Serge, *Year One of the Russian Revolution*, Chicago, Haymarket, 2015, Kindle edition, loc. 9513–9516.
2. Serge, *Mémoires d'un révolutionnaire et autres écrits*, op. cit., 834.

Works by Victor Serge in English

FICTION

Serge's fiction covers almost every period of his life, from his imprisonment after the Bonnot Trial in 1912 until the period shortly before his death in 1947. The novels are a reflection of Serge's life and evolution, and he is represented in each and every one of them. Only his early years as an individualist anarchist do not figure in his oeuvre, though such a novel was written and was "lost" by the Soviet postal service, the tale of which is told in this book. Serge considered himself above all a writer, and he wrote even under the most difficult circumstances, including his time in the isolator of Orenburg. His affection for the writings of John Dos Passos is clear in all his novels, with their wide geographical scope, their diverse characters, their insertion into the events of the time in which they occur, and their formalistic flights. Serge was a radical novelist who applied his radicalism to both form and content, the former at times obscuring the latter. The political world in which he moved and in which he was a controversial player from his teen years until his death is that in which Serge's novels take place. It is a world of ideological battles that often led to bloodshed. He dealt with themes we also find in the works of Malraux, Koestler, and Silone, always with great artistry and insight. And yet, Serge never received the attention he deserved in his lifetime and has never found a home in academia to this day. This list of Serge's novels, all of which are now available in English (only a volume containing three novellas hasn't been translated), is laid out in chronological order of the events within them. Despite their artistic importance, they are primarily dealt with in this book as sources of biographical information. No one has written more astutely of Serge the novelist than Richard Greeman in his introductions to each volume of fiction, and so I choose to defer to Richard and to refer those interested to his introductory essays.

Men in Prison (2014), translation of *Les Hommes dans le prison* (1930). Translated by Richard Greeman. Oakland: PM Press.

Conquered City (2011), translation of *Ville Conquise* (1932). Translated by Richard Greeman. New York: New York Review Books Classics.

Birth of Our Power (2014), translation of *Naissance de notre force* (1931). Translated by Richard Greeman. Oakland: PM Press.

The Case of Comrade Tulayev (2004), translation of *L'Affaire Toulaev* (1948). Translated by Willard R. Trask. New York: New York Review Books Classics.

Midnight in the Century (2014), translation of *S'il est minuit dans le siècle* (1939). Translated by Richard Greeman. New York: New York Review Books Classics.

Last Times (2022), translation of *Les Derniers Temps* (1951). Translated by Ralph Manheim and edited by Richard Greeman. New York: New York Review Books Classics.

Unforgiving Years (2008), translation of *Les années sans pardon* (1971). Translated by Richard Greeman. New York: New York Review Books Classics.

POETRY

A Blaze in a Desert (2017). Translated by James Brook. Oakland, PM Press.

Serge wrote in every genre except playwriting. His poetry has had less impact than his fiction or memoir, but it was a form he handled masterfully. Bay Area poet and translator James Brook's collection of Serge's verse is done with great skill and art.

NON-FICTION

Memoirs of a Revolutionary (2012), translation of *Mémoires d'un Révolutionnaire* (1951). Translated by Peter Sedgwick and George Paizis. New York: New York Review Books Classics.

Serge's classic autobiography, the necessary starting point for any reader. It's a classic of its genre, recounting the political and itinerary of its author, who participated in or witnessed the great revolutionary struggles of the first half of the twentieth century.

Notebooks, 1936–1947 (2019), translation of *Carnets, 1936–1947* (2012). Edited by Carlo Albertani. Translated by Mitchell Abidor and Richard Greeman. New York: New York Review Books Classics.

A necessary complement to Serge's memoirs, the *Notebooks* contain his real time reflections on events both large and small over his final decade. Prominent are his thoughts on the continued degradation of the Russian Revolution and the Communist movement, but also of the travails and frustrations of exile life.

Year One of the Russian Revolution (2015), translation of *L'An 1 de la Révolution russe* (1930) Translated by Peter Sedgwick. Chicago: Haymarket Books.

Serge, in his introduction to this volume, explains its goal:

> My chief aim has been to display, for the benefit of the proletarian classes, those lessons which can be drawn from one of the greatest and decisive epochs of class struggle in modern history: with this in mind, I could express no other point of view but that held by the proletarian revolutionaries.

Year One is thus committed history, a defense and explanation of events from the Bolshevik point of view. Despite his open *parti pris*, this history of the nascent Soviet state was highly regarded upon publication even by those who did not share Serge's politics. It remains a vital work.

The Life and Death of Leon Trotsky (2016) (with Natalia Sedova), translation of *Vie et mort de Leon Trotsky* (1951). Translated by Arnold J. Pomerans. Chicago: Haymarket.

Serge's final and most complete homage to the man he most admired, despite their frequent disagreements. An invaluable document written from close personal knowledge.

What Every Radical Should Know About State Repression (2024), translation of *Les Coulisses d'une Sûreté générale. Ce que tout révolutionnaire devrait savoir sur la répression* (1925). New York: Seven Stories.

A fascinating work based in Serge's research in the files of the tsarist secret police, the Okhrana.

The Serge–Trotsky Papers (1994). Edited by D.J. Cotterill. London: Pluto.

Though out of print, this collection can be found at used bookstores and sites selling out-of-print books. It is a must for anyone interested in either of the correspondents. Every letter is revelatory not just of their political stances but of the true nature of the writers.

Anarchists Never Surrender (2015). Edited and translated by Mitchell Abidor. Oakland: PM Press.

During his anarchist period, which covered Serge's late teens and most of his twenties, Serge was a prolific writer and at the heart of the now forgotten individualist anarchist movement. Serge tended to downplay and even hide the positions he took during this period. This collection makes available the foundations of all of Serge's later life.

Revolution in Danger: Writings from Russia 1919–1921 (2021). Translated by Ian Birchall. Chicago: Haymarket Books.
An uncompromising collection of articles written in defense of the beleaguered Soviet state during the Civil War, of its people and the government, forced to adopt repressive measures in order to survive.

Witness to the German Revolution (2020). Translated by Ian Birchall. Chicago: Haymarket Books.

A collection of articles Serge wrote in the early 1920s when he was a Comintern agent in Berlin. Though much of it is pretty standard propaganda fare, his analyses of the failure of German Communists are of more than historical importance.

ON THE WEB

The Marxists Internet Archive (marxists.org) contains dozens of works by Serge in its Victor Serge Archive (www.marxists.org/archive/serge/index.htm), covering the years 1908 through 1947, the year of his death. This includes his writings on Kronstadt, long excerpts from *Year One of the Russian Revolution*, and two books in their entirety, his novel *Conquered City* and his historical analysis the degeneration of the USSR, *From Lenin to Stalin*. The scope of the works on the site is broad and diversified and is an essential resource for anyone interested in Serge. There are gaps in the archive, but it is the single best place for a full view of Serge and his evolution.

Index

VS refers to Victor Serge

Action Francaise, L' 72,78
Ad Lumen (study group) 14
Aid for Political Prisoners 236
Alain (philosopher) 231
Alba, Victor 369–71
Albertani, Claudio 216, 288
Alexander II, Tsar 2
Alfonso XIII, King of Spain 36
Almereyda, Miguel 40, 59
Alter, Victor 312
American Rescue Committee
    see Emergency Rescue
    Committee
anarchie, l' 27–8, 31–5, 41, 45, 56,
    58–9, 62–6, 73–5, 77–8, 80,
    250
    and trial of Bonnot Gang 69,
    82–3
    move to Romainville 54
anarchism and anarchists 16
    see also French anarchism;
    Russian anarchism; Spanish
    anarchism
anarchist individualism 97–8,
    102–3
    dietary theories of 55
anarcho-syndicalism 119–20
anti-communism 336–9, 349–50,
    376–7
anti-semitism 129, 131, 166, 195
Aragon, Louis 196, 231

Armand, Émile 33–4, 55–6, 58,
    68, 71, 79, 87–8, 97–8, 90,
    99–100, 111
    Au delà de la melée 98
Aron, Robert 272
Artzybachev, Mikhail *Sanine*; *A
    l'extreme limite*; *Le Vieux
    Procureur Raconte* 31
Audry, Colette 272
Aujourd'hui (magazine) 362
Autant-Lara, Claude 272

Bakunin, Mikhail 124, 140, 315
Balabanoff, Angelica 272
Balmont, K.D. 31
Barbusse, Henri 163, 183–4, 205,
    208, 226
Barcelona uprising
    (1909) 36
    (1917) 106–8, 110
Baron, Aron 124–5
Batalla, La 264
Bataille, Georges 220
Bauer, Otto 272
Bayard, Pierre, and 'inner
    paradigm' vii
Bergery, Gaston 249–50
Berkman, Alexander 119, 120, 125,
    128–9, 133, 143, 154, 156, 158
Bernstein, Edward 358
Bidault, Georges 378
Birchall, Ian 338–9, 350

Black Hundreds (monarchist movement) 189, 190

Blanc, Louis *History of the French Revolution* 13

Bloch, Ernst 232

Bloch, Jean-Richard 197, 203, 226

Blum, Léon 253, 379

Body, Marcel 148, 155, 157, 272

Boë, Jean De 13, 14, 15, 25, 52, 64, 66, 76–7

Bonnot, Jules 62, 64, 66–7
    death of 67–8

Bonnot Gang 15, 28, 45, 46, 50–2, 54, 88, 105–6, 141, 219, 250, 325, 383
    robbery of Société Générale 46, 61–8
    trial of 68–88

Bookchin, Murray 106–8

Borghi, Armando 146–8, 158

Borodin, Mikhail 177

Brest-Litovsk Treaty (1918) 122, 179

Breton, André 244, 268, 272, 283

Bronstein, Alexandra (wife of Trotsky) 207, 213

Bronstein, Zinaida (daughter of Trotsky) 213–4

Bukharin, Nikolai 131, 156, 176

Bulgarian Communist Party 171

Bulletin Communiste 116, 140, 162

Bulletin of the Opposition 210, 211, 258

Buttiegieg, Joseph 166

Caballero, Largo 107

Callemin, Raymond 13, 14, 25, 52, 54, 58, 61, 64, 67
    trial and execution of 70, 74–7, 81, 84–6

Camacho, Manuel 309

Camus, Albert 277, 369

Cantinflas (actor) 294

Cárdenas, Lázaro 281, 294

Carlotto, Massimo *The Fugitive* 354–5

Carmaux Mining Company 16

Carnot, Sadi 32

Carouy, Edouard 13, 25, 52, 54, 58, 62, 66
    trial and suicide of 79, 72, 75–6, 78, 80–1, 856

Carrington, Leonora 298

Caserio, Sante 32, 59–60

Causeries populaires 33, 51, 53, 65

Céline, Louis-Ferdinand 246

Cendrars, Blaise 208, 272

Chadaev, Vassily 207

Challaye, Felicien 272

Chambers, Whittaker 350

Chapelier, Émile 22

Chardon, Pierre 111

Charnov, General 131

Cheka (secret police) 122–3, 126, 151–2, 195–6, 201, 258, 261, 351

Chernykh, V.M. 181

Chiang Kai Shek 176–7

China 176–80

Chinese Communist Party 177–8

Chirik, Marc 366, 367

Ciliga, Ante 272–3

Clarté (later *Lutte de Classes*) 162–4, 168, 178, 183

Cocteau, Jean 268

colonialism 320–1

Combat (newspaper) 369, 376

Cominform (Information Bureau of Communists and Workers' Parties) 373
Comintern (Communist International) 116, 160, 162, 167–71, 317, 346–7
2nd Congress (1920) 146
role in China 176–9
Cominternians 166
Comité Obrero 106
Commentary (magazine) 350
Commission on International Relations 355
Committee for the Defense of Victims of Fascism and the White Terror 183
Committee for the Investigation of the Moscow Trials 244, 251
Commune (journal) 235
Communist Review 132
Communiste, Le (later *Le Révolté*) 14, 15–17, 23
Confederación de Trabajadores de América Latina (CTAL) 343
Confederación Nacional de Trabajo (CNT) 106–7, 146, 158, 254
Confédération générale du travail (CGT) 27–8, 57
Congress of Democratic Action 311
Constitutional Democrats (Cadets) 131
Control Commission 182
Costa Iscar, Manuel 99–100, 105
Crapouillot, Le 245–6
Critique (journal) 338

Darwin, Charles *On the Origin of Species* 186

defense de rupture 75–6
Degrelle, Leon 241
Denikin, General 123, 153
Dettweiler, Georges 62
Dewey Commission 209, 212
Dieudonné, Eugène 64–7, 74–5, 84, 86
Dimitrov, Georgi 171
Dissent (journal) 350
Dommanget, Maurice 244
Doriot, Jacques 206, 246
Dormoy, René Marx 244
Dos Passos, John 185–6, 194
Dostoevsky, Fyodor *The Possessed* 243
Dr. Atl (Gerardo Murillo) 297
Drumont, Edouard 43
Duhamel, Georges 223–5, 229, 273
'The Value of a Man' 223
Durruti, Buenaventura 315
Durtain, Luc 224
Dzerzhinsky, Feliks 201

Eastman, Max 262, 278–9
École emancipée, L' 222, 251
Ehrenberg, Ilya 235, 362
Ehrlich, Henrykh 312
Emergency Rescue Committee 277–8, 285–6
Esenin, Sergei 196
Esprit 222, 238, 243, 273, 328–9, 330–1, 333, 335, 347–8
Esprit du Temps, L' 221
Estonian communist uprising (1924) 170–1
Estorges, Anna *see* Maîtrejean, Rirette
Europe 370–1
Europe (journal) 203, 226

Excelsior, L' 94, 110

Fabré, Attorney General 81
Fallières, Armand 43
Faure, Sébastien 32−3, 83, 138
Federal Bureau of Investigation
    (FBI), file on VS 279−80, 340
Fénéon, Félix 32
Ferrer, Francisco 35−8
Figaro, Le 38
Figner, Vera 2
Finland, 267−8
Fischer, Ruth 168−9, 206
Flèche, La 250
Fouchs, Paul 155
Fourth International 253−5, 307,
    316
France
    Gaullist era 373−80
    lois scélérates 32
    Third Republic 276
    WWII: 275−6
France, Anatole 43
Frankael, Michael 305−6, 363
French anarchism 32−3, 137−40, 144
French Association of Proletarian
    Writers 223
French Communist Group 148,
    155, 272
French Communist Party 162, 190,
    231, 344, 373, 377
French individualism 96−7
French Popular Front 241, 253
French Revolution 112, 168−9
French Socialist Party 220
Frolov, Vladimir 5, 8
Frolova, Vera *see* Podorevskaya,
    Vera
Frolova, Vera (half-sister of VS)
    8, 11

Frontism 250
Fry, Varian 277, 283, 286

Gaidar, Arkadi *A Tale About a War
    Secret About the Boy Nipper-
    Pipper and his Word of Honor* 4
Galtier-Boissière, Jean 245
Garnier, Octave 13, 54, 58, 61−2,
    64−5, 67, 70, 72
Gaulle, General Charles de and
    Gaullism 373−5, 372,
    378−80
Gazette des Tribuneaux 75, 77
Gelfman, Gesia 3
German Communist Party (KPD)
    167−70, 169, 206
German Revolution (1923) 167−8,
    206, 352
German Social Democratic Party
    182
Germany
    economic crises in 167
    WWII: 275−6
Germinal (review) 221
Ghezzi, Francesco 207, 273
Gide, André 232, 235−6, 238−40,
    246, 272
    Return from the USSR 240
Giono, Jean 272, 277
Giraudoux, Jean 222, 229
Gironella, Enqrique 306, 312, 319,
    356−7
Gogua, Irina 6−7, 287
Gold, Mike 231
Goldman, Emma 119, 120, 125,
    128−9, 133, 152−6, 158
Gorkin, Julián 306−7, 308−9, 311,
    312, 356, 363, 372
Gorky, Maxim 226−7, 236

GPU (secret police) 182, 209–14, 372

Gramsci, Antonio 165–6

Graulich, Michel 296

Grave, Jean 32, 33, 48, 54

Greeman, Richard vi, 2, 4, 9, 29, 182, 328, 377

Groupe anarchiste internationale (GAI) 20

Groupe communiste libertaire 15

Groupe révolutionnaire belge 15, 18, 21–3

Guéhenno, Jean 222, 231

Guèrin, Daniel 379

Guerre Sociale, La 38, 40, 43–4, 59–60, 81, 86–7

Guesde, Jules 14–15, 57

Guliai-Polei, Ukraine 122–4

Guzman, Eulalia 311–2

Hartenstein, Abraham 20–7, 49, 141
  trial of 25–7

Henry, Émile 13, 16–17, 32, 52, 59, 61

Henault, Semen 22

Hervé, Gustave 40, 42, 59, 81–2
  'The Apache's Example' 40–1

Hilferding, Rudolf 315

Hinault, Michel 11

Hitler, Adolf 170, 206, 264

House Committee on Un-American Activities 340

Humanité, L' 30, 40, 44, 71–2, 83–4, 87, 183, 227–8, 230, 246, 249
  'Panait Istrati: Agent of the Romanian Police' 190

Humbles, Les (review) 142–3, 243, 329

Huron, Le 229–30

Idée Libre, L' (journal) 64, 77

illegalism 16–18, 32, 49–51, 54, 73–5

Independent Labour Party (UK) 316, 356

individualism 34, 52–4, 90
  see also anarchist individualism; French individualism

International Congress in Defense of Culture 231

International Socialist Commission 358, 363–6,

Intransigeant, L' 267

Israel, Leon 59

Istrati, Panait 105, 187–93, 228–9
  La Russie nue 228
  Vers l'autre flamme 175, 187–90, 193, 228

James, C.L.R. 272

Jaurès, Jean 30, 37, 40, 43, 48, 87, 379

Jews 131, 166, 189, 278–9, 362, 364
  see also anti-semitism

Joffe, Adolf 179

Joseph, Albert *see* Libertad, Albert

Jouin, Deputy Chief 64, 67

Journal, Le 86

Juin, Ernest *see* Armand, Émile

Kahlo, Frida 274

Kalinin, Mikhail 188–9

Kamenev, Lev 175–7, 243, 251

Katz, Otto 307

Kerensky, Alexander 217

Kibalchich, Cecile (niece of VS) 12

Kibalchich, Helène (half-sister of VS) 8, 12

Kibalchich, Henri (nephew of VS) 12

Kibalchich, Jeannine (daughter of VS) 11, 113, 216, 236, 281, 286, 288–9, 295

Kibalchich, Leon (father of VS) 1–8, 287
  marriage to Maria Mouillard 7, 9
  in Belgium 7–9, 12, 28–30

Kibalchich, Nikolai Ivanovich 2–4

Kibalchich, Oleg 6

Kibalchich, Raoul-Albert (brother of VS) 9, 10

Kibalchich, Victor Napoléon see Serge, Victor

Kibalchich, Vladimir (son of VS) 2–3, 4, 6, 113, 166, 275, 279, 281, 298 375–6
  accompanies father to Orenburg 215–7, 220
  relations with father 11–12, 354–5
  relations with mother 288

Kirchway, Freda 310–1

Kisch, Egon Erwin 307, 310

Klement, Rudolf 255

Koestler, Arthur 338, 350
  Darkness at Noon 300–1

Kollontai, Alexandra 138–9

Koltsov, Mikhail 188–9

Kronstadt Rebellion (1921) 116, 126–36, 151–2, 156, 161, 258–60, 352

Kropotkin, Prince Peter 11, 15, 13, 33, 88, 117, 121–2, 124–5, 143–4
  death of 125

Kuomintang Party 176–8

Lam, Wilfredo 283

Laski, Harold 272

Last, Jef 232

Laurat, Lucien 220

Lazarevich, Nicolas and Ida 236, 238

Le Bon, Gustave The Psychology of Crowds 28, 52

Lecache, Bernard 183

Lecoin, Louis 143

Lefebvre, Raymond 149–50

Lefeuvre, René 230–1, 243, 338–9, 347, 378
  'Victor Serge is deported' 230

Left Opposition 139, 171, 176–7, 179–83, 198, 217, 266, 321, 383–4

Lenhoff, Herbert 358

Lenin, V.I. 28, 116, 121–2, 124, 148, 156, 171, 198, 241, 259, 261, 266, 326, 351
  death of 171
  on Kronstadt Rebellion 130
  The State and Revolution 121, 326

Lenin Enrollmennt 174

Lenin's Testament 176, 179

Leningradskaya Pravda 187–8

Lepetit, Jules 146

LeRoy-Ladurie, Jacques 273

Leval, Gaston, 132–3, 135, 138–9, 143, 150–2, 156
  'Victor Serge against Kibalchich : Kibalchich against Victor Serge' 150, 155

Lévi-Strauss, Claude 283–4
  Tristes Tropiques 283

Levitas, Sol 334–5, 341, 343, 346, 378

Liabeuf, Jean-Jacques 22–3, 38–45, 49, 59, 86
  execution of 44–5

Libertad, Albert 32, 33, 34, 46, 59, 88

Libertaire, Le 33, 119, 139, 140, 143–5, 149–50, 158

Liebknecht, Karl 113, 169

Ligue Communiste 'Still Silence on the Fate of Victor Serge' 221

Ligue des Droits de l'Homme 222

Limon, Léon 231

Líster, Enrique 345–6

Litvinov, Maxim 252

Londres, Albert 86

Lorulot, André 54, 55–7, 59–60, 64, 99, 106
  and trial of VS 73, 77–80, 83, 97–8

Lotta Continua Group 354–5

Lukács, György 165, 171–2

Lutte de Classes 183

Luxemburg, Rosa 113, 169

Macdonald, Dwight and Nancy 278–9, 281–6, 306–8, 309, 341–3, 366–7

Maertelinck, Maurice 31

Mahé sisters 59

Maîtrejean, Louis 34–5, 93–4

Maîtrejean, Rirette 45, 25, 29, 345, 54–6, 63, 66–7, 273, 276–7
  divorces VS 113–4
  marries VS 93–4
  memoirs of 98–9

review of *Birth of Our Power* by 108–10
on trial with VS 69–72, 76, 80–4

Maitron, Jean 33, 88, 231

Makhno, Nestor 116–7, 122–4

Malaquais, Galy 277, 358–9, 362

Malaquais, Jean 277, 298, 306
  dispute with VS 357–68
  Planète sans visa 367–8

Malraux, André 208, 231–2, 373–80
  Condition humaine, La 232
  Conquerants, Les 232

Mandelstam, Osip 207

Maritain, Jacques 326–7

Marshall, Bill 377

Martinet, Dr. J.D. 292–3

Martinet, Marcel 194, 198

Marx, Karl and Marxism 260, 324–6

Maslow, Arkady 168, 206

Masses (magazine) 230

Masses Nouvelle 231

Matin, Le 65, 77, 83, 98

Maura, Antonio 36

Mauricius *see* Vandamme, Maurice

Mayakovksy, Vladimir 163

Mayer, M. 25–6

Melée, La 111–2

Menils, Jean de 298

Merezhkovski, D.S. 31

Méric, Victor 72, 87

Mesnil, Jacques 198, 207, 220

Metge, Marius 54, 62, 85–6

Mexican Communist Party 378, 377

Mexican Revolution 295

Michon, Émile *Un Peu de l'Ame des Bandits* 15, 91

Modern School movement, Spain 36

Molins y Fabregas, Narciso 275

Monde (magazine) 205

Monier, Étienne 84–6

Moscow Trials 209, 212, 244, 246

Mouillard, Marie, marries to Leon Kibalchich 7, 9

Moulaert, Jan 15, 16

Mounier, Emmanuel 222, 232, 273, 347, 349, 377, 385

  'Manifesto in Service to Personalism' 330–1

  relations with VS 328–36

Mouvement républicain poopulaire (MRP) 378

Muhsam, Eric 235

Mundo (newspaper) 345–6, 356–7, 365

Munis, Grandizo 308, 311

Museum of the Revolution, Leningrad 233

Mussolini, Benito 189, 264, 312

Muste, A.J. 253

Narodnaya Volna (People's Will revolutionary group) 2–3, 6–7

Nation, The 309–11

National Socialist German Workers' Party (Nazi Party) 170

Naville, Pierre 208, 210, 255, 273

Neruda, Pablo 310

Neumann, Heinz 168

New Economic Policy (NEP) 136, 163, 259

New International 134, 260

New Leader 334, 341, 343–4, 345, 350, 367, 378

New York Times 376

New Yorker 278

Nietzsche, Friedrich 48–9, 99–101, 103–5

  Thus Spake Zarathustra 101

Nin, Andreu 208, 210, 254, 263–4, 309

  death of 267

Nizan, Paul 231

Nouvel Age 196–7

Nouvelle revue française 187, 190

Oeuvre, L' 223, 225

Okhrana (secret police) 8, 21–2, 31, 163, 213

Opposition *see* Left Opposition

Ordine Nuovo 165

Ordre, L' 273

Orwell, George 336

Pagès, Pere *see* Alba, Victor

Palante, Georges

  'Anarchism and Individualism' 53

  La Sensibilité individualiste 52–3

Palmier, Jean-Michel *Weimar in Exile* 364

Par delà de la melée (review) 98

Paris Commune (1871) 28, 32–3, 47–8, 116, 129, 169

Parry, Richard 28–9, 54

Parti ouvrier belge (POB) 13–16, 159, 314–5, 382

Parti populaire français 206

Partie socialiste ouvrier et paysan (PSOP) 231, 319, 356

Partido Obrero de Unificación Marxista (POUM) 208, 254, 260, 263–7, 272, 306–7, 316, 319, 321, 327, 345, 355–6

Partisan Review 350

Pascal, Pierre 128, 162, 188, 207, 220

Paz, Magdeleine and Marcel 198, 207, 210, 217, 232–6, 236, 239–40, 244, 327

Péguy, Charles 330

Pelloutier, Fernand 124

Peret, Benjamin 306

Personalism 201, 273, 327–31, 347–8, 385

Pestaña, Angel 106–7, 146–7

Pétain, Philippe 273, 275

Petit Bleu, Le 22

Petit Parisien, Le 58–9

Peuple, Le 21

Piechkova, Mrs 236

Pigeon, Alexandrine 39

Pilnyak, Boris 164, 185, 207

Pilsudski, Józef 351

Pivert, Marceau 231, 274, 306, 308–9, 311, 316, 319, 355–6, 359, 363, 367

Plekhanov, Georgi 358

Plisnier, Charles 208, 221, 223, 234–6, 238, 274

Poderevskaya, Vera (mother of VS) 1, 5, 8

Political assassination and the USSR [VS et al] 251

Politics (journal) 341, 350

Populaire, Le 183, 220, 234–5

Poulaille, Henry 196–7, 208, 217–8, 223, 236, 244–5

Povolovzky, Jacques *see* Serge, Victor

Preobrazhensky, Yevgeni 213–4

Prolekult 163

Proust, Marcel 164

Rassemblement, Le 373

Rassemblement démocratique révolutionnaire 336

Rassemblement du peuple français (RPF) 373–5, 377

Ravel, Maurice 42

Raymond la Science *see* Callemin, Raymond

Reclus, Elisée 88

Régler, Gustav 306, 308, 309–11

Reiss, Ignace, assassination of 243, 250–2

Relenque, Michel 160

Renkin, Jules 20

Renn, Ludwig 235, 307, 310

Renoir, Jean 304

Révolté, Le 15–16, 20, 22–4, 49, 140

Révolution Permanente, La 210

Révolution Prolétarienne, La 134, 158, 173, 198, 200, 210, 214, 221–2, 228–9, 248, 260, 262, 374–5, 380

Revolutionary History (journal) 338

Revolutionary Military Committee 120

Revue anarchiste, La 7, 108

Rex movement, Belgium 241

Rhillon 137

  views on VS 140–2

  'A Virtuous Revolutionary: Victor Serge' 140

Rière, Jean 29, 217

Rivera, Diego 274, 296–7

Rochefort, Henri 43

Rodriguez, Léon 77
Rolland, Romain 203, 218−9, 225−30, 236
  Jean-Christophe 225−6
Romains, Jules 272
Romanian fascism 346
Roosevelt, Franklin D. 344
Rosenthal, Gérard 210, 255, 258, 273
Rosenzweig, Arthur 168
Roshchin, Iuda 121
Rosmer, Alfred 244, 251
Rote Fahne, Die 167
Rules of the Game (film) 304
Russakov, Alexander 113, 186−9
Russakov, Anita 212−3, 221
Russakov, Liuba 186, 216
  marriage to VS 113, 268
  mental illness of 191, 217, 220, 268, 287−93
Russian anarchism 117−22, 160
Russian Civil War 115−6, 120, 124, 126−7, 163, 195
Russian Communist Party 118, 120, 124, 175
  10th Congress (1921) 129−30, 132, 151
  14th Congress (1926) 175−6
  15th Congress (1927) 179−80, 183
Russie nue, La 228
Rutkovsky (secret police chief) 209, 212−4
Ryner, Han 83, 102−3

Sadoul, Jacques *Trotksy's Advocate* 246−50
  reply by VS 248−9
Sahagian, Luc 155−6, 162−3
  Victor Serge: l'Homme Double 133

Saint-Exupéry, Antoine de 274
Salvemini, Gaetano 234
Samson, J.P. 278
Sartre, Jean-Paul 332, 336
Schachtman, Max 273
Schleiermacher, Friedrich *On Religion* 330
Schoots, Marie 76
Second International 315, 317
Sedov, Leon (son of Trotsky) 251−4, 274
  death of 255, 262
Seghers, Anna 231, 235, 283, 307, 310
Seguí, Salvador 106−7
Séjourné, Bernard 268
Séjourné, Laurette 277, 281−3, 285−6, 295, 291, 296, 298, 354, 372, 377
  marries VS 268−71, 273
Sejourné, René (son of Laurette) 268, 283, 286
Semnone, Jorge 7
Semprun, Jorge 36
Serge, Victor
  attacks on 137−45, 152
  belief in science 54−5
  birth and early years 8−10, 13
  death of 372
  defense of the human person 327−8
  deportation in Orenburg 215−37
  dispute with Malaquais 357−68
  divorced by Rirette Maîtrejean 113−4
  education 10−11
  expelled from Communist Party 183
  FBI file on 279−80, 340

imprisoned by GPU 182–4
imprisonment in Fleury-en-
  Bière 111
imprisonment in Melun 89–93,
  142–3
in Barcelona 96–114 383
in Belgium 13–28
in Berlin 165–7
in Brussels 236–44
in Canterbury 9–10
in Marseille 277–83
in Mexico 285, 294–313
in Paris 31, 34–6, 45
in Poland 236
in Russia 113, 115–8
in Whitechapel 10
interest in Mexican archaeology
  296
interrogation in Lubyanka
  208–9
interview with Victor Alba
  369–71
joins Russian Communist Party
  118
letter to Liuba 291
letters to Rirette 91–2
marries Laurette Séjourné
  268–71, 273
marries Lubia Russakov 113, 268
marries Rirette Maîtrejean 93–4
physical appearance of 284, 372
'Profession of Faith' 198, 202,
  204, 214, 384
pseudonyms of 1, 31, 45
relations with Trotsky 180,
  253–63
themes in writing 45–6
trial for possession of stolen
  weapons 68–89

turns to fiction writing 184–6
views on colonialism 320–1
views on duplicity 205–6
views on French novels 185
views on love and sex 91–2
views on the masses 19–20,
  46–7
views on Russian Communist
  Party 129, 173–4
views on Russian Revolution
  (critical of) of 181–2, 192–4,
  199–200, 339–40, 347–53
  (defence of) 100–1, 154–8,
  160, 165
views on socialism 200–1,
  316–20
views on Stalinism 336–7
views on the West 336, 338
views on WWI: 89–90
in Whitechapel 10
writing as Le Rétif 15, 17–20,
  24, 47–8, 74, 103–4, 111, 141,
  148, 169, 276, 305
WRITINGS
'1909' 19
'Against Hunger' 51, 73
'Against all Bastilles'(talk) 56–7
'Anarchist Bandits' 23
'Anarchists and Criminals' 74
'Bakunin's Confession' 140
'Bandits, The' 73, 79
'Birth of our Power' 96, 105,
  108–9, 186, 207
Case of Comrade Tulaev, The 195,
  298–305
'Christmas' 18–19
'Conquered City' 126, 156, 186,
  194, 207, 224, 236, 300
Derniers temps, Les 12

'Europe of Tomorrow: Neo-totalitarianism or Democracy' 318
'Expedients' 73
'The Experience of the Russian Revolution' 146
'Extreme Moments' 101
'Farewell to a Friend' 267
Fate of the USSR/Fate of a Revolution 244
'From Criminal Court to the Trenches' 94
From Lenin to Stalin 156, 245
'Good Example, A' 41–2
'Head Will Fall' 43
Hommes Perdus, Les 218–9, 236, 250
'Individual Against Society' 53–4
'Individualist Doctrine' (talk) 57–8
'Intellectual Life in Soviet Russia' 163
'Lettre d'un Emmuré' 112
'Man, A' 24
Memoirs of a Revolutionary vi, 1, 27, 28, 56, 108–9, 130, 328, 369
'Men in Prison' 89, 184, 186, 207
Midnight in the Century 215, 218, 240–1
New Russian Imperialism, The 320, 326, 347
'New Writers, New Literature' 164
'On Anarchist Life' 45
'Once More Kronstadt' 260
'Return to the West' 241
'Séisme, Le' 294

'Sixteen executed men in Moscow' 240, 243
'Socialism or Totalitarianism' 326
Soviets 1929: 175
'Substance of the Comintern, The' 346
'Thirty Years after the Russian Revolution' 350, 381
'Time of Intellectual Courage, The' 324
Tourmente, Le 236
'Tragedy of a Revolution' 130–1, 132
'Trotskyism' 316
'Tsar Falls, A' 100
'USSR: Can it Really Make War?' 267
What Every Radical Should Know about State Repression 31, 213
Year One of the Russian Revolution 184, 196, 207, 221
Service d'information et de la presse, Le 238
Séverine 43, 183
Shatov, Bill 120
Shattuck, Roger 232
Silone, Ignazio 273
Siqueiros, David Alfaro 297
Slansky, Rudolf, trial of 307, 385
Smirnov, Ivan 116
Sneevliet, Henk 251–2, 254–5
Sobolevicius, Abram (Z1-1) 210–1, 213
Sobolevicius, Ruven 210–1
social democracy 256–7, 315–6, 382
Socialismo y Libertad 306, 354

Socialist Appeal, The 259
Socialist Revolutionary Party, Paris 31
Solano, Wilebaldo 319
Solidaridad Obrera (newspaper) 36, 107
Souchy, Augustin 146
Soudy, André 66, 75–7, 84, 86
Souvarine, Boris 166, 220, 337
Soviet Union 115
  economic crisis in 126–7, 162, 186
  intellectual life in 163–4
  role in China 176–9
  role in Spanish Civil War 265–8
  War Communism era 127, 129
Spanish American Society 208
Spanish anarchism 158, 254
Spanish Civil War 158, 208, 241, 254–5, 263–8, 345–6, 362
Spanish communists 345–6
Spartacus (publisher) 243
Stalin, Joseph 117, 148, 199
  relations with Trotsky 173, 178, 233
  relations with Zinoviev 175–6
Stevens, Annick 101
Stirner, Max 325–6
  The Ego and His Own 49–50, 52
Study Group of the Twelfth 57, 73
Sulzberger, C.L. 376–7
Sun Yat-Sen 177
Svierteva (accuser of Russakov) 186–7, 189

Tagore, Rabindranath 225
Temple, Martin 285
Temps, Le 33, 87, 222
Temps modernes, Les 332

Temps Nouveaux, Les 20, 54
Thaelmann, Ernst 206, 231
Third International *see* Comintern
Tierra y Libertad (newspaper) 99–100, 105, 107, 248
Tikhonov, Nikolai 234–5
Toledano, Vicente Lombardo 308
totalitarianism 317–8, 323–4, 334, 341–2
Tottenham Outrage (1909) 49
Transatlantic (Netflix film) 277
Tresca, Carlo 312
Trial of the Thirty 32
Trotsky, Leon and Trotskyism 122, 167, 171, 175–8, 210, 249, 251, 253, 297, 316, 344, 384
  assassination of 309
  on Kronstadt Rebellion129, 133, 258–60
  relations with VS 180, 253–63
  relations with Stalin 173, 178, 233
  Lessons of October 171
  New Course, The 171
  'Their Morals and Ours' 254–5, 25
Truman, Harry S. 344

Union General de Trabajadores (UGT) 107
Unitary Federation of Teachers 231
Universalists 121

Vaillant, Auguste 16, 32, 59, 61
Vaillant, Jean 23–4
Valet, René 13, 62, 66–7, 70
Valiami, Leo 306
Valois, Georges 196

Vandamme, Maurice 29, 33, 34−5, 60, 149
Vandervelde, Emil 14, 236, 238, 273, 315
Vauthier, René 272, 281−2
Versailles Treaty (1919) 167
Vie Anarchiste, La 56
Vie Ouvrière, La 130, 132, 139, 258
Vietnam War 337
Vigo, Jean 40
Vilkens, Maurice 148−9, 152
Voline 123, 139

Wald, Alan 'Victor Serge and the New York anti-Stalinist Left' 338
Wallonie, La 238, 241, 263, 267, 294
War Resisters League 253
Weissman, Suzi 4, 6−7, 216, 271, 278, 372

Werth, Léon 208, 222, 274
White, Walter 339
Whitman, Walt 330
Winock, Michel 203, 330
Wolfe, Bertram 310−1, 367
Workers' Opposition 134, 138, 156−7, 260
World War II: 275
Wrangel, General 123, 131
Wullens, Maurice 142, 243, 251, 328−9

Yudenich, General 153

Zinoviev, Grigory 115, 131, 153, 165, 169, 171, 177, 243, 251, 259
  and Kronstadt Rebellion 126−7
  relations with Stalin 175−6, 342
Zola, Émile *Paris* 13